Critical Crossings

Critical Crossings

*The New York Intellectuals
in Postwar America*

NEIL JUMONVILLE

University of California Press

BERKELEY   LOS ANGELES   OXFORD

University of California Press
Berkeley and Los Angeles, California

University of California Press, Ltd.
Oxford, England

Library of Congress Cataloging-in-Publication Data

Jumonville, Neil.
Critical crossings : the New York intellectuals in postwar America /
    Neil Jumonville.
        p.   cm.
    ISBN 0-520-06858-0 (alk. paper)
    1. Intellectuals—New York (N.Y.)—History—20th century. 2. New
York (N.Y.)—Intellectual life. 3. United States—Intellectual life—20th
century. I. Title.
F128.52.J86 1991
974.7'1043—dc20   89-20517
                                                                CIP

Printed in the United States of America
1   2   3   4   5   6   7   8   9

The epigraph is from *One Hundred Years of Solitude,* by Gabriel
García Márquez, English translation copyright © 1970 Harper & Row,
Publishers, Inc.; reprinted by permission of the publisher. Part of
chapter four originally appeared in a different form in the *Journal of
American Culture* 12(1): 87–95, Spring 1989. Part of chapter five
originally appeared in a different form in *Queen's Quarterly*
97(2):290–304, Summer 1990.

For Annette Ansley Jumonville and
Lynn Chisholm Jumonville

It was Aureliano who conceived the formula that was to protect them against loss of memory for several months. He discovered it by chance. An expert insomniac, having been one of the first, he had learned the art of silverwork to perfection. One day he was looking for the small anvil that he used for laminating metals and he could not remember its name. His father told him: "Stake." Aureliano wrote the name on a piece of paper that he pasted to the base of the small anvil: *stake*. In that way he was sure of not forgetting it in the future. . . . With an inked brush [his father] marked everything with its name: *table, chair, clock, door, wall, bed, pan*. He went to the corral and marked the animals and plants: *cow, goat, pig, hen, cassava, caladium, banana*. Little by little, studying the infinite possibilities of a loss of memory, he realized that the day might come when things would be recognized by their inscriptions but that no one would remember their use. Then he was more explicit. The sign that he hung on the neck of the cow was an exemplary proof of the way in which the inhabitants of Macondo were prepared to fight against loss of memory: *This is the cow. She must be milked every morning so that she will produce milk, and the milk must be boiled in order to be mixed with coffee to make coffee and milk.* Thus they went on living in a reality that was slipping away, momentarily captured by words, but which would escape irremediably when they forgot the values of the written letters.

Gabriel García Márquez
One Hundred Years of Solitude

Contents

Photographs follow page 150.

Preface

Dwight Macdonald once referred to the late 1940s as "the gray dawn of 'peace.'" [1] It was an ambiguous image. His characterization reflected the beginning of a new day and the promise it brought in the wake of the war, but it also acknowledged the discouraging problems that clouded any optimism. At the time American intellectuals experienced the disillusionment of the Cold War, the threat of mass culture, the decline of radicalism, and an uncertain role for critics—to mention only a few of their most significant and unsettling fears.

This is a study of one particular group of American writers—the New York intellectuals, cultural and social critics prominent during what Randall Jarrell called the age of criticism. It was a time, Jarrell wrote, when for many writers "the act of criticism" became "the representative or Archetypal act of the intellectual." [2] The New York group's response to the unsettling gray dawn was to redefine and reshape the meaning of the term *intellectual* in order to exclude, undermine, and discredit those they thought at least partly responsible for the uneasy postwar situation. Their reaction to the problems facing their culture was to adopt a more rationalistic and pragmatic criticism than they employed before the war.

Although the New York intellectuals have had enough influence on the thought of mid-twentieth-century America to warrant a small shelf of studies, until recently we have had only their own accounts of themselves. Yet lately, as Jason Epstein once predicted, several historians have undertaken to serve as a "future Proust of Manhattan's Upper West Side" by recounting the story of the New York intellectuals.

The first mentions of the group appeared in the 1960s and 1970s but touched on it only tangentially. Daniel Aaron's pathbreaking *Writers on the Left* (1961), James Burkhart Gilbert's *Writers and Partisans* (1968),

John Diggins's *Up From Communism* (1975), and Peter Steinfels's *The Neoconservatives* (1979) all refer to the New York intellectuals, but the group was not the focus of these studies.

In the mid-1980s a second round of histories of the group appeared. Terry Cooney's *The Rise of the New York Intellectuals*, like Gilbert's book, ends at 1945 and again recounts the early story of *Partisan Review*. Alexander Bloom's *Prodigal Sons*, a general secondary account of the group, offers a comprehensive introductory survey whose central theme is the growth of Jewish identification among its members. Finally, Alan Wald's *The New York Intellectuals* provides a political account from a Trotskyist perspective. Wald focuses on the byzantine political factionalism on the left, mostly in the 1930s and 1940s, in order to indict those who departed from Trotskyism. Like the earlier wave of authors, Wald often lost the New York group in the story he was really telling: the history of American communism and socialism from the 1930s to the 1980s.

I have taken a different approach. This book tells the story of only a few of the most important debates the group waged, those that most sharply illuminate the passions and tensions of its members. Chronologically, although I discuss events from the early 1930s through the mid-1980s, my study focuses on these writers' most fruitful period—from 1945 to about 1970, when they were the most recognized, respected, influential, and prolific. In matters of interpretation, my emphasis falls on the group's development of what it means to be a responsible intellectual and critic. At each significant crossroad members of the group chose an allegiance to intellectualism rather than political leftism—and that is the real reason for their apparent journey from left to right of center.

Within this context I stress two themes. First, in the late 1930s and 1940s the New York intellectuals began to abandon their earlier ideological faith and prophetic partisanship for a more modest and precise outlook based on reason, analysis, and pragmatism. This crossover was a genuinely critical crossing: a critically important crossing from one conception of the critical role to another in the volatile Cold War world. In this reorientation that, in turn, influenced the rest of the intellectual community, they became rationalists and pluralists who opposed absolutism, moral crusades, ideology, and intuition.

Their intense rationalism was produced partly by their left-wing factional arguments in their youth, debates in which they learned to use reason to destroy an opponent's position. It was also a result of their disillusionment with ideology in the thirties and forties at the hands of Stalin, Hitler, and, later, Senator Joseph McCarthy. In the international arena their rationalist and pluralist outlook was usually referred to as antitotalitarianism. If anticommunism has been the official ideology of America in the postwar period, the New York critics not only helped shape it but also demonstrated how to integrate antitotalitarianism into culture as well as politics.

Over the decades their growing rationalism, pragmatism, and rejection of ideological simplicity produced a frustration with what they took to be simplistic liberalism and reform. Adopting a "tragic sense of life," they embraced complexity, irony, and ambiguity. For them the postwar period became a series of struggles against "romantic," "absolutist," or "intuitional" antagonists whom they considered insufficiently committed to reason and diversity: the Communists, the "totalitarian liberals," some theologians, the Beats, those who supported mass culture, and the counterculture and New Left in the 1960s.[3]

My second theme is that, contrary to the New York critics' interpretation of themselves, they were not committed political and cultural radicals in the 1930s who were pushed into neoconservatism by the antinomian uprising of the young in the 1960s. Nor were they trying in the 1960s to defend true reformism against the young radicals, only to turn in frustration toward neoconservatism to salvage whatever they could from an exhausted liberal tradition.

Instead, even in the 1930s these intellectuals had clear tendencies toward what later became neoconservatism.[4] Their crossing of the political spectrum was an evolutionary process, the natural outcome of their early outlook. Their political neoconservative leanings were discernible in their elevated, theoretical, intellectual socialism that was interlaced with a fear of the masses, just as their early cultural neoconservatism was evident in their highbrow and elitist criticism of mass culture. Their enduring fear of the masses leads us to an important question: Is this fear endemic to all intellectuals, since the intellectual's role as an evaluator entails the setting and maintaining of standards, and those standards, by nature, are exclusionary and not usually democratic?

Some historians have been persuaded by the New York group's autobiographical accounts, which stress the exhaustion of leftism and even reform liberalism in their time, that the neoconservative camp was the natural resting place for the group after the 1960s. But the alternatives to the neoconservatism of Sidney Hook, Irving Kristol, or Norman Podhoretz have been demonstrated by those who wrote for *Dissent* and remained "dissenters" during their entire careers. Irving Howe and Lewis Coser, for example, fought the implications of the group's early elitism more successfully than did their colleagues.

What difference does it make to argue that this group of writers be-

came anti-ideological rationalists who dominated much of the critical dialogue in the American intellectual community in the postwar period? Let
me begin to answer that by mentioning an observation made by Dennis
Wrong in 1970. He wrote that the 1960s (but one might say the entire
postwar period) represented the "Europeanization" of American politics,
the first large-scale importation of foreign ideologies into American political life.[5] Of course, a Europeanization of American culture had already
occurred with the triumph of modernism in the 1920s and 1930s. But
America, the New World, had always resisted the pull of Old World politics, and throughout the nineteenth and early twentieth centuries an iso-
lationist America had fended off the greater part of European political and
ideological influence. Yet after America assumed a role of international
leadership in the wake of World War II, the dangers were greater that
European political ideological tensions—in this case ideologies of the
right and left, fascism and communism—would penetrate American de-
fenses.

So the rationalism and pragmatism of the New York intellectuals after
the war was partly an anti-ideological impulse that attempted to fight off
the "ideological Europeanization" of America. The group was convinced
that a liberal society—open, humanely tolerant, and therefore nonideological—was necessary for intellectuals to survive. In order to preserve
the liberal outlook at the heart of the New World, they became determined to fight those who were not liberal rationalists, those who were
not "anti-ideological." These former ideologists, most of whom were second generation immigrants with strong Old World ties, stemmed the tide
of Old World ideologies in order to preserve their vision of the liberal
purity of the New World.

They did not wage the fight alone, of course. They found allies within
the American liberal intellectual community—for example, Reinhold
Niebuhr and the camp of neo-orthodoxy, and those we loosely label the
consensus historians—as well as among American conservative writers
who had their own agenda. But the New York intellectuals were the ones
who led the defense of liberal anti-ideology and pragmatism at mid-
century.

In this battle the New York group did not act entirely without self-
interest. Their efforts helped them gain a stronghold against the ideological totalitarian threats to intellectuals and Jews. In affirming the liberal
pragmatic consensus, they also came to feel better integrated into American society. Not least important, their leadership role enabled them to
exercise control over the definition of the term *intellectual*. Yet they as-
sisted American culture, too, by helping America restate and recommit

its intellectual resources to a liberal pluralism—after it had been pushed out onto stage in the postwar period as the leader of a very ideological and uneasy world.

Each chapter of this book has a half-dozen or more sections to it, two of which are biographical sketches of members of the New York group who prominently represented opposing opinions in the debate at hand. In order to articulate the group's attempts to define the proper role of the contemporary intellectual, I have organized my materials thematically rather than chonologically. Chapter 1 explores the question, What is sufficient intellectual integrity?; chapter 2, What is responsible intellectual criticism?; chapter 3, What is sufficient intellectual independence?; chapter 4, What is the intellectual's cultural responsibility?; chapter 5, What is proper intellectual radicalism?; chapter 6, What are the current and future prospects for the intellectual?

I also suggest how the New York intellectuals can be useful models. First, they set a good example for those who would like an alternative to academic confinement, and who would prefer to follow the pattern of freelance "high journalism" that the group employed in its early years. One legacy of the group's Marxist beginnings was an integrated interdisciplinary approach to thought; indeed, an interdisciplinary generalism was part of their definition of an intellectual approach.

Second, I reject the notion of the past two decades that intellectual history is elitist and social history is radical. Ideas are vital to radicals, and the New York critics are an example of those who employed ideas for intelligent radical ends early in their careers, and for liberal ends later. Even those who believe that the group did not find the right answers should recognize that they asked the right questions—about the proper relation of culture to politics, the worth of popular culture, the future of political and cultural freedom, and the role of intellectuals.

Acknowledgments

It is a pleasure to acknowledge the instruction and generosity I received while writing this book. I am especially grateful to Donald Fleming, who offered me guidance and support from beginning to end, and Alan Brinkley, who provided me with patient advice, encouragement, and insightful comments.

Despite disagreeing with me frequently, Daniel Bell has graciously read my work and commented extensively on it, rescuing me from mistakes and granting me more of his time than I had a right to expect. Daniel Aaron, whose work first prompted my interests, has shown an enthusiasm for this study and suggested the idea for the first chapter. George Rawlyk gave me his insight into each of my chapters at an early stage, and more importantly has served as a model scholar and friend. Michael Wreszin has fielded countless questions with good nature. Murray Hausknecht, Sidney Hook, and Dennis Wrong all read the entire manuscript and gave me beneficial and thorough advice.

I have also benefited from the help given me at various stages by Lewis Coser, Richard Gehr, Nathan Glazer, Irving Howe, Gordon Hylton, Robert Jumonville, Charlie McGovern, Greg Pfitzer, David Riesman, David Samson, Tom Siegel, Russ Sizemore, Cushing Strout, Jonathan Vietch, and David Watt. Further, it has been my good fortune to learn from those of my students at Harvard who shared my curiosity about the New York intellectuals. Andrea Nagin, David Rosenfeld, and Alexander Star wrote, under my supervision, undergraduate theses or summer research projects on aspects of the group. I also benefited immeasurably from the students in my three freshman seminars at Harvard (on the subject of the New York intellectuals and the letters tradition) who consistently challenged my views and provided me with fresh insights.

Without the assistance of several key libraries and their staffs, and their willingness to let me quote material in their possession, my research would have been more difficult. I appreciate the professional kindness of the Archives of American Art, Smithsonian Institution (Clement Greenberg Papers and Erle Loran Papers); the Henry W. and Albert A. Berg Collection, New York Public Library, Astor, Lenox and Tilden Foundations (Alfred Kazin's journal); the Columbia University Oral History Research Office (Richard Hofstadter project and Columbia Crisis project); the Harvard University Archives (Harlow Shapley Papers); the Manuscript Division, Library of Congress (Hannah Arendt Papers); the Rare Books and Manuscripts Division, New York Public Library, Astor, Lenox and Tilden Foundations (Norman Thomas Papers); Manuscripts and Archives, Yale University Library (Dwight Macdonald Papers); and, for their continual help, the reference librarians in Widener Library, Harvard University.

Several of the principals of this study were more charitable to me than I had a right to expect. Alfred Kazin was kind enough to allow me to be one of the first to read through over thirty volumes of his private journal, and I owe him a special thanks. Murray Hausknecht provided me with copies of an unpublished exchange with Louis Filler, and Nathan Glazer supplied an unpublished autobiographical essay. Other individuals have generously allowed me to quote from their personal letters or papers; for this I am grateful to Daniel Bell, Lewis Coser, Malcolm Cowley, Murray Hausknecht, Sidney Hook, Irving Howe, Mrs. Albert E. Kahn, Gloria Macdonald, William Phillips, Betty Rahv, and David Riesman. I am also indebted to those who found time to grant me interviews: Daniel Aaron, Daniel Bell, Lewis Coser, Robert Gorham Davis, Nathan Glazer, Murray Hausknecht, Sidney Hook, Irving Howe, Alfred Kazin, David Riesman, and Bernard Rosenberg.

One of the most enjoyable tasks in constructing this book was the collection of the photographs. I owe a special thanks to Daniel Bell, who kindly lent me nearly half of the photos I used. The other individuals who also lent me their private photos made this job a pleasant one, and I appreciate their generosity.

I am very grateful to Sheila Levine, Rose Vekony, and Amy Einsohn, my editors at the University of California Press, who have shared their knowledge and expertise with me and contributed immeasurably to the outcome of this book.

Finally, the most rewarding debt to acknowledge I owe the two women to whom this work is inscribed. This book is dedicated to my mother, Annette Ansley Jumonville, who, while raising six children by herself, encouraged in them the values of education and determination, stood by them always, and by her example taught them the power of the word and idea. And it is dedicated to my wife, Lynn Chisholm Jumonville, whose spirit of generosity and love, recognized by all who know her, has served as a fund of quiet strength for me during the completion of this project.

1 The View from the Waldorf

On Friday evening, March 25, 1949, the Waldorf Conference opened in New York. The weekend-long series of meetings of international intellectuals included sessions at the Waldorf-Astoria Hotel, Carnegie Hall, and Madison Square Garden. Since the hotel housed most of the meetings, the event immediately became known as the Waldorf Conference, though its formal name was the Cultural and Scientific Conference for World Peace.

During the preceding several weeks, as they tried to shape their final arrangements, the conference leaders had been treated to increasingly hostile criticism. The State Department, much of the media, many church leaders, and a variety of organizations, from war veterans to labor unions, all competed to issue the most strident denunciation of the conference. Although the conference planners and sponsors described themselves as international leaders of science and culture who wanted only to promote world peace in the face of increasing Cold War tensions, their opponents denounced the event as a Communist-front forum held to criticize the United States and defend Stalin's cultural and foreign policies.

Despite "considerable pressure" to cancel the conference, the Waldorf proclaimed its civic duty not to collapse under that weight.[1] Late Friday afternoon the gray, imposing Waldorf stood ringed with picketers and police. Inside, in a room twenty-five floors above the street, sat the chairman of the conference, Dr. Harlow Shapley, professor of astronomy at Harvard University, with his friend Martin Popper, a lawyer from the National Lawyers Guild, and their wives. The door to Shapley's room stood slightly open as the four sipped cocktails and chatted about the evening's plans.

Suddenly there was a loud knock at the door; then two men pushed it open and burst into the room. One was Sidney Hook, professor of phi-

1

losophy at New York University and an outspoken anti-Stalinist. The other was a reporter from the *Herald Tribune* whom Hook had brought with him to record the encounter. Shapley, according to the reporter, "rose from his chair with a startled look." During the previous two months Hook and Shapley had developed a mutual animosity that seemed to surpass mere intellectual disagreement. They stood on opposite sides of the Waldorf divide: Hook was the acknowledged leader of the intellectual forces opposed to the gathering. Neither regarded their dispute as insignificant.

Hook angrily accused Shapley of preventing him from addressing the conference, to begin an hour later, at 8 P.M. Shapley owed him a public apology, he insisted. Popper, in his anxiety, could not follow Hook's reasoning and thought Hook "talked incoherently." But Hook was a veteran of the most heated polemics, and passion produced intensity, but not confusion, in him. Shapley and Hook had traded accusations in the press for several weeks about whether Hook was being deliberately refused a spot as a speaker. Shapley maintained that Hook had not written him in time; Hook contended that he could prove otherwise.

"You have impugned my integrity, Dr. Shapley," Hook declared angrily, "by denying that my offer to read a paper at the conference was ever accepted by any members of the Program Committee. . . . Well, here's the evidence." He walked to a coffee table in the room and slapped down carbon copies of several letters that, he said, proved beyond doubt that he had sent several early requests to various members of the committee, including Shapley. Shapley responded that he had not received the letters personally but he knew they existed. More words were exchanged. Shapley, looking for a way to end the unpleasant confrontation, confided to Hook, "We can't talk about this in front of the ladies." He suggested to Hook that they saunter into the hallway and peacefully carry on their discussion: that way the women would be spared the argument. Putting his glass on a table, Shapley walked to the door and opened it. Hook and the reporter followed. Once the men were out of the room, Shapley turned back quickly over the threshold, locked the door, and refused to open it or come back out. Hook heard a confusion of voices in the room, among which he could distinguish Popper shouting: "Call the desk. Call Security." Hook left.[2] The confrontation was over.

This scene, for all its ideological hostility, was not uncharacteristic of other confrontations during that weekend in New York. Nor, for that matter, was it out of the ordinary during any of the period, from the 1930s to the 1980s, in that intellectual group to which Sidney Hook belonged—the group that became known as the New York intellectuals.

The New York Intellectuals and Cultural Criticism

Like the rest of the New York intellectuals, Sidney Hook was in conflict with other factions of the intellectual community—in the case of the Waldorf Conference it was the insufficiently anti-Soviet portion—over what responsibilities a proper intellectual had to maintain. Throughout the post-World War II period the New York group clashed with other sectors of the American intelligentsia about what constituted the function of intellectuals, and the appropriate level of criticism of one's own culture.

The New York intellectuals were the mid-century's most prominent group of generalist cultural critics—reviewers and essayists who wrote on contemporary issues of political, social, and cultural importance. As generalists, they took all of culture and society as their province, rather than restricting themselves to the specialized fields they also knew; as reviewers and critics, they were constantly evaluating and adjudicating ongoing cultural and political production; as intellectuals, they were involved in current issues and struggles, rather than detached and neutral scholarship.

Cultural criticism at its core is an intellectual activity that poses a nearly religious task. It undertakes what in the past was exclusively the function of theologians and philosophers: to evaluate and promote moral values and social ethics. It demands that we transcend the commonplace and judge ourselves, culture, and society against the highest standards. Criticism, at its best, is a debate about the purpose of life. This process requires challenging, remeasuring, and revising cultural traditions. It is founded on dissent. Performed properly, it reaches beyond the measurement of a particular artifact, explores the possibilities and boundaries of life, and informs the demands that culture places on our lives. It is, as Matthew Arnold noted, life's criticism of itself.[3]

The first American critics in this genre had taken some of their cues from the earlier British tradition of the literary review.[4] Benjamin Franklin, for example, emulated Joseph Addison's *Spectator* in producing his Silence Dogood pieces for his brother James Franklin's *New England Courant* in the 1720s. Fifty years later the Hartford Wits—Jonathan Trumbull, Timothy Dwight, and Joel Barlow—modeled themselves after such English authors as Addison, Pope, and Milton, although the Wits were more given to light verse than to the review. Washington Irving, at the beginning of the nineteenth century, contributed drama criticism and satirical essays under the pseudonym Jonathan Oldstyle to the *Morning Chronicle*, *The Corrector*, and *Analectic Magazine*. These early attempts in the letters tradition were significant but, in the absence of a healthy network of culture, they failed to produce any sustained critical interaction.

America's cultural anemia was less pronounced by the 1830s. In New England, and to a lesser extent in New York, an American critical sensibility began to take shape. Ralph Waldo Emerson, Margaret Fuller, Orestes Brownson, Elizabeth Palmer Peabody, Theodore Parker, Henry David Thoreau, and Walt Whitman were all engaged as reviewers and essayists who examined cultural, political, and social issues.[5] From 1840 to 1844 in New England *The Dial* functioned as the country's first forum for what came to be known as the "letters tradition"—a term that reflects that criticism was performed almost exclusively as a branch of literature or drama during the eighteenth and nineteenth centuries. Cultural criticism, still in a nascent condition, persisted after the waning influence of the Concord writers and the death of *The Dial*, although for the remainder of the nineteenth century the dialogue was weak.

During and after the Civil War, critics such as James Russell Lowell, William Dean Howells at the *Atlantic* and then *Harper's*, and Mark Twain and Henry James wrote about culture.[6] Although they added significantly to America's critical heritage, they were at heart novelists or poets, not critics whose primary role was to engage one another and society at large in broad cultural debate. Late in the century the Genteel Tradition produced several critics, including Thomas Bailey Aldrich, Charles Eliot Norton, Edmund Clarence Stedman, and Richard Henry Stoddard.[7] This group, however, was too correct and Victorian to preside over a vigorous cultural debate.

In this period Henry Adams—best known for his histories, autobiography, and novels—also functioned as a critical essayist and generalist during his tenure at the *North American Review*. Adams had written his brother Charles as early as 1862 to announce, "What we want is a *school.*"[8] Without any identifiable schools of thought, there was a lack of clearly defined perspectives for writers to criticize, little to beneficially polarize them and to create the basis for cultural debate. Adams, like Emerson in his "American Scholar," felt the need for distinctively American critical outlooks.

In the early twentieth century, however, there arose slowly the style of cultural and social criticism that anticipated the mid-twentieth-century fashion. In Greenwich Village young critics, artists, and political radicals gathered from around the country, cut loose from provincial America by the social and cultural changes created by industrialization. In the teens in New York the letters tradition came of age; what had been since Emerson's time a sporadic and uneven line of cultural criticism became steady and continuous.[9]

Van Wyck Brooks exerted the most leadership when he tried during World War I to prompt his generation to a new sense of their cultural responsibility. Brooks agreed with Emerson and Adams that Americans needed to develop a critical literary consciousness. Critics, Brooks said on behalf of his generation, needed to know they were "working in a great line." Despite Henry Adams's power, Brooks complained, Adams had failed to speak out forcefully enough to "become the founder, the centre, of the school that he desired." [10]

Brooks tried to rectify the anemic cultural condition. As Emerson had urged his generation to shun European models and depend on themselves, so Brooks implored his contemporaries to leave behind the arid Genteel Tradition and the pioneer culture and begin a cultural criticism that could serve as a foundation, or a "wind shield," for later generations. [11] He was joined in this project of escalating cultural criticism to a sustainable and recognizable level by various essayists in the letters tradition such as Harold Stearns, Gertrude Stein, and H. L. Mencken; by little magazines such as the *Freeman, Seven Arts,* and the recreated *Dial;* and by the poet-critics T. S. Eliot, Ezra Pound, and Amy Lowell, who served as models and mentors for many of the later literary generalists.

In the 1920s a slightly younger generation of literary generalists made its debut. Edmund Wilson, the most prominent of this generation and a direct influence on the New York intellectuals, wrote for *Vanity Fair* and then the *New Republic.* [12] The literary exiles of the Lost Generation in the years after World War I were led by critics such as Malcolm Cowley, Kenneth Burke, and Matthew Josephson. During the twenties the Harlem Renaissance bloomed, with critics and generalists such as James Weldon Johnson, Sterling Brown, Langston Hughes, Zora Neale Hurston, Alain Locke, Jean Toomer, and Paul Lawrence Dunbar. [13] Concurrently there was the Algonquin group, which included Dorothy Parker, Alexander Woollcott, and Ring Lardner—a group to which Malcolm Cowley in his younger days wished to belong. [14] The Nashville Agrarians, with such notable figures in the letters tradition as John Crowe Ransom, Allen Tate, Donald Davidson, and Robert Penn Warren, promoted a conservative and anti-industrial vision at the end of the 1920s. At the same time, the conservative New Humanist movement coalesced under the direction of critics Paul Elmer More and Irving Babbitt.

During World War I, a group of writers became active in Greenwich Village who, while interested in literature, were equally interested in radical politics. Led by Max Eastman, Floyd Dell, and Waldo Frank, the literary left wing edited and wrote for *The Masses* and the *Liberator.* Although the political impulse was muted in the 1920s, by the early 1930s there were literary leftists again—under the leadership of Granville

Hicks, Michael Gold, Joseph Freeman, Whittaker Chambers, and others—this time connected to the *New Masses*, or V. F. Calverton's *Modern Monthly* (which since 1923 had combined Freudianism and Marxism). In the early years of the Depression the newly radicalized Edmund Wilson left the *New Republic* to write criticism independently, and the newly radicalized Malcolm Cowley replaced him at the magazine. Later in the decade Richard Wright was among the new critics who arose on the left.

Cultural criticism, of course, consisted of more than the literary talents of the letters tradition. It included a mix of criticism by historians, economic philosophers, and political writers. America's best-known nineteenth-century historians—George Bancroft, Francis Parkman, William Prescott, and Henry Adams—wrote history as an avocation, saw historical writing as an extension of literature, and were self-consciously generalists in the letters tradition. When the field was professionalized at the end of the century, historians such as Frederick Jackson Turner, Charles Beard, Carl Becker, and Vernon Parrington continued to write as generalists who addressed the public as well as their professional peers. In the late 1920s members of the next generation of historians, including Allan Nevins and Henry Steele Commager, also crafted essays in the generalist tradition on political and social topics for widely circulated magazines. These generalist historians served as models for such New York intellectuals as Richard Hofstadter and Arthur Schlesinger, Jr.

There were generalists among economists as well, and although few of them were reviewers, they did act as broad cultural critics. Interested in political economy and its relation to the social and political structure, they viewed economic philosophy as an integral part of social thought and culture. Essays on American political economy extend back at least as far as Alexander Hamilton and Thomas Jefferson, and include those written by Orestes Brownson in the antebellum period and Henry George after the Civil War. In the first decades of the twentieth century, Thorstein Veblen achieved prominence as an economic generalist.

Among Veblen's successors at the University of Chicago, Frank Knight and Henry Simons were interested in political economy, although they were proponents of a laissez-faire system of economics and society and were skeptical of the benefits of socialism. At Harvard, the Czechoslovakian-born and Austrian-educated Joseph Schumpeter was an eminent political economist concerned with the workings of broad systems, as the title of his *Capitalism, Socialism and Democracy* (1942) indicates. These economic philosophers had widely ranging political and social interests, and as cultural critics they explored the relation of intellectual and political freedom to the economic and social structure. Among the New York intellectuals in this mold were social scientists such as Robert Heilbroner,

Daniel Bell, Irving Kristol, Ben B. Seligman, Robert Lekachman, and Edward Shils.[15]

Also among American critics early in the twentieth century were essayists whose primary focus was politics. Prominent in this group were Lincoln Steffens, John Dewey, Randolph Bourne, John Reed, and Walter Lippmann; they wrote for *McClure's*, the *New Republic*, the *Nation*, *The Masses*, and other publications. Sidney Hook was the member of the New York group whose work most directly reflected this political strand of generalist criticism.

Finally, some pioneering critics escape simple categorization. Lewis Mumford, for example, wrote literary criticism, architectural essays, and articles on the relation between urbanism, technology, and culture. His combined interest in politics and the arts led him to explore the relation between social life and the forms people create to express and shape it.

With the decline of religion in America in the nineteenth century, the responsibility for working with these central cultural values was thought by many to have moved from religious leaders to novelists and poets. In the early twentieth century, however, as those writers came increasingly to mistrust the ability of language and narrative to convey beneficial values, critics began to take over their function and replace them at the core of culture. Now, late in the twentieth century, criticism has been invaded in some quarters by a similar distrust of language and of the writer's subconscious intentions and perhaps will follow its predecessors into decline.

Among the themes of American cultural criticism from Emerson to the present, several have been recurrent concerns: for example, the importance of maintaining one's own independent analysis, the value of stubborn persistence in the pursuit of truth and justice, and the necessity of freedom, variously defined. Further, nearly every serious cultural critic in America has addressed the relationship between the intellectual and society, with many holding that the critic must be a detached outsider in order to be an effective observer.

Others, beginning with Van Wyck Brooks, hoped to prevent the cultural intelligence in America from becoming too ethereal, abstract, or disconnected from everyday real life. Cultural criticism needed to be grounded in the experiences of work and the streets, and not least of all it needed to be political. Yet another concern—especially in the 1920s and early 1930s from writers as diverse as the Nashville Agrarians, Edmund Wilson, and Malcolm Cowley—was whether artists and critics had a duty to assume social responsibility or commitment to a political cause. The issue of a political component in cultural criticism encompassed a long list of political—and ultimately ideological—considerations: Did intellectuals lose more in independence than they gained from the direction provided by political commitments? Did critics need to foster community—or even collectivism? Was collectivism the appropriate response, for writers or society, to social crises, or did it bring more trouble than it was worth? What form of society, economy, and culture produced the greatest benefits? Should intellectuals oppose industrialism? Did critics and society at large need a moral vision, and how did that differ from a political vision?

From their own unique background in the late 1920s and early 1930s the New York intellectuals stepped into a line of American generalist cultural inquiry that was increasingly political in nature. Most of them were raised in poor Jewish neighborhoods in New York City, attended City College, and came to share an ideological outlook. In general, they supported Soviet socialism until the mid-1930s. After the wrenching Moscow Trials of 1936, their bitter hatred for the centralization, deceit, murder, anti-intellectualism, and undemocratic nature of Stalinism led them to become anti-Stalinist socialists. (They called themselves independent radicals, though they were called "Trotskyists" by the Stalinists.)[16] In the late 1940s, as the outlines of the Cold War became clearer, they turned toward centrist liberalism.

They also shared institutional affiliations in their network of small intellectual journals. Between the mid-1930s and the 1980s various members of the group founded, edited, and wrote for the *Menorah Journal, Partisan Review, The Contemporary Jewish Record, Politics, Commentary, Encounter, The New Leader, Dissent,* the *New York Review of Books, The Public Interest, The New Criterion,* and the *National Interest,* among others. Finally, the New York intellectuals were identifiable socially. Members of their inner circle associated with each other, attended each other's parties, and recognized each other as members of the same crowd. They knew who they were.[17]

Observers of the New York intellectuals have ranked them by generation. The first generation includes members born between 1900 and 1915 who came to political maturity in the 1920s or early 1930s: Sidney Hook, Lionel Trilling, Dwight Macdonald, Philip Rahv, William Phillips, Meyer Schapiro, Harold Rosenberg, Lewis Coser, Clement Greenberg, and Mary McCarthy. The second generation was born between about 1915 and 1925 and came to political maturity during the Depression: Irving Howe, Alfred Kazin, Daniel Bell, Nathan Glazer, Irving Kristol, Seymour Martin Lipset, Norman Mailer, and William Barrett. A third generation arrived on the scene after World War II and included Norman Podhoretz, Susan Sontag, and Michael Walzer.[18] The group prior to 1950 had perhaps twenty-five members in its inner circle, but expanded by another twenty-five or so as one moved toward its periphery. After the early 1950s the larger group expanded into a more diffused entity, with about seventy-five people affiliated with it.[19]

Early in their careers these writers lived and published in relative obscurity, but after World War II they rose into positions of leadership in such fields as literary criticism (Trilling, Kazin, Howe), art criticism (Greenberg, Rosenberg, Schapiro), sociology (Bell, Coser, Glazer, Lipset), and intellectual high journalism (Kristol, Macdonald, Podhoretz). Among the most influential American intellectuals in the postwar period, they increasingly set the agenda for contemporary intellectual discourse.

This circle has also put its distinctive stamp on one strain of American social and literary criticism in the past forty years—the strand that is contextual rather than formalistic and deconstructive. The New York group's early mastery of Marxism in the 1930s, their abandonment of Marxism after the war, and their adoption of a pluralistic liberalism enabled them to introduce a synthesis of Marxist and liberal analysis into the American mainstream. Following the Marxist intellectual orientation, which has always resisted the categorization and specialization of disciplines, the New York circle has always taken a sociological and historical approach to both literary and social criticism. Even when many of the group became more conservative, they maintained a holistic and interdisciplinary approach, an intellectual generalism that discouraged distinctions between literature and politics, or art and social policy.

As critics and reviewers, they took the essay as their medium, and the literary and political magazine was their institutional forum. Their minds were critical rather than artistic, minds trained to cut through illusion and fiction and sharpened by internecine left-wing factional debates. They were reviewers, debaters, critics, interpreters, intellectual surgeons, polemicists—not poets, novelists, or painters. With the exception of Mary McCarthy, Norman Mailer, and Saul Bellow, there were no novelists among the inner circle, and McCarthy and Mailer were better essayists than novelists anyway.

These writers maintained a strong opposition to simplistic or total solutions, to reductionism and absolutism. Although they wanted a political cultural criticism, they opposed a political domination of literature and culture. Similarly, in literary criticism, members of the group like Lionel Trilling called for a moral component to literature (in the F. R. Leavis tradition) but battled against a moral absolutism in politics or culture. The group searched for a balance: for a combination of politics and culture that resisted any political domination of culture, for a combination of moral and cultural elements that avoided the sort of moral absolutism they despised. The need for this balance created in them a reverence for ambiguity and complexity, and produced a revulsion against what they came to call "ideology."

Their appeal for a political and moral element in culture confused many observers, however, who heard the group demand an ideological component in culture and yet heard them denounce certain political and moral positions as dangerously ideological. Because the New York intellectuals often failed to articulate their distinction between appropriate and inappropriate ideology—the latter comprising outlooks the group regarded as simplistic, absolutist, and inappropriately passionate—others had the impression that the circle both promoted and denounced ideology in culture.

At mid-century, as America emerged from a near-fatal contact with the European crises of the 1930s and 1940s, one might have expected even intellectuals to be optimistic and confident. After all, it was not a bad period for America. The war had been won; the American economy was beginning a meteoric rise that would not falter for nearly two decades; the country's military held an unchallenged international superiority. Yet despite the apparent success of the United States during the period that would be called the "consensus decade," American intellectuals were engaged in ideological battles that had seldom been fought with more passion.

In the postwar years, intellectuals could not shake their fear that America and the West were still strongly threatened by the dangers of totalitarianism and ideological absolutism. Largely as a result of those fears, the New York group embraced America as the only protection against totalitarianism. By the late 1940s their sharp criticism of American culture had given way to a mixture of optimism and pessimism. They grew increasingly optimistic about America's achievements in providing some democratic vision, civil freedoms, and economic success. Yet they were pessimistic about what they took to be a strong strain of pro-Soviet and anti-American feeling among the intellectual community, sentiments which, they were sure, would undermine America's strength if unopposed. Both their hopes and their fears were rooted in the group's relatively new identification with and support for America.

Between 1935 and 1955, as their new relationship with America was being forged, the position, status, and beliefs of the New York intellectuals changed significantly. This reorientation unsettled them and threw into question what they meant by the term *intellectual*.

One definition of an intellectual emphasizes occupational roles: intellectuals are those whose jobs require them to deal with ideas. In this category, for example, we might put scientists, teachers, journalists, and novelists, among others. While this description has been favored by conservatives, it has been put forward by such different figures as the conservative sociologist Talcott Parsons and the more radical sociologist Robert Brym.[20]

A second definition of intellectual transcends occupational divisions to include anyone who perpetually questions accepted truths, challenges orthodoxies, and adopts the stance of a dissenter. This approach is equally open to doctors, professors, or truck drivers because it describes a way of looking at the world and challenging it—on and off the job, in any job.[21] Among those who subscribe to this second definition, some conceive of the intellectual as a partisan, an advocate for a particular set of views, while others insist that the intellectual be a freelance dissenter who is neither institutionally nor ideologically committed to any class or political position.

A third constellation of definitions portrays the intellectual as fulfilling a sacred function. Here the intellectual is expected to exert a creative impulse, to synthesize and integrate diverse materials and apparently unrelated concepts into a new perspective, to step back and speak to larger, deeper, and more important values. This integrative task requires intellectuals to be generalists who can translate and popularize their specialized knowledge into culturally relevant meaning for the entire educated population. For some, the intellectual is seen to perform a secular version of a religious function, interpreting a confusing and chaotic world to a secular congregation, and creating myths, symbols, and scriptural literature to convey meaning and promote proper values and beliefs.[22] This latter function also suggests an anthropological conception of the intellectual as one who creates, as Malcolm Cowley once said of novelists, "the myths of the tribe."[23]

The act of cultural criticism, then, is one of the many ways of functioning as an intellectual. Critics are being intellectuals when they challenge orthodoxies, adopt the role of questioners and dissenters, write essays as freelancers, synthesize and generalize cultural trends, ask the culture to transcend the common, offer a sacred leadership by creating values and meaning, or construct myths of the tribe. Although all cultural critics perform an intellectual role, not all intellectuals need to work as cultural critics.

Partly because of the strong tie many of them had with Jewish immigrant culture, which caused them to feel like outsiders in America, most members of the New York group in the 1930s adhered strongly to the second definition: that intellectuals were those who opposed mainstream society from a radical and alienated position outside its comfortable confines. Intellectuals had to be free from institutional attachments to the mainstream. Partisans of a dissenting political position, intellectuals were not to avoid ideology but rather to confront dangerous political ideologies with a more beneficial and just ideology.

By the 1950s, however, the consensus had changed. Seymour Martin Lipset and other centrists in the group endorsed the more conservative occupational definition of the intellectual's task. Those who were radicals in the 1950s—including Lewis Coser, Harold Rosenberg, and Irving Howe—stayed with the group's earlier view that the intellectual is a dissenter, or, as Rosenberg once said, is one who turns answers into questions.[24]

Despite these disagreements about definitions, by the 1950s most members of the group had rejected the necessity of thinking ideologically.[25] Global events of the previous two decades had convinced them that ideology was dangerous. Now, with many members of the group being hired by the universities after the war, mainstream institutional attachments no longer seemed so compromising. Questioning the status quo was still deemed worthwhile, but increasingly they saw the intellectual's role as one of affirmation rather than dissent. They still wanted to believe that they opposed orthodoxies, but now they began to find it more important to "dissent from the orthodoxies of dissent," as Lionel Trilling described Nathaniel Hawthorne as doing.[26] Rather than being an advocate or a political partisan, the intellectual was to be a liberal cultural critic committed to open debate and to making important analytical distinctions about culture. Perhaps cultural enfranchisement could even make one a better critic or intellectual, by providing one with insights from the inside.

While many in the group believed they had abandoned ideology and partisanship, actually they had traded their earlier partisanship in leftist factions for a postwar partisanship in defense of political liberalism. Because liberalism was more diverse and open, their new partisanship was less narrow, but it was equally polemical and contentious, retaining much of the attitude, if not the strength, of their early partisanship. Further, none of their partisanship in matters of art abated. "There is no discrimination without partisanship to an ideal," Alfred Kazin wrote in 1962 about art criticism. "The critic who has the equipment to be a force, the critic who can set up standards for his age," he told the intellectual community, "must be a partisan of one kind of art and a bitter critic of another. . . . Such a critic will be not only unfair, he will pursue his prejudice to the point of absurdity."[27]

Their search for a new intellectualism was undertaken in the cultural sphere as well. Most of the group believed in the need for rigorous standards and the defense of high culture against mass culture. Although part of their hostility to mass culture was based on cultural anticapitalism, most of it reflected their preference for the highbrow and the avant-garde. As early as the 1930s their disdain for mass culture epitomized the tensions between their own vigorous commitment to intellectual values on one hand, and a commitment to a democracy in the cultural sphere that they never enthusiastically endorsed on the other hand. Their sharp antagonism to mass culture reveals that on cultural issues most of the group chose intellectualism over a cultural and aesthetic democracy, and maybe even over a vision of cultural and aesthetic pluralism. Although they argued for the international self-determination of countries and for the political self-determination of the individual, they opposed the self-determination of the individual consumer of culture.

Their cultural choices help us to clarify their political outlook. Even at their most radical, in the 1930s, they espoused a Talmudic highbrow socialism divorced from the common people, a radicalism for intellectuals. The group's constant hostility to populist politics and mass culture is hardly unusual: by nature, most intellectuals are antipopulist, especially in the realm of culture.

Their attempts to envision a new function for intellectuals were also shaped by the rapidity of postwar changes in technology, society, and power relationships. Among the questions they confronted were those pertaining to an intellectual's proper relationship to government power, patriotism, and propaganda. Should intellectuals defend individualism or collectivism, the political left or right? How could intellectuals best respond to political beliefs and alliances they now regretted, to current ideological outbreaks, to romantic movements of the young?

The New York intellectuals' involvement with the Waldorf Conference was a revealing episode in their fight to establish a code of responsibility and integrity among the American intellectual community in the years following World War II. Their opposition to the conference typified their lifelong battle with what they considered to be improper leftism, and their protests demonstrated the polemical style for which the group became known.

The Freedom to Speak

A cornerstone of an intellectual's identity, according to the New York group, was integrity of opinion. To function as an intellectual, one needed the freedom to speak honestly and candidly, even heretically. One's analysis had to be untainted by pressure from outside, whether political, economic, religious, or social. This issue of intellectual integrity was central to the Waldorf conflict.

The spring of 1949 was not a congenial time in America for a conference sympathetic to leftist domestic and international goals, a conference clearly more critical of the United States than of the Soviet Union. Cold War anxiety had reached high tide in America, and the political atmosphere of hostility to the left in general and to Communism specifically was not encouraging to those who organized the Waldorf Conference or to those sponsors affiliated with it.[28]

Just prior to the conference, the New York media were already reporting an anti-Communist fever in the country. On the Wednesday preceding the Waldorf weekend the "Communist Eleven" conspiracy trial opened in New York City with front-page coverage in the *New York Times*. Eugene Dennis, general secretary of the Communist party of the United States, and ten other party members were charged with holding secret meetings to train revolutionaries to overthrow the government through violence. During that same week Harold Laski, professor at the University of London and a member of the Executive Committee of the British Labour party, was banned from making two scheduled lecture appearances at UCLA because of his leftist writings.[29] In keeping with the national mood of anti-Communist enthusiasm, Yale University had refused to provide a hall for Dmitri Shostakovich, a member of the Soviet delegation to the Waldorf Conference, to give a concert and speak. When Professor John Marsalka of Yale tried to arrange for Shostakovich's appearance, the administration issued a statement warning that they saw "no educational value in opening the university halls to such a meeting," a position that shocked and distressed many in the intellectual community and delighted others.[30]

Harlow Shapley, in view of these conditions, decided to proceed discreetly and cautiously with the conference arrangements and not create trouble by defending those on the left who were under attack. "But let us be very careful . . . not to take part in some operation that can blackly smear us, before our peace conference, with being pro-communist," he warned in a letter to Hannah Dorner, executive director of the National Council of the Arts, Sciences, and Professions (NCASP, the sponsoring body). "I am tremendously anxious that we do a useful peace conference; one that by right-thinking people can be taken as non-partisan." Nonpartisan did not mean nonpolitical, but Shapley knew that if the Waldorf leaders became associated in the public mind with the Communist Eleven trials, the integrity of the conference would be destroyed. "If we directly or indirectly jump into the defense of the communist leaders at this time," he continued to Dorner, "we may feel all right inside, if there is persecution in actual operation, but we will not help our meetings in March. Sometimes it seems as though we just go out of our way to supply raw material to the Red-baiters."[31]

The immediate problem for Shapley in the months prior to the conference was to secure visas from the U.S. State Department for all the members of the foreign delegations who planned to attend. From the moment Shapley contacted the State Department, both State and the FBI began investigating the NCASP. An internal memorandum at State noted that the NCASP had disturbing similarities to the subversive National Council of American-Soviet Friendship, and a State Department telegraph to the American embassy in Rome noted that the conference was "largely COMMIE-dominated," though sponsored by "non-COMMIE individuals."[32]

During the week prior to the conference, increasing public pressure was put on the State Department to derail the meeting by refusing admission to the foreign guests. On March 16 the State Department granted visas to twenty-three delegates from Communist-bloc countries, but it had a more difficult time ruling on Western European and third-world delegates.[33] The following Monday, March 21, four days before the Waldorf Conference was to begin, the State Department declined to issue visas to almost all Western European delegates, citing alleged Communist connections—which were real in some cases, but nonexistent in most. The State Department concluded that the "Communist side of the case" would be presented thoroughly enough by the conference's Eastern-bloc delegates and the American fellow travelers, and that it was "not necessary to admit a score of additional spokesmen for the Communist viewpoint in order to permit an adequate presentation of the cause."[34] The FBI, which earlier had wiretapped Shapley's phone, would maintain surveillance on the foreign delegates during their stay.

That the State Department's policy angered the conference leaders and its supporters was not surprising. Less expected was the criticism of the State Department by Sidney Hook and his group, the Americans for Intellectual Freedom (AIF), the most outspoken and visible intellectual critics of the Waldorf Conference. For the AIF the visa action was an issue of intellectual freedom. On Tuesday, March 22, Sidney Hook and George Counts of Teachers College, the two serving as cochairmen of the AIF, issued a statement to the press. After characterizing the Waldorf Conference as "a perfect case study" of how Communists attempted to infiltrate the American intellectual community, the statement censured the State

Department for its refusal to issue visas to French and British delegates. "That contrast between our way of life and theirs," their statement read, "becomes blurred when our Government refuses entry to foreign nationals of any political persuasion." [35]

Dwight Macdonald also disapproved of the State Department's visa decision, but he noted, with some satisfaction, that the U.S. government had acted liberally by comparison with Soviet behavior. He acknowledged that the visa refusals and the mass picketing were unpalatable. "But," he continued, "the American government *did* let in the Russians, and it *did* permit the Conference to be held, and the local police *did* protect the delegates. So let us hear no more from Messrs. Shapley, Schuman et al. about the mote in the eye of the State Department until they have cast out the beam from the eye of the Kremlin." [36]

By the New York group's standards, the participants in the Waldorf Conference were not true intellectuals. Blinded by a party line, the Waldorf confederates were a danger not only to society but to the life of the mind. Yet if the delegates to the conference were prevented from entering the United States, then freedom of expression would be dealt an even stronger blow. Facing this choice, the group supported a more open visa policy than the State Department was willing to tolerate. The New York intellectuals upheld the freedom of expression, and then worked tirelessly and stridently to oppose and refute everything the Waldorf speakers had to say.

As Sidney Hook interpreted it, the New York group's right to speak freely, to express its opinions about the political and cultural treachery of the conference, meant instead that he had an individual right to address the conference personally. By the time Hook sought permission to speak at the Waldorf affair, he already had "suspicions" that it was dominated by the Communists. If this was a conference of intellectuals, Hook thought, it had to live up to that claim by giving him, a fellow intellectual, the chance to present his opinion on the conference issues. On February 25 Hook wrote Shapley asking to be allowed to deliver a paper, "Science, Culture, and Peace," and citing the support of Herbert Davis, president of Smith College and a member of the conference program committee. Hook told Shapley he would argue that there were no national, class, or party "truths" in science, and that international peace and science had been "seriously undermined" by those doctrines. [37] Since science was one of the intellectuals' methodological tools, Hook felt that its analyses should not be clouded by national or party doctrines.

The conference leaders, it is obvious from the record, did not want Hook's opinions to be dignified by a formal presentation to the delegates.

Howard Fast, the leftist novelist who was one of the most prominent and central of the conference planners, later wrote that Hook had "requested permission to speak at the conference. Quite properly, considering him outside the pale of either peace or progressive human endeavor, the conference denied this request of Mr. Hook."[38] Shapley, however, wanted the official response to be more diplomatic, and he urged that it express the regret of the conference leaders that Hook had not contacted them earlier, since "the first we heard from him was after the program was completed." Hook was sent a letter informing him that the program was full, but inviting him to attend one of the smaller panel meetings on Saturday afternoon. There, after the panel speakers had presented their papers and discussion was opened up to the floor, he could offer his remarks. Hook had requested fifteen minutes to speak; the responses from the floor in the panel discussions would be limited to two minutes apiece. The conference leadership obviously was trying to defuse the threat of Sidney Hook.[39]

What Hook considered to be a proper and legitimate attempt to do intellectual battle with the Waldorf minds by offering an opposing viewpoint and some necessary criticism, Shapley perceived as an underhanded attempt to disrupt a conference that its leaders had every right to stage for their own purposes.[40]

From the perspective of the New York group, the issue of whether Hook or other opposition voices would be given a spot on the program raised the question of whether the conference leaders were behaving as responsible intellectuals. Could the conference planners promote the Waldorf weekend as an open and inquisitive forum, and yet restrict the ideological variety of the critical analyses presented at the conference without undermining the intellectual vocation itself? Hook and his associates felt that the misrepresentations of the conference by its planners, and the absence of any analytical freedom or integrity in what appeared to be a party-line conference, were clear evidence of intellectual irresponsibility and fraud.

Hook was the most adamant of the New York group about the Waldorf Conference's betrayal of intellectual values, and his passion on this point was a hallmark of his life and ideals.

Sidney Hook

The intellectual forefather of the New York group, Sidney Hook was the most important generator of its ideas in its early years. Like many of them, Hook was raised in a lower-class Jewish neighborhood in New York

City. He was born on December 20, 1902, in Brooklyn and grew up in the Williamsburg section. Precocious—like Irving Howe and Daniel Bell years later—Hook by the age of thirteen was already politically aware and active as a socialist. "The first Socialist candidate I voted for," Hook remembered, "was Allen Benson, candidate for the Presidency on the Socialist Party ticket, in a straw vote in a public-school classroom at the age of thirteen. The time was 1916. My classmates, and I fear most other people, had never heard of him. Since then I have always considered myself a Socialist."[41]

The young Hook became intrigued by philosophy as a boy when Jack London's epistemological argument in *Martin Eden* set him on a road of discovery from which he never turned back. During his high school years the contentious young Hook "was denounced as pro-German" and "almost expelled" for challenging his teachers' conviction that the German army "cut off the hands of Belgian children" and used human bodies for industrial fat. Setting the standard he maintained throughout his career, Hook demanded proof.[42]

Like many poor Jewish boys talented enough for Harvard, but who could only afford to go uptown to Morningside Heights, Hook then enrolled at the College of the City of New York (now City College), where he was influenced by the galvanizing teaching of Morris Cohen, one of the college's most prominent faculty members. Hook was among Cohen's best students, receiving the Ward Medal in Logic from the college in 1922 and the Certificate of Merit in Philosophy upon his graduation in 1923.[43]

Cohen had also attended City College as an undergraduate, and then completed his graduate studies in philosophy at Harvard, working under William James, Josiah Royce, and others. Never a disciple of any of his teachers, Cohen later called himself "a stray dog" in philosophy. Irving Howe, another student of his, described Cohen as the "culture hero of the City College boys," a philosopher who was "alien to systems, indifferent to converts, forever a man of questions." Cohen had a "terrifying," grueling, almost "sadistic" style of teaching, "and only the kinds of students that came to Cohen could have withstood it—Jewish boys with minds honed to dialectic . . . indifferent to the prescriptions of gentility, intent on a vision of lucidity."[44]

Hook always acknowledged Cohen's influence on his own intellectual approach and stressed his admiration for Cohen's method and perspective. Cohen taught his students to be critical, taught them that understanding was a process not of intuition but of the methodical application of reason.[45] Hook thus received from Cohen some of the same emphasis on experimental rationalism that Dewey would later impart to him. "Every position," Hook wrote of Cohen's teaching, "is to be understood in the light of its consequences." Yet that is not to suggest that Cohen was a pragmatist, for he was very critical of that outlook. A logical realist, Cohen believed that the rational order is independent of the human mind. Pragmatists, much to his horror, degraded the status of the rational order by judging truth and reality in terms of practical consequences—thereby reducing logic to a set of practical tools without any independent status.

Cohen also encouraged the opposition to religious systems and philosophical absolutism that Hook had earlier learned from reading William Lecky, Henry Lea, and John Draper; this antiabsolutism would become central to many of Hook's philosophical battles in the 1930s and 1940s. Cohen was, at heart, a naturalist philosopher, and he found no place in his system for knowledge that came from methods other than the scientific and the natural. Cohen stressed, according to Hook, "the rights of reason against the oppression of authority, the irresponsibility of intuition, the vagueness, obscurantism and hidden absolutism of immediate experience, natural or supernatural."[46] These tenets became central to Hook's belief.

Following his years at City College, Hook became a teacher in the New York City public school system for five years. He also enrolled as a part-time graduate student at Columbia University on a scholarship in philosophy. At Columbia Hook first fell under the influence of Frederick J. E. Woodbridge, who taught a "modified Aristotelianism," but he was led away from Woodbridge by the intellectual magnetism of John Dewey. Hook received his master's degree in 1926 and was awarded a university fellowship. He continued studying under Dewey, submitted his dissertation, "The Metaphysics of Pragmatism," and received his doctorate in 1927. The following September Hook was appointed as an instructor in philosophy at Washington Square College of New York University. A Guggenheim research fellowship enabled him to spend the academic year 1928–29 studying at the universities of Berlin and Munich and at the Marx-Engels Institute in Moscow. He returned to NYU, rose quickly to the chairmanship of the philosophy department, and remained his entire academic career in Greenwich Village.[47]

By the early 1930s Hook was already acknowledged to be America's leading Marxist theoretician, and as Dewey's most promising student he had inherited the leadership of the pragmatic tradition that passed from Peirce to James to Dewey. Hook's great early achievement was his combining of the philosophies of Dewey and Marx in *Towards the Understanding of Karl Marx* (1933). His intention, he later explained, was to "develop a kind of Americanized Marxism strengthened by John Dewey's activist theory of mind and knowledge, as well as his philosophy of education and naturalist humanism, that would be consonant with the American revolutionary tradition."[48]

Because Hook found in Dewey and Marx a congenial emphasis on action, he combined the two philosophers into what might be called a Marxist instrumentalism. Dewey's instrumentalism was a philosophy of action that proposed evaluating the meaning of a concept by its consequences. Dewey's philosophy of education, for example, postulated that people learned by experiencing the consequences of their own actions. Marx also stressed action, in his case praxis, and as Lewis Feuer, a scholar of Marxism, put it, Hook's book provided an image of Marx as the "great scientist-activist." Marx's eleventh thesis on Feuerbach, urging philosophers to change the world rather than merely interpret it, might well have been written by Dewey.[49]

Here, from both Marx and Dewey, were the impulse and justification that pushed Hook and the New York group headlong into the public arena to change the world as intellectuals and critics. No matter that one was a literary critic, a philosopher, or an art critic; the job of ideas was to affect the outcome of life, all life. The separation between idea and the real world was only the difference between the brush and the canvas: one was made to influence and change the other.

It has been argued that Hook was one of several social theorists of the 1930s—along with Mumford, Lynd, Dewey, and Niebuhr—who were trying to preserve "a tenuous balance between liberalism and Marxism . . . private thought and collective action, individual freedom and the search for community," trying to find an ideology to replace the insufficient and bankrupt liberal ideology of progressivism without tumbling irretrievably into the inflexible strictures of Marxism.[50] Therefore, the liberal variant of Marxism that Hook proposed was, in his mind, actually the fulfillment of the liberal ideal.

Dewey, like Hook after him, combined competing ideas to create a middle way. Early in his career Dewey was a Hegelian, and his first articles attacked British empiricism. From this early outlook Dewey adopted a tendency to unify competing forces, and this impulse followed him throughout his career. While Dewey was impatient with dualisms, he used those dualisms as the bricks and mortar to create a new position. This emphasis on unity also led Dewey to admire Emerson, as he wrote in a respectful essay in 1903. Dewey viewed Emerson as a bridge between the individual and society, one who saw that "every individual is at once the focus and the channel of mankind's long and wide endeavor, that all nature exists for the education of the human soul."[51] That the human soul is educated by the contingencies of the natural world appealed to Dewey and Hook as pragmatists.

Moreover, Dewey's view that individuals are not "given" but are created by society was useful to a social democrat such as Hook. Social laws were not made to make individuals happy but to create them, and individuality was something to be wrought, to be achieved.[52] Yet Dewey realized in the late 1920s, when Hook was studying with him, that America had entered a new corporately collectivist age, and that its citizens needed to remake their outmoded individualism so society was not a "house divided against itself." He now felt that individualism was to be realized through its manifestation in collectivism.[53]

The importance that Dewey placed on individual development naturally led him to insist on an environment of free choice and diversity in society. Knowledge and opportunity had to be open to all, for the monopolization of knowledge by the few had only served to enslave the many. A democratic society had to provide for the free communication of experience and the free participation of its members.[54]

Dewey also emphasized using the experimental scientific method in social analyses. In fact, he went so far as to equate democracy and the experimental method, tying the two together in mutual cause and effect. In 1918 he told the Philosophical Union of the University of California that there was "a coincidence in the development of modern experimental science and of democracy." Because a democratic philosophy construes liberty as meaning that the universe is incomplete and forever in the making, Dewey told the philosophers that a democratic philosophy must consider the future to be "a genuine field of novelty . . . a field for experimentalization and invention."[55] It can even be argued that both Dewey and Hook elevated method above program in society, since method was neutral but program had the potential for both evil and ossification.

There are commonly thought to be two kinds of philosophy: pure (theoretical) and applied (practical). Hook, who believed that pure philosophy is pure foolishness, rejected this distinction. Instead, following Dewey, Hook construed philosophy as an empirical discipline with methods similar to those of the natural and social sciences. Like Dewey, Hook also thought that philosophy should serve, in Paul Kurtz's words, as "a normative guide for thought and action." Hook's experimental pragmatism posited that mankind lives in an open universe, the open universe that all pragmatic philosophers found around them, a pluralistic universe that is not predetermined but is the effect of actions—and therefore can be affected by actions.[56] But this belief in the open universe required Hook, early in the 1930s, to begin jettisoning and refuting Marx's deterministic course of history, the inevitability of the inexorable dialectical process.

Here again, Hook found in Dewey's work the tools he needed. For Dewey, the philosopher of change and experimental method, spent nearly an entire career arguing against those who defended static, fixed systems—against the philosophical absolutists who believed that absolute truths and values exist, and who discovered and defended those truths. In an article in the *New Republic* in 1918 Dewey announced his amazement that anyone could praise "the established order as though there were any order except that of change," and was disturbed that people could "argue as if stability and alteration, order and innovation, were to be discussed as possible alternatives."[57]

Two years later, Dewey took up this theme in *Reconstruction in Philosophy*, arguing that conservatives opposed pragmatic philosophy because by changing the world pragmatism undermined their self-interested status quo.[58] Instead, the forces of reaction hid their intentions behind unquestionable total theories that they themselves had constructed. In an article published in 1938, Hook echoed Dewey, contending that an experimental approach was the method of the social reformer and that the vested interests hid in the fog of idealistic philosophy. A "significant connection," he wrote, "is to be found between social movements and philosophical doctrines."[59]

The opposition to absolutism that Hook learned first from Cohen and then from Dewey was the most abiding gift his teachers provided. The New York group as a whole joined Hook in his respect for the experimental approach and his rejection of comforting idealistic philosophies. This orientation supplied the group with the intellectual armor they needed in the following decades to wage war on philosophical absolutists and idealists across the political and philosophical spectrum—from the Catholic Church to the fundamentalists, from fascist to communist totalitarians, from the intuition of the Beat bohemians to the alienated Marxism of the New Left radicals.[60] Even when holding their absolutist visions benevolently and attempting to produce social good, these various groups contradicted the pragmatic approach, the scientific method, the Marxist dialectic of experimental action, and the open pluralistic universe.

In addition to Hook's longstanding battle with Communist absolutism, of which he considered the Waldorf episode part, he also attacked religious and philosophic absolutism. Prominent was his barrage in the early 1940s against Jacques Maritain, Reinhold Niebuhr, and Mortimer Adler. He complained that the religious dependence of Maritain and Niebuhr represented a "failure of nerve," and announced that "Catholicism is the oldest and greatest totalitarian movement in history."[61] Similarly, Hook thought the idealist philosophers who insisted on eternal moral laws and fixed ethical standards were also dangerous, although not totalitarian in the Communist or Catholic sense. At a conference at the Jewish Theological Seminary in New York in September 1940, Hook and Mortimer Adler debated whether philosophical absolutism or skeptical positivism was more responsible for Hitler and the European political crisis. Adler accused the positivists of abandoning a fixed system of the good, the abandonment of which allowed Hitler to rise unopposed. Hook countered that the philosophical absolutists only fed the arsenals of leaders like Hitler who used expansive theories of the good to shelter their intentions and actions, which no one was allowed to question; it had worked the same for all official repressions in history, of no matter what religious or political stripe.[62]

But part of the reason for Hook's antagonism to the *a priori* and idealistic philosophy of Maritain and others might have been due to his polemical nature. Hook himself noted the connection between temperament and philosophy in his own case. The temperament, he wrote, that cares for peace above all other values will probably embrace an outlook of theology, idealism, or invariance. The temperament that enjoys battle, contention, and variety, on the other hand, will probably adopt an outlook of experimentalism, action, and pragmatism.[63]

Among the New York intellectuals, Hook was probably the first to turn against Soviet Communism and yet remain a Marxist—the position that the group's Stalinist adversaries derided as Trotskyism. The epithet had little to do with whether or not one supported Trotsky's socialist vision or tactics. Indeed, Hook frequently argued in the 1930s and 1940s with committed Trotskyists such as Howe, Macdonald, and others.

Hook refrained from joining the Communist party because it was "insufficiently Marxist both in its slogans and its practices." He and others did collaborate with "Communist-party stalwarts" in the League of Professional Groups for Foster and Ford in 1932, partly out of their antifascist commitment. By following the Communists rather than the Socialists, they were also rejecting Socialist timidity, according to Hook—the sort of timidity seen when Socialists in office would not follow their own programs. Those who voted Communist in 1932, Hook admitted, were mistakenly convinced "that the liberal philosophy was inadequate to cope with the danger" presented by the recent crises. But he set out to formulate a set of Marxist principles that could draw the allegiance of independently critical minds. In order not to render himself unwelcome and irrelevant within party circles, he omitted in *Towards the Understanding of Karl Marx* criticism of the Soviet Union. Still, by the mid-1930s Hook was an independent leftist, opposing Stalin and unable to accept the "Trotskyist line" of those anti-Stalinists who still believed in the Communist future.[64]

At NYU in the early 1930s Hook had a reputation as a sharply brilliant professor who exercised a noticeable influence on his students, among them his future colleagues in the New York group Delmore Schwartz and William Phillips. Phillips remembered Hook in this period as "already an anti-Communist but still a maverick Marxist." "Many of us learned a great deal from Hook," Phillips reflected. "I remember in his graduate class one day . . . he said to me, with the concern and authority of a good teacher, that I had a very good mind but that I would ruin it if I continued to mistake Marxist cliches for thinking."[65]

William Barrett, a future editor of *Partisan Review*, was rooming with Delmore Schwartz when Schwartz was taking undergraduate classes from Hook at NYU, and Barrett heard the stories of Hook's teaching and his unpopularity with those who still admired the Soviet Union. Hook rejected Stalinism, according to Barrett's account, only because he was such a dedicated socialist that he could not bear Stalin's perversion of socialism. "Hook as a young instructor at New York University," Barrett recalled, was "hissed by Stalinist students as he walked through Washington Square. Not that anything like public hissing would have deterred him for a moment from his self-appointed course, for he had the absolute integrity and courage of the single-minded." The pressure on Hook's anti-Stalinist position increased during the decade. "The latter thirties," Lewis Feuer remembers, "were Hook's most polemical period; a few years earlier he had been the only Marxist professor in an American university; in the latter thirties, it often seemed that he was the only professor who had the courage to speak out against the evil of Stalinism."[66]

If anti-Stalinism was one of Hook's political obsessions in the 1930s and 1940s, democracy was the other side of the same coin. The two concerns were inseparable. To advance on one issue was automatically to advance on the other; in discussing the one issue, a person found himself inescapably using the rhetoric of the other. As a socialist in the mid-thirties, Hook had already realized that the important political question was how much democracy was to be permitted in a socialist state. As early as 1936 he had set his enduring agenda, about which he became more strident as he aged. It was not enough to support collectivism, he told *The Nation's* readers: Since there were now totalitarian collectivists, it was vital to be clear about what kind of collectivism one envisioned. Was it democratic or minority-led collectivism? Were culture and science to be independent or subject to political control? "We cannot begin soon enough," he warned, "to make the necessary distinctions between the various kinds of collectivism—not only in the interests of intellectual clarity but because the battles of tomorrow will in all probability be fought around the issues they raise."[67]

Over the course of the 1930s, Hook's politics were transformed. Early in the decade he was a politically active socialist, helping James Burnham and A. J. Muste organize the socialist American Workers party in 1933 and acting as a leader within American Trotskyist circles. By the end of the decade, however, he was clearly more interested in forming the Committee for Cultural Freedom with John Dewey to battle the forces of totalitarianism. Socialism and antitotalitarianism were not mutually exclusive concerns, but gradually Hook focused so much of his attention on international repression that it served to disengage him from many of his earlier socialist goals. As James Gilbert has pointed out, "The Dewey-Hook organization was essentially nonradical, and its most important stand, since almost everyone was opposed to Nazism, was its repudiation of the Communists."[68]

By the mid-forties Hook's fund of enthusiasm for socialism was running dangerously low. Hook began his evaluation of "The Future of Socialism" in *Partisan Review* (1947) by announcing: "I am a democrat. I am a socialist. And I am still a Marxist in the sense in which one may speak of a modern biologist as still a Darwinian."[69] This is one of the most memorable and remarkable passages Hook ever wrote. In a few lines he affirmed his primary allegiance to democracy, declared himself a socialist, and repudiated his Marxism in all but its most historical sense. In this passage he showed clearly the extent to which he, like the other members of the group, would carry the mark of his youthful Marxism well into the time when his radicalism had passed, and he demonstrated the New York intellectuals' assumption that it was natural and somewhat inevitable to do so. One could continue to think of oneself as holding an identity long since abandoned.

In the body of the article, Hook again testified that a democratic socialist society could be successfully democratic if it adopted and maintained a "mixed economy," although he thought the likelihood of America adopting a democratic socialist plan only moderately better than "very dim." This did not distress him, because he was "first a democrat and then a socialist" and was "more profoundly convinced of the validity of the democratic ideals than of any specific way of achieving them."

By the late 1940s, no matter what Hook said, his socialist sun was setting. Hook reminded his *Partisan Review* readers that for two decades his unorthodox, if not maverick, Marxist view had made him an enemy of traditional Marxists. "It would appear," he wrote with a clever irony, "that if I were justified in my interpretation of Marx's meaning, I would be perhaps the only true Marxist left in the world. This is too much for my sense of humor, and so I have decided to abandon the term as a descriptive epithet of my position." Henceforth Hook would begin to wear the label of social democrat. "Certainly," he acknowledged without much regret, "if the Stalinists and their international salon of fellow-traveling litterateurs and totalitarian liberal politicos . . . are Marxists, then I am cheerfully resigned to being non-Marxist."

Here, at the end of the forties, Hook was partly right about himself: He was not only no more of a Marxist than modern biologists were Darwinians; he was also hardly more of a socialist than Max Eastman, Edmund Wilson, and others in his generation who once had believed but who since had lost faith.

Hook felt connected to the tradition of social democrats, who he thought were "all right-wing." His favorite was Eduard Bernstein. "Truth to tell," Hook later wrote of Daniel Bell, Irving Kristol, Melvin Lasky, and himself, "we are all offspring of Eduard Bernstein, whose intellectual and moral stature has grown with the years." But many observers also felt that, although Hook would not admit it, his continuing to call himself a socialist became as untenable as Milton Friedman's insistence on calling himself a liberal. Norman Podhoretz, himself increasingly conservative after the 1960s, later wrote that "many people would snicker privately whenever [Hook] declared himself to be a socialist." Philip Rahv, late in his life, underscored the contradiction of those "of whom Sidney Hook is a prime example, who at opportune moments still choose to call themselves socialists but who in practice support and defend the American capitalist drive for world hegemony."[70]

Others in the New York group regretted Hook's narrowing of focus and the greater inflexibility it brought, although they would not admit that many of them had shared in this same narrowing process. William Phillips, an enthusiastic anti-Communist, noticed that Hook's "preoccupation with the evils of Communism" distorted his overall social outlook and led him to underestimate the "faults" of American society. "It also led to a lessening of his earlier enthusiasm," Phillips observed, "at least in practice, for the free play of the mind—which was particularly disturbing to see in someone who had one of the most agile and disciplined minds I had ever encountered."[71] Hook struck his same note repeatedly, hammered at it endlessly like a blacksmith pounding on an anvil in the shed from breakfast to dinner. "Within that first-rate mind," remarked Irving

Howe, also an anti-Communist, "there had formed a deposit of sterility, like rust on a beautiful machine."[72]

Nonetheless, Hook's intellect and polemics continued to outdistance those of many other analysts in America. One aspect of his contribution to intellectual life was his belief that thinkers must rise above the polarized dogmas of inevitable systems. That is what intelligence and discourse meant. "More important than any belief a man holds is the *way* he holds it," Hook told Max Eastman. "Any fool or fanatic can embrace a doctrine. Even if true, it remains a *dogma* unless evaluated in light of its alternatives, and the relevant evidence for them. The whole enterprise of intelligence consists in envisaging alternatives before embarking on action."[73]

Many antagonists of Hook thought him an intransigent Cold Warrior whose inflexible positions were matched only by the stridency with which he fought for them. Hook disagreed: Pragmatism was the antidote to intransigence. Rather, pragmatism led one to value responsibility, which must be defended strongly. After wrestling with the problem of Tolstoy's pacifism, Hook decided that "rational ethics is the ethics of responsibility, and that rational politics is the choice of the lesser evil. . . ." Although impressed with Tolstoy's refusal to destroy human life under any circumstances, he explained that he abandoned that outlook when he "realized the human costs of holding it in the same way Tolstoy did—absolutely without qualification." Some values *were* worth dying for or killing for: "It is better to be a live jackal than a dead lion—for jackals, not men; . . . those who are prepared to live like men and, if necessary, die like men, have the best prospect of surviving as free men and escaping the fate of both jackals and lions."[74] The Cold War, he felt, would have to be waged with an unblinking resolve.

Of Hook's philosophical works, his early books—*The Metaphysics of Pragmatism*, *Towards the Understanding of Karl Marx*, and *From Hegel to Marx*—were the most theoretical. Theory was the means by which he sought to reconcile the past he shared with his associates (Marx, socialism, immigrant identity) with the future he dimly began to see for himself (defender of American democracy, liberalism, and capitalism). Once that tension was resolved, once Marx had been melded to Dewey, Hook had no more need to wrestle with theory, and he moved on to the arena of social and political thought.

When he did venture back into philosophy, as in *Quest for Being* (1961), he did so to uphold his conviction that all knowledge was to be gained from the scientific method and that traditional categories such as metaphysics were of little importance. A parallel hostility to linguistic analysis precluded any interest in the linguistic turn philosophy took after the 1960s, under the influence of continental literary deconstructionism and poststructuralism. Although Hook and the linguistic radicals held different views on politics and culture, one critic, noting the similarity of their assumptions, has written that "American pragmatists were just as skeptical as any contemporary poststructuralist about all privileged—they called them 'idealist'—claims to truth or meaning" and were similarly hostile to "a metaphysics of 'absolutes.'" [75]

But Hook was so explicitly nonacademic in his writings and essays—preferring the intellectual to the scholarly—that he became entangled in relatively few academic exchanges with other philosophers. Instead, he was that rare philosophy professor whose counsel to fellow citizens (usually on the theme of anti-Communism) appeared frequently in the *New York Times Magazine* or the *Saturday Review*. As his ordering of the significant confrontations in his autobiography indicates, Hook thought of himself less as a professional and scholarly philosopher, and more as an activist in the realm of antitotalitarianism, the scientific method, democratic liberties, and other social and political elements of liberal thought. Like Marx, Hook believed that a philosopher had to be concerned with history, with the fate of society, with the future of political relations.

Hook had a noteworthy influence among the New York intellectuals, and at least up through World War II he played the decisive leadership role in the group, "the part of a strategist and elder statesman." [76] It was from that position of leadership that he directed the assault against the Waldorf Conference.

Americans for Intellectual Freedom

In searching for the proper intellectual response to the Waldorf Conference, the New York group realized more was required than merely unmasking the pretensions of ideological neutrality behind which the conference leaders operated. They needed to do something affirmative, create their own alternative conference where real intellectuals behaved responsibly and practiced their function of independent analysis and criticism.

Nor was Sidney Hook willing to let the intellectual army of the ideological opposition charge thundering into New York unchallenged by an organized response. As he wrote to Albert Einstein in a letter years after the conference, "I am old-fashioned enough to believe that truth is the best answer to the propaganda of the lie—not counter-propaganda. But I have learned enough from modern psychology to know that silence is no answer at all." So the weekend before the Waldorf Conference began, Hook met the press and announced the formation of a new organization, the Americans for Intellectual Freedom (AIF), to rally the forces of freedom in opposition to the Stalinist conference and to sponsor, on the Saturday of the Waldorf weekend, a counter-rally at Freedom House on West Fortieth Street in New York City.[77]

Upon learning of the plans for the Waldorf Conference, Hook made "extensive inquiries" among his radical friends throughout the East Coast. None had been invited to participate in the forum, he learned, and the conference, in his words, was to be "a family affair among Communists and 'honest liberals,' the quaint expression used by the Communist Party to designate formally unaffiliated individuals who were willing to echo the party line or go along with it in uncritical complicity."[78]

While many others joined in the AIF organizing effort, including some members of the New York group, Hook was its driving force. Hook and Dwight Macdonald both claimed that the impetus for creating the AIF was Hook's exclusion from the program of the Waldorf Conference.[79] A preliminary meeting to plan the AIF, held at Macdonald's apartment, was attended by Hook, socialist leader Norman Thomas, novelist James Farrell, labor editor Arnold Beichman, historian Bertram Wolfe, social philosopher Horace Kallen (one of the founders of the New School for Social Research), William Phillips, George Counts, and about a dozen other anti-Stalinists. Some of those at Macdonald's apartment had been members of the earlier Committee for Cultural Freedom, started by Hook and John Dewey in 1939.

Lewis Coser and Alfred Kazin later remembered that they had not been invited to join the AIF because, they thought, Hook considered them to be insufficiently anti-Communist. Hook disagreed, and maintained that the AIF was prepared to include "anyone who had any academic or literary or scientific standing" who would endorse the AIF position, "which seemed axiomatic to the life of mind." The AIF sought to exclude only "confirmed CP fellow travellers" who might have tried to infiltrate it and then resign with false information to discredit the organization. Coser believed that few of those who later became the *Dissent* crowd were interested in the sort of anti-Communism that the AIF represented, and indeed many of the later dissenters, including Harold Rosenberg, Paul Goodman, and Coser, ignored the conference.

Yet Howe and Macdonald were important exceptions, and were interested enough to attend the Waldorf meetings and publish criticisms of the sessions. Hook maintained that he had no objection to inviting the "Dissentniks" to join the AIF because, although they might have "scorned" the offer, he would have considered their involvement a sign of their "political sanity." Hook accounted for Kazin's absence by noting that he was not yet "a big shot," but he found Harold Rosenberg's lack of involvement "a mystery." In truth, the AIF needed signatories badly enough that it would not have been very particular about members. Further, if he was willing to allow Macdonald in the AIF planning group, Hook was not overly worried about potential members subscribing to a narrow orthodoxy. Indeed, Hook later wrote that although he considered Paul Goodman "an irresponsible pacifist I would have had no more objection to him than I had to D. Macdonald." [80]

Hook chaired the AIF planning meeting amid the "Spartan simplicity" of Macdonald's hospitality, and he proposed an educational countercampaign to expose the Waldorf Conference as a Cominform front. About $200 was collected at the meeting, and the group was launched. Originally Hook wanted to call the group the Committee for Cultural Freedom, to stress the connection with the earlier group, but the others wanted a new name. It became the Ad Hoc Committee for Intellectual Freedom. [81]

With the lack of subtlety characteristic of Hook, the AIF announced that its objective was to hold a meeting at the Freedom House conducted "in the spirit of free inquiry and honest difference of opinion—the true hallmark of a gathering of intellectuals whose minds are not twisted into the straight jacket of the Communist party line." The AIF plan was also "to keep up a running barrage in the press," according to Macdonald. [82]

Waldorf leader Howard Fast, however, charged that the AIF was the creature of the State Department. After watching "the entire monopoly press" flog the Waldorf Conference, Fast alleged, the State Department was still unsatisfied with the damage done, so it then "turned to those old and tried jackals of reaction, the Social Democrats and the Trotskyites, and inspired them to organize, for the same date, a rival 'conference.'" Fast complained that the "worn and battered philosophical pillar of Trotskyism, Sidney Hook, was called upon to head up this effort. Such bruised stalwarts as John Dos Passos, John Dewey and James T. Farrell shored him up," followed by "a choice collection of renegades, traitors and cheap turncoats," including "the latest Soviet 'refugees.'" The AIF counter-rally, Fast wrote, "was held in that misnamed but resplendent pile known as 'Freedom House,'" but despite their efforts "it proved to be a dismal failure. . . . It represented no trend or aspiration of the American people, but only an aberration of the ruling class." [83]

One of the more important AIF activities, not referred to by Hook, Howe, or Macdonald in their projected plans, was a campaign to persuade Waldorf sponsors to withdraw their affiliation with the conference and renounce its Stalinist backing. It was an "intensive telephone campaign," of which Lillian Hellman reportedly remarked that "Nothing so intense has been seen since the pyramid clubs." Hook felt that many of the more naive conference sponsors could be convinced of their error; about one fourth of the 650 sponsors "clearly did not belong there."[84]

Many sponsors were neither Stalinists nor fellow travelers, and had supported the Waldorf plans hoping it would be a useful peace conference and an opportunity for discussion. Such sponsors included Leonard Bernstein; Marlon Brando; Aaron Copland; Albert Einstein; Robert Lynd, professor of sociology at Columbia University; Norman Mailer; Kenneth Murdock, professor of English at Harvard; and Rexford Tugwell, the professor of economics at the University of Chicago who had been a leading member of Roosevelt's New Deal brain trust. Yet the AIF never acknowledged that one could support the conference with hope or integrity, and treated everyone associated with the event as pro-Stalinist or a Stalinist dupe. The AIF thought the Waldorf sponsors, even the casual ones, had a duty as intellectuals to make finer distinctions about the kinds of leftism that could be supported. Meanwhile, AIF members also failed to make the necessary intellectual distinctions, and consequently branded all associates of the Waldorf proceedings as equally guilty.

The AIF telephone drive met with mixed success, dislodging a few sponsors along the way, yet also arousing some animosity in those who might have agreed intellectually with some of the AIF's criticisms of the Waldorf Conference but who were offended by the pressure tactics. Among the sponsors who withdrew, either because of AIF pressure or their own last-minute misgivings, were Sarah Gibson Blanding, president of Vassar College; Rabbi Mordecai Kaplan, professor at the Jewish Theological Seminary; Irwin Edman, professor of philosophy at Columbia; and John Gillin, a professor at the University of North Carolina.[85]

The AIF was not as careful as it might have been when announcing the list of withdrawing sponsors on the eve of the Waldorf Conference. On Thursday, the day before the conference began, the AIF went public with the names of eight people they claimed had withdrawn their affiliation from the conference. But according to the *New York Times*, "Five of them denied having withdrawn and some of them said attempts had been made to 'high pressure' them into withdrawing." The mistake was an embarrassing boomerang for the AIF, and its error was covered widely in the Thursday afternoon newspapers and on the radio. Among those who said the AIF report of their withdrawal was false were Rexford Tugwell and Ernest Hocking, the latter a professor of philosophy at Harvard. The confusion prompted Howard Fast to complain that the "first move" of the AIF "was to attack the growing group of sponsors; and every device, every cheap subterfuge was indulged in here."[86]

William Phillips later agreed that the AIF employed some questionable tactics, but he assigned the blame to overly zealous underlings. He acknowledged that the AIF had committed some unfair acts, "such as intercepting mail and messages and issuing misleading statements in the name of the conference—tactics that upset all but the most hardened veterans of Communist and anti-Communist organizational fights. Even Sidney Hook, himself not a political virgin, was annoyed at the things done in his name when he became aware of them." Phillips felt caught in a dilemma. Did one repudiate the AIF, resign the battle, and by that action cede the contest to the opposition with one's righteous purity intact? Or did one "recognize the unpalatable political reality that the ones who do the work control the organization," that, as the Communist wisdom went, "those who ran the mimeograph machine had the power." [87]

With Hook as the chief spokesman, the AIF spent the week preceding the conference trying to put their adversaries on the defensive. Shapley, Hook charged, was a "captive" or "willing tool" of the Communists. (A month later Hook was to call Richard Wright, Jean-Paul Sartre, and Maurice Merleau-Ponty "reluctant accomplices of Stalinism.") Hook and the AIF accused both Alexander Fadayev, secretary of the Union of Soviet Writers and leader of the Soviet delegation to the Waldorf Conference, and Ivan Rozhansky, a Soviet scientific writer who was a member of the Soviet delegation, of being agents of the MVD, the Soviet secret police. A spokesman for the AIF was unable to reveal to the *New York Times* the evidence supporting the accusation, claiming it was based on confidential information. The spokesman pointed out, however, that it was "apparent," because Rozhansky was translator for the Soviet delegation and "it is well known that every Soviet translator must be an MVD agent." [88] Though the accusation may well have been true, this type of reasoning did nothing to enhance the AIF's credibility.

Another major offensive launched by the AIF was its press release listing six points the Waldorf Conference should adopt to demonstrate its belief in democracy and freedom: Those attending the conference should condemn "officially interpreted orthodox philosophy"—a request obviously written by Sidney Hook—should condemn the suppression of free speech "in whatever country it may occur," and condemn the "policy of imprisonment, exiling and execution of scientists." Further, the conference should name a commission to investigate the extent of repression of scientists and artists, and should also commend the U.S. government's efforts to reestablish cultural relations with the Soviet Union. Finally, the AIF asked the Waldorf Conference to endorse the statement made by the Soviet scientist P. L. Kapitsa before the Academy of Sciences of the Soviet

Union in June 1945: that there is no such thing as a Soviet or British science, but rather only one international science devoted to "the betterment of human welfare."[89] This last concern, of course, was the theme of the paper Hook had wanted to read at the Waldorf Conference.

The AIF's anti-Stalinist counterconference was held at Freedom House, across from the New York Public Library, on Saturday afternoon, from three o'clock until after six in the evening. All 450 seats inside Freedom House were filled, and loudspeakers transmitted the speeches to an overflow crowd in Bryant Park, estimated at 500 by the *New York Times* and more expansively estimated at "several thousand" by Macdonald. Unlike the opposition drawn by the uptown conference, only one solitary picket wandered back and forth in front of Freedom House, carrying a sign: Defend All Victims of the Smith "Gag" Act. Read the Court Testimony of the First Victims in the Trial of 18 Trotskyist Leaders.[90]

The speakers at Freedom House stood under a sign that read One World—Or None; another sign framed the podium: Freedom of the Mind Knows No Frontier. As chairman of the proceedings, Hook gave the keynote address—apparently the paper he wanted to deliver to the Waldorf Conference. Wearing a dark three-piece suit and waving a pencil for emphasis, he argued against the Soviet notion that "science is national in form and class in content." The "evils that threaten the integrity of the life of the mind and of free creative activity of any sort," he admitted, "are found in many countries, including our own." In summarizing the AIF position, Hook told his audience: "We are an independent group of scholars, writers and artists interested in preserving and extending freedom. We disapprove the action of the United States in barring any delegate to [the Waldorf] conference. We disapprove picketing where it interferes with free discussion."[91] Whether the picketing was any more disruptive to the Waldorf dialogue than the telephone campaign he orchestrated to dislodge and intimidate Waldorf sponsors, Hook did not indicate.

Among others who spoke at the AIF meeting were Bryn Hovde, president of the New School for Social Research; Arthur Schlesinger, Jr., professor of history at Harvard; and Louis Fischer, the journalist who that same year contributed to the landmark book *The God That Failed*. Also addressing the Freedom House audience were A. J. Muste, a noted American pacifist and activist on the left, and Bertram Wolfe.[92]

The AIF did not disband as an organization after the Freedom House conference. A representative of the AIF told a *Herald Tribune* reporter that the group had planned no further meetings after the conference, but would continue "certain activities" against Communist power and influence in America. Despite Macdonald's belief that the AIF enjoyed only a "brief week of existence," Sidney Hook was still making statements ex cathedra as chairman of the group and invoking its power a month later. Hook and James T. Farrell left for Paris from LaGuardia Airport with as much fanfare as they could muster on the afternoon of April 21, nearly a month after the Waldorf Conference, traveling as delegates of the AIF to the April 30th anti-Stalinist conference. The AIF was far from dead, at least in the minds of Hook and Farrell, who claimed that the AIF still comprised 200 members. The role of the AIF in Paris in April 1949 was nearly identical to its role during the Waldorf Conference: it opposed a Communist "peace" conference formally called the World Congress of Partisans of Peace. The AIF, along with its anti-Stalinist counterparts from other countries, held their own conference in Paris, the Peace Through Liberty Day, to counter the Communist influence on intellectuals.[93]

There was more to the Paris trip of Hook and Farrell, however, than merely an effort to offset the Communist conference. It was their intention to prolong the life of the AIF by expanding it into a larger organization, perhaps connected into an international network of anti-Stalinist intellectual groups. Prior to their departure from LaGuardia, Hook and Farrell told the press, as reported by the *New York Times*, that they planned to create "a continuing anti-Communist world federation for intellectual freedom." Realizing that the Stalinists were at work across the globe, and never one to be outdone, Hook told the press that their own main objective was to establish an international organization "independent of all governments which will represent independent thinkers and artists concerned with the least common denominator of a free culture."[94]

In the process of joining with an international anti-Stalinist network, the name and identity of the AIF were transformed. The American contingent, started as AIF, after the Paris trip took on the name of the organization that Hook and Dewey had operated for a few years in the early 1940s, the Committee for Cultural Freedom. As Hook recalled years later, the AIF "grew into a revived Committee for Cultural Freedom in 1949."[95] Before long the new group was renamed the American Committee for Cultural Freedom (ACCF), an organization that lasted into the 1960s. The international organization that was developed to help orchestrate and contain the various national groups came to be known as the Congress for Cultural Freedom (CCF).

Although the AIF was founded to resist what the New York group considered to be the intellectual irresponsibility and deceit of the Waldorf Conference, the AIF was open to the charge that, despite its loud defense of open and free analysis, it promoted its own ideological narrowness in its Freedom House conference. Especially as the AIF evolved into the ACCF, it became increasingly more interested in sustaining and promoting anti-Communism than in polishing and protecting an ideal of open intellectual analysis. To understand why and how the AIF developed as it did, we first need to know something of Dwight Macdonald who, along with Hook, was the most prominent of the New York intellectuals involved with the AIF. When one examines Macdonald's background and career, it is more apparent why the Waldorf proceedings should have so outraged his sensibilities.

Dwight Macdonald

Among the first generation of the New York group, if Hook was the anti-Communist leader, and a leader of the postwar centrism that slowly overtook the circle, Macdonald represented the political alternative. Although Macdonald was anti-Communist, he was too much of an iconoclastic dissenter to allow his leftist energies to be sapped by an anti-Soviet fixation. Hook's pragmatic Cold War outlook constantly demanded that in every decision one choose the "lesser evil." Macdonald's strong moral principles led him to different conclusions.

Macdonald had the sharpest wit and cleverest sense of irony among the New York group and was its most polished and engaging writer. He helped originate, with Edmund Wilson, the wide-ranging style of intellectual journalism that became the group's trademark. "Yes," Macdonald once told Diana Trilling, "I always thought of myself as what Edmund Wilson called himself, a literary journalist." [96]

He was a cultural critic in the purest sense: even when he wrote of politics his subject was politics as culture and morality. His enthusiasm for many forms of culture spurred him to write on literature, popular culture, film, journalism, politics, and intellectual events. Macdonald seldom wasted time writing to validate accepted opinion—that was done enough by others. Instead he reevaluated reputations or challenged settled conclusions. In the 1930s and 1940s his focus was politics, which he judged by the standards of justice and moral integrity; representative essays from this period appear in *The Memoirs of a Revolutionist* (1957). In the fifties he increasingly measured mass culture and reassessed recognized American authors and cultural institutions that he considered "middlebrow"; a selection of these articles was published as *Against the American Grain* (1962). A final set of his essays from the sixties on culture and events was collected in *Discriminations* (1974).

Macdonald was born in New York City on March 24, 1906. Unlike most of the New York intellectuals, the young Dwight was raised in a relatively happy and affluent family. His father was a middle-class lawyer who had married the daughter of a rich Brooklyn merchant. Until his father died, when Dwight was twenty, the family spent summers vacationing at their summer house in Sea Girt, New Jersey. If many other members of the New York group were sharp and polemical products of political childhoods and Jewish lower-class neighborhoods, Macdonald was a preppie. He attended Collegiate School in Manhattan and then enrolled at Barnard School for Boys in New York, where he became interested in books and writing. At Phillips Exeter Academy he was class poet, began writing for publication, and helped edit the school's weekly paper and monthly literary magazine. As an undergraduate at Yale, he majored in history, edited the *Yale Record*, wrote a column for the *Yale News*, was managing editor of the *Yale Literary Magazine*, and won various literary prizes. He received his bachelor's degree in 1928.[97]

After being graduated from Yale, Macdonald took a job in Macy's executive training program so he could help his family with its finances, which had declined since his father's death two years earlier. "My plan," he later remembered, "was to make a lot of money rapidly and retire to write literary criticism." After six months of training at a salary of $30 a week, he was offered a job behind the tie counter at the same salary. He quit. A few months later a Yale classmate got him a position with the new *Fortune* magazine, where eventually he made $10,000 a year. Covering business during the Depression radicalized Macdonald and the other *Fortune* writers: "I became increasingly skeptical about American capitalism, which I saw at close quarters. . . . The New Deal was inspiriting to me, as to my fellow writers on *Fortune*. To Luce's dismay, we became increasingly liberal." By 1936 Macdonald's radicalism was too strong for Luce's corral, and the young writer resigned.[98]

By education and heritage, then, Macdonald was a scion of the middle-class white Protestant Yankee and midwestern intellectual radical tradition, in the footsteps of Max Eastman, Floyd Dell, Waldo Frank, Lincoln Steffens, and John Reed. In the 1930s this old Yankee radicalism was washed over, swamped, transformed, and assimilated by the wave of radicalism from Europe and the second-generation American Jews.

The New York intellectuals represented a clear departure from the earlier tradition. They had none of the benefits of the middle-class radicals who could comfortably slum it in Greenwich Village without losing self-respect or family name, who had good educations and could command professional and intellectual respect and positions of power if they chose. For the earlier radicals America was their country and, like peevish lovers, they made demands, acted out scenes of disaffection, and turned their backs on it. Not so for the New York group, whose members often bore a different set of values and principles from those of the Yankee Ivy League culture. Although the New York intellectuals had been raised in America, in their early years they were European radicals banging on the outside of the American power structure, not establishment radicals rattling the windows from inside the edifice.

So, at least by education and heritage, Dwight Macdonald was an emissary from the early radical tradition. Had he been born a few years earlier he might have been an Imagist poet, voted for Debs, read Mencken, and traveled with Harold Stearns to France. Instead he integrated himself into the New York group in the mid-1930s. Mary McCarthy was another from an established background who joined the group, following an affluent Midwestern childhood, schooling in a Catholic girls' school in Seattle, and four years at Vassar. Edmund Wilson (Princeton) and Malcolm Cowley (Harvard) could have joined had they wished. Both were critics with the requisite scope and force of intellect, but Wilson was too independent to belong to any group, and Cowley was always on the other side of the Communist/anti-Communist fence from the *Partisan* circle—or at least they thought so, forever branding him a Stalinist, a totalitarian, or an anti-American long after he had abandoned any real Communist sympathies.[99]

Within a year after leaving *Fortune*, Macdonald had formed a partnership with these predominantly Jewish New York intellectuals and *Partisan Review*. The differences in background aside, it was an odd marriage, since the lanky writer with the glasses and goatee was still only a political newborn in the mid-1930s. The trait that cemented the relationship was that Macdonald loved to argue. At a party he would pin a contentious soul into a corner and argue until his victim managed to escape.

With his enthusiasm for polemics, Macdonald began to bridge the gap between his political innocence and the group's fund of experience. "I came late to the revolutionary movement (or what we then took to be such)," Macdonald confessed, "partly because I went to Yale instead of, for example, 'City College.' . . . Many of my Trotskyist comrades had begun handing out antiwar leaflets and marching in May Day parades while they were in short pants. . . . At thirty, when I first read Marx, they were scarred veterans of several left-wing parties and numberless 'faction fights.'" In his last days at *Fortune* he had started to read Marx, Lenin, and Trotsky, and, being "a pragmatist . . . I leaned toward the Communists because they alone on the American Left seemed to be 'doing something.' I became a mild fellow traveler."[100]

When Macdonald first read Marx in 1935 he was bored: "Not my style at all." But the Moscow Trials in 1935 and 1936 appealed to his moralism. After reading the transcript of the second trial, he, like a flood of other American leftists, abandoned any sympathy for the Communist party in Moscow or America. As Diana Trilling once told him, "as soon as you were really learning about the Soviet Union you were learning it in the spirit of dissent from it," which was "not the common experience" of others in the group.[101]

In immediate succession Macdonald joined the Committee for the Defense of Leon Trotsky, led by John Dewey (to exonerate Trotsky from Stalin's charges, brought against him in absentia in the Moscow Trials); "became politically *non grata* with the liberal weeklies," *The Nation* and *The New Republic*; and, by the end of 1937, joined Philip Rahv, William Phillips, F. W. Dupee, Mary McCarthy, and George Morris as one of the founding editors of the revived *Partisan Review*. They were able to get *Partisan Review* off the ground again in the late 1930s partially because George Morris financed the project, and because "Rahv and Phillips had a mailing list which, after all," Macdonald joked, "is all that matters in such a magazine."[102]

It soon became apparent that Macdonald was not as disenchanted by socialism as was Hook, and in the early years of the *Partisan Review* Macdonald remained a more active critic of America. The two also disagreed about the position intellectuals should take on the war, with Hook advocating American intervention and Macdonald opposing it, viewing the war as a fight between capitalist countries. In 1943 this rift drove Macdonald to leave *Partisan Review* and begin his own magazine, *Politics*, which lasted until 1949.

Although Macdonald was more radical than Hook, he never compromised his anti-Stalinist credentials. After the Moscow Trials he maintained a bitter opposition to Stalinist Russia and the Communist party. Like other members of the New York group, he called himself part of the anti-Stalinist or independent left.

His anti-Stalinist outlet was usually to attack the "liberal weeklies" (*The Nation, The New Republic*, and the daily *PM*), which in 1944 he considered "shooting-fish-in-a-barrel." In *Politics* he complained about the "spineless and moral insensibility of present-day American liberalism," and called the liberal editors our "modern Pilates" who printed "Stalinoid rationalizations" and promoted "liblab evasion." Macdonald used *Politics* to accuse "totalitarian liberals" of justifying Soviet slave labor, propaganda, and imperialism "in the name of social progress" and "democratic re-education," because liberals, blinded by a narrow ideological vision, believed that "Soviet Russia is the repository of all political virtue." Their "totalitarian liberal" approach prompted them to believe that "Society is the end: human beings the means. Hence, no concern for the Rights of Man (or of nations), for even-handed justice or the freedom of the individual, but simply for the effective perpetuation of the existing social systems." Unfortunately, the liberals failed to notice that the Soviet myth "preserves the *means* of 19th-century Progressivism—such as rational planning, scientific advance, democracy, popular education, industrialization—while quietly dropping overboard the humanitarian *ends* which led both Marxism and bourgeois liberalism to accept these means." [103]

Aside from the liberal magazines, Macdonald's favorite target in the 1940s was Henry Wallace, who he claimed "never analyzes a problem; he barges around inside it, throwing out vague exhortations." He described the enemy territory: "Wallaceland is the mental habitat of Henry Wallace plus a few hundred thousand regular readers of *The New Republic*, *The Nation*, and *PM*. It is a region of perpetual fogs, caused by the warm winds of the liberal Gulf Stream coming in contact with the Soviet glacier. Its natives speak 'Wallese,' a provincial dialect." [104]

But Macdonald was careful not to be construed as an unbalanced anti-Communist whose passion made him as narrow-minded and doctrinaire as totalitarian liberals. So he reserved equal derision for those zealots who operated from his own side of the fence, especially "the kind of simple-minded Moscow-baiting *The New Leader* goes in for (in which *any* anti-Communist personality or institution, regardless of other considerations, acquires superhuman virtues)." Macdonald issued this warning in 1945, well before Truman or McCarthy roused the intellectuals to any sort of caution. He was simply worried that the brains of those who read *The New Leader* were being "addled" by "the corrupting influence of an editorial line whose major and often apparently sole criterion of value is anti-Stalinism." [105]

Macdonald was the very human conscience of a group that sometimes became so enraptured by enthusiastic polemics or logical analysis that it forgot its humanity. Even Malcolm Cowley, an adversary of the group, liked Macdonald because he "wasn't self-righteous or a careerist" like others in his crowd. [106] The alternative voice of the group, Macdonald was its countervailing force, its counterbalance. Among the serious critics he was clever and witty. If the rest were sometimes stodgy socialists, after the mid-forties he was outrageous enough to announce that he was a pacifist and an anarchist—a deliberate provocation, perhaps, but also a testament to a sober American individualism and libertarianism. In this, Macdonald was something of a twentieth-century Thoreau, an antistate philosopher who judged politics by a very personal and moral standard.

Of course, supporting individualism and anarchism was not necessarily a radical stance in the twentieth century. Macdonald knew that. "Everybody thinks I'm a wild man," he once confided, "but I'm always in the middle. . . . I'm not the stuff of martyrs. It would never have occurred to *me* to go to Spain in 1939, the way it occurred to Orwell and all those others. I'm absolutely squarely in the middle. . . . I'm always in this middle position it seems to me." [107]

A contentious, if clever, cultural critic, Macdonald showed his fellow intellectuals how a witty and polemical criticism could be written. He had a much nimbler mind and sense of humor than anyone else in the New York group, and his spirit rescued their magazines from becoming dull theoretical journals. Regarded as one of the group's most sharply critical minds, he also supplied a stylishness, a *New Yorker* sensibility. Finally, by engaging the moral aspect of issues, Macdonald demonstrated how to move moralism from an intellectual gentility to an intellectual contentiousness in cultural criticism. His moral influence extended beyond the intellectuals, especially in the 1940s and 1960s, when his advocacy of draft resistance brought him wide publicity and a substantial following.

Standards for Intellectual Integrity

The most interesting exchanges in the Waldorf debate occurred after the meetings had ended and the delegates departed. Then the two ideological armies—the anti-Stalinists and those they considered fellow travelers—battled over the heart of the issue. Had there been diversity of opinion at the Waldorf Conference? Was the Freedom House conference any better in this regard? Why should one group try to prevent another from staging whatever kind of conference it pleased, with or without diversity? Had the AIF tried to silence the free speech of the Waldorf participants? Did the Soviet Union really want cultural exchange? Could the Waldorf Conference have been held in the Soviet Union? What did it mean to be an intellectual, a critic, or to hold a responsible conference?

The AIF was most upset at the lack of diversity at the Waldorf Conference. Macdonald upbraided it as "strictly a Stalinoid affair" that "excluded from the speakers' platform all known anti-Communists." He found it ironic that a peace conference could not spare "five minutes" for the pacifist voice of A. J. Muste and instead had only "reliable" speakers. Their one exception to excluding critics of Russia, in Macdonald's opinion, was Norman Cousins, "a pennyworth of bread in an intolerable deal of sack." [108]

Margaret Marshall, editor of *The Nation*'s book section and one of the few outspoken anti-Stalinists at the magazine at the time, was held in high regard by the New York intellectuals—whom she published when she could. Her attitude caused some friction among the staff, as Freda Kirchwey, editor of *The Nation*, was a favorite target of the anti-Stalinists. Soon after the conference ended, Marshall wrote that she did not regret that the issue of "freedom of expression" had "haunted the conference from its very inception," acting "like an invisible picket." Although the issue was not on the conference agenda, still, "Since it is my incorrigible belief that the free expression and exchange of ideas will do more in the end than a thousand peace conferences to bring about genuine peace, I cannot regret that the conference was thus pulled off its appointed course." [109]

Not to be left out of a Waldorf argument, Hook joined Macdonald and Marshall in their criticism in the pages of *The Nation*. In a letter printed in the magazine, Hook complained that there were no anti-Stalinists at the Waldorf podium, no "well-known critic of Soviet totalitarianism" such as Edmund Wilson. "A few questions from the floor," Hook wrote impatiently, "do not constitute a discussion," but rather an "intellectual fraud." That dishonesty, Hook stressed to the magazine's readers, was the heart of the AIF's opposition to the Waldorf Conference—that their rigging of the speakers "made honest discussion impossible." [110]

The defense offered by some conference associates on the question of diversity was beguiling. Howard Fast informed the public that, although the Waldorf Conference did not represent all the varied intellectual opinions in America, "it most certainly represented the aspirations of most American intellectuals." Even more disingenuous was leftist author Albert Kahn's statement in a letter to Shapley before the conference that, yes, "there are aspects of Soviet life which warrant criticism," but "the leaders and people of the Soviet Union are constantly indulging in all sorts of criticism about themselves." Kahn told Shapley that he opposed having the conference criticize the Soviet Union and was against "presenting a fully rounded picture," because of his respect for Soviet accomplishments, their "great contributions, particularly in the last war, to the Jewish people," and because he did not want others to think he was criticizing the Soviet Union merely to promote his reputation. [111]

Kirchwey's defense of the conference, however, had an obvious integrity. In response to the AIF's accusations that the Waldorf leaders had invited only reliable leftists, Kirchwey named a list of the invited who would surely have rocked the boat if they had attended. Only Cousins had accepted the invitation. [112]

Rather than be put on the defensive, Kirchwey had questions of her own. For all its sanctimonious evangelizing about intellectual freedom, she asked, how much diversity was there at the AIF's Freedom House conference? Leafing through the record of the Freedom House program, Kirchwey decided that the AIF had omitted to make space "for even the limited ideological differences that emerged at the Waldorf." She found no "pro-Communist speakers" thundering behind AIF microphones and marveled that "Dr. Hook's refusal to permit T. O. Thackrey [editor and publisher of the *New York Post*] to speak at the counter-rally was amazing in view of his own righteous indignation over Shapley's refusal to permit him to speak at the Waldorf."

After all their moral breast-beating, how did the AIF explain its own one-sidedness? "If the answer," she told Hook, "is that no one can claim to talk about peace who is bound by the dogmas of communism or the interests of Moscow, then the question arises: What is left, under that dictum, for any further negotiation between West and East?" How could Hook exclude one party to the debate and yet assert that interchange and dialogue were the path to truth? "If we do not want to fight communism," Kirchwey counseled, "the only alternative is to deal with it, try to work out ways of accommodation. Most anti-Communists of the Hook school insist that neither they nor this country desire war with Russia. If they are sincere, and I think they are, then they should be wary of rejecting as a frame-up every attempt to talk to Russians or other Communists."[113]

Perhaps intellectual openness and responsibility, she implied, required a conception of freedom that included encouraging a dialogue with odious groups such as the Communists. If dialogue was encouraged to break down, were intellectuals being intellectuals? Was this not exactly the sort of dialogue, Kirchwey asked, that the Waldorf Conference had tried to promote?

The editor of *The Nation* was not alone in chiding the AIF for transgressing its own highest principle. Margaret Marshall, who stood much closer to the AIF than to the Waldorf position, had attended both the Waldorf's opening dinner on Friday night and the Freedom House program on Saturday afternoon. At Freedom House she reported finding some of the same narrowness of opinion as at the conference ten blocks uptown, but the AIF speeches, to their credit, were more "specific and informative," and benefited from exploring the issue of intellectual repression. "Here also there was unanimity," Marshall wrote of the anti-Stalinist program, "and it too would have been more interesting if the other side had been present." But worse, in her opinion, was the AIF's defensive claim that inviting the opposition only plays into the hands of the enemy. That logic, Marshall pointed out, supported rather than undermined the Soviet belief that repression has a future.[114]

Hook was offended by Kirchwey's assault on the integrity of the AIF.

"We invited Dr. Shapley or anyone he delegated to speak at our meeting," Hook insisted. No, answered Kirchwey, that statement is "wholly disingenuous." Since Hook had already harshly attacked all those taking part in the Waldorf program, his invitation was not "a friendly offer of cooperation," and he could not have expected Shapley to accept. Hook manned the AIF defense without flinching. He sharply denied her allegation that the AIF rejected "as a frame-up every attempt to talk to Russians or other Communists." It was the AIF that wanted honest dialogue between the two sides, Hook argued, and the Waldorf leaders were the ones who had rigged it to make that impossible. How dare Kirchwey and *The Nation* presume to speak of intellectual freedom? "As anyone knows who listened to our speakers, especially the noted pacifist, A. J. Muste, more differences on foreign policy were expressed than have ever been voiced at the dinner forums of *The Nation* since the days of Oswald G. Villard."[115]

Here Hook referred to the Reverend A. J. Muste, secretary of the pacifist group Peacemakers, which the *New York Times* described as "an organization advocating non-violent resistance to war and the draft," and which Muste himself described as an association of "non-violent revolutionaries." Muste sent requests to both Shapley and Hook asking for time to present his proposals for peace to both the Waldorf Conference and the Freedom House meeting. Only the AIF offered Muste a chance to speak, although, in all fairness, it is not clear that Muste asked for a spot on either program any earlier than two days before the Waldorf Conference opened. Hook later described Muste's speech at the AIF conference as one in which he "denounced the American government as equally responsible for the cold war as the Soviet Union."[116]

Some observers felt that the AIF had stifled the freedom of speech of the Waldorf participants, whether intentionally or not. One of the more outspoken of this opinion was Hook's colleague Theodore Brameld, professor of educational philosophy at NYU. In a letter to the *New York Times* following the Waldorf events, Brameld warned of "the need to withstand the pressure of certain 'liberals' to scare and intimidate others of us from daring to identify ourselves with such a conference." Lest any reader mistake the subject of his letter as the AIF generally rather than Hook specifically, Brameld quickly clarified the portrait. Referring to Hook's role as a leading pragmatist, Brameld complained that "By the kind of philosophic test which they themselves usually employ to settle important problems—the test of practical consequences—it is entirely plausible to argue that the consequence of their own tactics may turn out to be vastly more injurious to the cause of democracy than any which could possibly follow from sponsorship."[117]

Hook was not amused. He and George Counts fired a letter to the

Times in reply, complaining that Brameld had misrepresented their position toward the Waldorf program's freedom of expression. The AIF did not want to prevent the Waldorf meeting, but rather to assure a diversity of opinion there. When they could not do so, they concluded that Shapley's forum was "a propaganda weapon of the Soviet Foreign Office," and planned their own gathering. The AIF invited representatives from the Waldorf meeting to speak at Freedom House, but the invitations were not accepted. If the Waldorf leaders really intended "a fair give and take between different points of view," as they claimed, then sponsors such as Brameld should have insisted upon an honest program or else resigned. "Those who, like Dr. Brameld, remained as sponsors and did nothing whatsoever to prevent Communist domination of the program became accomplices in the perpetration of an intellectual fraud upon the public." But instead of criticizing the Communists who designed the fraudulent conference, Brameld and others "now direct their fire against those American liberals who have opposed repressions of freedom in every country in the world, including our own. This testifies to a bad conscience." Hook and Counts found it especially inconsistent that Brameld criticized the picketers for disrupting freedom of expression at the Waldorf, while "he failed to condemn the widespread booing of the few speakers at the conference who sought to criticize ever so slightly the drastic purge of intellectuals in the Soviet Union." [118]

With a heavy heart, a somewhat discouraged and wounded Brameld answered their letter in the *Times* with another. Discovering unnecessary roughness, he first called foul play. Hook and Counts had shifted the discussion "from an impersonal level to that of one's own integrity," accusing him of a "bad conscience" and pronouncing him "guilty by association." Brameld instead described his concerns as the stifling of opinion under the guise of promoting greater diversity of opinion. He was worried about an anti-Communist offensive that would transgress liberal boundaries, the impulse that would later be known as McCarthyism. "I did issue the warning," Brameld admitted, "which I repeat, that their continuous, too all-inclusive, almost totally negative attack upon communism at home and abroad is one of the most dangerous boomerangs which could at the present moment be placed in the hands of those powerful reactionary forces for whom many of the picketers were merely a front." The late 1940s were not a safe time to encourage domestic attacks; they could too easily get out of hand. "For while the boomerang would perhaps miss my critics and their associates on its return trip," Brameld pointed out, "it could scarcely miss vast numbers of liberal, socially oriented trade unionists, Jews and others who are so often the indiscriminate victims of every attack from the extreme right." [119]

Brameld's point was well taken, for Hook's rough rhetoric was not intended to promote a flourishing of opinion on the left. Hook would have been the first to admit that he had no tolerance for what he considered to be dangerous opinions, but the last to admit that his definition of dangerous opinions sometimes loomed stiflingly large. Nor did Hook seem to appreciate how his caustic polemical style was at odds with the AIF's professed concern with promoting intellectual dialogue and free expression. In his argument in *The Nation* with Freda Kirchwey, he fulminated against her "totalitarian liberalism" that was blind to "red totalitarianism." Of her writing during the previous decade, Hook maintained that it had been "a record of intellectual and moral double-dealing." [120]

In her reply to the AIF's concerns about the lack of diversity at the Waldorf affair, Kirchwey entertained, for argument's sake, Hook's premise that he and other anti-Stalinists were omitted from participation in the Waldorf program because of their political views. "Is even this evidence of 'fraud' or of 'organized Communist duplicity'?" she asked. "I'll confess I don't think so. I think it only proves what hardly needed proof: that the Waldorf conference was a left-wing affair run by an organization which has never concealed its leftist complexion." She agreed that the NCASP was composed of "people of about the same range of opinion as the Wallace party—Communists, near-Communists, and assorted liberals who believe peace requires a policy of conciliation with Russia." She found nothing especially shocking, deceptive, or covert about this. "The sessions were 'free' within the range of opinion represented above. But it would be nonsense to pretend that the speakers or delegates comprised a cross-section of American opinion, or that a vigorous interchange of conflicting views was the order of the day. At a meeting like the Waldorf conference one hears variations on a theme rather than discords."

Given that the Waldorf leaders never pretended that theirs was anything but a leftist conference, how could Hook and the AIF try to deny the group its right to stage a sectarian meeting? "Why can't Dr. Hook admit the simple, not very shocking or fraudulent fact that when partisan organizations, left, right, or center, hold meetings, they act like partisan organizations, favoring people of their own general point of view and rejecting most of those who detest and oppose them?" Were Presbyterians invited to Baptist conferences, or were Catholics invited to Jewish policy meetings? And was it really so intellectually traitorous that it was so? Admit that there was nothing underhanded and dishonest about a leftist group holding a leftist conference, she advised, "and there is still plenty of room to denounce the opinions expressed at the Waldorf meetings as lop-sided, dangerous, seditious, or anything Dr. Hook pleases."

Indeed, Kirchwey disagreed with "a large part" of the pronouncements of the Waldorf program, its "concentration of fire on American foreign policy and the whitewashing of Russia," but that did not convince her of the planning committee's sedition. "There was no attempt to analyze the balance of responsibility," she admitted, "and few sensible proposals for ending the cold war. But all this does not add up to 'fraud,' in my opinion."[121]

Despite Kirchwey's intelligent response, the Waldorf Conference clearly had called down upon itself the wrath of the AIF and other opponents. The Waldorf leaders had foolishly billed the affair as a free forum for a discussion about world peace, a nonpolitical event. Further, as Margaret Marshall pointed out, in choosing the conference participants on the basis of their political beliefs, the Waldorf sponsors "threw down the gauntlet to other writers, scientists, and artists who stubbornly regard themselves, and surely with reason, as also representative. It was a challenge that could hardly be ignored, and the response of Sidney Hook and Americans for Intellectual Freedom was not only inevitable but necessary." By sending representatives such as Fadayev and Shostakovich, the Soviets "were surely inviting the attention of the curious on the one hand and the furious on the other."[122]

The crime was not that the Waldorf sponsors had chosen leftist speakers, as Kirchwey knew they had a right to do. The error was that after the leaders had designed their program they insisted that it was not a leftist political gathering at all. The New York intellectuals, along with most of the rest of America, were not willing to let the conference sponsors have it both ways.

For their part, the anti-Stalinists delighted in pointing out that an anti-Soviet counterpart to the Waldorf Conference could never have been held in Russia. William Barrett imagined "what the analogue to this Conference must be: a conference held in Moscow in which the Russian delegates would vigorously attack the Soviet Union while the American delegates spoke in jingoist terms of the United States." Macdonald, in his wry style, rendered a more caustic scene. Let us hear no more from the Waldorf participants about American repression, Macdonald suggested. "That is, until they have prevailed on the Politburo to permit, in, say, Moscow's Hotel Lux, a similar gathering of 3,000 pro-USA Russian citizens (especially released from the labor camps to attend), which will be addressed by a seven-man American delegation chosen by Dean Acheson." Macdonald drew up the cast himself. "Clarence Buddington [*sic*] Kelland would do very well, politically and esthetically, for Comrade Fadayev's opposite number . . . and Comrades Fadayev, Shostakovich and Pavlenko can have three minutes each, from the floor, to ask awkward questions of Mr. Kelland."[123]

The skirmishes about the Waldorf Conference demonstrate several attributes of the New York group. First, the contentious manner in which they waged their opposition to the conference reflected the polemical style they brought with them into adulthood from their youthful Marxism, factional debates, and educational training. Second, it revealed the seriousness they attached to their fight against improper and irresponsible leftism. Third, the Waldorf antagonisms showed the group at work helping to form the acceptable boundaries to an official ideology of American liberal anti-Communism.

But most important, the Waldorf conflict demonstrated the tension within the intellectual community over the role and function of the intellectual. Intellectual responsibility was needed, all agreed, but there was little consensus about what defined responsible behavior. Between Hook and Shapley, or between Macdonald and Kirchwey, there were sharp disagreements about what constituted intellectual integrity and intellectual fraud. Although Kirchwey thought that the exclusion of some viewpoints from the conference was not fraudulent, Hook, Macdonald, and others in the New York group had no confidence that her approach would preserve the intellectual's role as independent critic. In that regard, the group felt that the Soviet Union and the Waldorf Conference represented the same threat to free society, and to allow the conference to proceed unchallenged could undermine American pluralism, individualism, and intellectual independence. So the AIF had a duty to unmask the conference's real nature and to provide at their Freedom House counter-rally alternatives to what they considered to be irresponsible leftism.

The New York group's opposition to the Waldorf Conference demonstrated that they placed a higher premium on their identities as independent intellectuals than on their images as political radicals. They were more driven by their intellectual responsibilities to rationalism, tolerance, and freedom of inquiry than to their political dedication to the concepts of socialism, equality, social justice, and planning. During the 1930s the group's primary commitment to the intellectual necessities of free debate and a diversity of opinion had already caused them to turn slowly away from a radical socialism and toward a greater concern for democracy and liberalism. From their beginning as a group in the 1930s, they were above all intellectuals. Only secondarily were they radicals.

The Waldorf struggle was merely the most recent event in the string of anti-Communist battles the independent leftists had waged, beginning with their furor over the Moscow Trials in 1936. Maybe it was inevitable that the great intellectual warriors of the time were drawn into the anti-Communist battles, for they felt as though they were defending the province of free intellect by protecting the sanctity of the West. "In the last few decades," William Phillips wrote shortly before the Waldorf affair, "politics has made greater claims on intellectual life than ever before in modern history. The reason, of course, is that our intellectual fate is bound up with our political fate; and . . . our political fate has constantly been at stake. It has been a time of extreme situations." [124] So much, according to the group, hung in the balance in the tensions between East and West: national destiny, political democracy, social pluralism, cultural freedom, and not least of all the intellectual function. This was the view of the New York group from outside the Waldorf at mid-century.

Yet the New York intellectuals were not unified in their response to the period of "extreme situations." Although the divisions were less evident in their response to the Waldorf Conference, from the late 1930s through the 1980s the group split over the proper amount of criticism intellectuals should direct toward their culture. Certainly those on the left who sponsored the Waldorf proceedings were too critical of America, but how much criticism should responsible intellectuals aim at their own country? Conversely, how much dissent could critics avoid before they ceased to perform a useful intellectual function? That disagreement framed most of the debates among the New York intellectuals in the postwar period. Since the group's inception in the 1930s there had been a division between those members who were "affirmers" and those who were "dissenters."

2   Affirmers and Dissenters

From the outset, more than a decade before the Waldorf Conference, the New York intellectuals split into two camps. The more idealistic faction, originally led by Dwight Macdonald, conceived of themselves as perpetual dissenters, critics continually in opposition to mainstream culture. The more pragmatic camp, led at first by Sidney Hook, saw no benefit to perpetual opposition and instead hoped to reshape the world through a skeptically minded affirmation of culture.[1]

Despite the significant fissure, members of both camps pondered the same problems, shared almost the same enemies, and employed the same style of analysis. The group's unity in opposition to the Waldorf Conference showed that the affirmers and dissenters could combine to fight a common threat, and that they viewed the Stalinists and fellow travelers as a greater danger than the differences within the group. Although the political outlooks of the two camps diverged, their practical politics were often nearly identical. For most outsiders looking in, there was little difference between Macdonald's circle and Hook's.

The Split: 1937–1943

In 1934 Philip Rahv and William Phillips launched the first *Partisan Review* under the auspices of the New York John Reed Club, a Communist organization for proletarian writers. The literary counterpart to the Communist *New Masses*, the *Partisan Review* supported proletarian literature and revolutionary Marxist politics, continuing the tradition of *Symposium*, published from 1930 to 1933 and edited by James Burnham and Philip Wheelwright. Writers in the *Partisan Review* circle who had written for *Symposium* included Macdonald, Phillips, Hook, Harold Rosenberg, and Paul Goodman.[2] But almost immediately Rahv and Phillips grew weary of the drudgery of proletarian realism and cultural orders from the Party, and the magazine suspended publication in 1936.

In 1937 *Partisan Review* was reborn with a new cast of editors: Rahv, Phillips, Macdonald, F. W. (Fred) Dupee, George Morris, and Mary McCarthy. The new magazine supported modernist literature and an anti-Stalinist politics of the left, and was intent on Europeanizing what they considered an inferior American naturalist culture.[3] The shift from communism to a more moderate cultural and political position brought it nearer the American mainstream, and enabled it to attract over the course of the next several decades an impressive sampling of American and European intellectuals as contributors and readers.

But politics and culture were not simple matters of agreement among the intelligentsia, and by 1938 there was already friction. During that year Hook was attempting to organize a League Against Totalitarianism (LAT) and sent Macdonald a manifesto that had already been endorsed by Dewey, Eugene Lyons, and himself. Macdonald thought it was not leftist enough and declined to sign it. "Unless the LAT states that its sympathies are on the left, with the masses and against their exploiters," he wrote to Hook, "its program is as empty and even politically red-baiting" as the Dies committee. By June 1939 Hook and Macdonald had founded separate organizations to oppose totalitarianism. Hook started the Committee for Cultural Freedom with John Dewey as its head, the forerunner of both the Americans for Intellectual Freedom and the American Committee for Cultural Freedom. Macdonald's League for Cultural Freedom and Socialism was a more outspokenly Trotskyist organization that opposed totalitarianism and believed that cultural freedom was impossible without socialism, an opinion that Hook rejected.[4]

Hook did not appreciate Macdonald's splitting the antitotalitarian unity. "When the first Committee for Cultural Freedom was organized in 1939," Hook wrote to Richard Rovere in 1952, "a small group insisted that only under socialism was cultural freedom possible. Instead of trying to convince the rest of us that this was so, they split away to organize a 'Committee for Cultural Freedom and Socialism' [*sic*]. We survived it."[5] Narrow at first, the differences between the Hook and Macdonald committees soon expanded into an ideological rift that nearly sank the *Partisan Review* for good. The issue of the proper response to the war ignited the hostility.

Of the six original *Partisan Review* editors, Rahv, Phillips, and Macdonald wielded the strongest influence in the first years of the forties. Rahv and Phillips, together with Hook (a prominent contributor but not an editor) represented one power bloc within the magazine. Macdonald and Clement Greenberg represented another.

Hook became associated with the magazine through Phillips, who had been his student at NYU. In *Partisan's* first decade Hook was the review's principal political voice alongside, until 1943, Macdonald. "In the late 30's *Partisan Review* and everybody on it leaned on Hook politically," William Barrett, an assistant editor at the magazine, recalled. "He was the acknowledged master of Marxist theory, and the spearhead in the attack on Stalinism from the Left; and therefore ideologically indispensable to the magazine."[6] Hook, with the blessing of Rahv and Phillips, wanted the journal to acknowledge that both America and the *Partisan* community should support the Allies against the growing fascist totalitarianism in Europe. Although some other liberal and leftist intellectuals had reached similar conclusions, Hook was the first in the *Partisan* circle to press for American involvement. About this Hook was adamant, and Rahv and Phillips, unaccustomed as most of the New York group had always been to think of America as *their* country, were only slowly coming to support his position. Macdonald, on the other hand, regarded both America and Germany as exploitive, repressive capitalist countries to which no socialist intellectual could offer his loyalty. Macdonald, like many Trotskyists of the time, believed that principled intellectuals had to support a "third-camp" position that rejected the moral claims of both the Allies and the Axis powers with the hope that from the ashes of war would rise a viable third position of democratic socialism.

As Macdonald recalled, Rahv and Phillips initially agreed with him that it was an imperialist war, but their minds "changed the day of Pearl Harbor when the United States got into it." Irving Howe, however, located the turn of the magazine against Macdonald in the issue of November–December 1941, where Rahv attacked Macdonald and Greenberg's earlier article "Ten Propositions on the War," a formal declaration against American involvement in the imperialist war. Rahv's "Ten Propositions and Eight Errors" was the Rahv-Phillips-Hook repudiation of Macdonald's position.[7]

Macdonald resisted the wish of Rahv and Phillips to throw the magazine's support behind the Allies, and he insisted on *Partisan Review* having a divided editorial voice. He felt that the journal had started in the 1930s as a vehicle of opposition rather than an affirmation of American culture, and he now thought that stance should not be compromised by the war. Throughout the 1940s, from before the war until after the Waldorf Conference, Macdonald urged on the intellectual community a third-camp ideal that was first Trotskyist, then in the late 1940s pacifist.[8]

According to Hook, the split between the Trotskyists and him came in 1940 or 1941. Until then, he recalled, he had been the darling of the Trotskyists because he had led the fight against the acceptance of the Moscow Trials, despite his disagreements with the Trotskyists and their political line. Until 1940 everyone on the left, including the liberals, opposed involvement in the war; but around 1940 Hook publicly changed his mind, and the Trotskyists turned on him and attacked his war position.[9]

In the early forties it looked as though the power at *Partisan Review* might shift toward Macdonald by default when Rahv considered giving up his editorship because his wife, Nathalie, had work that had taken them to Chicago. He told Macdonald to find an editorial replacement for him. But Rahv's identity was bound to the magazine he had helped conceive seven years earlier, so in the spring of 1941 he changed his mind and wrote to Macdonald that Nathalie's work was going quickly enough for them to return soon to New York. "Hence I think I'd better reverse my decision to take my name off the magazine. This also puts a new construction on your search for new editors. I hope you haven't committed yourself to anyone." Meyer Schapiro and Lionel Trilling had both declined offers to become editors, much to Rahv's relief.[10] Had Rahv left, Macdonald might have been able to steer the magazine to his course, although Phillips and Hook would still have been formidable obstacles. The obvious irony is that by the 1940s, among the *Partisan Review* editors, the Jews of the group were supporting the U.S. against its enemies while the old Yankee on the staff was America's sharpest critic.

By the end of 1941 Rahv and Macdonald were corresponding about their differences on the war. "I think our controversy is exciting," Rahv wrote Macdonald from Chicago, "though in my opinion you begged most of the questions I addressed to you. You seem to think that a mere listing of the failures of the democracies is enough to prove the validity of the revolutionary case you have outlined." Rahv thought Macdonald unreasonable. "To make the revolution in America is a much more difficult task than to win the war against Hitler on the present basis—hence your position amounts to saying: let's do the more difficult thing first. There is no logic in such a policy."[11]

(Five years later, in 1946, Rahv would still be making the same charge against Macdonald, but with regard to Stalin rather than Hitler. What Macdonald's "position comes down to—in objective terms—is a complete surrender to Stalin," Rahv and Phillips warned. "With a truly oriental passivity, Yogi Macdonald prostrates himself beneath the wheels of the advancing juggernaut."[12] By 1950 Macdonald had come to agree entirely with Rahv's complaints and issued essentially the same warning to others about the need for more than a passive stance against the Soviet Union.)

Hook was disgusted with Macdonald and other Trotskyists who criticized the capitalist war and would not oppose fascism. He believed that for socialism to be successful in America, Hitler had to be defeated. The best plan for socialists, in Hook's opinion, was to organize their political program around a democratic socialist approach to fighting and winning the war: labor should participate in war councils, and all levels of the nation should be offered a greater stake in a victory.[13]

Macdonald was not convinced. By 1942 his faith in his third-camp position was strong enough that he was willing to tear the magazine apart over the war issue—to fight for control of the magazine and abandon it if he lost. His friend Lewis Coser, the sociologist who a decade later would be one of the founding editors of *Dissent*, wrote to him that "there is no use denying that there *is* a change between the old and the new *PR* and this change is on the whole not a very beneficial one. The question is only if one should abandon it or not, and I still think that it is worth while to stick to it and to make the most one can out of it."[14]

The other founding editor of the future *Dissent*, Irving Howe, was also more sympathetic to Macdonald than to the other editors at *Partisan Review*. Assessing *Partisan's* internal struggle over the war, Howe praised Macdonald for having moved the magazine to the left for a considerable period of time before it turned against him and moved to the right. Howe mistakenly thought Macdonald acquiesced in the magazine's rightward swing, but when Macdonald later left *Partisan Review* and started his own magazine Howe again was sympathetic to his general outlook.[15]

Macdonald disagreed with Coser about the value of remaining with *Partisan Review*. Concurrently, the magazine's prospects began to dim because of a serious lack of financing. To resolve the editorial and financial impasse, the editors decided that if Rahv and Phillips could obtain the money to keep the magazine going they would receive editorial control; but if they failed, and *Partisan* folded, Macdonald could revive the review under his control. Even as Rahv and Phillips worked through the spring of 1943 to find a sponsor, Macdonald was preparing an announcement to run in the magazine. It explained that the journal would fold because of financial hardship, but assured readers that "*Partisan Review* will not disappear, however. It will be carried on in the fall, with a different format and editorial policy, under the editorship of Dwight Macdonald. It will become a magazine of political and social comment with cultural overtones (instead of, as at present, a literary magazine with political overtones)."[16]

Macdonald's statement was never printed; Rahv and Phillips found a sponsor in Mary Herter Norton, who pledged $2,500 a year to the magazine, although she guaranteed only the first year's funding. She was more interested in a cultural than a political magazine, which Rahv evidently assured her it would be. "Mrs. Norton is a woman of the finest sensibility," Rahv wrote to Macdonald, explaining his success, "but politically she is an indifferentist more or less. What she liked particularly about the mag is its sustained contact with European literary art and ideas." [17]

Macdonald wrote a letter of resignation and asked that it be printed without change. It was. In his letter he lamented that *Partisan Review* had abandoned whatever political position it once held, and in the future would be only a cultural forum. Rahv and Phillips strongly objected to this accusation, with Phillips complaining to Macdonald, "Your note is inaccurate, misleading, and it, in effect, knocks the magazine, somehow suggesting that you stood for a good magazine and we for a lousy one." [18] Rahv, whose perpetual scowl made him look "like the chairman of a grievance committee," was more to the point. [19] "It is not true," he advised Macdonald, "that *PR* will now be thoroughly de-politicized; there are a thousand and one ways of slipping political discussions into the magazine—reviews, ripostes, etc.—despite our agreement with Mrs. Norton. Let's not be too literal-minded about it." [20]

Hook later claimed that Rahv, Phillips, and Macdonald were not very influential in changing political and cultural attitudes. *Partisan Review*, according to Hook, ended up taking the same political and cultural line as most of the rest of the intellectual community. Further, the editors were not even "serious revolutionists" since they took no risks and were not active in revolutionary events of the period. "They called themselves socialist and occasionally Communist, but the terms had no real content in their minds, except that they were against things as they were," Hook remembered. The *Partisan* editors "read no economics or sociology or philosophy but mainly literary criticism," which was insufficient to educate or fuel a revolutionary. "Their chief contribution," Hook wrote, "for which they deserve commendation, is that they provided a forum for nonsectarian writing during a highly sectarian period in intellectual political life." In Hook's estimate he was the political intelligence and savvy behind the magazine: the editors invited him to associate with them "as a kind of political guide." [21]

Yet after the war Hook's position "was already subtly on the wane" at the magazine. His influence began to dissipate, according to William Barrett, because of his anti-Stalinist "single-mindedness," his narrowing of vision. For Rahv and Phillips, Barrett wrote, Hook "had become a kind of Johnny One-note, clear and forceful but also monotonous in the one issue he was always pursuing. When the question came up one day of Hook's possibly doing an article that was then needed, Rahv rejected the suggestion in his usual corrosive and reductive way: 'No. Sidney will only tell you once again that Stalin stinks.'" [22]

Perhaps Rahv and Phillips were correct to insist on the futility of the third-camp position in the early 1940s. But that issue aside, Macdonald was accurate in noticing the effect of the war on members of the *Partisan* community. *Partisan Review* had been founded by leftist outsiders, most of whom felt little in common with American values. Many in the founding generation had middle-class aspirations, but most of them also felt alienated by a culture with which they only partly identified. Those who were least alienated from American culture—Alfred Kazin, Norman Mailer, Norman Podhoretz—were members of the group's second and third generations and were not part of the power struggle over the magazine during the war.

So, as Macdonald realized, the depoliticization of *Partisan Review* was a significant shift. It was a notable sign that many of its first generation editors and readers (as well as the younger crowd) were being pulled into the orbit of American cultural values by the gravity of the international tensions. The magazine had gained such high regard among the American intelligentsia that Richard Hofstadter was later prompted to call it "a kind of house organ of the American intellectual community." [23] But in the 1940s the magazine and the group itself were slowly becoming transformed, evolving toward a more affirmative outlook and a greater respect for America. At the same time, the division between the affirmers and the dissenters was growing more pronounced.

Politics *and* Commentary: *1944–1950*

Unwilling to abandon the stance of cultural opposition upon which he and others had founded *Partisan Review,* after he left the magazine Dwight Macdonald carried on his own vision of its original critical intention and posture by starting his own publication, *Politics,* in 1944. [24] *Politics* was a fulfillment of the editorial statement he had planned to use for *Partisan Review* if he had inherited it: a political magazine with cultural overtones. The magazine lasted only five years, folding on the heels of the Waldorf Conference in 1949. Within the New York group *Politics* became required reading, and it lived on as a legend after it died. It was a small operation—edited and orchestrated by Macdonald and his first wife Nancy, although they drew articles from members of the group such as Irving Howe, Lewis Coser, Meyer Schapiro, Paul Goodman, Harvey Swados, Daniel Bell, Irving Kristol, Nathan Glazer, and Lionel Abel. [25]

Throughout the war years, Macdonald, like other members of the international intellectual community, felt that "new roads" in politics should be explored. He was influenced by Nicola Chiaromonte and the young postfascist Italians, and by the new Canadian Commonwealth Federation. When Macdonald began thinking of a new magazine, others were interested as well. Zellig Harris at the University of Pennsylvania (a linguist whom Noam Chomsky and Nathan Glazer studied under) showed interest, as did Frank Marquart of the United Auto Workers. Paul Goodman was discouraged with *Partisan Review* because, like Macdonald, he was more of an anarchist than the others, and he too was looking for new outlets. Several planning meetings at Macdonald's apartment were attended by Goodman, Harold Orlans (representing Zellig Harris), and Daniel Bell. "It soon became clear that Dwight could not work easily with others," Bell remembered, "and as it was his money (or Nancy Macdonald, the sister of Selden Rodman, who had founded *Common Sense*), and his magazine, he took up the marbles and began shooting them himself. But we all contributed articles and ideas to the early issues."[26] *Politics* began speaking to the intellectual community the year before the war ended.

"I am very glad that you have definitely decided to go ahead with the new revue," Lewis Coser wrote Macdonald shortly before the first issue appeared. "Everything seems to be crying for some new and fresh radical magazine." Coser advised him to "rely to a rather large part on younger elements who are not yet very well known but could become a homogeneous group under your direction." He warned Macdonald not to allow the new magazine to "sound like an agglomeration of foreign specialists in Marxism." Among other names, Coser suggested as contributors Meyer Schapiro, James Farrell, Harold Laski, and Daniel Bell. The magazine, Coser recommended, could function for those on the left who had been tied to the Young People's Socialist League ("YPSLs" is what those young members called themselves), which he estimated at about two hundred. Though it would not be wise to write it for the YPSLs, he thought they could be a "backbone for the revue" and help spread the magazine on campuses.[27]

Coser was born in Berlin in 1913 to a middle-class Jewish family. Although he was the son of a banker, as a young man he became a socialist. With the failure of the Weimar Republic and the increasing threat from the Nazis, he left for Paris in 1933, where he studied comparative literature and then sociology at the Sorbonne. After France fell, Coser lived in the unoccupied zone until 1941, and then found his way to America on a special visa with a few hundred émigrés who had opposed the Nazis. Late in 1941 he arrived in New York.[28]

There Coser decided he wanted to become "a highfalutin Walter Lippmann type of journalist." While working at the Office of War Information, he wrote a few articles for *Partisan Review*, submitting the pieces under the pseudonym Louis Clair to circumvent the OWI policy that employees clear their writings with the government. When Macdonald left *Partisan Review* and began *Politics*, Coser maintained his allegiance to Macdonald and wrote under the same pseudonym for that journal. After reading Macdonald's letter of resignation printed in *Partisan Review*, Coser wrote him that "There is absolutely no point of disagreement between us." Sometimes Macdonald would ask him: "Why can't you say that in a simpler way? Why be so Germanic?" Coser felt that Macdonald had taught him "what an American writing style was" and found him to be "a wonderful editor."

Through parties at Macdonald's apartment in the Village, Coser met Paul Goodman, Harold Rosenberg, and Meyer Schapiro, among others. Seymour Martin Lipset, Irving Kristol, and Martin Diamond invited Coser to contribute to *Enquiry* magazine. At the Shachtmanite paper *Labor Action* Coser came to know Emanuel Geltman, Stanley Plastrik, and its editor, Irving Howe.[29]

Irving Howe was then a precocious twenty-year-old, and Coser was twenty-seven. *Labor Action* was published in "a grubby loft on Fourteenth Street," and about half the "four-page sheet" was composed by Howe himself "under various pen names." Coser wrote a weekly column on European events under the pseudonym Europacus for *Labor Action*, but Howe considered him formal, shy, "a somewhat strange bird," and they maintained only a business relationship.[30]

In summer 1948 Coser registered for graduate study in sociology at Columbia. Shortly after, he was called by Nathan Glazer: "Do you know David Riesman?" Coser didn't. Glazer told him that Riesman was hiring people to teach at the University of Chicago. So Coser met Riesman for a walk in Central Park and was offered a job teaching American history. Unfamiliar with American history, Coser declined. Two weeks later he was offered a job in sociology at Chicago, and this time he accepted. He had not yet started graduate work at Columbia, although he had studied at the Sorbonne. Coser wrote Macdonald about his new job, "the same job Daniel Bell used to have," and told him how pleased he was with his good fortune. "Got this mainly through Dave Riessman [*sic*] who must have told them that I am a little genius." Coser signed off his letter: "Professor (former hatchecker) Lou." Riesman, a regular reader of *Politics*, admitted he was "very much taken with Louis Clair," and confided that "in Coser's case I alone" brought him to teach at Chicago. Riesman then hired Coser's wife, Rose, as a research associate for *The Lonely Crowd*.[31]

In *The Functions of Social Conflict* (1956), Coser developed a view that has been called "conflict theory," an approach drawn largely from Marx, Max Weber, and Georg Simmel that underscores the tensions, competitions, and hostilities between classes and groups. In the 1960s Coser became expressly interested in the sociology of intellectuals, which led him to write *Men of Ideas* (1965) and *Refugee Scholars in America* (1984).

Riesman knew many of the New York intellectuals individually, but he "wasn't that conscious of them as a group." When he was in Chicago in the late 1940s he learned of Glazer by reading *Commentary*. He thought Glazer and *Commentary* overestimated the impact of American communism, and wrote and chided him for thinking American communists were so important. Glazer told Riesman that his wife was disturbed that she could not walk down Riverside Drive without running into readers of the fellow-traveling *New York Post*. Riesman thought this story illustrated how New Yorkers, even after 1948, oddly persisted in seeing communists and fellow travelers as a threat—and he took this as an example of the entire New York group's insularity and parochialism. Not sharing their obsession with their city and with the danger of communism, Riesman "felt very remote from these people because of their provincialism."[32]

While Riesman thought the New York circle excessively anticommunist, he had other concerns and was somewhat indifferent to their ideological battles. One could share the New York group's interest in the general cultural and political landscape without being preoccupied with the Soviet or communist threat.

His studies of the impact of mass society and affluence on character formation and political perceptions in individuals produced two influential volumes written in collaboration with Glazer and Reuel Denney, *The Lonely Crowd* (1950) and *Faces in the Crowd* (1952). The books explored the loss of autonomous individual behavior and beliefs and their replacement by peer pressure. Many of Riesman's notable essays on individualism, popular culture, leisure, Veblen, Freud, Tocqueville, intellectuals and populists, the nuclear threat, totalitarianism, national character, affluence, and suburbanization were collected in *Individualism Reconsidered* (1954) and *Abundance for What?* (1964).

Riesman respected Macdonald. "Macdonald I knew from quite a different vantage. I was on the *Crimson* when he was at Yale putting out his little irreverent sheet." Trilling was the member of the group who most influenced Riesman, although Riesman felt his own interests were nearest to Glazer's and was a closer friend of his.[33]

Macdonald had thought to call his new magazine *The Radical Monthly* or *New Left Review*. But *Politics* was suggested by C. Wright Mills, a sociologist who taught first at the University of Maryland and then at

Columbia during the 1950s. Sharply iconoclastic and outspoken, Mills was associated with the dissenters, influencing such members of the group as Dennis Wrong, but his commitment to radicalism put him at odds with even the dissenters by the end of the 1950s.[34] Mills's criticisms of the American power structure appeared in *White Collar* (1951) and *The Power Elite* (1956).

Macdonald met Mills in 1943, "a few years after he had broken out of his native Texan corral, like a maverick bull, to seek greener intellectual pastures up north." The two men were drawn together in a wartime atmosphere that was not particularly radical; both were cynical, skeptical, and rebellious iconoclasts. According to Macdonald, Mills "could argue about practically anything even longer and louder than I could." While writing for *Politics*, Mills met Coser. Though Mills taught graduate courses in the Columbia sociology department, where Coser earned his doctorate, Coser never took classes from him. Nevertheless, the two "were very close" according to Coser, and he claimed that it was he who later brought Mills "into the *Dissent* fold."[35]

Richard Hofstadter was another figure who inhabited the periphery of the New York group and shared many of their concerns but kept a separate identity. Daniel Bell, a member of the inner circle who had attended City College, said of his friend, "Dick wasn't a New York intellectual—I use 'New York intellectual' in quotes—to the extent, let's say, that Alfred Kazin was or even I might be, namely, a great interest in ideas and constantly racing around to discuss ideas."

Nor was Hofstadter a cultural generalist in the letters tradition: "Dick was less interested, in the evenings, in sitting around, getting involved in a large-scale discussion of what was going on in politics, what was going on in the cultural world. . . . his orbit essentially was his own particular intellectual preoccupations." Hofstadter also did not share the group's freelance literary-cultural outlook, the approach of the New York street intellectual raised on factional politics—the sort of person who felt as comfortable in an editor's chair as in a university chair. A scholar more than a freelance intellectual, Hofstadter took to the classroom, library, and scholarly writing rather than journalism, essays, and talking. Hofstadter, Bell reported, was not as engaged in "the more general world of abstract ideas, which is, you know, the great stuff of discussion in the '50's." Bell concluded that Hofstadter "was intellectual in the range of his interest, but he wasn't in that very simple and slightly invidious distinction, a 'New York intellectual.'"[36]

Hofstadter's fellow historian Arthur Schlesinger, Jr., however, had no trouble serving as the sort of involved intellectual Bell described. Schlesinger shared little background with the group, for he was raised in Cambridge as the son of a Harvard historian and never thought of himself as anything more radical than a reformist liberal. When the politics of the *Partisan* circle had cooled into liberalism after World War II, Schlesinger shared their liberal anticommunism, wrote *The Vital Center* (1949) in defense of that outlook, contributed to some of their publications, attended an occasional conference, and joined their American Committee for Cultural Freedom.[37]

Alfred Kazin, Bell's brother-in-law, was another who fit Bell's model of the New York intellectual better than Hofstadter. Like Macdonald, Kazin during the war described himself as "a man of the third camp." He read *Politics*, but after the war he was frustrated by Macdonald's emphasis on "abstention and perpetual alienation." "What I object to in McDonald's [sic] position," Kazin wrote in his journal in 1946, "is not that it is 'impractical,' but that it is self-righteous to the point where it identifies *all* power with evil and its own powerlessness with good."

In Kazin's view an intellectual had to be a dissenter, but if dissension solidified into intransigence, one's power necessarily diminished. An intellectual needed to be creative and flexible. In contrast, Kazin felt that Macdonald "does not distinguish between opposition to the established culture, which is good, and the *ceremony* of alienation, which is a self-protective neurotic device." Further, Macdonald set unrealistic goals which led to a feeling of futility. He "errs initially and almost fatally," Kazin observed later, "by setting himself the smallest possible amount of primary alternatives, usually in terms of the external organization of the state, and then despondently, finding them equally abhorrent, writes them all off."[38] Criticism could be both useful and moral in Kazin's view, and its utility should not be surrendered easily.

Yet Kazin found much to admire in Macdonald. In the late 1940s several of these writers belonged to a Europe-America discussion group, and Kazin sometimes felt, after the evening meetings, that "Rahv is a commissar out of a job and Macdonald [is] an utter fool." But in his journal Kazin also found himself "regretting, as I always do when I see Macdonald, that I have so often poo-pooed him superficially; in his strivings and daily attitudes, [he is] more creative than anyone else in his group." Because Kazin was more interested in art than journalism, Macdonald could bore him, but Kazin at least considered him a clever and thoughtful "utopian journalist."[39]

Irving Howe was another of the contributors to *Politics*. "Only Macdonald's personal zest as editor of *Politics*," Howe remembered later, "created the possibility—perhaps the illusion—of preserving some sort of left-wing community" in this period. Howe had returned from the army in 1946 and again worked for the Shachtmanite *Labor Action*, but his horizons had expanded too far for him to remain in a sect. Macdonald hired him at fifteen dollars a week as a part-time assistant at *Politics*. There Howe again ran into Lewis Coser. Howe and Coser considered themselves unorthodox Marxists, but they thought Macdonald went too far, in "The Root Is Man," toward "a kind of anarcho-pacifist-moralist declaration stressing his new commitment to absolute values." Howe and Coser each wrote "rather turgid" criticisms of Macdonald's idealism, and, according to Howe, "Dwight was good-natured enough to print them." Later Howe admitted that those criticisms "probably helped sink that admirable magazine." [40]

While Howe was criticizing Macdonald's political outlook, the two men existed in a friendly tension of ideas. Macdonald was paying him to write a review of articles in various periodicals, for *Politics*, and Howe sent him several each month. Macdonald received a letter from Howe in late summer 1946, when Macdonald was considering printing Howe's attack on him, explaining that "our political lines have diverged so widely that all we can really do is note the differences and let it go at that." Two weeks later Howe again wrote Macdonald that "the two political lines of thought we represent have diverged so radically that there is less and less common ground for polemic." They remained friends, although they did not try to hide their disagreement. [41]

Those at *Partisan Review* took a different course during the 1940s than the dissenters at *Politics*. After Macdonald left *Partisan Review* in 1943, the magazine continued to support America in the war, and for the remainder of the 1940s it was increasingly sympathetic toward America in the Cold War. Along with *Commentary*, which was founded by the American Jewish Committee under the editorship of Elliot Cohen in 1945, *Partisan Review* became the home of the affirmers among the New York group. In the 1940s the division grew more pronounced between the Hook group at *Partisan Review* and *Commentary* and the Macdonald circle at *Politics*.

It is usually assumed that Hook's politics originated in his strong Marxism of the late 1920s and early 1930s, and that as his passion cooled it solidified into a social democratic vision close to that of Eduard Bernstein. Although this version is not wrong, it underestimates the extent to which Hook, after his initial Marxist period, settled into the political outlook of his mentor John Dewey.

Dewey had always been interested in individualism, especially in the first few decades of the century. By the late 1920s, when Hook studied with him, Dewey realized that collectivism was the new order and that America's only choice was whether that collectivism would be operated under private, corporate, and somewhat fragmented auspices or under a more coherent social control. Yet he thought that even if that increased planning and integration remained in private hands, the economic system might as well be called socialism because of its collectivism. "We are in for some kind of socialism, call it by whatever name we please, and no matter what it will be called when it is realized," Dewey announced on the eve of the stock market crash.[42]

His vision of what planning would entail did not change perceptibly from World War I to the market crash. The planning agency would be a partnership of government, labor, business, and consumer representatives. If it sounded vaguely like the Swope Plan or the National Recovery Administration of the New Deal that is not surprising, since the visions of Dewey, Swope, and the NRA were all roughly based on the planning partnerships established in Britain and the United States during World War I. While the war was still at a peak Dewey announced his plan. "This does not involve absolute state ownership and absolute state control," he reported, "but rather a kind of conjoined supervision and regulation, with supervisors and arbiters, as it were, to look after the public interests, the interests of the consumer, the interests of the population as a whole, others to represent those who have their capital immediately invested, and others to represent those who have their lives (in the form of work) immediately invested."[43]

Thirteen years later, just prior to the stock market crash, Dewey wrote a similar piece, although this time he mentioned the Soviet Union. His plan, he said, would need to be voluntary rather than imposed by the government. "A coordinating and directive council in which captains of industry and finance would meet with representatives of labor and public officials to plan the regulation of industrial activity," he suggested, "would signify that we had entered constructively and voluntarily upon the road which Soviet Russia is traveling with so much attendant destruction and coercion."[44] Although in 1932 Dewey supported Norman Thomas and the Socialists, he never abandoned his fundamentally liberal outlook.

Both of Dewey's proposals, over a decade apart, envisioned a partnership between government and the major interests of society, with the government serving as the orchestra leader—much as he suggested should occur in his liberal associationist theory of society. Hook, except for the decade of his fascination with Marxism, shared this Wilsonian progressive liberalism with Dewey—and mixed it with a dash of the social democratic vision to which he paid rhetorical allegiance. Many of the ostensibly more radical members of the New York group followed Hook, if not always intentionally, along his political course. Even the young firebrand Irving Howe over the decades grew closer to the politics of liberalism than Marxism.

This insight did not escape Hook, who felt that Howe viewed everything Hook did after announcing his support for American involvement in the war in the early 1940s as only a sign of betrayal to the left. Yet Howe, according to Hook, followed Hook's own political journey toward the center at a lag of ten or fifteen years. Hook always felt alienated from Howe, whom he thought had never stopped judging him. But Hook softened toward Macdonald, at least after his death, in part because Macdonald was not a party person, not doctrinaire. Hook saw virtues in Macdonald that he did not detect in Howe—Macdonald was flexible, more interested in culture than politics, more freewheeling and willingly irresponsible—and Hook continued to think of Macdonald as a first-rate journalist.[45]

As Howe remembers it, Hook was respected by the group during the 1940s as the best anti-Stalinist voice, and they were proud to have Hook deal with that controversy. But the dissenters recognized that Hook's moral outrage about oppressed peoples (other than those oppressed by totalitarian regimes) had left him. In the tension between the affirmers and the dissenters, Harold Rosenberg and Paul Goodman, both dissenters, were frozen out of writing for *Partisan Review* because they were considered to be too far left. Yet Howe, though he was a vocal critic of *Partisan Review* and the Hook group, continued to write for the magazine, and assumed it was because he was too young to be resented.[46]

The third significant publication of the New York intellectuals in the 1940s was *Commentary*. It succeeded the *Contemporary Jewish Record*, which the American Jewish Committee had published since 1938, and for which both Rahv and Greenberg had served as managing editor in the early 1940s.

Commentary's first editor was Elliot Cohen, who was in his midforties when the magazine began. Born in 1899, Cohen was only three years older than Hook and six years older than Trilling. Raised in Mobile, Alabama, he had been a brilliant and precocious youngster and at age fourteen he went to Yale. Despite being an exceptional student in English, he sensed there was an anti-Semitism in English departments, which Trilling and others would later feel, and he did not pursue graduate studies.

From 1924 to 1932 Cohen was an editor at the *Menorah Journal*, where he became another kind of teacher, gathering around him promis-

ing young Jewish writers like Lionel Trilling, Tess Slesinger, Herbert So-
low, Clifton Fadiman, and others. Trilling wrote that "no one—certainly
none of our teachers—ever paid so much attention to what we thought
and how we wrote." At Cohen's death Trilling said, "I would wish to
acknowledge him as the *only* great teacher I have ever had." [47]

After leaving the *Menorah Journal* in 1932 under strained relations
with its head editor, Cohen for the next decade and a half served as a
fundraiser for a Jewish organization. Despondent at such an insufficient
outlet for his talents, Cohen leaped at the opportunity to edit *Commentary* in 1945, and he established a strong presence there. [48] Again he became a teacher. His lesson now was that Jewish writers needed to become
involved in American culture, that there was a connection, in Trilling's
words, "between the seemingly disparate parts of a culture, and between
the commonplaces of daily life and the most highly developed works of
the human mind." [49] Baseball, stump politics, popular culture—all of it
should be evaluated, addressed, and engaged by the American Jewish
community and then made to correspond and interact with the higher
realms of thought. More than any theme other than persistent anticommunism, Cohen's advice about interaction with American culture characterized the tradition of *Commentary*.

Within a few years of its birth *Commentary* functioned as a new voice
of the New York group, and after the early 1950s it became the most
prominent of their publications. Among its editorial staff were Clement
Greenberg, Nathan Glazer, the young film and cultural critic Robert Warshow, and Irving Kristol. Sidney Hook was a contributing editor, and contributors included Harold Rosenberg, Mary McCarthy, Paul Goodman,
Alfred Kazin, Hannah Arendt, Sidney Hook, Irving Howe, Daniel Bell,
Philip Rahv, Diana Trilling, and William Barrett. [50]

Commentary was not limited to affirmers, although they came to predominate over time. For one, Clement Greenberg scarcely qualified as an
affirmer, and Howe wrote Macdonald in 1946 that Greenberg had been
helpful getting him published there. Macdonald remained unimpressed
with *Commentary*. He answered Howe that "I don't agree that the journal is worth calling attention to." [51]

Midge Decter, who went to work for *Commentary* in the early years,
acknowledged that her editorial friends such as Warshow, Glazer, and
Kristol had all become affirmers. "My new friends," she recalled later,
"had been radicals who became pro-American because of World War II,
and then afterwards they went to work at *Commentary*. . . . I think it
could be said that they were more anti-Communist than they were merely
pro-American. They had looked upon the face of totalitarianism and were
finished with their early flirtation with radicalism." [52]

This was a key issue between the dissenters and the affirmers in the 1950s: Had the affirmers at *Commentary* abandoned their radicalism? If so, were they justified or not? Were they merely anticommunists rather than affirmers of mainstream American culture? Did their strong anticommunism lead them into affirmation? Or were the dissenters merely defending an outmoded and irrelevant stance of critical opposition that contained more intransigence than intelligence?

As the mid-century mark approached, at least some of the affirmers and dissenters began to reach a closer agreement on the inadvisability of a third-camp outlook that tried to straddle the tensions between the Soviet Union and America. Hannah Arendt's *The Origins of Totalitarianism* (1951) was representative of the increasing hostility in the intellectual community toward any type of totalitarianism—right or left. By her analysis, the totalitarianism prevalent in the Soviet Union was not the natural product of Marxist or socialist principles, but an analogue of the situation in Nazi Germany. The influence of her book helped sink any traces of third-camp ambivalence that remained in the New York group.

Hard to classify, Arendt was probably more of a dissenter than an affirmer. She admired Macdonald, and in 1946 wrote to Houghton Mifflin, recommending him and his manuscript *The Root Is Man*. Arendt called him "an honest, stubborn, restless thinker" who was "struggling with the problems which perplex our age." It was the strength of Macdonald's dissenting unorthodoxy that attracted and impressed her. "What I like best about Mr. Macdonald," she told the publishers, "is his courageous willingness to go beyond the fashionable and orthodox unorthodoxies which constitute so great a danger for any person who is really trying to think today." [53] She was close to others as well. Alfred Kazin found himself so galvanized by her that he had to remind himself in his diary that he was not in love with her. "So drawn to Hannah these days," he noted to himself, "that I resent [Heinrich, her husband]. I'm not in love with her, just adore her as a human being, with all my heart." [54]

Arendt, like Coser, had escaped from Germany to America early in the war. In Germany she studied under Karl Jaspers and received a doctorate from Heidelberg. More than others in the New York group, she wrote deep and complex philosophical works rather than critical essays. Her work, like theirs, shared significant themes with the critical theory developed in the 1930s and 1940s by the Frankfurt School in Germany and the United States.

The Frankfurt School had been established as the Institut für Sozialforschung in Frankfurt in 1923, but was exiled to the United States in the mid-1930s. There it took up residence at Columbia University as the Institute for Social Research under the leadership of Max Horkheimer, until it was reestablished in Frankfurt in the early 1950s. Its key figures were Horkheimer, Theodor Adorno, Leo Lowenthal, Franz Neumann, Erich Fromm, Herbert Marcuse, and Walter Benjamin. The Frankfurt School was characterized by an anti-Bolshevik and then anti-Stalinist Marxism, a neo-Marxist criticism of the Marxist heritage, and an outlook that found neither capitalism nor Soviet socialism satisfactory.[55] In that regard it was compatible with the independent radicalism of the New York group.

Among the topics that the Frankfurt School explored were the growth of the state and bureaucracy, the domination of the individual by the government apparatus and the cultural hegemony of the dominant class, the spread of mass culture and the growth of commodification in the culture industry, and the development of authoritarian and totalitarian societies. This constellation of interests was obviously prompted by an attempt to explain the social transformations and extremism that had surfaced around the globe during the 1930s and 1940s. It was an inquiry in which the New York group was also engaged, and the Frankfurt School and the New York intellectuals influenced each other, wrote for each other, and helped establish a cross-pollination of European and American intellectual culture around these important concerns.

In the late 1940s, for example, Adorno led a study, published as *The Authoritarian Personality* (1950), in which he postulated a personality type that under modern conditions of the growth of mass culture and the state was potentially fascist or absolutist in outlook and susceptible to racism and extreme nationalism. Parallel projects by the New York intellectuals on the dangers of mass societies and movements included Riesman's *The Lonely Crowd* (1950) and *Faces in the Crowd* (1952), and Arendt's *Origins of Totalitarianism* (1951).

While Arendt's thesis reassured leftists that Marxist or socialist principles need not produce a Soviet totalitarianism, she also warned readers not to make the mistake—as third-campers did—of equating the dangers of American illiberalism with those of Soviet totalitarianism: totalitarianism was the ultimate danger.

Even the dissenters agreed with Arendt on this judgment by the time her book appeared. Macdonald became increasingly convinced by the argument that Rahv, Hook, and Phillips had made before World War II: the third-camp position was meaningless in the reality of the 1940s, and one had to choose between East and West. Macdonald's change of heart was accompanied by another shift for which he had criticized *Partisan Review* years earlier: becoming less political. His depoliticization was born of despair. As a political critic looking at the disturbing aftermath of the war, he saw only futility; as a pacifist faced with the reality of having to choose sides in the Cold War, he stared blankly at a choice he did not want to make.

In addition, in Macdonald's case the personal and political were intertwined at that moment to increase his despair. His first marriage was breaking apart, and he left the bohemian life of Greenwich Village to move uptown, marry his second wife, and live after that at a more fashionable location on East 87th Street off Park Avenue.[56] These events marked a deeper change in his life that was reflected in his move from politics to culture, and from *Politics* to the *New Yorker*. It was not an easy time for him. There was a crisis in his soul that reflected the crisis of postwar America.

As Macdonald looked about him in 1947 from his position at *Politics*, he told his readers that "now the clearer one's insight, the more numbed one becomes." It was remarkable for a leading member of a group committed to rational criticism and intelligence to admit that he was dazed by the world. Even as recently as a decade before, the New York group had assumed that intelligence could transform the world. Most of them still believed that, if in a slightly more modest way. Macdonald was the most discouraged of the group, perhaps because he had been the most idealistic and hopeful. "But on the world scale," he wrote in confusion and sadness, "politics is a desert without hope." Hook and the rest of the group in the aftermath of the war flinched only slightly, almost imperceptibly, as the reality of the new world situation swept over them; then they recommitted themselves to their course—although most of them now took paths that were a little more cultural than political, and centrist than leftist.

Politics and ideology were no longer the maps to the future. "Instead it is discouraging," Macdonald wrote blankly. "For our positive ideas have not worked out, either: the world seems farther than ever from either pacifism or socialism. As one brought up in the Progressive tradition, which assumes that if we only 'know enough' about any situation, we can master it . . . I find it disconcerting to be confronted with a problem that shakes this assumption." The path to the future, which had been so clear during his socialist days, was now uncertain. "We radicals are faced with a split between knowledge and action; we may overcome it, but we cannot any longer assume that we will."[57] He felt all options were closed to him. Violence could not settle the Cold War tensions because of the threat of atomic weapons. Nonviolence would not work because of the Soviets' immorality and inhumanity. A pacifist, he decided, was in an inescapable "dilemma."[58]

By spring 1948 Macdonald was increasingly willing to support the

West against the Soviet Union, rather than merely to criticize the Soviets. In *Politics* he wrote a long list of comparisons between the two countries that showed how on each score America was better. Again he regretted that the liberals would not admit this. In the thirties the New York group and others had discovered the evils of Stalinism, but a decade later the "younger generation in America, on the other hand, seems to be not even at the level of sophistication I had reached in 1938." He used the image of a pair of "scissors" cutting America in half: the anti-Stalinist intellectuals becoming even more anti-Soviet, while the younger generation was becoming less critical. Macdonald was worried lest the "scissors gape even wider" in the future.[59] The scissors that Macdonald feared did cut sharply across the fabric of the American intellectual community in the 1940s and 1950s, and an example of that incision occurred a year later at the Waldorf Conference in New York.

While it lasted, from 1944 to 1949, *Politics* maintained the viability of the third-camp position and offered a perspective that Macdonald described as "anarchism and pacifism." *Politics* existed in that short span of years Macdonald aptly labeled "the gray dawn of 'peace,'" in which the reality of the Nazi death camps, the atomic bomb, and Stalinism began to settle on people—like the dust descending after a great explosion.[60] Most of the New York intellectuals were more prepared than the rest of the country for the "gray dawn." They had few illusions left. They had watched the approaching daybreak for years. They had lived with the soured reality of their dreams in a long, protracted, polluted sunrise that began to dawn with the Moscow Trials in the mid-1930s. They had seen another shade of light added to the gray morning with the Nazi-Soviet Pact in 1939. They had watched the continuing brightness of the dull light with the disappointing perversion and destruction of ideologies in World War II. Now with the arrival of the atomic bomb and the beginning of the Cold War in the late 1940s most of them were witnessing without surprise or illusion, even without despair, the glaring bitter morning to the postwar period.

Macdonald was not exempt from the pressures that had transformed his fellow writers from antagonists to supporters of America. As late as 1944 he could still write in *Politics* that the only hope for "a humanly tolerable world" following the war was a succession of "popular revolutions" by the common people of Europe (America was not advanced enough, to his disappointment) which would be "socialist as to economics and democratic as to politics."[61] By the end of the decade he was not nearly so pessimistic about the value of America's ideals and potential for good.

By 1952, three years after the Waldorf Conference had ended, Macdonald publicly admitted that he was ready to side with America against its Stalinist enemies. He later called this "a 'lesser evil' choice," and rolled his eyes, acknowledging "the pages and pages of argumentation I have written exposing the illogic and immorality of this position" against Rahv, Phillips, and others in earlier years. At Mt. Holyoke College in the winter of 1952 Macdonald debated Norman Mailer; Macdonald defended his statement "I choose the West" against Mailer's (formerly Macdonald's) "I cannot choose." The following year Macdonald again complained about the lack of alternatives to choosing either the East or West, though he remained committed to the West—if without exuberance. "This is one reason," he explained, "I am less interested in politics than I used to be." [62]

Macdonald's slow turnabout in support of the West is testimony to how even the staunchest dissenters were reoriented by the international conflict. One need only look at how the names of the New York intellectuals' organizations changed over the decade for an example of how readjusted their outlook about America became. Before the war the names of their groups were the Committee for Cultural Freedom, or the League for Cultural Freedom and Socialism. After the war they identified themselves more closely with American culture, and by the late 1940s their organizations were named the Americans for Intellectual Freedom, and the American Committee for Cultural Freedom.

At mid-century, about a decade after the first of the New York group began to make their peace with America, Macdonald reluctantly joined his associates "on native grounds." For Irving Howe, Lewis Coser, and others who remained more critical, the reconciliation took a few years longer, although even the most adamant critics had become more sympathetic to their adopted culture by the late 1940s. Significant differences remained between the dissenters and the affirmers, but each side had grown closer to America.

Irving Howe

Along with Lionel Trilling and Alfred Kazin, Irving Howe was among the most serious and productive literary critics in the New York group. But Howe was more political than Trilling or Kazin: he wrote more explicitly political articles and edited the political journal *Dissent*, and even his literary criticism had more political engagement and imagination. Trilling and Kazin were the more powerful and inspired literary critics, but Howe, as a spokesman for culture at the intersection of literature and politics, was often a much more interesting and instructive presence.

Although Howe was actively engaged in reviewing literary and political trends in Western Europe and the Soviet bloc, particularly the political literature of oppression and resistance, he was overwhelmingly interested in American subjects. This focus marked a departure from the first-generation New York literary critics, such as Rahv and Trilling, who were at least as interested in foreign modernism. In mid-career, Howe developed an interest in Yiddish literature and Jewish history, but his essays continued to be primarily American in emphasis. His first book was on Walter Reuther and the United Auto Workers, but he then switched more solidly to literary criticism and wrote studies of Sherwood Anderson, William Faulkner, politics and the novel, literary modernism and politics, Thomas Hardy, and Ralph Waldo Emerson, among others. Interspersed with these literary works were a study of American communism (with Lewis Coser), several collections of political essays, a book on Trotsky, a history of American Jewish immigration and cultural life, and edited collections of Yiddish stories, articles from *Dissent*, and Trotsky's writings.

From his earliest literary writing Howe, like the rest of the group, was opposed to formalism in cultural criticism, against the construction and application of a set of formal "scientific" principles or structures for evaluating literature apart from its social and historical context. Thus in the 1950s he rejected New Criticism, and in the 1970s and 1980s resisted deconstructionism and related forms of postmodernist continental literary radicalism. Instead Howe informed his criticism with biographical, social, and political considerations of the author, work, and environment. He judged literature by how much one could learn from the author's or characters' dissenting intelligence, individual courage against official oppression, moral propositions, or commitment to justice. [63]

Howe was born in a poor Jewish neighborhood in the Bronx on June 11, 1920. The five-story walk-up tenements of the East Bronx, Howe remembered, formed a clutter of streets overflowing with poor Eastern European Jewish immigrants. The old brownstones were run down, with dingy staircases and overcrowded apartments. People moved in and out. Milk was still delivered in the morning by horse and wagon. In the neighborhood "Yiddish was spoken everywhere," and the Yiddish newspaper the *Forward* sold as well as the other dailies. Howe's parents were representative of other first-generation Jewish immigrants who fixed their hopes on their children but feared their children's journey into mainstream America "almost as much as they desired it." When his father's West Bronx grocery went bankrupt in the early 1930s the older Howe became a "customer peddler" selling door-to-door. Howe's family had to crowd in with relatives to live, "dropping from the lower middle class to the proletarian—the most painful of all social descents." His parents then became laborers in the garment industry for low wages, his mother an operator, his father a presser.[64]

From this background Howe's socialism was born—apparently more from the neighborhood than from his family. At the age of fourteen he joined the Young People's Socialist League (YPSL) chapter on Wilkins Avenue in the Bronx, and he began to take part in leftist factional arguments. Before long he and six or seven of his friends became street orators for the socialist cause. By the time he was at City College he was one of the leaders of the lunchroom arguments between the Trotskyists (the anti-Stalinist left) in Alcove One and the Communists (the pro-Stalinist left) in Alcove Two of the school cafeteria. Alcove One in the 1930s was a training ground for nearly a generation of the New York group, fostering Irving Howe, Irving Kristol, Seymour Martin Lipset, Daniel Bell, Nathan Glazer, and Melvin J. Lasky, among others.[65]

It is hardly surprising that members of the group were radicals when they were young. Studies have shown that an overproduction of educated persons (intellectual underemployment) causes intellectual radicalism. Those who think of themselves as intellectuals tend to be the most radical in society, as do those in the "critical" disciplines of the humanities and social sciences. Further, intellectuals most likely to be radical are those born into a leftist class or group, those schooled by such a group, and those occupationally and politically tied to such a group in young adulthood. Finally, discontented intellectuals remain radical only if they have the power to change their conditions—otherwise they become apathetic.[66] The New York group met all of these criteria.

Yet, linked as most of the New York intellectuals were to Jewish immigrant labor in the garment and other industries, and tied also to the European Jewish socialist tradition, socialism for them was more than merely a theoretical stance. It was part of their cultural identity, nearly the same as their ethnic heritage and religion. "Socialism, for many immigrant Jews," Howe recalled, "was not merely politics or an idea, it was an encompassing culture, a style of perceiving and judging through which to structure their lives."[67]

There was obviously something about growing up in the 1930s, coming into personal and political consciousness during the Depression, that made the second generation of these critics more aware of their Jewish background and their political unity. Unlike the first generation, most of whom were more affected by the 1920s, the second was more reflective about their poor Jewish childhoods and their self-conscious identification with socialism and with each other in the developing New York group.

The oldest of them—Hook, Trilling, Macdonald, Rahv, Phillips, Mary McCarthy, Harold Rosenberg, Meyer Schapiro—had discovered that the group formed around them and *Partisan Review* in the mid-1930s without their consciously thinking about it. The next youngest of them— Howe, Kazin, Bell, Coser, Mailer, Glazer, Kristol—were young enough to have read *Partisan Review* and to have aimed deliberately at an institutional and social affiliation with the *Partisan* circle. For intellectual Jews in the 1930s and 1940s, *Partisan Review* was both a political cause and the career vehicle that university teaching and some other professions could not be.

Alfred Kazin, another member of the second generation, was one of the first to look back to his beginnings to determine what it meant to be part of the New York group.[68] Kazin remembered a socialism that was so pervasive that "though I felt it deeply, [it] did not require any conscious personal assent or decision on my part; I was a Socialist as so many Americans were 'Christians'; I had always lived in a Socialist atmosphere."[69]

Despite his socialist background, Kazin was less political than most members of the group and in his early years placed more emphasis on literature, culture, and the letters tradition. In his youth, when his friends gravitated toward Marx and other political models, Kazin was more interested in literary figures such as Van Wyck Brooks. His literary sensibility also colored his reaction to the group's magazines. "Reading *Partisan Review* this morning (a magazine I admire and am indebted to)," Kazin wrote in his journal in 1941, "I cannot help but feel how strikingly a certain kind of Marxist disputation has become pure scholasticism."[70] At the time, though, few others in the *Partisan* circle had yet tired of its political polemics, and few would have sympathized with Kazin's essentially literary reaction to it.

Similarly, Kazin's literary inclinations informed his appreciation of John Dewey. Like others in the group, Kazin was influenced by Dewey, although not in the same predominantly political manner. In early 1942 Kazin wrote in his journal, "my own impression of his career and significance is so curiously different from that of most people." "For me," he acknowledged, "Dewey represents not the pragmatic adaptable twentieth-century intelligence which was going to fit philosophy into a new age; rather, he seems to speak with the security and quiet serenity of a vanished world." Kazin's literary perceptiveness and understanding of American culture allowed him to identify the side of Dewey that owed so much to Emerson. In Dewey, Kazin saw "The tang of the Vermont woods; the philosopher of the frontier; the good American teacher and scholar, doing his work, teaching with real integrity and quiet—if not audible—originality."[71]

Just before World War II Kazin wrote *On Native Grounds,* his widely celebrated study of American literature from 1890 to 1940. As that book and his journal reveal, Kazin was more imaginatively attached to American culture than the others in the group. "Every once in a while some token, a sentence in a book, a voice heard," Kazin wrote in his journal in 1942, "will recall for me the fresh instant delight in the sense of being a student of the American landscape and culture that I felt first two years ago, only after I had begun serious work on the book. . . . Yet what it does for me is to recall the excitement under which I lived for weeks on weeks early in 1939, when suddenly I realized, and for the first time consciously, that I had a passionate and even professional (sic) interest in American culture and literature" (the *sic* is Kazin's). His desire to participate in the letters tradition prompted him to write a continuous flow of essays and reviews on American and European authors, many of which were first collected in *The Inmost Leaf* (1955) and then *Contemporaries* (1962). His interest in landscape, noted first in his journal, culminated in his *A Writer's America: Landscape in Literature* (1988).

Kazin was also fascinated with American history texts and biographies, and experienced an "incommunicable delight" in viewing the early American portraits at the Metropolitan Museum. "I have never been able to express the pleasure I derive from the conscious study of 'Americana.' . . . I love to think about America, to look at portraits, to remember the kind of adventurousness and purity, heroism and *salt,* that the best Americans have always had for me."[72] No other member of the New York group would have considered making such an intimate statement about the American cultural heritage in the early 1940s, and only a few of them were ready to do so a decade later.

Howe acknowledged how difficult it was for those raised in the Jewish immigrant culture to identify with the American pantheon. "With American literature itself, we were uneasy," he admitted. American romanticism meant little to them. What were they to make of Emerson, a frigid and denatured "spiritual godfather of Herbert Hoover" who lived, of all places, in the country? "Our own tradition," he explained, "long rutted in *shtetl* mud and urban smoke, made little allowance for nature as presence or refreshment." Of course, the distance they felt from American culture did not leave them bereft. They found the source of their romanticism not in nature but in the Russian romanticism directed toward social justice. "We had *other stories.*"

The individualism central to the American tradition also left Howe and the others baffled, since community and family were paramount values to them. Further, Emerson and Thoreau, Howe reported, were "deficient in those historical entanglements we felt to be essential to literature because inescapable in life." But if American individualism at first drove them from the American canon, in the end it brought them back. The young Jewish intellectuals, according to Howe, finally saw that the individualistic American writers were also profoundly alienated from American culture. Emerson, Thoreau, Melville, and Whitman "had also regarded themselves as strangers" in the land.[73]

Kazin was also attracted to the outsiders in American literature. When he was young he wondered whether his fascination with American culture was because he was an outsider, and whether "only for the first American-born son of so many thousands of mud-flat Jewish-Polish-Russian generations is this need great, this inquiry so urgent?" Like Howe, Kazin was drawn to "the terrible and graphic *loneliness* of the great Americans. Thinking about them composes itself, sooner or later, into a gallery of extraordinary individuals; yet at bottom they have nothing in common but the almost shattering unassailability, the life-stricken I, in each." Kazin, as the first of his group to make the journey into an appreciation for the American tradition, identified poignantly with this loneliness of the pioneering genius. "Each fought his way through life—and through his genius—as if no one had ever fought before," he wrote in his journal about the American figures. "Each one, that is, began afresh—began on his own terms—began in a universe that remained, for all practical purposes, his own."[74]

In Kazin's journals and Howe's autobiographical texts, there is an element of psychological and sociological analysis that sets the second generation apart from the first wave of the New York group. In a retrospective passage, for example, Howe offered one of the more resonant observations about why young Jewish intellectuals were drawn to the political left. They were poor, without power and influence, alienated from their surroundings, but actively involved in trying to shape the future of the world they hoped someday to control. Howe felt that "there is a more fundamental reason for the appeal of the Movement. Marxism involves a profoundly *dramatic* view of human experience. With its stress upon inevitable conflicts, apocalyptic climaxes, ultimate moments, hours of doom, and shining tomorrows, it appealed deeply to our imaginations." Imagination and hope were important to immigrant youths. "We felt that we were always on the rim of heroism, that the mockery we might suffer at the moment would turn to vindication in the future, that our loyalty to principle would be rewarded by the grateful masses of tomorrow."

The rewards would be the sort that the intellectually ambitious wanted: the pleasure of seeing their version of justice enthroned, but also a taste of influence and power in the realm of politics and culture. "Often enough these disputes concerned issues of genuine importance, in which the Movement found itself groping toward problems that most political analysts had not even begun to consider. . . . But," Howe remembered, "I think the faction fights had another purpose that we could not then acknowledge: they were charades of struggle, substitute rituals for the battles we could not join, ceremonies of 'acting out.' Through them we created our own drama in our own world."[75]

Indeed, looking at the group's history before 1950, one finds that they had an increasing need to move beyond their isolation into positions of influence, leadership, and power in setting and shaping opinion on political and cultural matters. After World War II, the nation's need for intellectuals to stock its universities and design its expanding welfare state, combined with the decline in anti-Semitism in America, provided the group with new outlets for their ambitions.

Working for Macdonald's *Politics* in the mid-1940s showed Howe the way to combine culture and politics in an influential journal. Under the pen name Theodore Dryden, Howe wrote a monthly review of periodicals for the magazine, and he did editorial chores around the *Politics* office. From his early adolescence until the late 1940s, though, Howe had been a committed Trotskyist, working with Trotskyist organizations and publications. *Politics*, in Howe's opinion, "became a stopping place for independent leftists who were bored with Marxist sects yet refused Cold War conservatism," a magazine full of "deviations" from Trotskyism that was "increasingly unreliable in its ideology." Howe would not admit, however, that working for Macdonald was evidence of disloyalty to the Trotskyist orthodoxy, though the contradiction of a professed Trotskyist working at *Politics* was amusing to some observers. "Macdonald was kind enough not to tease me about this," Howe remembered gratefully; "perhaps he saw that I was already heading down the slopes of apostasy and there was no need to push."[76]

In 1948 Howe began to write occasionally for *Time* magazine, and he and his wife moved to Princeton, where she had found work. He resented the conformist pressures that both *Time* and the proper town of Princeton exerted on him, and perhaps those pressures hastened his desertion from Trotskyism. Macdonald in 1948 playfully tweaked Howe by signing a letter to him: "Are you still a Trotskyist?" Howe took the comment seriously and responded: "As to your question about my politics: I haven't considered myself a Trotskyist in any strict sense of the word for some time now. I've been undergoing a rather painful soul-searching and will probably arrive at a terminus soon. My ideas are changing."[77]

Following the same arc of change as Hook before him, Howe had slowly started to develop a greater concern for democracy, although he did not abandon, as most of the group did, the role of oppositional critic and socialist. "A critical point came in my own intellectual development," Howe confessed, "when I began to see that certain elements of traditional political theory could not be reduced to categories of class analysis. The stress of *The Federalist Papers* on the need for countervailing powers in a democratic society represented an important truth, not rendered any less so by Madison's conservative opinions."[78] By the eve of the Waldorf Conference, Howe's continuing socialist commitment had become infused with Hook's respect for the liberal and pluralist tradition in American democratic theory.

Yet while Hook's pragmatism influenced Howe's socialism, Howe never abandoned the socialist ideal.[79] He followed the same journey from Marxism to liberal democracy that Hook pioneered—but stopped short of crossing out of camp and remained a democratic socialist. Never content with merely a theoretical political position, however pure, Howe became a coalition-builder between the democratic socialists and the left wing of the Democratic party, joining Michael Harrington in that effort in the 1970s and 1980s through the Democratic Socialist Organizing Committee and the Democratic Socialists of America. By mid-century, factional squabbles were in his past.

Yet Macdonald, not Hook, was the member of the first generation whose influence was clearest on Howe. *Politics* was the obvious model for Howe's *Dissent*, and it is *Dissent* as much as his literary essays that stamped Howe's identity and for which he will be remembered. Howe took from his close association with Macdonald the latter's wide-ranging concerns, the mark of the intellectual journalist.

During the late 1940s, then, the second generation of the New York group became assimilated with the first. Howe was representative of what the younger learned from the older members, although there was enough contentiousness within the group for any of them to have bristled at the thought of having been influenced by anybody about anything.

The Creation of Dissent: 1950–1955

By mid-century the affirmers in the New York group had become less distressed by the country's self-satisfaction, conformity, and postwar affluence. The dissenters, however, were alarmed at the American celebration and the dissipation of the political left. Kazin felt "the reaction in America creeping around me like the blast of a cold wind," and Rahv warned the intellectual community about abandoning their dissenting outlook. Yet, like most of their colleagues, neither Kazin nor Rahv was willing to say or do much to combat the situation. Howe, in contrast, decided to mount a campaign against the new conformity and carry it to the American intellectual community.

At the point in the mid-1940s when *Partisan Review* was turning toward the political center, it was joined in its position of increasing affirmation by the new *Commentary* magazine. This double-barrelled swing from the political left alarmed the dissenters, who began more frequently to target *Commentary* for their criticism. In 1951 Howe wrote *Commentary* to complain about "the *quality* of some of the anti-Marxism" in its pages, with "its indiscriminate and unscholarly zealousness" and "its air of rude certainty." He went on to criticize articles that had appeared by Robert Gorham Davis, Alfred Kazin, and William Barrett. In response, Kazin dismissed Howe as "outraged" and confused. Davis also found Howe confused, could not determine "what kind of Marxist he is," and did not understand what Howe really wanted from *Commentary* articles. Undeterred, Howe continued to write letters to the editors of *Commentary* rebuking the uncritical position the magazine represented. "It is in the pages of the influential magazine *Commentary*," he warned the dwindling band of dissenters who heeded him, "that liberalism is most skillfully and systematically advanced as a strategy for adapting to the American status quo."[80]

Then in *Partisan Review* in 1954, Howe printed a prominent attack on the affirmers entitled "This Age of Conformity." He complained that former critics were now too comfortable in America, and that "intellectuals, far from thinking of themselves as a desperate 'opposition,' have been enjoying a return to the bosom of the nation." Despite the "tremendous pressures" to conform to the zeitgeist, there were "very real virtues in preserving the attitude of critical skepticism and distance." *Partisan Review* and many of its contributors, according to Howe, had abandoned the radical intellectual orientation that was its founding principle. Once, *Partisan Review* had combined radical politics and avant-garde culture, but that "union has since been dissolved, and there is no likelihood that it will soon be re-established. American radicalism exists only as an idea, and that barely."[81]

A letter to *Partisan Review* by *Commentary* editor Robert Warshow accused Howe of sporting an outdated Marxism. But Howe denied being "a thorough-going or systematic Marxist" at all. "One need not be a

Marxist to accept the main theme of my article," Howe replied. "The very terms of the article are not Marxist; and deliberately so. I used the rather loose phrase 'conformity' instead of a more precise political one simply because I wished to emphasize that my complaint was not that certain intellectuals had abandoned this or that ideology but that they had abandoned the traditional idea of keeping a critical distance from state power, *any* state power." How could intellectuals function without some distance between themselves and the forces of political or cultural power? "Whether people call themselves socialists or not interests me less than the values and standards they try to maintain in this age of locusts," Howe told Warshow. "My complaint against *Commentary*, for example, was not that it ceased to be socialist: it never had been that; but rather that it has become an apologist for middle-class values, middle-class culture and the *status quo*, and that on the issue of civil liberties it has squirmed, evaded, and played possum." [82]

The affirmers thought Howe and the dissenters were passé, and they were prepared to defend themselves. When, David Riesman wondered, would the second-generation immigrant critics finally stop parading their alienation and settle down into a normal pattern of life and thought? For some of them, Riesman conceded, "it may still be necessary to go through a novitiate of emotional expatriation in order to establish securely a claim to the intellectual's function—as we can see in a somewhat analogous case when we ask: how soon can the descendants of immigrants again eat garlic and other savory foods after a bland, self-inhibited period of 'Americanization'?" He hoped that "As we get second- and third-generation intellectuals, these problems may for many become less intense." Although Riesman respected dissenters such as Macdonald and Coser, in Coser's case enough to hire him, he still felt a distance between his political outlook and theirs. He thought Howe and Coser "had too much left rhetoric." [83]

The dissenters' perception that many fellow New York intellectuals had abandoned radicalism was sharpened by their conviction that *Partisan Review* and *Commentary* were insensitive to the dangers of McCarthyism. Indeed, the dissenters suspected that the magazines not only acquiesced in but also approved of some of McCarthyism's anti-leftist effects. Howe and sociologist Bernard Rosenberg considered *Commentary* worse than *Partisan Review* in this regard, since Rahv, although timid, had at least opposed McCarthyism. *Commentary*, according to Howe, thought the "anti-anti-communists" more dangerous than McCarthy and his followers. Because of their disapproval of *Commentary*'s outlook on McCarthyism, dissenters Howe, Coser, Meyer Schapiro, and others were not invited by the affirmers to join the American Committee for Cultural Freedom, an organization the dissenters, in any event, considered too stridently and indiscriminately anticommunist. Had they been invited, Howe admitted, "we would of course have refused." [84]

Many of those involved in the ACCF, however, agreed with Hook that charges of their being soft on McCarthy were silly and irresponsible. "Everything that one can reasonably mean by McCarthyism," Hook wrote Richard Rovere in 1952 about an ACCF publication, "is excoriated in this pamphlet." What, Hook wondered, did the dissenters want? "For myself," he told Rovere with frustration, "a *general* resolution against McCarthy is like a resolution against sin or a resolution against Communism or Fascism, and I can say this without misunderstanding, I hope, because I have publicly and repeatedly denounced the 'irresponsible and morally scandalous methods of McCarthy.'" A generalized opposition was not the method of a pragmatist. "But I have no objection in principle to such a resolution," Hook explained to Rovere. "A resolution to have point and effect, however, should center on specific acts, particularly as they bear on cultural issues." [85]

With *Partisan Review* and particularly *Commentary* controlled by the affirmers, the dissenters became restless. Howe and Coser discussed the lack of publishing opportunities for those who maintained standards of critical opposition. Anti-Stalinist leftists cared to write for the book section of the *Nation* only until Margaret Marshall, who was sympathetic to them, was fired. Dissenters, after *Politics* had died, lacked a voice and a home. [86]

"When intellectuals can do nothing else," Howe once wrote, "they start a magazine." Yet in the spring of 1949, just as *Politics* folded, Macdonald and Howe had a disagreement about what constituted a worthwhile radical magazine. Howe had written an article, printed in *Partisan Review*, about the need for good small political magazines. When Macdonald complained that Howe had omitted mention of *Politics*, Howe explained why the magazine did not fit the description. "What I was *clearly* referring to, I think," Howe wrote in reply to Macdonald, "was a nonparty Marxist magazine defending the general view of revolutionary Marxism but not supporting any kind of group. If, for instance, a magazine were started with Meyer Schapiro, Jim Cork, Louis Clair, perhaps Mills and myself as editors, it would, for good or bad, fit that description. Again for good or bad, *Politics* does not." [87]

Howe's conception of a useful radical magazine anticipated *Dissent*, which, as he hinted about his ideal magazine, would roughly follow in the tradition of *Politics* but depart from it in important ways. "*Politics* as now constituted," Howe continued, "does not, I think, fit into the 'mainstream' or mainpuddle of American radicalism—that may be a compliment, but I think it's a fact. And I want to puddle or muddle along in a way you don't."[88]

Macdonald disagreed that *Politics* was more of a "party" or sectarian magazine than Howe's imaginary ideal. He wrote back to Howe that "with the best will in the world, I cannot see why a magazine edited by the Marxists you mention and dedicated to 'defending the general view of revolutionary Marxism but not supporting any kind of group' is any more or less a 'party magazine' than *Politics*, which defends the general anarcho-pacifist position and is likewise not committed to any group." Why did Howe think his ideal magazine was so different? "Your mag would slant toward Marxism," Macdonald told him, "mine does slant toward anarchism; if yours is non-party why in the world isn't mine?" Macdonald failed to see a difference. "Mabe [sic] you think of Marxism as being less 'party'-sectarian than anarchism," he wrote Howe, "since, as you correctly say, anarchism 'does not fit into the mainstream of American radicalism'; but this is to mistake popularity for nonsectarian broadness. Anyway, as you also write, maybe it's not a stream but a puddle in both cases—and the puddle shouldn't call the smaller puddle wet!"[89]

Soon after *Politics* died, Macdonald was again at the heart of discussions about a new publishing venture. Hannah Arendt, Mary McCarthy, Richard Rovere, Arthur Schlesinger, Jr., and Macdonald were hoping to begin *The Critic*. McCarthy did all the fundraising and collected pledges totaling $55,000, but, according to Macdonald, "since we figured it would take twice that at the very least to carry on [the] mag for [the] first two years, we dropped the project." Kazin assumed that McCarthy had "backed out" of it for personal reasons, but Macdonald said no such reasons were known to her colleagues.[90]

At about the same time, Howe and Coser started to plan their new magazine. Through Robert Lynd, who was teaching sociology at Columbia (where Coser was doing graduate work), and Max Lerner, who was at Brandeis, Coser was hired at Brandeis in the spring of 1951.[91] When Howe was still living on Grover Avenue in Princeton he drove up to visit the Cosers at their home in Wellesley, Massachusetts. They talked in Coser's living room, and, as Howe recalled, at length they discussed "the glory our magazine was going to be: it would avoid every fault, every sin of previous radical journals." Coser remembered that they wanted a journal "unhampered by the cowardice and caution of what passed at the time for the left-of-center press." Later they were joined in the planning of the project by Stanley Plastrik, Emanuel Geltman, Bernard Rosenberg, Mever Schapiro, Norman Mailer, and Harold Orlans.[92]

Plastrik and Geltman had been brought into the planning circle by Howe, as all three were chastened and somewhat disillusioned former Shachtmanites who wanted to remain involved in a nonsectarian politics of the democratic left. Bernard Rosenberg was introduced to the group through Coser; the two of them together at the time constituted the entire sociology department at Brandeis. Rosenberg, an independent sort of radical, had never belonged to political organizations. When a few members of the planning group met to decide on a name for the magazine, according to Plastrik's account, Rosenberg "destroyed the attractive notion of naming the magazine *No!* with the quip that it would be too 'affirmative.'" Coser suggested the title *Dissent*.[93]

Howe and Coser next decided to see whether they could interest a sufficient number of their friends in the project. Howe assembled a group of about fifty people, many of them former Shachtmanites, at a conference in New York to discuss the viability of the magazine. He invited both potential writers and donors. "To our great surprise," Coser remembered, "they almost all came, and there was a good deal of enthusiasm." Howe asked those in attendance whether they would be willing to contribute articles for nothing, and whether they would be willing to contribute money. The response, according to Coser, was gratifying. Meyer Schapiro said he would write, although he never did. Yet he did lend his name and moral support which, given his stature, was significant. Schapiro also persuaded some of his wealthy art friends to contribute money.[94]

The dissenters knew that a radical journal could not be self-supporting, so they agreed not to begin the project unless they could guarantee at least one year of four issues. They determined it could not be done for less than six thousand dollars. "Well, two, three, four issues and then of course we go bankrupt and that will be that," Howe told Coser, "but we will have made a heroic effort." Their best luck came from Joseph Buttinger, an Austrian socialist émigré whom Rose Coser knew. The editors did not want any one contributor to be in a position to control the magazine financially, however. Although Buttinger gave enough to assure the existence of *Dissent*, he never tried to control it. Even the editors were not exempt from having to donate money to the project. Coser said that the privilege of being a *Dissent* editor meant you had to contribute a few hundred dollars a year to the magazine.[95]

In spring 1953, as the planning for the magazine was under way, Howe wrote Macdonald and asked whether he would allow *Dissent* to use the old *Politics* subscribers' list to solicit funds. Howe explained the new venture as "a socialist magazine: non-party, without a 'line,' but with a general radical outlook." He told Macdonald they planned to operate "on a shoe-string, if we can get the shoe-string." Macdonald agreed to let Howe have the subscribers' list, and he also sent along a prospectus for *The Critic*. Howe thought the prospectus "interesting," and felt there was no "real conflict" between the two magazines. *Dissent* was "on a much more modest scale," Howe admitted. "Very likely, both projects won't pan out," he told Macdonald. "If by some miracle, they did, it would be fine; and people writing for one could write for the other, if they cared to." [96]

The *Dissent* editors courted Macdonald as a writer but he was never very interested. By the early 1950s he was writing for *The New Yorker*, was fatigued by political arguments, and would not rise to the lure of politics again until the New Left confrontations caught his imagination in the 1960s. Coser did his best to persuade Macdonald to write for the new magazine. He joked to Macdonald in a letter that since he was "some 7 years younger than you are I still can afford to have some political passion prevail over the normal inclination to academic quiescence," and therefore he would help edit *Dissent*. "It will be by no means as good as *Politics* used to be," he wrote flatteringly, "but at least it will be an effort to provide a Forum for dissenters of various stripes and hues." It was important that there be "a place where dissenters can express their ideas. The repenters seem to have conquered almost all the other existing mags."

The young *Dissent*, Coser knew, would profit from an affiliation with Macdonald. "Now we would like to extend to you a most cordial invitation to contribute to the magazine," Coser wrote. "We will not be able to pay a red penny, we will not have a circulation much above 2000 [it was 4,000 after two years], we will not be considered as 'glamorous' as *Politics* was—all we are really able to offer you is a place in which you can say whatever you please." Coser renewed his offer two years later, writing that "*Dissent's* pages are always open for you, we would love to have you among our contributors. If there are things you prefer not to say in *Encounter*—*Dissent* is yours for the saying them." [97] Macdonald did not accept the invitation.

An important difference between *Politics* and *Dissent* was that the former was an "anarcho-pacifist" publication mostly written and edited by one person, while the latter was a democratic socialist magazine not individually controlled. But the similarities between the two journals included the host of *Dissent* contributors who had written for *Politics*: Coser, Howe, C. Wright Mills, Harvey Swados, and Paul Goodman, among others. As *Politics* was created in the mid-1940s to replace the critical function that *Partisan Review* had abandoned, *Dissent* was formed in the 1950s to replace the radical forum lost when *Politics* folded in 1949.

On the editorial board for the first volume of *Dissent* were Coser and

Howe, Travers Clement, Harold Orlans, Stanley Plastrik, and Meyer Schapiro. The contributing editors were Erich Fromm, University of Chicago economist Bert Hoselitz, Norman Mailer, labor leader Frank Marquart, peace activist A. J. Muste, and University of Washington English lecturer George Woodcock. Frequent contributors from 1954 to 1960 included Coser and Howe, Bernard Rosenberg, Stanley Plastrik, Ben B. Seligman, Norman Mailer, C. Wright Mills, Harold Rosenberg, Michael Harrington, Harvey Swados, Michael Walzer, Henry Pachter, and Paul Goodman.[98] Most of the editorial work was done by Howe and Coser, with Howe—who was then teaching at Brandeis—performing most of the "line-by-line routine editing and rewriting." Emanuel Geltman did the technical work of makeup and general editing. Howe thought those were "pretty good years" for Coser and himself. "We were still in our thirties; we were starting to make our mark professionally, he as a sociologist and I as a literary critic," and the editing at *Dissent* "gave us genuine pleasure." He felt there was a complementary difference between *Dissent*'s two head editors. Howe "tended to be more empirical, looking for opportunities on the American scene to make even a small dent, while Lew tended to make of his radicalism a stance primarily moral, yielding criticism from intransigence."[99]

A statement of intentions published in the first issue of *Dissent* pledged to combat conformism, "defend democratic, humanist and radical values," fight totalitarianism "whether fascist or Stalinist," begin "a frank and friendly dialogue with liberal opinion," investigate American cultural life, and reassess "socialist doctrines." Not wanting to concede positive values to the *Commentary* side of the group, *Dissent* acknowledged that its project "would be meaningless if in dissenting it did not also affirm. We are united in the affirmation of a positive belief," the magazine declared, "—the belief in socialism." *Dissent* would carve out a middle position of independent radicalism between the Stalinists and the new affirming liberals at *Commentary*. "Our magazine will be open to a wide arc of opinion," *Dissent* announced, "excluding only Stalinists and totalitarian fellow-travelers on the one hand, and those former radicals who have signed their peace with society as it is, on the other." Hardly a description of "a wide arc of opinion," this narrow span offered the magazine only a self-righteous isolation. One of its own editors, Harold Orlans, in the second issue criticized this statement of exclusion, and thereafter the magazine omitted the sentence from its statement of purpose, which for a few years continued to appear inside its front cover.[100]

The *Dissent* editors quickly identified the *Commentary* wing of the New York group as an enemy. Coser drew the battle lines in the first issue. "Radicals of the thirties," he reported, ". . . can be classified as repenters and dissenters. The former predominate. Some magazines, such as *Commentary*, specialize in documents of repentance." To illustrate how *Commentary* promoted the ex-radical position of affirmation, Coser cited sociologist William Petersen's article in the November 1953 issue. Petersen's thesis, Coser explained, was that the strength of America's postwar economy demonstrated the country was still a land of opportunity, and that arguments to the contrary were only "scholarly myths." Petersen, Coser continued in disbelief, thought that America's mixed economy was socialist. According to Coser, that kind of thinking was aimed only at helping the repenters find a defense for affirming the status quo. [101]

Howe joined Coser's attack on *Commentary*. The "sophisticated liberals who read *Commentary* and think of Sidney Hook as their spokesman" could do much better, Howe alleged, since the *Commentary* liberals did not even appear to know that threats to civil liberties existed in the America of Senator McCarthy. If *Commentary* would not, the dissenters themselves should "try to raise the traditional banner of personal freedom that is now slipping from the hands of so many accredited spokesmen of liberalism." Hook's followers had "lost their capacity for integral response," according to Howe, and the most discouraging development was "not that the reactionaries attack but that the liberals hardly remember how to counter-attack." [102]

If Howe and Coser were genuinely convinced that the *Commentary* group had lost their skill at "integral response" or their expertise at "counter-attack," they had only to wait for the following issue of *Commentary* to be treated to a stinging refutation of that belief. Nathan Glazer decided to write the rejoinder because he liked neither *Dissent's* tone nor its positions. Howe later remembered that Glazer's attack on *Dissent* "delighted us, since the one thing a new magazine needs is attention." [103]

Glazer began by noting that "in the abstract" starting *Dissent* had seemed like "a fine idea," as there was always a need for good political magazines. The reality of the magazine, however, he found depressing. "The whole thing is an unmitigated disaster as far as what is left of socialist thought in this country is concerned," he told his *Commentary* readers. "If this is socialism no further explanations are required for its failure to catch on in America." *Dissent* was against conformism, but did not document the spread of conformism nor suggest specific ways to combat it. The new magazine was no better than the despised *Nation* in its disregard for "fact and authenticity." Similarly, the new project was against war, but did not bother to say whether some wars were necessary, and if not how they could be avoided. If the third-campers at *Dissent* had their way, according to Glazer, the Soviets would be "comfortably established" throughout the world—in Rome, Paris, London, Saigon, and Hanoi.[104]

Particularly offensive to Glazer was the new magazine's hostility toward *Commentary*. *Dissent* "carries on the unpleasant tradition of vituperative intemperance begun by Marx," and in the same heritage its "greatest violence is reserved for renegades and those politically closest to you." Why, he wanted to know, did the self-righteous editors of *Dissent* have to imply that "the former radicals" had "sold-out" rather than merely changed their outlook? Did *Dissent* need a scapegoat? "Marx had his 'nigger Jew Lassalle,' Lenin his 'Kautskys and their ilk,' and the editors of *Dissent* have their 'Sidney Hook and other writers for *Commentary.*'" Unwilling to let *Dissent* monopolize all the vituperation, Glazer excoriated the magazine's intention to exclude totalitarians and former radicals: "Perhaps no more remarkable spectrum has been conceived of since *Mein Kampf*." *Dissent* did not represent anything but "the left wing of socialism," and Glazer urged other socialists to disassociate themselves from the magazine and join him in condemning it.[105]

The third-camp position *Dissent* took on international issues particularly troubled Glazer, who attributed the third-campism mostly to the influence of Lewis Coser, but also to the lingering influence of Dwight Macdonald. Glazer also thought it a weakness that *Dissent* writers argued against specific people whom they thought took a wrong position, rather than arguing about the issue itself. For example, Coser sanctimoniously criticized Glazer's friend William Petersen and other affirmers for reconciling themselves to American culture, but, Glazer noted with irritation, Howe and Coser both had academic jobs at Brandeis at the time. Had either of them sold out less than Petersen, *Commentary* writers, or other ex-radical affirmers?[106]

Glazer's question encapsulated the tension between the dissenters and the affirmers in the New York group in the first years of the 1950s. Were the affirmers reconciling with America in a way that the dissenters were not? Did the dissenters' critical and nonconformist stance have anything to do with genuine leftist or radical convictions, and, if so, what did leftism or radicalism mean? Did the dissenters' critical orientation have any more inherent intellectual validity or analytical integrity than the affirmers' approach? Did either of them have the right to claim the correct intellectual outlook?

As the disagreement between Coser and Glazer about William Petersen's article showed, the extent to which members of the New York group believed America had changed from the 1930s to the 1950s was vitally important, since, if there had been no change, some former critics were reconciling themselves to the same culture that they had previously despised and derided. To affirm that culture, it became necessary to show that it had changed for the better. The documentation of that change became the theme of much of the writing done by the affirmers from 1945 to 1960, and their work contributed to a new respect within the intellectual community for American institutions and culture.[107]

Nathan Glazer

Like Irving Howe, Nathan Glazer was a member of the second generation who had been involved in magazines since early in his life. Three years younger than Howe, Glazer was born the youngest of seven children to a tailor from Poland and his wife in New York on February 25, 1923. His father was a quiet man, and Glazer's parents pushed him into neither an education nor their view of politics. Although his parents could speak English, they seldom did, and they spoke only Yiddish at home. They were moderate in their opinions, and critical of the extremes of communism, religious orthodoxy, anarchism, and Zionism. His family's socialism was unionist rather than revolutionist. Glazer described his background as "Socialist, but not too socialist; Orthodox, but not too Orthodox; friendly to Palestine, but not Zionist; Yiddish-speaking, but not a Yiddishist."[108]

At James Monroe High School in New York, Glazer discovered he had little aptitude for math or science, and somewhat more talent for drawing and writing. Since art was not thought to be a vocation, he decided to become a writer in some field. Within the context of his working-class family, Glazer was free to pursue what education he wanted. For him as for others in the New York group, this meant attending City College, which he entered in February 1940. He began studying history but ended as a sociology major.

Again like others in the group, he focused his education outside the classroom in his involvement in magazine work. In his case the magazine was the Zionist *Avukah Student Action*, the national organization's newspaper, which he edited. In retrospect Glazer felt it was a "left sectarian" organization whose anti-Stalinism fitted well with the Trotskyists at City College. In the Avukah group he learned a moderate nonrevolutionary socialism whose outlook was between that of the social democrats and the Leninists.

With his Avukah friends, Glazer read *Partisan Review*, the *New International*, *Politics*, and the *New Leader*. Through Avukah Glazer met Harold Orlans, who preceded Glazer as editor of *Avukah Student Action*;

Dwight Macdonald, who addressed the Avukah summer camp; and Daniel Bell, who was then managing editor of the *New Leader*. Glazer "was sometimes present at the informal *New Leader* shmooze sessions that took place at their offices Friday afternoons, after the paper had been sent to press." He also met Seymour Martin Lipset and Philip Selznick. It was Lipset who first told Glazer about Lewis Coser and arranged for Glazer to be invited to a study group at Coser's apartment in Queens.[109]

At City College Glazer became intrigued by community studies and ethnographic sociology, known as the "Chicago style" of sociology, which was the beginning of a continuing intellectual interest. Glazer received his bachelor's degree from City College in 1944, and a master's degree in social anthropology later the same year from the University of Pennsylvania.

On the recommendation of Daniel Bell, Glazer called on Max Horkheimer at the American Jewish Committee in 1944 for help on a study of anti-Semitism. The committee also supported the *Contemporary Jewish Record*, and Glazer maneuvered himself into an editorial position there. When the *Contemporary Jewish Record* was transformed into *Commentary* in 1945, Glazer found himself aboard the new ship.

In the late 1940s Glazer met David Riesman and decided to take a leave from *Commentary* to work with him on *The Lonely Crowd*. That was the first of several collaborative projects that also included *Faces in the Crowd* and the noted article "The Intellectuals and the Discontented Classes," a response to the McCarthyist right. While Riesman thought some of the New York intellectuals possessed a doctrinaire theoretical aridity, he felt Glazer shared some of his own love for fieldwork and curiosity about society.[110]

During the early 1950s, back at *Commentary*, Glazer was slowly taking graduate courses in sociology at Columbia. Some years he took no courses; other years he spent a day a week at Columbia. He studied with Robert Merton and Paul Lazarsfeld, and worked gathering and analyzing interview data for C. Wright Mills's *White Collar*. Glazer finally submitted a book he had already published, *The Social Basis of American Communism*, to fulfill his dissertation requirement, and he received his doctorate in 1962.

He decided later that he had learned more at *Commentary* than in graduate school. One of his lessons as an editor was to be suspicious of generalizations, but he also learned the intellectual synthesis of fields and interests that was the style of a general intellectual magazine. One of his final acts at *Commentary* was his critical review of the first issue of *Dissent*.

Glazer was bound to be offended by the young *Dissent*. He had been raised in a moderate household that avoided ideological excess, and he was trained in a sociology that had specific demographic and cultural interests and avoided generalizations and overt ideology. Further, *Dissent* had attacked not only *Commentary* and his friend William Petersen but also Sidney Hook, whom Glazer saw as a broad and beneficial influence in the 1940s and 1950s. Hook had advanced the intellectual agenda by helping to destroy the illusion of Marxism as a science; as a result, the rest of the group did not have to worry about battling it so vehemently on their own.[111]

After leaving *Commentary* in 1954, Glazer went to the new Anchor Books as an editor. He produced a shortened version of *The Lonely Crowd* for Jason Epstein's new scholarly paperback house and stayed at Anchor for three years as an editor. But he was too interested in sociology to stay longer, and he began a series of teaching jobs: as an instructor in sociology at Berkeley in 1957–58, at Bennington College the next year, and at Smith College the year after.[112] He taught race relations, the sociology of ethnic groups, and urban sociology.

In 1959 Glazer began writing *Beyond the Melting Pot*, and at Irving Kristol's suggestion he recruited Daniel Patrick Moynihan to write a chapter on the Irish. Glazer finished the book in 1962 and spent a year in Japan studying urban life. When he returned, Moynihan, then working at the Labor Department, set up an interview for him at the Housing and Home Finance Agency in Washington. Glazer was hired.[113] While in Washington Glazer was recruited by Lewis Feuer to teach sociology at Berkeley, where he taught until 1969. He then went to Harvard with an appointment in the Graduate School of Education, and also became a member of the Sociology Department. Throughout the 1960s and after, Glazer remained a frequent contributor to *Commentary* and other publications, and served as an editor of *The Public Interest*.

From the 1960s on, Glazer maintained a keen interest in the relations between blacks and Jews and how pressures toward social funding and affirmative action influenced society and altered the relations between various ethnic groups. In December 1964 he wrote an article for *Commentary* on the tensions between blacks and Jews, and in 1975 he published *Affirmative Discrimination*.[114] In his writing on ethnic groups and affirmative action, Glazer combined the New York intellectuals' support of pluralism and diversity against absolutism and unity, on one side, with their commitment to meritocracy instead of stifling egalitarianism, on the other.[115]

In *Affirmative Discrimination*, Glazer complained that after liberals had struggled for decades to reach a point where no distinctions were made on the basis of race, religion, or national origin, many of the same liberals were attempting to make just those distinctions with affirmative action requirements. He lamented that the nation was moving from a goal of equal opportunity to "statistical parity." Glazer and others in the New York group opposed that trend because, as he wrote, individual equality must be a higher concern than group equality.[116] The worth of the individual and individual rights remained a central tenet of the New York intellectuals' outlook both when they called themselves socialists and later when they did not. Their sympathy for the individual and fear of excessive egalitarianism prompted many of them to embrace the work of Tocqueville in the postwar period.

Before, during, and after college Glazer thought of himself as a socialist, if only by family inheritance, but by 1947 he no longer identified himself as one. Never among the more stridently committed of the New York group, he suggested that his beliefs "were not to be defined as socialism then, nor sociology now." Although generalization made him uneasy, like others in the New York group he was too much an intellectual generalist to classify himself—yet he did not want to be mistaken for a socialist. The empirical nature of his sociology after the war increasingly undermined the faith necessary to sustain a visionary socialism.

To acknowledge that he had abandoned socialism was not to say that he had abandoned politics, for politics was the common foundation of all the various outlooks and interests among his fellow critics. Like many of them, Glazer turned to sociology at least partly to wage the political struggles of the present. Alfred Kazin noted to himself in 1959 that Glazer's "comparative intellectual success is not accidental," and found him bright and aware of what he was doing. He had been "kidding" Glazer about sociology and mass culture, and Glazer had answered that "sociology for him is a way of writing contemporary history." Writing contemporary history, Glazer might have added, is contributing to contemporary social and cultural politics. "Exactly the phrase that haunts me," Kazin confided to his journal about Glazer's remark. "And I know why. For to write contemporary history is, by covering the present to the best of one's ability, to seek the future, to press the future for a solution."[117] This shows that the critics in both the social sciences and the humanities were devoted to a similar enterprise: cultural criticism, that generalist intellectual project whose mission, at heart, is to seek the future in present conflicts and to derive future solutions from present polemics.

Glazer recognized the political content of his scholarly writing and reflection. "Sociology," he acknowledged in retrospect, "is still for many socialists and sociologists the pursuit of politics through academic means, though it is today a far different politics, pursued with different means." Part of the impact of the New York group on American intellectual life is that they dignified that outlook of political pursuit. They were never embarrassed to admit the political content of their scholarly work, and in fact brought into the intellectual mainstream the idea that all strong work had ideological and political overtones. They tried to balance that axiom with the assertion that intellectuals, in order to maintain a proper function, could not become the uncritical voice of one party or position. It was a fine line between engaging the world as scholars and remaining critical and independent enough to be of use to that world. Glazer's comment that his work could be seen as pursuit of politics through other means could serve as a fitting epigraph to the careers of most of the New York intellectuals.

Dissent *and* Commentary: *1955–1965*

The threat of the Soviet Union, felt especially keenly by intellectuals and Jews who would be prominent targets of repression in the Soviet system, had pushed many of the New York intellectuals into the arms of America by the late 1940s. The problem was how to stop Stalinism without forfeiting radicalism; however, if forced to choose, most of them were willing to sacrifice their former socialist aims.

As Diana Trilling saw it, intellectuals needed to reclaim a proper sort of chauvinism. In the justifiable attempt in the twentieth century to combat "excessive nationalism" and "imperialism," the effort had gone too far. In 1951 she complained to the American Committee for Cultural Freedom that a "decent feeling for one's own country" was thought to be chauvinistic. Idealist liberals and third-camp intellectuals, she felt, did not allow one to support America properly against the Soviet threat. Trilling hoped that without becoming overly chauvinistic, and while continuing "to criticize our own country as we must," American intellectuals would no longer "undervalue what is our own." [118]

That the fear of the Soviet Union's postwar power was chiefly responsible for the new intellectual reconciliation with America is dramatically illustrated by the "Our Country and Our Culture" symposium in *Partisan Review* in 1952. Sidney Hook, in his contribution, recognized the polarization caused by the Cold War, but he asked his fellow critics for a more complex intellectual response than a Manichaean duality. The real choice, Hook suggested pragmatically, one to be made without embarrassment, was "between endorsing a system of total terror and *critically* supporting our own imperfect democratic culture with all its promises and dangers." Nonconformists in the West might not be honored, but at least they survived; in the Soviet Union a nonconformist could only earn "a bullet in the neck." [119]

However, even while the affirmers were defending American culture against the Soviet alternative and praising recent beneficial changes in the culture that had brought them into middle-class occupations and life-styles, they resented others pointing out the signs of their affirmation. Hook wrote impatiently to Norman Thomas in 1954, defending himself against an allegation by Waldo Frank: "worst of all is the invention that I ever surrendered my belief in socialism and became a defender of capitalism or free enterprise." He told Thomas that his affiliation with Americans for Democratic Action "expresses my point of view." The ADA, of course, was not a socialist organization. [120] Hook was also indignant at *Dissent* for having branded him a counterrevolutionist, a right-wing social democrat who uncritically supported American culture. *Dissent*, he complained, simplistically interpreted his attacks on communism as mindless pro-Americanism. Despite thinking of himself as a person of the left, Hook never wrote for *Dissent* and admitted that he never read it carefully. [121]

Yet it was not only those at *Dissent* who were uneasy about the new mood of cultural reconciliation and intellectual anticommunism. Writers such as Philip Rahv, Reinhold Niebuhr, and Archibald MacLeish all voiced their concerns. Although, as an editor of *Partisan Review*, Rahv piloted a journal that was accused of having reached its own peace with America, Rahv himself rode the fence between the dissenters and the affirmers. He acknowledged the "incontestable virtue" of American democracy, but he was dismayed by the intellectuals' "recoil from radicalism," and their "complacence and spiritual torpor." The "ex-radicals and ex-Marxists" could hardly be distinguished "from the common run of philistines," and the "petrified anti-Stalinists" could not separate the real danger of the Soviet Union from the illusory danger of domestic communism. [122]

Reinhold Niebuhr was harsher. He found it foolishly arrogant for the affirmers to attribute contemporary American power to the nation's "virtue" rather than to events and circumstances. Our economic and military power led us to the "conceit" that our status was a result of "the American way of life." Although the Soviet Union did in fact pose a real threat, the affirmers were "in greater peril from their own illusions than from their neighbors' hostile designs." Moreover, that our competition with the Soviets produced such "hysteria" was evidence we had little confidence in ourselves and our institutions. [123]

Archibald MacLeish, unconnected to the New York group except as an occasional antagonist, shared Niebuhr's distaste for the strident anticommunism of the period. In 1949 he predicted that later historians would describe the immediate postwar period in America as dominated entirely by the Soviets. A future historian, he imagined, might write that, in the late 1940s, "American foreign policy was a mirror image of Russian foreign policy: whatever the Russians did, we did in reverse." This historian would conclude that "American domestic politics were conducted under a kind of upside-down veto: no man could be elected to public office unless he was on record as detesting the Russians, and no proposal could be enacted, from a peace plan at one end to a military budget at the other, unless it could be demonstrated that the Russians wouldn't like it." [124] MacLeish did not aim his criticism at the *Commentary* anticommunists, but he rejected the notion that the evil of Soviet society implied anything about the virtue of American society. America needed to recognize its own Jeffersonian virtue, rather than merely react to the Soviet threat.

Irving Howe, at about the time *Dissent* first appeared, told the *Partisan Review* community that it was not necessary to be pushed into the arms of middle-class America by the Soviet threat. He pointed out that "the danger of Stalinism may require temporary expedients in the area of *power* such as would have seemed compromising some years ago, but there is no reason, at least no good reason, why it should require compromise or conformity in the area of *ideas*, no reason why it should lead us to become partisans of bourgeois society." [125] He urged intellectuals to separate foreign-policy power issues from critical considerations of ideas. For him that meant that an intellectual could remain a dissenting radical, could maintain a third-camp position of not supporting totally either the East or the West, yet still remain a certified and enthusiastic anticommunist.

Those at *Dissent* could have been called third-camp anticommunists. Their anticommunism was so strong that they took it for granted and did not discuss it much among themselves. Within the context of the New York intellectuals, they thought of themselves as leftist anticommunists, but they did not see the issue perfectly polarized between left and right within the group. Instead they perceived a continuum, from Hook and many affirmers with an enthusiastic anticommunism on one side, to most of the dissenters with a less strident but active anticommunism on the other. Howe felt that during the Cold War the distinction between left and right anticommunism became harder to maintain. [126]

Third-camp anticommunism did not mean neutralism for the dissenters. In *Dissent's* second issue, in 1954, Stanley Plastrik criticized the Western European desire for neutralism. The editors declared themselves "unalterably opposed to all forms of totalitarianism" of both left and right. Throughout the 1950s *Dissent* hammered at the Soviet Union and Stalinism. In spring 1956 Coser vented his disgust at the lack of discussion in the Soviet Communist party, and in the following issue Howe dismissed the significance of the changes in Soviet rule between Stalin and Khrushchev. The New York group's anticommunism had been correct for a generation, Howe proclaimed. "It would be a great error," he announced, "if we did not insist upon reminding people that we were right—whatever our shade of socialist or radical opinion, we who for thirty bitter years kept up the fight against the lies of Stalinism. Modesty or immodesty is irrelevant here: there is a deep moral-political necessity for keeping the record clear."[127] In the next issue Howe was at it again, this time taking Paul Sweezy and Leo Huberman of the *Monthly Review* to task for their support of Stalinist Russia, and calling them "left authoritarians" who supported "the radicalism of the blackjack."[128]

Throughout the Cold War, especially after 1950, the third-camp anticommunism of the dissenters was tilted toward America and against the Soviets. The dissenters felt they could no longer, as they had during World War II, cast "a plague on both your houses" equally, could no longer "pretend that we were spectators in a fight that was not ours."[129] Yet they were neither as anti-Soviet nor as pro-American as the writers at *Commentary*. In the mid-1950s, for example, Howe's articles in *Dissent* were more critical of American foreign policy than anything that appeared in *Commentary*. His "The Politics of Moderation," published in *Dissent* in 1956, was written from a third-camp perspective that was hostile to both American and Soviet foreign policy. In the early 1960s the dissenters continued their third-campism. Harold Rosenberg told *Partisan Review* readers that the Cold War was a "delusionary struggle" in which the East and the West both limited freedom in the developing world whenever that freedom encroached upon either the profits of the West or the dictatorship of the East. To believe that such issues were worth nuclear war—perhaps an offhand reference to Hook's position—Rosenberg felt "one would have to have lost his mind." Hook later said that he felt Rosenberg's article "openly came out for what was in effect unilateral nuclear disarmament for the U.S."[130]

For his part, Howe told *Partisan* readers in the "Cold War" symposium in 1962 that although Soviet Communism had to be opposed there was "no longer any possibility" of Western "intervention" or "roll back" without nuclear war—and war would be insanity. Howe rejected both excessive anticommunism and "unilateral disarmament." One had to be balanced, but one could not be "neutral or indifferent to the world struggle." He admitted that there was an "identity of interest" between radicals and the West, "a sharing of certain limited goals" that required the dissenters as well as others to "depend on Western power." [131]

The dissenters took the same approach to the Vietnam war. Although they were hostile to North Vietnamese communism, they also opposed the intense American military involvement in the conflict. They hoped that in the wake of the conflict a more democratic socialist force would rise in Southeast Asia. By 1967 Rosenberg was willing only "to fight Communism with economic aid but not with napalm, and to help anti-Communist peasant movements but not anti-Communist dictators." Because the theory of containment undermined radical politics, he was willing to repudiate containment. [132]

Dissent's third-campism drew criticism not only from those to its right at *Commentary*, but also from those on its left, such as C. Wright Mills. Mills was interested in *Dissent* in the 1950s, and, although he declined to join its editorial board when asked in the beginning because he was opposed to such a formal ideological affiliation, he came to *Dissent's* defense when its inaugural issue was attacked by Glazer. Mills contributed several articles to the magazine during its first five years, but his books and articles were skeptically received by some *Dissent* editors, and friction developed. In 1959 Howe criticized Mills for comparing the use of power in the Soviet Union with its use in America. There were qualitative as well as quantitative differences, which Howe thought Mills failed to recognize. Mills's analysis bordered too closely on that "neutralism" that the *Dissent* editors rejected. Unlike neutralism, *Dissent's* third-campism would not tolerate a "moral coexistence" with the Soviet Communists. [133]

Mills was disappointed and angered by Howe's attack, and before severing his relations with the magazine he wrote a response. "I had thought that you had abandoned the foot-dragging mood of the Cold War and were trying to make a new beginning," he told Howe. Mills expected Howe's third-campism to be more of a departure from the group's anticommunism. Instead he felt that Howe's anticommunism would fit well with the conservative and strident State Department. If Howe opposed moral coexistence with Soviets, how, Mills wondered, did his view differ from that of Dulles or Adenauer? Was that a position for an editor of a magazine that encouraged opposition? "To dissent is lovely," Mills chided him. "But Irving, as regards foreign policy, from what, tell me, do you dissent?" [134]

It was not only on foreign policy that *Dissent* tried to straddle the fence. In its general political orientation it sought a middle position—similar to its third-camp stance—between socialism and liberalism. At its inception the magazine was a somewhat Marxist socialist publication, but after five years it had all but abandoned Marxism for a democratic liberalism that its editors combined with their socialist outlook to produce a democratic socialism.

At the time *Dissent* began publication, Howe told *Partisan Review* readers that he hoped "that any revival of American radicalism will acknowledge not only its break from, but also its roots in, the liberal tradition," and he wrote with admiration of "the liberal-radical vision of the good society." For the first several years *Dissent* proclaimed inside its front cover that it would "reassert the libertarian values of the socialist ideal." Central to Howe's criticism of Stalinists such as Paul Sweezy and Leo Huberman was their failure to advocate a multiplicity of political parties in Russia and their failure to deem democracy and pluralism essential. For years, Howe wrote in 1957, he and the *Dissent* editors had kept alive the idea of libertarian socialism. Seeing the liberalism of the 1950s in a crisis similar to the problem socialism faced, he tied the future of the two together in 1959 and proposed a dialogue between them.[135]

Journeying from Marxian socialism to liberal socialism, Coser and Howe both admitted the benefits of decentralization over centralization of power in society, and they thought society should be pluralistic instead of unitary, participatory rather than imposed, and material and practical rather than ideological and visionary. Like Howe, Coser was willing to recognize common aims "with those radicals who do not consider themselves socialist."[136]

One of the more interesting voices in the magazine to argue for the synthesis of liberalism and socialism was Ben B. Seligman, who wrote on economic theory. In a series of articles published during *Dissent*'s first half-decade, Seligman worked to reject the economic philosophy of both conservatives and Marxists and to carve out a place between them for the democratic socialists.

Seligman began with an admiring piece on Joseph Schumpeter, characterizing him as a conservative who, like Marx, wanted to discover the internal laws of capitalist motion. He followed with an essay on Keynesian economics that sought to fuse the best of Marx and Keynes, as Hook had earlier fused Marx and Dewey. Both Keynesian and Marxian economics, he explained, described breakdowns in capitalism that resulted "from internal insufficiencies." Keynes's shortcoming was that he focused too much on gadgetry like multipliers and liquidity and not enough on "underlying social realities"; he relied too much on price theory rather than on the human, political, and social. Overall, Seligman faulted Keynes as "essentially a conservative thinker."[137]

Next Seligman examined Marx. Too bad, he thought, that Marxists took Marx's words as the "absolute truth," for it rendered his followers the sort of fools Marx detested. The Marxian labor theory of value could not explain price changes and it "fails as an analytical tool," yet his work still was useful in explaining "the internal drive of the capitalist economy." Marx could help one understand the "long view," the direction in which the economy was moving, so his theory could not be "blithely ignored." Marx was a useful thinker, but one who had been taken too literally by the true believers. [138]

Having touched on both poles of economic theory—Marx and Keynes—and having found something to admire and something to dismiss in each, Seligman in 1959 advocated a move to the middle ground of market socialism, the transplantation of a normal market system into a socialist economy and society. Under this hybrid model, the economy was to run by a market price mechanism that set production levels and distribution, gauged demand, and promoted decentralization. Proponents of market socialism, in fact, believed that only in a socialist context that allowed the market to exist in its pristine neoclassical state—without the interference of the inequalities of income and the barriers to entry in some industries—could a market actually function correctly. As Seligman argued, since it is only in a market socialist system "that the textbook version of the market really comes into existence, it may be said, somewhat paradoxically, that perfect competition can only exist in a socialist society." [139]

Seligman, like Howe and Coser, believed that democratic socialists had to place the values of individual autonomy, personal freedom of choice, and decentralization of economic and political power above all others in the socialist vision. For him it meant that socialism had to be combined with democratic liberalism. "Simply enough, socialism can no longer be discussed purely in economic terms," Seligman concluded. "In fact, it seems reasonable to suggest that the way in which a socialist economy works must be in consonance with the moral and political aims that socialists seek to attain. In such a framework the competitive solution of market socialism seems by far the more desirable objective." [140] Seligman, however, was one of the few dissenters to endorse market socialism; curiously, Howe, Coser, and many others ignored it.

When the dissenters became involved in the economic issues of democratic socialism in the 1950s they were visiting a territory that some European and American political economists had already charted. Ludwig von Mises, Friedrich Hayek, and Joseph Schumpeter, three prominent economists who had been educated at the University of Vienna, all opposed market socialism, but in the process had at least addressed themselves to the difficult problems of weighing the free market against economic planning and collectivism.[141] In 1935 Hayek, then teaching at the London School of Economics, edited *Collectivist Economic Planning*, a volume in which some key essays on market socialism appeared, including articles by Mises and Hayek himself. Schumpeter arrived in America to teach at Harvard in 1932, and Mises in 1945 was appointed professor of economics at New York University—the same faculty as Sidney Hook.

Their opposition to market socialism as incompatible with intellectual and economic freedom was also taken up in America in the 1930s by the newly forming Chicago School of economics at the University of Chicago, under the leadership of Frank Knight and Henry Simons. Although the Chicago School was known for its endorsement of laissez-faire and its hostility to economic planning, Knight acknowledged that economic theory alone could provide no refutation for market socialism—although he felt there were clear political, moral, and historical reasons to oppose it.[142]

In Europe a few political economists wrote sympathetically on market socialism, particularly Henry Dickinson in Britain and the Polish economist Oscar Lange. Dickinson's remarkable book *Economics of Socialism* proposed a libertarian economic and political socialism. Lange was recognized for his short but seminal *On the Economic Theory of Socialism*, in which he outlined the benefits of market socialism. But Lange soon gave up on the theory and, as a member of the Polish government, began to endorse traditional centralized planning instead.[143]

So Poland, Britain, Vienna, the University of Chicago, and Harvard all had economic philosophers who shared with the New York intellectuals a belief in the importance of the decisions about socialism, capitalism, democracy, planning, intellectual freedom, and ideology. This was not the New York group's most important tie to European cultural criticism—not nearly so strong as its connection to the Frankfurt School, or to that collection of European writers who operated almost as an extension of the New York group: Arthur Koestler, George Orwell, Raymond Aron, Ignazio Silone, André Malraux, and Nicola Chiaromonte. But the shared interests between the New York intellectuals and political economists on both sides of the Atlantic showed the extent to which economic issues were understood as cultural and ideological issues as well—and that the enterprises of economic criticism and cultural criticism overlapped. The conflation of those disciplines and identities was most apparent in the work of such figures in the group as Seligman, Robert Heilbroner, and Robert Lekachman, who were both economists and cultural critics.

While working out this new ideology that combined liberalism and socialism, *Dissent* in its early years was at the same time trying to de-emphasize ideology. It was a curious and ambivalent attitude. Most of the ideology they shed was Marxist. Throughout the 1950s, as Howe recalled, "we kept shedding more and more ideology; by about 1960 most of us no longer thought of ourselves as Marxists." Instead the dissenters tried to "work piecemeal, treating socialist thought as inherently problematic." Yet, if trying to lose ideology, they did not want to lose ideas. They felt that for dissenters it was especially a time of ideas, "that socialism in America had to be seen mostly as an intellectual problem before it could even hope to become a viable movement." [144] One of the ways they sharpened their ideas was by grinding them against the whetstone of Communist ideology. By denouncing Communists, Stalinists, and their sympathizers, they showed that their new democratic socialism was all-American and worthy of respect. They were trying to ground intellectual leftism on an American rather than a European ethic.

Trying to save leftism (now an increasingly centrist and liberal leftism) from extinction in America in the postwar period, the *Dissent* group tried to bridge the distance between their Old Left background in European debates and the newer American orientation of a younger generation of radicals. Coser wanted to teach the young that they could not change the country in the current conservative period, but that it was enough for leftists merely to endure. Faith in radicalism and in history had been lost by Americans, even some, like the affirmers, who had once been members of the left. In such conditions, the remaining radicals had to be content with "fostering" each other, constructing "little oases of radical thought," and looking to the future while being interested critics of the present. Radicals in the postwar period, Coser counseled, must drop their Marxism and have "wider and deeper" orientations. They had to be concerned with individual liberty and personal autonomy, with democracy. Above all they had to survive, so they could pass their radical outlook on to others when the mood of the country changed. "It might be," Coser wrote without illusion, "that the most significant answer that radicals could give in the future to a question about their 'action' in our period would be 'I stayed alive, Sir and I remained sane.'" [145]

Radicals realized that they were in the minority, and the affirmers' attacks only added to their fear of extinction. Bernard Rosenberg complained that "the number of dissenters *or* Dissenters in American intellectual life today is pitiably small; and if the ex-radicals didn't keep sourly kicking us while we're more or less down, we'd be even more obscure than we are." [146] *Dissent*, however, launched its share of attacks on the affirmers and was hardly a timid victim. The magazine in the early years was a small group of social and cultural critics besieged, wagons pulled up into a circle for protection, but emitting louder whoops than their assailants.

By the end of the 1950s *Dissent* began to note that the changing temper of the country offered radicals a new opportunity. Howe detected "a significant change in political mood, a shift toward liberalism." The "hostility" to radicalism so prevalent in the 1940s and 1950s "has begun to evaporate," and radicals no longer needed to feel "beleaguered." It was time for dissenters to develop programs that would take advantage of the new unrest in the country. Time, too, for *Dissent* to move forward: "Our first five years were devoted to cleaning up a little our own intellectual heritage," Howe told the magazine's readers; "let the next five be devoted, in part, to seeing what we can say usefully about American society as it operates today."[147]

So during the 1940s and 1950s the group moved from leftism to liberalism. Even the dissenters evolved into liberal socialists and social democrats. For some members of the group, affirmers such as Lionel Trilling, that change occurred in the early 1940s. For others, dissenters such as Irving Howe and Lewis Coser, the transformation did not take place until the early 1950s. By the 1950s, however, both the affirmers and the dissenters, with different levels of enthusiasm, supported the welfare state. Totalitarianism and communism in foreign policy remained their predominant interest, but they were also concerned in the postwar period with the Civil Rights movement, civil liberties issues, and general problems of equality in the domestic political realm.

They now approached these matters as liberals and centrists rather than leftists. The desire for a wide-ranging political or social transformation in America had dissipated. The dissenters had moved from the left in the 1930s to the liberal left by the late 1950s. The affirmers had evolved from the left, before the war, to the liberal center by the late 1940s and early 1950s, and then to the right of center in the late 1960s and after. For the affirmers it was a gradual and relatively smooth transition from left to center-right. For the dissenters it was a shorter journey from left to center-left.

The dissenters and affirmers disagreed on many issues in the postwar period, but one commitment that bound them in a common enterprise was their view of what it meant to be an intellectual. Both dissenters and affirmers agreed that an intellectual must be a nonconformist who maintained some tension with society, yet they disagreed about what constituted nonconformism and about the proper level of tension with one's culture.

The dissenters' opinion of the proper intellectual orientation was articulated by Howe and Harold Rosenberg. Howe described the intellectual as a "noise-maker," one who could not watch silently. He seconded Rosenberg's definition that an intellectual "is someone who turns answers into questions," the challenger of orthodoxy and accepted wisdom, the upsetter of apple carts. The intellectual was someone pledged "to freedom above all." Like Julian Benda, Howe believed that an intellectual "stands apart, as critic and observer," from the interests of a particular party or state, or else is transformed into a propagandist.[148] He worried that the "whole idea of the intellectual vocation" was being abandoned. The postwar opportunity of affluence and power had harmed the intelligentsia, because whenever the intellectuals "become absorbed into the accredited institutions of society they not only lose their traditional rebelliousness but to one extent or another *they cease to function as intellectuals*."[149]

Harold Rosenberg, constantly satirizing the affirmers' views on various subjects, lampooned their outlook on intellectuals as well. "Who but one with a taste for priests would desire this particular caste to flourish?" he asked about intellectuals. "Except perhaps that portion of it that works quietly in the laboratory, the study, the classroom. The others, the ideological ones, those who want to remake the world, the revolutionists in everything from paint to politics, those who never stop talking save when someone puts to them a pertinent question, these people have proved themselves as a group more trouble than they are worth." Those dissenters, he continued, were "traitors both to their ideas and themselves" out of a loneliness and conceit. "This type has manifested the same disagreeable traits throughout the world, in the 'new nations' as in the old, wherever the breakdown of authority has given prominence to ideas."[150] What good were intellectuals, Rosenberg wrote with a wink to his readers, if all they did was cause trouble? The affirmers, according to Rosenberg, thought that intellectuals only got in the way and caused an unnecessary fuss.

Yet none of the *Commentary* crowd proposed giving up cultural criticism; they asked only that it be employed intelligently. Granville Hicks, a literary critic who occasionally wrote for the group's magazines, pointed out that "'Blind unreasoning rejection' may be, as Irving Howe says, 'healthier' than blind unreasoning acceptance, but it is not more intelligent."[151] One should be allowed to be independently affirmative as well as independently hostile.

Similarly, Sidney Hook, the bête noire of the dissenters, felt that the intellectual was "no more un-American when he is intelligently critical of the United States than he is chauvinistic when he is intelligently appreciative." To be intelligent and useful, critics had "to discriminate, to make relevant distinctions." Be pragmatically critical and intellectual, Hook suggested. Unthinking dissent was not intelligent criticism, it was "fashion," and that was no better than unthinking affirmation. "It is sufficient for the majority to believe anything," Hook wrote of his radical detractors, "for them to oppose it." A habitual response, in Hook's estimation, did not qualify as an intellectual process whether one was an affirmer or a dissenter. Real intellectuals, in his view, had to "criticize what needs to be criticized in America, without forgetting for a moment the total threat which Communism poses to the life of the free mind."[152] Yet some of Hook's critics believed that the affirmers' same automatic reaction against the danger of Communism caused a reflex reaction against all dissent.

Few of the dissenters criticized Hook's animosity toward the intellectually corrosive effects of habitual positions. Instead of his rhetoric, it was his actions and commitments that made the dissenters doubt his sincerity. Hook, it seemed to the dissenters, had put all his energy into criticizing the Communists and had forgotten to be a critic of America as well. His actions, it seemed to them, suggested that an intellectual's primary responsibility was to criticize the Communists, and his example suggested that intellectuals should not criticize the West at all.

Affirmers might have adopted the example of David Riesman, who was not excessively anticommunist, and who felt it was the intellectual's responsibility "to remain in some tension with his audience and his immediate milieu."[153] Many of the radicals, however, doubted whether Riesman ever functioned as a dissenting critic of American culture. Moreover, most of the affirmers were more anticommunist than Riesman, and so did not fit his example.

Therefore, despite a nominal agreement between affirmers and dissenters that intellectuals should be nonconformists and questioners, in practice the agreement collapsed into arguments and accusations about what really qualified as significant nonconformism. The two sides of the group were bound by a common ethic that each side interpreted and practiced differently.

A special case of nonconformism arose in the decade following the end of World War II, as the New York group struggled to establish a role for intellectuals in what, in their view, was a postcommunist and postideological world. During that decade many former members of the Communist party published books or essays of atonement. The New York intellectuals' ambivalent response to that confessional impulse, and disagreements about the extent to which it was specifically aimed at stifling radicalism, produced a significant and revealing friction between affirmers and dissenters.

3   Pragmatism and the Repentant Sense of Life

The most tragic moral conflict, Sidney Hook wrote in 1960 in his essay "Pragmatism and the Tragic Sense of Life," arises when two rights (decisions dictated by conscience, contract, or law) conflict with each other—for no matter how the conflict is resolved, some good will be sacrificed. Hook's formulation was a restatement of Reinhold Niebuhr's argument, presented earlier in *The Irony of American History*, that had influenced the New York intellectuals so deeply. Niebuhr had argued that in the postwar world nations faced the tragic (because unwanted, unavoidable, and complex) responsibility of making "conscious choices of evil for the sake of good," bearing guilt in the name of some higher responsibility, or sacrificing some high value for another even higher.[1] The affirmers and dissenters faced similar tragic moral conflicts of conscience throughout their careers, but those choices seemed particularly difficult in the decade following World War II.

Many values and orientations the group had considered useful before the war now had to be questioned in the postcommunist and postideological world they began to envision. Above all, ideology, once hailed by an ideological New York group whose intellectual function had been to interpret and sustain it, was now to be challenged and denounced as a form of absolutism. Further, during the late 1940s and early 1950s many ex-Communist and former fellow travelers in the American intellectual community wrote books confessing their past mistakes, repenting their political sins, and asking atonement. Here, too, the New York group might have to sacrifice high values for those higher: Were the works of repentance cleansing to the intellectual community or stifling to intellectual independence and further dissent?

"After the signing of the Nazi Soviet pact," Granville Hicks wrote in the *Antioch Review* in 1945, "a number of specialists on Russia came forward to tell us all the things that they had not found it expedient to tell us in earlier years, and one wonders if there will be a second outburst of true confession on some future occasion."[2] Hicks would have been surprised to know how prophetic he was at the moment he wrote—standing, as he was, at the threshold of the very period he foresaw.

From the end of World War II until the mid-1950s, a confessional literature of ex-Communist repentance and disillusionment spread across portions of the intellectual community. (In the next generation, the New Left radicals would also have their day of repentance.)[3] Before the war only two confessional books surfaced—J. B. Matthews's *Odyssey of a Fellow Traveler* (1938) and Benjamin Gitlow's *I Confess* (1940)—both of which were dismissed by the New York group as intellectually insignificant. Matthews was thought to be a huckster, the Billy Sunday of the ex-Communists, and Gitlow, a former party functionary, was considered uninteresting. After the war Louis Budenz's *This Is My Story* (1947) and Elizabeth Bentley's *Out of Bondage* (1951) were also ignored by the New York group because of the authors' unintellectual or sensationalist approaches.[4]

The content and reception of three quite other books, however, take us to the heart of the controversy. The first of these, Lionel Trilling's insightful *The Middle of the Journey* (1947), was ignored on publication because the time was not yet right for a novelistic consideration of the tensions created within the intellectual community by the disillusionment with Communism and the apostasy it produced. Trilling's novel was a study of several political types, one of which was based on Whittaker Chambers. "So far as *The Middle of the Journey* had a polemical end in view," Trilling wrote later, "it was that of bringing to light the clandestine negation of the political life which Stalinist Communism had fostered among the intellectuals of the West."[5] The writing was consciously in the style of Henry James, with some of the virtues of James's dialogue and manner, but it featured a political sensibility that James lacked.

Two years later the second momentous book, a celebrated collection of autobiographical essays from European and American ex-Communists, was published as *The God That Failed* (1949). Although its impact was felt in the intellectual community at large, it did not have a reorienting influence on the New York group, since it reproduced arguments they had been voicing for more than a decade.

With the publication of the third book, Whittaker Chambers's *Witness* (1952), the left-wing landscape in America was changed unmistakably. Despite its weaknesses, *Witness* looms as the book of an era: an autobiography of enormous power, a nonfiction novel of unequaled psychological and philosophic choice, a story of political espionage and intrigue taut with tension, a compelling courtroom case, a tragedy of personal and family horror, of suicide and madness. Above all *Witness* riveted the reader to the dramatic question of what humanity's vision of the future should be, and what role individuals and collectivities must play to realize that vision.

As Chambers explained it, two competing faiths were forever battling for dominance in the world. One faith was the belief in Man, a logic that led unfalteringly to Communism; the other was the faith in God, which manifested itself in Christianity. No neutrality was possible in this mortal combat, and before the end of the century one of the opponents would wholly prevail. Chambers was pessimistic about the chances of Christianity to triumph, yet a person of courage needed to speak out anyway. After he had issued his warning to the world, even his most heated critics acknowledged his talent as a writer and the book's many solid accomplishments.

In responding to Chambers and other apologists, the New York group had to face some difficult questions about their own identities. Most ex-Communists did not disturb them, especially if the converts embraced liberal values. It was the missionary ex-Communists who kept a sense of divine purpose who unsettled them. Touched off by the tensions of the McCarthy period and the Cold War, their response to the literature of repentance partook of the same hostility to ideological inflexibility that prompted them to oppose the Waldorf Conference with such enthusiasm. Yet their contentiousness was tempered by their recently acquired sophistication in sociology and literary criticism, and their new appreciation for complexity, irony, tragedy, and ambiguity.

Absolutism, Ideology, and Pragmatism

The strong impulses of faith, absolutism, and ideology in Chambers's message alarmed the New York group. It would be difficult to imagine a more theological title than *Witness*, and his book became a symbol for them of the dangers involved in a religious orientation afoot in the public sphere. Hook, who throughout the 1940s criticized the Catholic church and other forms of corporate faith, reviewed *Witness* for the Sunday *New York Times* and called it "a minor classic in the history of religious conversions." Howe wondered whether "an unsympathetic reader might, in fact, conclude that God spent the past several years as a special aid [*sic*] to the House Committee on Un-American Activities."[6]

To both Howe and Rahv, Chambers seemed Dostoevskian in his pursuit of faith and certainty. According to Howe, Chambers aspired to be "a twentieth-century Dostoevsky" who would fight "the Moscow anti-Christ." Rahv, who had studied and written about the Russian author, found Chambers "Dostoevskyean in essence" from the first time they had met in the early 1930s when both were still Communists.[7]

Communists and missionary ex-Communists appeared to the New York group as seekers of mystical truths in an irrational realm. Chambers, in Rahv's words, was "essentially a mystic" who was unconcerned with empirical politics. Richard Crossman, fresh from editing *The God That Failed*, drove Chambers's image even further, portraying him as caught not merely in a mystical, irrational world, but in a "nightmare" state. "If these were scenes from a novel, I should say that another Edgar Allan Poe had risen across the Atlantic." Crossman went on to compare *Witness* to Hitler's *Mein Kampf*, demonstrating that even Chambers's critics could lose a sense of proportion.[8]

Alfred Kazin, in contrast, was more sympathetic in his approach to the ex-leftist true-believers. "No man ever lightly reverses the faith of an adult lifetime, held implacably to the point of criminality," Kazin copied into his journal from his volume of *Witness*. "He reverses it only with a violence greater than the force of the faith he is repudiating." Chambers's religious outlook did not repel Kazin, who wrote a short time later that "Last week, reading the Chambers book, I was still grateful to anyone for proclaiming belief in Him."[9]

But for the New York group as a whole, the need for an all-encompassing faith was a misguided quest for psychological and intellectual certainty. Robert Gorham Davis, a literary critic who occasionally wrote for *Partisan Review* and *Commentary*, made that point in his testimony before the House Un-American Activities Committee (HUAC) hearings in Washington in February 1953. Asked by Congressman Donald Jackson why an intellectual would submit to Party discipline, Davis replied: "Because those who join desire certainty. . . . The communists always have an answer to everything. . . . This is part, unquestionably for many people—the part of the psychological satisfaction of being a communist."[10]

If these traits accounted for the psychological attractions of Communism—the reassurances of faith, the irrational and mystical, the certainty—they were also the characteristics found in many ex-Communists. That kinship between Communists and ex-Communists, indeed, was one of the central themes of *The God That Failed*. Ignazio Silone, in his essay in the book, confided that he avoided joining any ex-Communist groups, since they had "all the defects of official Communism," especially the sort of fanaticism and centralization conducive to fascism. "It is not easy to free oneself from an experience as intense as that of the underground organization of the Communist Party," he warned. "Something of it remains and leaves a mark on the character which lasts all one's life. One can, in fact, notice how recognizable the ex-Communists are. They constitute a category apart, like ex-priests and ex-regular officers." In their contributions to the book, Arthur Koestler and Louis Fischer each observed the same phenomenon in converts to ex-Communism.[11]

Those driven by faith, the New York group assumed, found themselves embracing total solutions. Faith led to monolithic rather than partial beliefs and plans, the sort of absolutist approach that could endanger freedom in postwar America. Over the course of the 1940s, the ideal of the New York group was increasingly articulated in terms of values such as pluralism, moderation, tolerance, pragmatism, diversity, democracy, and freedom. Increasingly the New York intellectuals began to celebrate the tentative, provisional, and experimental. A postcommunist vision (now that intellectuals were less likely to be communists or ideologues) had to rid itself of the vision of totality that underlay totalitarianism. As the Cold War began to appear more threatening, so did the absolutist characteristics of some ex-Communist intellectuals.

In this regard, *Witness* evoked the New York group's worst fears. Because they equated pragmatism and Americanism, several of them wondered whether Chambers's inflexibility represented part of true American culture at all. Rahv found Chambers pursuing the absolute first in history and then in God, and thought this quest was "an idea so utterly unpragmatic that one is almost tempted to call it 'un-American.'" Howe shared Rahv's amazement, asking of Chambers's lust for totality: "how could Dostoevsky be an American, or an American be Dostoevsky?" Chambers's "vision of apocalypse," Howe told his readers, "is not highly regarded in this country." Hook joined the chorus. "The American experience itself," Hook declared confidently, "is after all the best answer to Chambers."[12]

Although Rahv, Howe, and Hook correctly identified the pragmatic impulse as important, they conveniently forgot the millennial, apocalyptic, and evangelical strains so predominant in American history. They thought the ex-Communist could not tend an absolutist garden in our native soil, although from the Puritan beginning to the present a portion of the population has always rallied to apocalyptic and millennial visions. Both Chambers's millennialism and the New York group's pragmatism were the products of American traditions. There was a precedent for each, as America has had a culture that has encompassed commonsense, empirical figures on one side, utopian, apocalyptic, and evangelical figures on the other, and many combinations of the two in between.

Equally disturbing to Howe was Chambers's insistence that his outlook provided a plan of action. Prophecy, in Howe's opinion, did not equal plan. To be productive, a historian or social critic needed to make useful distinctions. Chambers, for example, desperately urged Western intellectuals to save the West before it was too late. But of what use was such a large, unwieldy, and imprecise concept? "What is this 'West' that is to be saved?" Howe inquired. "The Salk vaccine or Jim Crow, anesthesia or torture, Shakespeare or Spillane, the seven-hour day or child labor? Why must some undifferentiated entity be saved or not saved?" In the end Howe denied that Chambers had a social theory at all, only a "Manichaean demonology." [13]

For the New York group, Chambers's apologia was yet another chapter in the conflict that had begun in the late nineteenth century, the battle in American intellectual history between the forces of philosophic absolutism and the forces of pragmatism, relativism, and scientific naturalism. [14] The most concerned of the New York intellectuals about the ex-Communists' lack of pragmatism, naturally, was Hook. As early as 1920, Hook's mentor, John Dewey, had argued against traditional philosophers who spoke in absolutes. "They tell us about *the* state when we want to know about *some* state," Dewey complained. Social philosophers needed to supply hypotheses to be tested rather than talking about absolutes, which closed the inquiry. Later in the 1920s, in an essay for the *New Republic* on Soviet Communism, Dewey wrote that "Not being an absolutist of either type, I find it more instructive to regard it as an experiment whose outcome is quite undetermined." [15]

Hook's pragmatism, though, was so strict in its standards of which positions qualified as anti-absolutist that he often berated the dissenters along with those like Chambers. He found it ironic, for example, that Howe set himself as a critic of Chambers's absolutism, since "during this whole period Howe was a Trotskyist—as absolute a Leninist as the Stalinists." He later claimed that Howe and the Trotskyists were attacking social democrats like himself "for being half-hearted, timid, opportunistic, etc.," while at the same time they were attacking Chambers for lacking those traits. [16]

In response to *Witness*, Hook admonished Chambers that with regard to "social programs and political strategy" religion was insufficient. There was "no substitute for creative intelligence." [17] For Hook that meant flexible, scientific, and empirical intelligence—of the sort descended from

Dewey rather than Hegel. "But perhaps the greatest lesson to which this literature points," Hook instructed his readers, "is that good sense in the quest for the good life in the good society depends not so much on *what* ideals are held as on *how* they are held; not so much on the nature of our beliefs as on the methods by which they are reached."[18] This is perhaps the most representative statement of Hook's entire philosophical system.

Still, Hook downplayed the absolutism of most of the ex-Communists. In an article for the *New York Times Magazine* in summer 1954, he argued that "there is no such thing as *the* politics of the ex-Communist," among whose ranks were found a diverse collection of political outlooks and party identifications. The confusion arose because we have generalized "from a few conspicuous illustrations." Hook reassured America that "The Communist generalization that most former Communists embrace the fanaticism of some other totalitarian creed or party is false. Most of them return to an earlier form of liberalism." Americans could now breathe a sigh of relief, since "having fled from what they regard, rightly or wrongly, as a political church, most ex-Communists are not likely to embrace another church, or to accept any source of spiritual authority except their new and hard-won faith in free intelligence and autonomous morality."[19] Ex-Communist absolutists were dangerous, he agreed, but he felt it important to acknowledge that most ex-Communists had not become fanatics.

Because the New York intellectuals perceived doctrinaire or passionate systems as the most salient form of absolutism endangering the interwoven fabric of international and domestic culture, the group's antiabsolutism manifested itself prominently as an anti-ideological preoccupation.[20] In the 1950s and 1960s observers came to call this the end-of-ideology impulse, partly because of a series of papers with that theme delivered at the Future of Freedom conference in Milan in September 1955, sponsored by the Congress for Cultural Freedom.

The anti-ideology outlook remained a strong component in the group's thought even after the 1970s, when Irving Kristol began to argue for a reinvigoration of conservative ideology in the American business community.[21] Like others in the New York group, and like the economist Joseph Schumpeter, who also wrote about the interplay between economic and political systems, Kristol realized that it was important for intellectuals to construct an appropriately moderate and flexible ideology to guide and legitimize their own culture, while at the same time it was necessary for them to oppose ideological systems that were excessively passionate, moralistic, demagogic, or absolutist.

By the term ideology, the New York critics meant abstract and fanatical thinking of the sort that constructed a complete and rigidly connected world view. Ideology was utopian rather than practical, passionately committed to an ideal rather than rationally analytical, and promoted an absolute vision that embodied total solutions rather than tentative hypotheses. Theirs was not the Marxist definition of ideology as false consciousness, the illusions that a class harbors about itself.

Because large political visions and passionate social movements were assumed to have led in Europe to fascism on the right and totalitarianism on the left, it was thought dangerous to deal any longer in these volatile commodities. It was safer to approach the present with the pragmatic instruments of realistic and moderate public policy changes. Keynesian countercyclical policy was less likely than a more total and inflexible ideological vision to produce absolutism. Common sense was an intellectual virtue.

Rather than creating a grand vision of the good society, which would have to be achieved through several visionary leaps and pirouettes without touching the ground, it was assumed safer to consider the good society more modestly—as nearly achieved already. This is human society, the anti-ideologists felt, and what can we really expect of it? The good society, they thought, needed only a few periodic adjustments by technicians to keep it on course. This outlook complemented the new consensus school of history, some of whose members—such as Daniel Boorstin in *The Genius of American Politics* (1953)—celebrated the pragmatic forging of common values and assumed no significant conflicts between sectors of society throughout the course of American history.

The importance the *Partisan* group attributed to the anti-ideological vision was revealed by their choice of European friends. The most prominent of their European colleagues were Arthur Koestler, George Orwell, and Stephen Spender in Britain; Raymond Aron and André Malraux in France; and Ignazio Silone and Nicola Chiaromonte in Italy. Several of these associates contributed essays to *The God That Failed*. Like the New York group, the European circle was split between affirmers and dissenters—with Raymond Aron among prominent affirmers, and Stephen Spender and Ignazio Silone the leading dissenters—but differences were subsumed under a common outlook, a shared commitment to purifying socialist thought of any totalitarian elements and the desire to create a benign socialist or liberal welfare state with an essential democratic component. The bond between these Europeans and the New York group lay in their opposition to destructive utopianism, inflexibility, and visionary ideology.

Further, there was a mutual respect on both sides of the Atlantic. The

Americans admired their European friends for having been on the front lines of the totalitarian oppression in the 1930s and 1940s. The Europeans knew firsthand of the horrors the New York group could only darkly imagine. The Europeans, in turn, admired their American colleagues for having been among the first to analyze and publicize the fatal flaws in the Stalinist world. Who had been earlier than Hook, on either side of the Atlantic, first as a knowledgeable ally of the Soviet Union and then as a thorough and rational critic of its dangers? It was *Partisan Review* that first helped to discredit Stalinism and totalitarianism, and led an assault on utopian social visions that called for sacrificing present generations for promises of abundance and equality beyond the horizon. When the Europeans came later to repudiate Stalinism and ideology, many found themselves repeating the New York group's earlier formulations—one of the first times that European intellectuals looked to their American colleagues for leadership.

During the 1940s and 1950s, then, anti-Stalinism and anti-ideology became a shared cause across the Atlantic, with each side contributing significant ideas to the common fund. In this cross-pollination of the intellectual communities, the Europeans wrote for *Partisan Review*, *Commentary*, and *Dissent*, and the Americans contributed to *Encounter*, and even sent Irving Kristol and Dwight Macdonald to London to help edit it. Within this transatlantic community, tensions between affirmers and dissenters persisted, but anti-Stalinism and anti-ideology cemented the factions together.

The most evocative statement of the New York group's position about the danger of absolute visions in the postwar world was Trilling's *Middle of the Journey*—a novel that examined the tensions between an ex-Communist, two fellow-traveling liberals who sympathized with the Communists, and a democratic liberal who chose moderation and pluralism. He had gone to Columbia in the 1920s with Whittaker Chambers, and had known him through the years, although not well. But Chambers had a riveting effect on those he met, whether one liked him or not, and Trilling decided to pattern Gifford Maxim, one of the major characters in his novel, on Chambers. Although Trilling said that Chambers "had never been a friend of mine," he admitted that "there was also something that engaged my interest and even respect." In court Trilling had said publicly, "Whittaker Chambers is a man of honor." He considered Chambers courageous. "In Whittaker Chambers there was much to be faulted," Trilling wrote near the end of his life, "but nothing I know of him has ever led me to doubt his magnanimous intention." [22] Chambers surfaced in Trilling's novel a year before he emerged into national prominence at the HUAC investigations.

Among Trilling's characters—Gifford Maxim, John Laskell, and Arthur and Nancy Croom—the fears troubling the New York group were played out. John Laskell, the character who represents Trilling's outlook, is a former fellow traveler who throughout the course of the story falls away from the camp of Soviet sympathizers but who is moderate and pragmatic enough not to join the ex-Communist extremists. Even when he was a sympathizer, Laskell always had a realistic bent, as illustrated by his interest in writing technical social-scientific monographs on housing policy. Unlike the fellow-traveling Arthur and Nancy Croom, Laskell has his feet on the ground, a trait to be admired in the postwar world of confusion. (Some thought that the Crooms were patterned after Alger and Priscilla Hiss, but, as Trilling later pointed out, who had even heard of the Hisses when he was writing the book in 1946?)

Soon after the book opens, Laskell convinces himself "that life was really a matter of routine, of clean face and neck and ears and shirts, not of such betrayals of the mind as led to being in love with death, or such things as the madness and treachery of Gifford Maxim." [23] Maxim, caught in the revelations of spirit and history that projected his vision into ethereal realms, was always dirty and unkempt—having sacrificed appearances in this world for an investment in the future.

The woman with whom Laskell relates most intimately in the story, Emily Caldwell, is also a practical anti-ideological person—although not on intellectual grounds. Asked by Nancy Croom, the most committed Communist sympathizer in the novel, whether people should not aspire to think of and be concerned about "mankind in general," Emily is indifferent and responds to Nancy that the best motto is "Carpe diem," or "Snatch the day and put very little trust in tomorrow." Emily's practical image is sharpened further. In keeping with the anti-ideologist's preference for making small adjustments in society with the help of public policy and social scientific tools, Emily and her husband Duck (a carpenter and handyman) live in a reconstructed tool shed. "I'm so proud of the house," Emily tells Laskell, "I must show it to you. This was an old tool house, you know." [24]

Arthur and Nancy Croom are not portrayed kindly. Nancy, an even more dogmatic fellow traveler than her husband, refuses to see what is occurring in the world. She has an "aura of self-deception," and "sets her chin sternly against any knowledge of the world in which she will have to make her sentiment prevail." The Crooms, for example, employ Emily's husband Duck as a handyman. Duck is a drunkard, rebellious about their authority, and slow and unreliable. Yet the Crooms adore him and speak reverently of him. Laskell cannot imagine why the Crooms, whose philosophy urges hurrying the present into the future, can be so taken by a person who maintains a slow pace and will not be hurried. It finally becomes apparent to Laskell that, to the Crooms, Duck is like Communism: something that they purposely refuse to understand.[25] The Crooms insist on taking Duck for something he is not: noble, a reliable workman, a trusted friend. The Crooms will not admit Duck's real nature, as they will not admit the real nature of Communism, and so they do not see the contradiction between either of them and their ideals.

Through Laskell, Trilling deals with the relationship of the present to the future, rejecting, as other anti-ideologists did, large "ideological" visions of the future that sacrificed democracy, individualism, civil liberties, and pluralism in the present for some greater recompense later. Trilling's advice, through John Laskell, is to forget about the future and live carefully in the present. It becomes clear to Laskell "that the present could no longer contrive and manufacture the future by throwing forward, in the form of expectation and hope, the desires of the present moment." Only children "live the life of promises," and those who insist on looking to the future will miss their chance for maturity and remain children.[26] Responsibility is immediate; it exists in the present.

Gifford Maxim, the ideologist who first wears the uniform of the Communist and then the holy robes of the ex-Communist Christian, thinks Laskell is naive. He uses Melville's story of Billy Budd to illustrate to Laskell how important it is that the spirit cleave to certain necessities in life. *Billy Budd*, Maxim assures Laskell, "is a political parable, but on a higher level than we are used to taking our political parables. It is the tragedy of Spirit in the world of necessity." Captain Vere becomes Maxim's vision of the ex-Communist believer, and Nancy Croom agrees with Maxim, though Laskell does not. "If you think about it," muses Nancy, "you see that it is really quite applicable to the Moscow trials. Even if those men were subjectively innocent—I mean even if they had good motives for what they did, like Budd—I don't believe that's so, but even if it were so—they may have had to be executed for the sake of what he calls Law in the world of Necessity."[27] Like Captain Vere, the believers on each side—Communists and ex-Communists—have to uphold absolute principles to maintain their ordered vision of the future. The anti-ideologists, the pragmatists, the dissenters, those who will not believe: they must hang from the yardarm in this world of necessities. Is it any wonder, believing as they did that they had been sentenced to the yardarm, that the New York intellectuals reacted with such intensity to the two camps of believers?

Between the pair of absolutisms, the Communist-sympathizing absolutism of the Crooms and Maxim's newfound ex-Communist religious faith, Laskell chooses a middle path of practical moderation. Trilling and Laskell will not be bound to ideological visions. Near the end of the story Maxim recognizes Laskell's choice and has a "sneer" for it. "Neither beast nor angel!" he accuses him. "Like any bourgeois intellectual, you want to make the best of every possible world and every possible view. Anything to avoid a commitment, anything not to have to take a risk." Laskell accepts Maxim's anger, understanding it as "the anger of the masked will at the appearance of an idea in modulation." But Maxim's anger cools when he realizes that ultimately he himself will triumph. "Yes, you were right," he apologizes to Laskell. "The Crooms and myself are at hopeless extremes. The child and the metaphysical essence—you put it very well. . . . And you spoke for something between. Call it the human being in maturity, at once responsible and conditioned." [28]

Although he considered Laskell right, Maxim still thought him a poor prophet. It was Maxim rather than Laskell who stood on the side of history, as only Communists and ex-Communists knew how. Maxim is convinced that he understands history, including the present, and the present is a time of extremism where only extremism will prove useful and victorious. Laskell's liberal tolerance is outdated, passé. "You could have kept that kind of mind up to fifty years ago," Maxim instructs Laskell, "vestigially even up to ten years ago. But now it is dead and what you feel is only a ghost. You know it as well as I do—the day for being human in the way you feel now is over. Gone. Done for. Finished." He offers Laskell little optimism about the future of moderate liberal humanism. "Maybe it will come again. But not for a long time, John, not until the Crooms and I have won and established ourselves against the anarchy of the world."

The Crooms are repelled by the idea of joining forces in an absolutist mindset with a traitorous apostate from Communism like Maxim. But history will not allow them to be deterred. "I'm sorry," Maxim confides to them, "—but we really must go hand in hand. Let it be our open secret. You will preach the law for the masses. I will preach the law for the leaders." The Crooms flinch at the prospect, but Maxim ignores their uneasiness. "We will hate each other and we will make the new world. And when we've made it and it has done its work, then maybe we will resurrect John Laskell." [29] The world was back at Matthew Arnold's "Dover Beach" with the clash of armies in the sinister moonlight, and Laskell, Trilling, and the anti-ideologists gave themselves little chance of prevailing in the battle. It was a time of extremism.

As Trilling's novel suggests, the New York intellectuals were in a paradoxical and somewhat untenable position with respect to their criticism of Communism in the late 1940s and 1950s. Could anti-absolutists who opposed Communism as an absolute evil do so without falling into another form of absolutism? Some of them came dangerously close. Diana Trilling, for example, complained that "totalitarianism is nothing if not a totality," but then went on to fashion her own inflexible dualism: "Either you have a free vote, or you do not. Either you have the freedom to criticize your government and change it, or you do not. Either you can write and speak and work as you choose, or you cannot—and all such criteria as 'free for whom,' 'free for what,' are only rationalizations."[30]

Granville Hicks was even clearer about the impossibility of taking a neutral stance toward Communism, although in the end he became confused and wanted to have it both ways. In an article in *Commentary* in 1951, Hicks warned his readers that Communism could not be treated as merely another idea to be tolerated or subjected to liberal freedoms. "It is one of the real absolutes of our time," he wrote of Communism as an ex-insider, "perhaps the only absolute, and by its nature, by virtue of what it has made of itself, it permits no neutrality. The liquidation of neutrals is one of its specialties." According to this view, the initiated such as Hicks understood the nature of Communism, while liberals such as *Nation* editor Freda Kirchwey, by their misjudgment, provided the nooses for those who would happily be their executioners.[31]

Yet Hicks tried to play both sides of the fence, denying he favored an absolute opposition. He realized the precariousness of his balancing act. "To call Communism an absolute is, I realize, to invite an absolute anti-Communism," he admitted, "and the absolutists do exist and grow more numerous. That, however, is one of the chances that have to be taken in these constricted times." In a period of excess in which the very existence of liberalism might be destroyed, liberal principles could not be extended to those whose goal was to destroy liberalism without debate or referendum. "At least the assumptions of the absolute anti-Communists are in the open and can be openly examined and openly fought," Hicks wrote in defense of his position, "whereas the assumptions of the pro-Soviet liberals are concealed—often, one suspects, from such liberals themselves."[32] Here he might have referred directly to Nancy Croom.

The task for the New York group was to construct an opposition that was absolute enough to be effective in combating absolutism, without falling into the enemy's absolutist approach, an error that would allow the adversary to win the battle without having to fight. Hicks was the only figure to wrestle consciously with the paradox, but all he could do was to waltz rhetorically through an intellectual minefield. In consecutive sentences he admitted that no neutrality was possible against Communism, but then warned that "opposition is not, in my vocabulary, synonymous with 'fanatical hatred'—a fact that has won me some hard words from certain professional ex-Communists." In another pair of consecutive sentences he reported that "I believe that the struggle against Communist espionage must be unremitting," and yet "I don't believe that this fight against Communism requires all our energies or that we can afford to give all our energies to it." [33]

The best interpretation one can put on Hicks's position is that he favored an absolute orientation against Communism but opposed an absolutist means of expressing that position. Such a theoretical distinction, however, was difficult to maintain in practice. Many of the New York intellectuals, and many liberal intellectuals who agreed with them on this point, were less practical, empirical, and pragmatic in their social philosophy than they assumed during the 1940s and 1950s. Opposing absolutism did not by itself make them flexible.

In a different context, Howe mentioned the same point about the affirmers in the mid-1950s. "One of the curiosities of our intellectual life at the present moment," Howe observed, "is the thoroughness with which the dominant school of liberalism—the school for which Sidney Hook is the philosopher-politician, David Riesman the sociologist and Lionel Trilling the literary moralist—exempts itself from its own analysis and recommendations. Few things are more dogmatic today than the anti-dogmatism of the liberal intellectual, few things more closed than his famous open mind." [34]

On these grounds Richard Crossman drew the connection between Chambers and the country Chambers hoped to save. "Whittaker Chambers personifies the American epoch in which he lives," Crossman reported, "the divided loyalties, the swiftly alternating moods of exaltation and despair, the conflicting urges, now to put the world to right and now to retire into lonely isolation; now to appease and now to smash the enemy." An Englishman, Crossman saw America wobbling under extremist impulses—impulses evident in Chambers's book. "All these features of his autobiography are a microcosm of American political life—or rather, to change the image, a distorting mirror, in which one aspect of America is reflected, monstrously distorted, yet still recognizable, an American [*sic*] which prophetically demands the destruction of anyone and everyone who questions the validity of the American way of life." [35]

Crossman's portrait of America was insightful: a culture caught in a whirl of changing positions that, if not as absolutist as Communist ideology, were often coopted by inflexibility. In this stormy period, the New York intellectuals were trying to sail a course toward an intelligent and calmer vision of society, and trying to convince society to follow their lead. Battered by fierce conflicting pressures, members of the group, not surprisingly, occasionally became immoderate themselves.

This stormy period also threw together unlikely collaborators. For example, Chambers, who was very involved in the public confessional process, was associated—if more in fiction than in reality—with Trilling, a rather politically uninvolved literary critic. Although Trilling's *Middle of the Journey* contained anti-ideological themes and criticism of liberal fellow-travelers during the Cold War, he was not actively involved in most of the group's heated polemics. In that regard he was unlike Sidney Hook. If Hook was the New York intellectuals' early political voice, Trilling was their literary guide. Yet an examination of Trilling's background and career makes it evident why he devoted his only novel to the conflict against ideological extremism.

Lionel Trilling

Trilling's *Middle of the Journey* and his scattering of short stories went mostly unnoticed. Rather, his reputation rested on the strength of his literary criticism. The defining feature of his work was that he viewed his subject from a distance and perspective much like that of an intellectual historian. Instead of functioning as a judge of a work, as a participant in the process of literary criticism, he ascended to serve as an arbiter of the rules of that process and the culture under which it operated.

He once noted that after a certain point in literary history a poet's work was no longer judged by whether it measured the reality of his audience; instead, after that, the poet's work was assumed to measure the poet's inner authenticity. The relationship was then inverted: the poet was no longer required to fulfill the audience's standards, but rather the reverse.[36] As a critic, Trilling similarly reversed the relationship between himself and his culture—so that he sat in judgment of the system of culture rather than merely following its dictates. The critic had to employ a system of meanings and values rather than let the system employ him.

Trilling wanted to know how culture related to life, and how criticism related to culture. In that pursuit, he felt that good "criticism, like science, occupies itself with questions of causation." Unlike literary formalism, Trilling's causal criticism "committed itself to the belief that the comprehension of a literary work can be advanced by knowledge of the conditions under which it came into being, which may be supposed to explain why it is what it is." To explain a text, therefore, the contextual critic sought a biographical causation (of the author), an environmental causation (the historical, economic, social and political context of the work), and a psychological causation (of the work, characters, and author).[37]

More than others in the New York group, Trilling was engaged with England and with British literature. His two book-length literary studies treat British writers Matthew Arnold and E. M. Forster. Of the essays in his major books (*The Liberal Imagination, The Opposing Self, A Gathering of Fugitives, Beyond Culture,* and *The Last Decade*), roughly one third are on British authors and one third on American subjects. In the latter group are essays on authors such as Henry James, Henry Adams, Hawthorne, and Edith Wharton—the Americans Philip Rahv referred to as "palefaces" rather than "redskins."[38]

Three years younger than Hook, Trilling was born July 4, 1905, in New York City. He was an undergraduate at Columbia in the early twenties and received his bachelor's degree there in 1925 and his master's in 1926. Throughout his student years, Trilling was aware of how his Jewishness set him apart. "Being a Jew," he wrote in his journal in 1928, "is like walking in the wind or swimming: you are touched at all points and conscious everywhere." In the mid-1920s Trilling fell in with several fellow Columbia students who became the core of young contributors to the *Menorah Journal,* published by the International Menorah Society. (The Menorah Society had been founded by Henry Hurwitz at Harvard to combat Jewish isolation there.) Trilling became attached to the magazine after he had a story accepted by it during his senior year, and at the end of the 1920s he served as assistant editor for a year.[39]

The greatest intellectual influence on the young Trilling was Elliot Cohen, managing editor of the *Menorah Journal.* Scarcely older than those who wrote for him, Cohen, whom Trilling described as a tormented "genius," instilled in his writers the same interdisciplinary attitude that Dewey, Morris Cohen, and Marx had encouraged in Sidney Hook. As Trilling later remembered, "Elliot's own mind was dominated by his sense of the subtle interrelations that exist between the seemingly disparate parts of a culture. . . . Indeed, he taught the younger men around him that nothing in human life need be alien to their thought." Norman Podhoretz, Trilling's student and friend in the 1950s, believed that Cohen was Trilling's political guide, first leading him into Stalinism, then into anti-Stalinism, and finally into a greater appreciation of America.[40]

Trilling was the first Jew to break into an English department in a major American university. Other Jews bore scars from their attempts. When Ludwig Lewisohn completed graduate school at Columbia and sought a job, he was faced with hostility from English departments. His

Columbia advisor merely shrugged his shoulders and noted "how terribly hard it is for a man of Jewish birth to get a good position." Elliot Cohen had been one of Yale's most promising English students, but, finding an English professorship closed to him, he had gone into magazine editing. Trilling knew the risks. "When I decided to go into academic life," he remembered, "my friends thought me naive to the point of absurdity, nor were they wholly wrong. . . ."[41]

After receiving his master's degree, Trilling was appointed as an instructor during 1926–27 at the University of Wisconsin at Madison, and then as an instructor at Hunter College in New York from 1927 to 1930. In the interim he met and married the writer and critic Diana Rubin. In a move that he felt was "pretty openly regarded as an experiment" by the university, he was hired as an instructor at Columbia in 1931. The young scholar began to write an intellectual biography of Matthew Arnold, but made little progress on it. In 1936 the department informed him he was being dropped because "as a Freudian, a Marxist, and a Jew" he would be "more comfortable" somewhere else.

The normally passive Trilling decided to stand up for himself and persuaded his department to keep him for another year. The one year turned into three, and Trilling found a new confidence within himself. By 1938 he had finished his dissertation and received his doctorate, and the next year he published, at his own expense, his biography of Arnold. Advised by a friend that Columbia president Nicholas Murray Butler appreciated receiving faculty books, Trilling sent him one. Butler was an admirer of nineteenth-century genteel culture and therefore interested in Matthew Arnold. He was impressed enough with the book that he held a faculty dinner in Trilling's honor and used his "summer powers" to appoint him assistant professor. Butler also let the English department know that he wanted them to make the appointment permanent. During the dinner party the university president told a story that concluded with the line: "At Columbia, sir, we recognize merit, not race."[42]

Trilling never expressed any sharp hostility about the anti-Semitism he experienced. Rather, as he explained it, anti-Semitism provided him a means of establishing an outsider's position. "If the anti-Semitism that we observed did not arouse our indignation," he pointed out, "this was in part because we took it to be a kind of advantage: against this social antagonism we could define ourselves *and* our society." Yet, a few of Trilling's fellow critics thought he distanced himself from Jewish culture and religion, even though some of his stories, published as *Of This Time, Of That Place*, dealt with Jewish themes. "In this respect," William Barrett observed, "though in many other ways they were radically different personalities, Trilling's case seems to me perhaps comparable with that of Walter Lippmann, who eschewed religious attachment lest it exclude him from the American mainstream."[43]

Perhaps the pressure to get along at Columbia affected Trilling's different orientation to Jewish culture, but so had his family background. Unlike many others in the group, Trilling was not the product of the ferocious economic and intellectual conditions of the Jewish ghettos. As Diana Trilling was quick to remind others about her husband, "The message of Lionel's upbringing was of a different order. . . . as naturally as [his parents] breathed they thought of themselves, and always had, as middle-class people—were they not honest, respectable, committed to the solidity and progress of their adopted country?" She remembered a stable economic and social childhood for her husband. "Unlike others of his intellectual generation, that is, Lionel had no need to make for himself the strategic leap into the American middle class, with what this so often involves in defensiveness. . . . It was not his sense that life was a contest of minds or that intellect was a weapon; it was more an instrument of conscience."[44]

Some in the group felt Trilling was more cultured than the rest. Barrett thought him to be "a graceful man" whose grace had "something of a moral quality." In a backbiting group like the New York intellectuals, Barrett found it amazing that Trilling was almost never criticized—partly because he never got drunk, pushy, and abrasive at parties as the others did. Both Diana and Lionel acted as though "they had a life of their own to lead and were intent on living it."[45]

Whether consciously or not, Trilling had distanced himself from the lower elements of society and the lowness of political analysis. Alfred Kazin viewed Trilling "as a writer who had absorbed the casual, more gentlemanly style of the twenties much as Bellow and I had absorbed the social angers of the lower-class thirties." But it was not merely that Trilling was older, for so was Hook—one of the most intellectually combative of the group. Trilling's whole manner and interests had a detached and elevated style about them. After all, he was not drawn to writing about Marx or Trotsky, even in his early years, but rather engaged himself with Matthew Arnold and nineteenth-century Britain. "He seemed to feel more than the usual literary connections to things English," Kazin observed about Trilling's vision, "and proudly told me that his mother had been born in England. Victorian England was his intellectual motherland." In the beginning his style was a curiosity among the group, although a respected curiosity—as though he operated in a higher, more ethereal world than their own. "When I first encountered the gravity of

Lionel Trilling," Harold Rosenberg once remarked in his acerbic style, "I did not get the joke; it took me some time to realize that there wasn't any." [46]

Trilling and Kazin did not get along well, probably because of both personal differences and professional rivalry. Kazin felt as though Trilling could not abide his "temperament," and he noted in his journal that Trilling "cannot stand the ghetto Jew in me—he cannot stand my vitality." Kazin wrote of Trilling's "long repugnance to me, thoroughly based, I see now, on a *fear* of the 'extremism' or whatnot he finds in me." [47]

Kazin criticized Trilling for being a "would-be gentleman," and he disliked Trilling enough that it even made him angry with Diana Trilling's writing. (Kazin called her "Mrs. Cooking Spoon.") He complained in his journal of Trilling's "specious air of reasonableness which he gives to his prudencies and fears and prejudices," and felt that his "writing is so completely audience-minded, in this sense; it is the style of a lecturer, whose very turns and pauses and connecting phrases show that he is thinking of the audience." Kazin noted to himself that Trilling's "contrived and external reasonableness seems to me the mark of an imitative and timid and second-rate mind; a mind that does not have a particular vision to bring out from its own depths, but is trying to fit its convictions to the existing usages and standards and prejudices." [48]

Beyond the professional rivalry, the two had conflicting sets of values, some based on class differences. Trilling was urbane, reasonable, successful, and perhaps slightly pretentious, while Kazin was more actively involved in the thrust and grapple of ideas outside the purely literary realm—as well as continuing to identify with his lower-class origins. The animosity between Trilling and Kazin was one of the rare instances of class tensions within the New York group. Trilling's manners and aspirations provided a spark of tension for those others in the group who were sensitive to class differences and pretensions. Sidney Hook later claimed that Trilling's critics such as Barrett, Kazin, Delmore Schwartz, and Rahv were merely jealous of Trilling, and therefore accused him of gentility and trying to suppress his Jewishness. Hook thought those accusations unwarranted. "Only after Trilling died," Hook alleged, "did they all find a kinship in him." [49]

By 1936 whatever radicalism Trilling had once felt was already beginning to dissipate. Like Hook, Trilling found Marx fading into the intellectual background. Ironically, this was the point at which the English Department at Columbia thought him too radical. Trilling, however, was already confiding to his journal that he was "no longer certain that the future will be a certain—Marxian—way. No longer measure all things by linear Marxian yardstick." [50] Here already were glimpses of his character John Laskell, a decade or more before Laskell was conceived on paper. Although he was well-respected for the intelligence of his literary criticism, after World War II Trilling's centrist conservative impulse did not fit in perfectly at *Partisan Review*.

In the mid-1940s Harold Rosenberg asked Rahv whether Trilling's pieces foreshadowed a new more conservative future for *Partisan Review*. Rosenberg did not stand alone in his assessment of Trilling. In Irving Howe's opinion, although Trilling "continued to think of himself as a liberal and felt hurt by the suggestions that he was not," his "critique of 'the liberal imagination' facilitated a turning away from all politics, whether liberal, radical, or conservative," and "provided a rationale for an increasingly relaxed and conservatized liberalism." Kazin agreed. Trilling "was the most successful leader of deradicalization—which was conducted in the name of the liberal 'imagination' against those who lacked it or had the wrong kind." Kazin summed up the indictment succinctly: "Arnold smote the philistines: Trilling the liberals." [51]

Trilling was surely stung by the accusations, but probably agreed with them in principle. He understood the path that Matthew Arnold had forged for him. "Arnold, I need hardly remind you, called himself a liberal," Trilling once acknowledged to a group of students, "yet his major effort in criticism was to bring into question the substance of liberal thought—the liberal assumptions, the liberal line of reasoning, the liberal conception of the *quality* life should have." [52]

There is another way to frame Trilling's role in the group. The New York intellectuals in the 1930s found two essential revolutions to be fought. The first was the revolution in the arena of intellectual politics, and it pitted the more democratic and Trotskyist elements of the socialist left (the New York intellectuals) against the Stalinists on their left and the defenders of capitalism on their right. This first revolution was led by Sidney Hook.

The second revolution, concurrent with the first, set the forces of literary and cultural modernism from Europe against the forces of mainstream American culture. In this battle the New York intellectuals championed modernism (Joyce, Kafka, Gide, Picasso, Stravinsky, and even some American modernists such as Pollock and de Kooning) against the proponents of American naturalism on their cultural right (Dreiser, Farrell, MacLeish, Wilder, and Frost) and the communist forces of proletarian realism on their cultural left (Michael Gold and others at *The New Masses*). This second revolution had no formal leader, and was fought equally by Trilling, Rahv, Phillips, Macdonald, Howe, and others. Yet

Trilling, who was the most interested in culture and the least political of the New York group, might for that reason be the best representative of the cultural battle fought over modernism.

The irony is that Trilling was perhaps the first of the group to become disenchanted with modernism, in the late 1940s or early 1950s, because he felt it helped to produce an "adversary culture" of alienation and dissent that opposed cultural authority and, in this case, opposed America. As Barrett remembered, because Trilling "was ahead of his time" with this conservatism, those who later would be neoconservative leaders admired Trilling after the war "and virtually took him as a master."[53] At the time, most of the group unhesitatingly affirmed the value of alienation in producing independent social critics and avant-garde cultural critics. Indeed, alienation was such a byword among the *Partisan* crowd that Norman Podhoretz was asked by a *New Yorker* editor in the 1950s "whether there was a special typewriter at *Partisan Review* with the word 'alienation' on a single key."[54] But Trilling was never as convinced as the rest of them about the positive role of alienation.

Trilling also stood apart from other literary essayists in the group— Rahv, Phillips, and Howe—who often used the review of a novel as a polemical platform. Trilling, as Podhoretz later put it, did not have a "puritanical ferocity" about his work. (The group's polemical political style of criticism was evident, for example, in Rahv's review of *Tender Is the Night*, in which he advised Fitzgerald not to avoid discussing class conflict and the impending social revolution. "Dear Mr. Fitzgerald," Rahv warned him, "you can't hide from a hurricane under a beach umbrella.") Trilling rarely used such direct political and social references in his work because it was grounded in a different vision of the critic's responsibility: A critic subtly enlightened rather than actively engaged. "Trilling's eyes," Podhoretz noticed, "did not blaze with a fierce Calvinist light upon the written word; he did not erect the capacity for 'true judgment' into the very principle of being; he did not conceive of criticism as the rod of the Lord's wrath."[55]

Though Trilling was far less political than other members of the New York group, in comparison to critics outside the group his work was notably political and social in its themes. Like others in the group, Trilling was influenced by the historical and social criticism of Edmund Wilson. But, as Giles Gunn has pointed out, Trilling located the obstacles to fulfillment and expression within the individual, while Wilson located those barriers in the social or political environment.[56] The other New York critics followed Wilson more closely than Trilling in this respect.

To Wilson's interest in the social and historical context of a work of literature and the biographical and ideological background of its author, Trilling brought the moral criticism of the British critic F. R. Leavis. Like Leavis, Trilling was at least as interested in the moral intention and impact of the work as in its historical context.

In Leavis, Trilling saw a critic who was not dogmatic in his approach, who required "no formulated first principles for his judgment but only the sensibility that is the whole response of his whole being." Trilling wanted to bring to criticism some of Leavis's "vital capacity for experience, a kind of reverent openness before life, and a marked moral intensity." Like Leavis, he strongly endorsed Matthew Arnold's belief that "Literature is the criticism of life." To be a moral critic of life was not to be "narrow and dour," but to interpret life and imagine the possibilities that could make life better. The moral approach made a declaration "about the qualities life does not have but should have." It would ask "for more energy and fineness of life, and, by its own communication of awareness, bring these qualities into being." Leavis's criticism had been devoted to the idea that "literature presents to us 'the possibilities of life,' the qualities of energy and fineness that life might have." [57]

That literature and criticism could illustrate the potentialities of life was compatible with the position of the affirmers in the New York group, and even the dissenters endorsed the role of affirmation in criticism. But Trilling went further and by the early 1960s was antagonistic to the "antisocial utterances of many modern writers" whose "expressions of antisocial feeling are nothing but imbecile." [58] Trilling was a leader among the New York group in his sympathy for intellectual affirmation—after all, he had been drawn to Matthew Arnold as early as the mid-1930s—and was a guide for others in that regard.

Leavis's "moral directness" and Trilling's intellectual affirmation did not preclude social concerns. "Sooner or later, of course, any critic of large mind will touch upon social matters," Trilling reported, "because what we call culture may be defined as the locus of the meeting of literature with social actions and attitudes." Politics was important. "What we address ourselves to is politics," he wrote of his vocation, "and politics of a quite ultimate kind, and to the disposition of the modern mind." [59]

This social and historical approach was evident in Trilling's influential *The Liberal Imagination* (1950), a collection of articles written in the 1940s that represented some of the clearest preoccupations of the group. In the first essay, Trilling criticized liberal writers such as Vernon Parrington and Theodore Dreiser for adhering to the simplistic and tired reform outlook of the liberal left. They were only a step away from the ideological blindness of the fellow travelers, and, especially in Parrington's case, they judged both art and personal motive by the standards of political correctness. Trilling preferred Henry James and Nathaniel Hawthorne, who he thought were more complex, nuanced, and conservative than Dreiser and Parrington, and less given to simplistic political judgments. Hawthorne's "dissent from the orthodoxies of dissent" was the mark of an intellectual who properly insisted on independent analysis.[60]

The New York group's hostility to romanticism surfaced in Trilling's criticism of Sherwood Anderson and others as too romantic and insufficiently intellectual and rational. It was also apparent in Trilling's quest to capture Freud from the romantics and for the pragmatic critics. Against those intuitive and emotional writers, those authors "of the myth and the dark irrational ways of the mind" who claimed Freud as their own, Trilling announced that "the rationalistic element of Freud is foremost; before everything else he is positivistic."[61] Trilling also vented the group's hostility to scholarship (which was ivory tower and archival) instead of criticism (which was socially involved and intellectual). The New Critics—Allen Tate, John Crowe Ransom, and others—he reproached for abandoning the historical elements of literature to focus on its formalist (and scholarly) properties.[62]

The Liberal Imagination was Trilling's attempt to draw a responsible line for proper cultural intellectuals to follow—between the dangers of culture with too little social and political content (such as the New Critics), and culture with too much political or visionary content (the romantics with their visionary irrationalism, or Parrington and Dreiser with their leftist ideological orthodoxies and cliches of dissent). Instead Trilling wanted complexity in criticism and literature. In criticism that meant enough intellectual independence to free one's analysis from the orthodoxies of dissent. In fiction that meant refusing to mount a simplistic soapbox, and instead producing a "culture's hum and buzz of implication."[63]

Literary critics, Trilling advised, should "recall liberalism to its first essential imagination of variousness and possibility, which implies the awareness of complexity and difficulty." Literature and its criticism, he urged, is "the human activity that takes the fullest and most precise account of variousness, possibility, complexity, and difficulty."[64] This complexity and ambiguity were allied to an awareness of the tragic sense of life. That tragic outlook was intelligent, but also fundamentally conservative, for it acknowledged the extent to which society was unable to control itself. Tragedy understood that there were unintended consequences to the most well-intentioned actions. The tragic outlook suspected that we could not control the various aspects of our lives—through reform or good intentions. The tragic view did not counsel despair, but neither did it campaign for reform. In that sense it had a clearly conservative component.

In effect, members of the group were moving from an idealistic and revolutionary vision of their earliest years that echoed Thomas Paine and the revolutionary generation of the 1770s, to a more practical and less optimistic view of society that echoed James Madison and the constitutional generation of the 1780s. As Madisonians, they no longer believed in the inherent goodness of the individual or the total salvation of society by a sweeping and apocalyptic change. They no longer subscribed to the most idealistic element of the socialist revolution. Instead they wanted to work within the contingencies of fallen mankind, to hope for the best but to guard against the worst. At first they combined this Madisonianism with their leftist commitments, but it soon led them into the camp of liberalism.

Trilling did not reject liberalism. He thought of himself as a liberal trying to improve liberalism, a centrist liberal who respected cultural tradition and the status quo. He wanted to be a liberal, but everywhere around him liberalism was a discouraging prospect. By the early 1950s, Trilling's early radicalism was a distant memory.

He shared this disillusionment about left reformist visions with Reinhold Niebuhr, Sidney Hook, and Richard Hofstadter, among others. Daniel Bell has said that at midcentury Trilling and Niebuhr were the key influences on the intellectual community, and Hook and Hofstadter only slightly less so. Trilling was so influential, according to Bell, "because of *The Liberal Imagination,* and the whole emphasis on complexity, irony, the simplicities of liberalism, and the pieties of liberalism." [65]

Trilling's emphasis coincided with Niebuhr's influential outlook. Niebuhr's *The Irony of American History* (1952) introduced the concepts of irony, tragedy, and complexity into historical analysis at the same time that Trilling announced the need for complexity and nuance in critical analysis, and that Hofstadter and other consensus historians repudiated the simplicity of the Progressive historians. "The thing which put together Niebuhr, Trilling, and Hofstadter," Bell remembered, "and which Sidney always in a way resented . . . is the emphasis of these people on the tragic sense of life." According to Bell, Hook's essay "Pragmatism and the Tragic Sense of Life" was a response to their concerns. Hook's article, Bell felt, "came really as a reaction to all the arguments that all of us had with Sidney and his feeling that somehow his role was sort of being leached away by the influence of Niebuhr." [66]

Hook's essay was an attempt to show that the pragmatic scientific naturalism he shared with Dewey could recognize a tragic view of life, to prevent that theme being monopolized by Niebuhr's emphasis on a Calvinist evil inherent in individuals. Yet some critics were skeptical of the ability of the Dewey-Hook outlook to be tragic. Because Dewey's educational philosophy proposed that individuals were not "given" but "created," bad individuals were not the product of inherent evil or flaws but had been trained that way. Its optimistic implication was that educational and social contingencies, properly designed, could produce good people. In addition, because pragmatists depended centrally on the experimental method and the system of open debate, their critics assumed that there was an optimism that a reliance on the system would produce an increasingly better world. That belief was hard for many observers to accept in the wake of the 1930s and 1940s. Further, the philosopher Horace Kallen observed that a vital difference between William James and Dewey was that the latter failed to realize the actuality of mystical experience.[67] Without a belief in the mystical, how could a tragic view be constructed? The same might be asked of Hook.

But Dewey had his defenders in the conflict. The Harvard philosopher Morton White assailed both Niebuhr and Walter Lippmann for their criticisms of Dewey. White scoffed at the popular intellectual portrait of Dewey as an optimistic child of the Enlightenment and Niebuhr as a "shrewd Pauline" who was realistically aware of human limitations, a tough Christian realist who navigated between "idiotic optimism and equally idiotic pessimism." If Niebuhr objected to the scientific method to judge political issues, White inquired, "one can only ask: What other ways are there?" If he criticized Dewey's method he must provide an alternative, but he only provided theology. Niebuhr believes we are too close to the serpent to trust persons to do socialist planning, White reported, and many liberals thus see him as very profound, but to judge from them he thinks humankind is far enough from the serpent to allow Keynesian planning and control. White, however, was not convinced that economic disagreements between Marx and Keynes could be settled by an appeal to the Bible. "Neither Paul nor Augustine tells us, so far as I know," White concluded, "why Keynesian advisers are less likely to dupe us than planners of production are."[68]

Trilling's commitment to irony and tragedy was influenced more by Freud than by Marx. "Only for a very short time," Trilling wrote, "and then quite presumptuously, did I think of myself as a Marxist. To Freud as a systematic thinker I became more committed and I remain so." Although Trilling acknowledged that Marx and Freud were in many respects incompatible, he saw both as thinkers who rejected "the settled, institutionalized conception of reality and how it works." Both Marx and Freud felt that institutionalized reality was only a mask, and believed "that the great work of intellect was to strike through the mask," to understand the individual, society, and the relations between them. [69]

Both thinkers also suggested that one's outlook was formed by a dialectical interplay between material or physiological forces on one hand (economic relations or biology), and forces of intellect or individual perception (superstructure or self) on the other. Therefore both of them provided a way not only for culture to resist material forces but also for the individual (or subordinate group) to resist the larger culture itself. Both Marx and Freud, that is, opened a way for intellectuals to move, in Trilling's phrase, "beyond culture" and its determinations. [70]

As a first-generation member of the New York group, Trilling held out the challenge of striking through the mask of culture. An anti-ideologist, he composed one of the group's most imaginative and articulate statements on the dangers of ideological thinking in the postwar world. His cultured, learned example provided a sense of authority and dignity that helped establish the group's intellectual preeminence. In this regard he openly questioned the "dispute and acrimony" of the others' polemics and wondered aloud whether Morris Cohen's antagonistic teaching style was a good influence, alleging that "there was a disproportion between the degree of his intellectual contentiousness and what it produced." [71] A cultured intellectual gentleman enthusiastically engaged in rational debate was, in his opinion, a better model, and the one he himself tried to provide. As one observer has noted, Trilling's essays showed others how to think rather than telling them what he thought. [72] He took this more sedate approach with him from the *Menorah Journal* to the *Partisan Review*, where it only partly offset the polemical styles of Hook, Rahv, Phillips, and others at the magazine.

The Effect of Confession on the Intellectual's Role

In evaluating the worth of the repentance literature, the New York group pondered the intellectual effect of confession on the individual penitent and on society as a whole. To make such judgments, the group again had to reconsider what it meant to be a proper and responsible intellectual in America.

Two in the *Partisan* community who portrayed the process of confession in a favorable light were Leslie Fiedler and Sidney Hook. An entire generation of liberals was responsible for the illusions that culminated in the Hiss trial, Fiedler told his readers, and they must bear the collective responsibility and issue a collective sigh of sorrow and regret. They must confess. The confession would be difficult, he knew, "yet the qualifying act of moral adulthood is precisely this admission of responsibility for the past and its consequences, however undesired or unforeseen." A squalid or self-serving confession such as Julian Wadleigh's in the Hiss trial would not do. The liberal community had to admit nobly and honestly that it had been wrong.[73] The function of confession, for Fiedler, was to bring society into "moral adulthood," prompt it to throw off its innocent and dangerous illusions, and allow it to struggle into maturity.

Sidney Hook also saw the confessions as an important step toward intellectual maturity, as well as an expression of grand spiritual humility (a trait not often recognized by members of the New York group). Fiedler and Hook adopted the reassuring tones of intellectual reverends: Members of the intellectual community, they counselled, could all grow up, chin in the air, if only they would unburden themselves about past mistakes. "We should be grateful to [the repenters] for providing texts not only in the costs of human folly," according to the fatherly Hook, "but in the grandeur of human faith and humility." He cited the noble example of the penitent Chambers, "the magnificent courage of this stubborn and sensitive man," and hoped that his example would "inspire others who until now have feared the wolf-pack of the anti anti-Communists to come forward to testify to the truth not only for the sake of their own country but for the sake of their fellow-men everywhere."[74]

Yet as early as the end of World War II, Alfred Kazin began to notice the pressure toward social conformity that the confessions encouraged. In Dostoevsky's work, for example, Kazin saw confession was much more important than "proof," for proof was merely a "cold" and scientific Western concept. For the Russians, Kazin noted to himself, "the confession is the terrible human meeting. Or is the speech of the living soul." It was a potentially more revealing means than mere conviction by evidence. Further, Kazin felt that the Soviets transferred this process from literature to "contemporary Russian politics. The confessor has betrayed the living community of souls—the 'people's state'—he can rejoin it only by confessing that he has sinned against it."[75]

A decade after Kazin noted his misgivings, several others of the dissenters, most notably Mary McCarthy and Harold Rosenberg, wrote unsympathetic essays about the crowded line of confessors bleating their regret. In McCarthy's contemptuous lampoon of the ex-Communist penitents, their moans of regret were really only a lurid and "sensational fact-fiction" that produced "a keyhole to which [the public's] eye is pasted." The confessions were peppered with people who were "seduced by Communism," and the stories pandered to the public's "almost prurient avidity for the details of political defloration." Their "shuddering climaxes" belonged in "the confessions of a white slave." McCarthy chuckled in scorn at the melodramatic protagonists who were subject to "a lightning storm of revelation, on the road to Damascus."[76] Never a Communist herself, she considered herself close enough to the battles as an editor of the reconstituted *Partisan Review* in 1937 to know drivel when she read it. None of the real story was as the ex-Communists told it.

No, for her there were no lonely and cataclysmic decisions made wrenchingly as the cymbals pounded around her. "It has never been like that for me; events have never waited, like extras, while I toiled to make up my mind between good and evil." The big choices—whether to be a Communist, anti-Communist, ex-Communist, or nothing at all—were all made accidentally, almost without her awareness. "Too late to do anything about it, I discover that I have chosen. . . . For me, in fact, the mark of the historic is the nonchalance with which it picks up an individual and deposits him in a trend, like a house playfully moved by a tornado." Conversions were not absolute and dramatic; they sneaked around and caught one unaware, long after the fact. Her own relation to Communism, important as it was, "had this inadvertence that seems to me lacking in the true confessions of reformed Communists," those which "the simpler comrades, with their shining eyes and exalted faces, seemed to have in copious secretion."[77]

In fact the typical confession was inverted by McCarthy. Most ex-Communists, on their knees, pleaded that their motives were good although their actions were bad. Not so with McCarthy, who claimed that her actions were good (helping the causes she supported) but her motives were bad (that as a young woman she was merely a "contentious" and embarrassing "show-off"). She did not initially realize the lasting consequences of her alliance with the anti-Stalinist New York group, but was drawn into her anti-Communism "by accident and almost unwillingly." So the process of breaking with Marxism or Communism was not a battle fought in the way Chambers or Elizabeth Bentley described it. Instead, it "was a break or a rupture, not very noticeable at first, that gradually widened and widened, without any conscious effort on my part, sometimes to my regret. This estrangement was not marked by any definite stages; it was a matter of tiny choices. . . . I did not 'give up' these things; they departed from me, as it were, on tiptoe, seeing that my thoughts were elsewhere."[78]

To be fair to the ex-Communists, McCarthy hardly went through the harrowing fear, imprisonment, or threat of death borne by Chambers and some of the others. She became an anti-Communist without having ever been a Communist, and it was that experience that informed her essay. Most of the other penitents talked about the experience of becoming ex-Communists—quite a different matter from becoming an anti-Communist.

Harold Rosenberg, with an even more biting irony and satire, made a more substantial point in an essay written in response to Fiedler's piece on Hiss and Chambers. In Rosenberg's view, the function of the confessions was merely "the manufacture of myths" by those who had taken part in the actual events. American ex-Communists had paid attention to the way the Soviets, in the Moscow Trials, had rewritten and transformed their previous history, and so "the formula for the production of historical fictions is no longer any more secret than that for the atom bomb." Through the public, social process of confessing, "recent history is being re-made," he claimed in 1955. "If the Soviets have purloined our nuclear know-how, we have evened the score by mastering her technique of the fission and fusion of memory. To be able to dissolve segments of time is at least as important in modern politico-military struggle as the capacity to sear areas of space. With Communist help, it is now definitely in our power to alter at will the contents of the past twenty years." [79]

Confession was a social act, Rosenberg suggested, an extension of that perennial American theme of the intellectuals' search for community. And in this bonding there was also a social conformity. A penitent was alone no more. "His confession will not only bestow upon him solidarity with other confessing culprits," he reported, "it will supply him with a community definition. Out of the solitude of the dungeon he marches in an ensemble of comrades into the full tableau of prefabricated history. That the scene is a hoax matters less than that he is no longer alone and has a role to play."

As he wryly described it, "Though confessing in America lacked the fatal finale of Iron Curtain confession, it was not without its hardships. The very absence of the bludgeon created special problems. It is possible that without the inspiration of the Russian originals, as an earlier generation of American actors was inspired by the Moscow Art Theatre, the entire effort would have failed." Having viewed the Soviet example, the American confessors invented their own enthusiastic initiative. "Far from being goaded to their parts by police agents hidden in the wings, the guilty here had to all but force their way on to the stage. . . . In time, we know, the barriers went down and whoever had a story to tell found a campfire waiting." [80]

Social conformity was also the theme of a key article in the *Antioch*

Review in 1954 by Murray Hausknecht, a sociologist later associated with *Dissent*. Hausknecht wrote the first penetrating analysis of the social and intellectual function of ex-Communist confessions, and the effect of public penitence on the role of the intellectual in society.[81] Did the ex-Communist confessions, he wanted to know, damage the critical independence of the intellectual?

"There is a connection between confession and the perennial problem of nonconformist behavior and the maintenance of a social order," Hausknecht argued. Public penitence was an important symbolic social act whose function previously had been ignored: it was a "dramatic symbol" that reaffirmed the prominence of one set of beliefs over another. The ex-Communist martyr, according to Hausknecht, by lamenting his past and chanting hosannas to America, was a "living symbol" of the "traditional values of society," and was engaged in a theatrical spectacle that "testifies to the force and validity of the moral code which condemns his behavior." A bargain was made with society. In exchange for being accepted back into the fold the penitent agreed to let his example "be used as a means of intensifying belief" and positioned himself as "an 'official' guide to approved behavior and belief" by making "his confession a *manual for conformist behavior.*"[82]

It occurred to Hausknecht that nonconformist behavior was actually being used to undermine itself through the process of public lamentations. "Confession," as he explained it, "is a unique means for making the inevitable existence of nonconformist behavior a means for strengthening the tendencies toward conformity." But, as he realized, the ranks of the ex-Communists were not unified. A penitent could be a "returner" who affirms society, or he could maintain a critical nonconformist stance while still rejecting Communism. That is, an ex-Communist could abandon the critical intellectual role when he returned, or he could maintain it. But as Hausknecht pointed out, those who kept a critical intellectual posture were not sympathetically received.

The nonconforming ex-Communists, Hausknecht explained, "still represent a threat to the social order; possibly a more unnerving threat to some than that of Communism." The nonconforming ex-Communist leftist was too much of an intellectual, a questioner: "he retains a critical attitude toward the world and himself. Such an attitude is never entirely welcome in any society, and in times of severe ideological conflict," such as the Cold War, "it is certainly not conducive to harmonious relations." Finally, he reported, the confessions usually opposed reason and analysis with belief. So the confessions were anti-intellectual acts performed, ostensibly, by intellectuals, but serving only to enforce conformity within the intellectual community.[83]

Part of the disagreement among the New York group over the repentance literature can be seen in microcosm in the animosity Hausknecht's manuscript created within the editorial staff of the *Antioch Review*. When the article was first accepted at the journal, some of the staff were for it and others against. Louis Filler, a professor of American civilization at Antioch College and a member of the *Antioch Review* editorial board, objected to Hausknecht's essay and asked to write a rejoinder to be published with it. When he had finished, many of the *Antioch Review* editors thought Filler's piece was too hostile and irrelevant. Among the staff, Everett Wilson supported Hausknecht, Paul Bixler supported Filler, and the tension produced a heated argument at the November 24, 1953 editorial meeting. The result was that Hausknecht was invited to write a rebuttal to Filler's rejoinder. Hausknecht accepted the opportunity and wrote the reply. By February 1954 nothing had yet been published, and Filler had added still another rejoinder of three pages to Hausknecht's rebuttal. As a consequence of the escalating tension and length of the project, the debate was cancelled and Hausknecht's original essay was printed alone, with no mention of any disagreement.[84]

In his unpublished rejoinder to Hausknecht's original article, Filler objected to Hausknecht's portrayal of Chambers and others as deviants from the mainstream who were trying to move, by their confessions, into the in-group. Chambers and the ex-Communists, according to Filler, never felt like outcasts, but rather insiders who had the petite bourgeoisie on the run. They were not alone, but supported by the workers of the world, by the Soviet Union. They were the triumphant, Filler wrote, not the vanquished. The ex-Communist confessions were not apologies, they were revelations of information. Stop worrying about conformist pressures, Filler advised Hausknecht, and start worrying about the Communist threat. It was discouraging, Filler concluded contemptuously about Hausknecht and his soft-hearted leftist friends, that they worried more about the ex-Communists damaging individual freedom with their stories of Communist activity than they worried about the Communist activity itself.[85]

In his unpublished rebuttal to Filler, Hausknecht claimed that Filler had missed the point. Hausknecht wrote that, for the purposes of his study, he was not concerned with the psychological phenomenon of an outcast like Chambers trying to move into an in-group. He was instead "concerned with the *social* functions of confession," the pressures of intellectual conformity it encouraged. The important question to ask about the confessional autobiographies was, "What are their consequences for human freedom?"

This was the heart of the disagreement between Hausknecht and the dissenters on one side, and Filler, Hook, and some of the more stridently anti-Communist affirmers on the other. "It is not enough, it seems to me," Hausknecht wrote in answer to Filler, "to be exclusively concerned with the past or with the ever necessary task of combating totalitarian ideologies and forces. We must also be concerned with the consequences of that fight, e.g., former deviants, confessions, etc." [86] Totalitarianism was not such an external threat to American society, in his view, that antitotalitarianism should be allowed to corrupt society first. The repercussions of anti-Communism had to be assessed.

By looking at the ex-Communist confessions themselves in this larger interpretive context, Hausknecht changed the nature of the question the confessions represented. Asking first what intellectual and social function the confessions represented, the question to be answered then was no longer whether Communism or ex-Communism was good or bad—a question most of the intellectual community agreed upon—but whether intellectual dissent or conformity was good or bad. If one could define the prescribed role for the postwar intellectual, one would know, by inference, whether the ex-Communist confessions were beneficial or detrimental.

The disagreement did not concern whether one should *be* an ex-Communist or anti-Communist. Most American intellectuals, and certainly all of the New York intellectuals, supported both—since there was nothing more shameful and intellectually scandalous than a Communist. The disagreement was over whether the literature of penitence had a beneficial impact on American culture, and especially on the intellectual's role as critic in postwar America. The group split over whether or not the confessions were a useful public process. The dissenters thought the confessions were confining and mandated a consensus. The affirmers viewed the public process of confessions as healthy for America and without intellectually harmful consequences.

Hausknecht later maintained that the difference between Hook and himself on the value of the confessions paralleled their different orientation toward McCarthyism. Hook, according to Hausknecht, was much softer on McCarthyism, saw it as much less of a threat, and thought the literature of repentance confirmed Hook's anti-Communism and his support for loyalty oaths. Hausknecht, in his own description, was much more worried about McCarthyism than Communism, and felt the confessional literature only fed the McCarthyist impulse. Hook, however, disagreed that Hausknecht's writings ever showed more opposition to McCarthyism than his own. [87]

Some among the affirmers argued that far from being an anti-intellectual process, the ex-Communist confessions exposed the anti-intellectual nature of Communism by telling the truth. There was wide agreement in the New York group that Communism was entirely anti-intellectual. The Communist Party line and the dialectic of history made no positions available for intellectuals—those whose independence of mind could only undermine the certainty of history and necessity. Even dissenters acknowledged that. "The Communist belongs to an elite of the knowing," Rosenberg phrased it. "Thus he is an intellectual. But since all truth has been automatically bestowed upon him by his adherence to the party, he is an intellectual who need not think. . . . what good is mental activity if one can know more by giving it up?" The Communist shakes his head at the sad foolishness of the non-Communist intellectual, since he "goes through all the motions of thinking, but at best he can only hope to arrive at what is already known." [88]

Sidney Hook elaborated this point. Looking back to the thirties, he argued that the real failure of intellectuals was not their endorsement of Communism, but "their renunciation of their vocation to think." An intellectual needed to experiment with ideas, and would perhaps support incorrect ideas occasionally, so "one should not reproach intellectuals for thinking their way to conclusions which turn out false." Intellectuals will "make mistakes not only because they think more than others but because they think more freely." But "the sin of the intellectuals who fell under Communist domination was that they yielded to this demand and stopped thinking." [89]

Despite their differing assessments of the ex-Communist confessions, all the members of the New York group were motivated by a common concern: to protect the role of the intellectual. Hook and the affirmers viewed the confessions as assertions of intellectual honesty and integrity and proof of Communist anti-intellectualism. Harold Rosenberg, Hausknecht, and the dissenters warned against conformist pressures that would repress intellectual independence and undermine the role of the intellectual critic.

Among the most visible of the dissenters on the subject of conformity and dissent, Harold Rosenberg was a commanding and influential presence in the New York group. His life and image illustrate what it meant to be a critical intellectual.

Harold Rosenberg

Harold Rosenberg's criticism of Fiedler did not surprise the New York intellectuals, all of whom knew Rosenberg's work well by 1955. Others, however, might have been startled to find an art critic writing on political and social questions in *Partisan Review* or *Dissent*. But like his colleagues in the New York group, Rosenberg was a former Marxist who took all of political and social life as his intellectual province.

Born in Brooklyn on February 2, 1906, Rosenberg was a member of the first generation—about three years younger than Hook, half a year younger than Trilling, and a few weeks older than Macdonald. In 1923 he enrolled at City College, but then transferred to St. Lawrence University and received his degree in 1927—although he claimed later to have been "self-educated on the steps of the New York Public Library." [90]

From 1938 to 1942 Rosenberg worked for the Works Progress Administration (WPA), a New Deal agency that sporadically employed many writers during the 1930s. While with the WPA, Rosenberg was national art editor of the American Guide, a series of books produced by the state and regional offices of the Federal Writers Project that were introductions to the history and culture of each of the states. During his time in Washington, he was uneasy about being a leftist with a government job. In 1940, for example, he sent Dwight Macdonald's wife Nancy a dollar for a copy of the leftist *Labor Action* (for which Irving Howe was an editor), but asked to be kept off her subscription list. "For all lists in their time, if not at once, fall into the hands of the investigators," he cautioned, "—and the way things are going now, with spies already reported in most divisions, a name on a list is as good as a hammer in the fist." [91]

During the war Rosenberg was employed as deputy chief of the domestic radio bureau in the Office of War Information. After the war he worked briefly as a consultant for the Treasury Department in 1945 and 1946, and following that he was a program consultant to the Advertising Council of America from 1946 until 1973. His teaching career included lecturing at the New School in the academic year 1953–54, Princeton in 1963, and the University of Southern Illinois in 1965. By 1966 Rosenberg's reputation among the intellectual community had grown sufficiently that he was appointed to a professorship in the Committee on Social Thought at the University of Chicago, and the following year he became the art critic for the *New Yorker*. During the 1960s and 1970s he spent half of each year in East Hampton with his wife, May, taught for a semester each year in Chicago, and spent the rest of his time in his "big World War II bargain apartment" on East Tenth Street in Greenwich Village. [92] The best of his essays are collected in *The Tradition of the New* (1959), *The De-Definition of Art* (1972), and *Discovering the Present* (1973).

Physically, Rosenberg was imposing. He stood taller than six feet, with broad shoulders and an arresting face. His brows were dark and bushy, as was his mustache, and he could look threatening even when he did not intend to. His forehead slanted out over his eyes as if to cut the wind for the rest of his massive figure. The *New York Times* suggested that he looked "like a philosophical eagle that had just finished feasting on bear meat," and the *New Yorker* said he had the "sculptured face of a prophet." He was also said to look like Captain Ahab. His friend Seymour Krim put it best: "Harold looked and shone like the Lion of Judah. He was about 6'4", a really heroic-looking prince among the bookish intellectuals, added to which he had a congenital game leg that had to be propped up like a bayonet when he was sitting. It gave him a Byronic wound, which increased his romantic air—the ladies were not immune—and probably made a number of his thick-lensed intellectual peers defensive as hell." [93]

Saul Bellow taught with Rosenberg in the Committee on Social Thought at the University of Chicago, and after Rosenberg's death Bellow wrote a story about him (as art critic Victor Wulpy). His face, Bellow wrote, might have been found in "the old Mediterranean or in Asia," or "on the cover of a book about the ancient world: the powerful horizontal planes—forehead, cheekbones." Wulpy "towered" and "tilted" because of his "surgically fused knee," and with "his leg extended like one of Admiral Nelson's cannon under wraps" he was to be reckoned with: "the way he gimped was formidable, not as if he was dragging his leg but as if he were kicking things out of the way." In Bellow's description, this produced "one of the most dramatic-looking men in the world." [94]

Like his real-life counterpart, Bellow's Wulpy has a respect for "people who lived out their *idea*." And ideas are related to power. "I thought what I would do with power," Wulpy tells a companion. "It gave me an edge over other intellectuals who never tried to imagine power. . . . My ideas had more authority because I conceived what I would do in authority." Bellow's art critic is an intellectual who wants to shape the world. "I would have done well in a commanding situation," Wulpy explains. "I have the temperamental qualifications. . . . Naturally political, and I have a natural contempt for people in private life who have no power-stir." [95] Or as Dwight Macdonald described the real Rosenberg in a letter to Hannah Arendt, he "certainly is a power-man who conceives of thought and art as pugilistic arenas, who wants to 'make' history, to push things around with his will." [96]

Rosenberg's energy and "power-stir" came through clearly in his art criticism, the body of work for which he is best known. In a celebrated interpretation he suggested that Abstract Expressionism be called "Action Painting," an idea he borrowed from the Dadaist critic Richard Hulsenbeck, who suggested that literature should be action and made with a gun in the hand.[97] On his canvas an Action Painter recorded "not a picture but an event," and the intention was "'to abolish art' in favor of the meaningful gesture." The moment of creation was not the transference of an image, however scrambled, from the artist's memory to the canvas, but rather an encounter that expressed the physical act itself and taught the artist something about himself. In the process the painter tried to extinguish the object of art.[98]

Unlike Clement Greenberg, who wrote frequently about Abstract Expressionism, Rosenberg wrote little—though his single article on the Action Painters rivaled Greenberg's entire critical output. Those painters were important to Rosenberg for several reasons. First, they were the perfect example of individualistic rather than mass thinking, an important consideration for one who disliked mass culture and ideological rigidity. Second, he could transform Expressionist painters from artists into actors, and as pragmatists these painters were Americans who fit well with the New York group's outlook. Finally, as painters who committed acts rather than art, they had no connections to the past and therefore were the best example of the Tradition of the New.[99]

The idea of Abstract Expressionism as action rather than image was a fitting product for a critic who had such high regard for event, spectacle, and action. At a party Rosenberg was an event; in life he was a spectacle; in his criticism he practiced action. In a period when art was in a constant act of patricide, a constant abolition of tradition in favor of the recent, what else could bind the painter and the art critic but action and event?

Rosenberg called this modern orientation the Tradition of the New because, even though it was founded on an insatiable "appetite for a new look," it had existed long enough to have established its own heritage. In effect, he was restating the accepted definition of modernism—a cultural movement that was predicated on an avant-garde compulsion to undermine tradition and produce constant change—while pointing out that a constant production of the new, an enshrinement of a vanguard, can become a tradition in itself.

The prospect of the vanguard mired in a tradition against its will appealed to Rosenberg's sense of humor. He instructed the artistic community that "the only vital tradition of twentieth-century art to which criticism can appeal is that of overthrowing tradition. This makes every attempt at criticism of contemporary art inherently comical." In this "ridiculous" situation, he remarked devilishly, "revolutionary art is a contradiction. It declares that art is art in being against art; and then tries to establish itself as the soundest kind of art. It demands of the critic that he take 'explosiveness' as an esthetic principle, and that he protect this principle against being blown to bits by the 'conscious negation' of principles."[100]

The tradition of modernism, as he saw it, was hostile to materialism and bourgeois capitalist society. But bourgeois society, not wanting to be philistine, accepted modernist art as its own—the more hostile the better. Artists realized that an embrace from their adversaries would be a death grip that would render real art impotent. The Tradition of the New tried to outrun that embrace by changing its style even more quickly, but with no success—for society adopted the "radical" idea of avant-garde art itself. So the only avenue left for the true artistic revolutionaries was suicide: they were forced to destroy the ammunition before the enemy captured it. "Painting today," Rosenberg concluded upon viewing this scene, "is a profession one of whose aspects is the pretense of overthrowing it." Art, in his phrase, was in a process of "de-definition" of itself.[101] This was the final, wildly frenetic impulse of the Tradition of the New.

Because the Tradition of the New was based on a revolution against the established, Rosenberg suggested that it was the engine of the twentieth-century fascination with self-transformation and political revolution as well as artistic style. "In such circumstances," he noted about the interconnectedness of culture, "criticism cannot divide itself into literary criticism, art criticism, social criticism, but must begin in establishing the terms of the conflict between the actual work or event and its illusory context."[102] Political revolution, and those who like the Stalinists had created a threat to humanity with its excesses, could not be separated from the Tradition of the New that created a revolution in the world of art. Friends and enemies had to be taken seriously in both realms, and had to pass the inspection of knowledgeable critics.

Although he claimed that "anything but art criticism" was "relevant" to Action painting, he did acknowledge a role for critics. Because the "painter has become an actor," the critic-spectator "has to think in a vocabulary of action" and has to join "the adventure of playing a part in events." Here again was Rosenberg's thirst for combining action and event in the critic's function. Even the radical component of artistic modernism arose from action rather than idea. For artists, he argued, "the *decision to be revolutionary* usually counts for very little. The most radical changes have come from personalities who were conservative and even conventional—a powerful recoil from the radical present threw them backwards, so to speak, into the future."[103]

Especially for those politically aware critics like himself, a major task of criticism was to distinguish in the world of art "the difference between a genuine uprising and a simulated uprising, that is, one fabricated according to the revolutionary 'craft' by professionals who deliberately design it to resemble a spontaneous upheaval." Not all revolutions were equally beneficial, so "to judge an event within the process of the revolution, you must first identify what is happening, in order to decide if at that moment you are hearing the voice of insurrection or the voice of the police." [104] In Rosenberg's opinion, at least in the 1940s and 1950s, both the Tradition of the New and Action Painting were revolutions that were a cause for optimism.

Some observers have proposed that Rosenberg was an early postmodernist. In this view, because he focused on the making of art rather than its finished product, and because he saw artistic "signs" as a result of human activity (which was close to Raymond Williams's definition of culture), he was a pioneer of postmodernism. Rosenberg, accordingly, was not interested in the historical origin of art but in deconstructing works (the central approach of postmodernism) to reveal their creative activity. The de-definition of art swept aside all canons, another representative activity of postmodernism. [105] Yet Rosenberg was never one to ignore the historical origin of anything, least of all art, and his passion for context puts him at odds with the postmodernist formalism of deconstruction and signs. Still, although he was hardly a postmodernist, Rosenberg, like Susan Sontag later, straddled the line between embracing interpretation and context, and rejecting them in favor of action and spontaneity.

Rosenberg was not a typical art critic. Whereas Clement Greenberg was a critic who judged art, evaluated the process of painting and the development of its styles, and measured its impact on the individual, Rosenberg was an intellectual who just happened to take painting as the lectern at which he would deliver his insights about changing cultural patterns. Rosenberg was always restlessly asking himself about relationships between painting and other corners in the culture. What was going on in politics that related to new styles in painting? What was happening in literature or in the intellectual community at large?

What might be called Rosenberg's "action criticism," combined with his caustic satire, made him prominent among the New York intellectuals, but also assured him of enemies. Nearly all members of the group had strained relations with at least a few others in the circle, as was natural in a collection of assertive and polemical critics. Feelings were hurt, jealousies generated, rivalries groomed. Rosenberg was no exception.

Already by the summer of 1938 Rosenberg was not getting along with Rahv and Phillips. The new *Partisan Review* barely had time to take its first breath before Rosenberg and its editors were at odds, and Macdonald tried to intervene so that Rosenberg would not be lost as a contributor. Macdonald wrote Rosenberg that he knew how he felt about Rahv and Phillips, and assured him that he felt "to a large extent" the same. Within "serious limitations," Macdonald confided to him, Rahv and Phillips were "extremely intelligent," and if one used "tact" and "patience" one could work with them. He did not want Rosenberg to leave the magazine's orbit because of "personal animosities," rather than ideas. "But perhaps I'm exaggerating the friction between you and the Rahv-Phillips camp anyway," Macdonald told him. "I hope so." He ended by encouraging Rosenberg to write for them: "Come on in, the water's fine!" [106]

Despite this friendly gesture, both Macdonald and Clement Greenberg eventually became Rosenberg's adversaries. Part of the reason was professional rivalry. Rosenberg and Greenberg were struggling for preeminence over each other as art critics, and, along with Macdonald, the three of them all wrote influential essays interpreting mass culture in America. The irony does not end there. As it turned out, Rosenberg and Macdonald for twenty-five years lived in the same four-story whitestone on East Tenth Street in the Village and rarely spoke to one another, "often barely grunting hello." To add to this, both found themselves working for the *New Yorker* as well—where Rosenberg was art critic and Macdonald wrote on culture. As Rosenberg's friend Seymour Krim pointed out with amusement, "O. Henry would have had a field day with a plot that began like this." [107]

Rosenberg had other opponents as well. Daniel Bell and Sidney Hook later claimed that Rosenberg, despite his role as a leading dissenter, was no radical. [108] Bell dismissed him as a person who was out to make statements and to impress others. Rosenberg and Hausknecht, according to Bell's account, were people who criticized things; they were flaneurs. Rosenberg was not totally serious, in Bell's view, whereas others such as Manes Sperber, Arthur Koestler, Ignazio Silone, and Nicola Chiaromonte were very serious and tried hard to capture the feelings of a generation that was moved by its involvement with the far left and agonized over breaking with it. [109]

Hook claimed that Rosenberg pretended to be a revolutionary but never took risks, and if he could skewer for being a revolutionary somebody who did take risks, he would do it. Rosenberg, Hook concluded, "was a shameless political opportunist." He found it ironic that Rosenberg "headed public relations for the Advertising Council of America celebrating the virtues of American business and at the same time was 'a closet revolutionist' or a 'parlor social nihilist' attacking everyone for selling out." [110]

Rosenberg, according to Hook, played both sides of the fence, but became known for a courageous radicalism he never demonstrated. "Rosenberg's remarks about people like Chambers and others who suffered as a result of telling their story," Hook wrote resentfully, "is shameless in the light of his work for the American Advertising Council glorifying America when we were being considered 'conformists.'" Hook thought himself a more courageous nonconformist, and was so disgusted by Rosenberg that he "rarely read what he wrote" and considered him a charlatan. "Neither I nor most of those who agreed with me," Hook reported, "regarded him as a politically active figure or a non-conformist in any open significant sense." He thought Rosenberg's work with the Advertising Council "made phrase-making natural to him" and "was celebratory rather than critical" of America. Why then, Hook wondered, was Rosenberg constantly cast as a heroic dissenting nonconformist?[111]

Hook was right that phrase-making was natural to Rosenberg, and that it might have been the result of his connection with the Advertising Council. There was something of the advertising perspective in his fascination with the catchy expression or proverb, and it also showed itself in his event-oriented art criticism and slogan-oriented criticism. Rosenberg did coin phrases in his work: "Action Painting," "orgmen," "herd of independent minds," "Orgamerican Phantasy," "couch liberalism," and "the Tradition of the New," to name only the most obvious. Whether his arresting sayings and the activity of his outlook rendered him less radical, however, is doubtful. His cleverness was not inconsistent with radicalism at all.

Yet one might question Rosenberg's radicalism on other grounds. In keeping with his advertising outlook, he once wrote that "American Life is a billboard; individual life in the U. S. includes something nameless that takes place in the weeds behind it."[112] But as intellectuals who were antagonistic to the common masses in politics and art, the New York group, Rosenberg included, never explored the weeds behind the billboard. If the billboard happened to be in a lower-middle-class neighborhood in Omaha, the weeds and life behind it would have been too common for the group, with not enough intellectual flavor to propel an essay. Besides, weeds had a rural flavor, and the group was connected to the city and hostile to the rural.[113] Rosenberg was radical, but, like the other affirmers and dissenters, he kept to intellectual matters and stayed out of the weeds.

Was Rosenberg less of a dissenter than Hook? It is true that Rosenberg, like many other dissenters, wrote lamentations about the postwar institutionalization of the intellectuals but partook of that trend himself.[114]

He was connected with the Advertising Council, the University of Chicago, and the *New Yorker.* Yet if we expect no institutional affiliations from our dissenters we will have no dissenters. It was self-defeating for Rosenberg to make the rejection of institutional affiliations the measure of one's intellectual function or radical intentions. As Hook saw, there were inconsistencies in Rosenberg's outlook. Still, that did not change the fact that Hook was an affirmer and Rosenberg was not.

Alongside his dissenting skepticism, Rosenberg's other notable feature was his humor. He had a great respect for humor, and he reminded his fellow social critics that "the oldest form of social study is comedy." Sociological studies needed the irony that arose from setting "whole cultures side by side," just the sort of irony that comedy provided. Irony was what ideologues lacked, and what Trilling and Niebuhr encouraged. Rosenberg regretted "the absence of comic perspective" in "moral reformers and utopians." When a writer is aware "that the joke is on him too," then he is a participant in his analysis, can unmask its disguises, and achieve some distance from the study as well. "What sociology needs," he concluded, "is to bring comedy into the foreground."[115]

Humor pierced almost all of Rosenberg's work. "He was, in part, a humorist," remembered Mary McCarthy, "and the ferocity of his look and voice had a hint of playfulness, as though he were casting himself jovially as King Herod in a pantomime ordering a massacre of innocents."[116] Those who knew this side of him saw a humorous and skeptical iconoclast, one whose humor was a shield against the dogmatism around him. In this sense, his humor not only sprang from his intellectual independence, it protected and defended it. Because humor was characterized by this undogmatic and independent individualism, it fit well with his belief that art's function was to keep open a space for individual values (the reason mass culture was so dangerous), which was the point of his celebrated essay "The Herd of Independent Minds."

Rosenberg, with Macdonald, was among the more independent of the New York intellectuals and was a model of their independent leftism. In the early 1970s he remained firm in his radicalism, although he no longer thought that the modernist Tradition of the New would serve as the road for radical change. "To champion new works because they are new," he wrote of the spent vanguard impulse, "is as orthodox an approach as to attack them for the same reason." The avant-garde had been purchased and domesticated by the bourgeoisie, and modernism was not as radical as it had been when he was younger.

"The cultural revolution of the past hundred years has petered out," he reported. "Only conservatives believe that subversion is still being carried on in the arts and that society is being shaken by it. Today's aesthetic vanguardism is being sponsored by the National Endowment for the Arts, by state arts councils, by museums, by industrial and banking associations." These organizations would not produce real radicalism, so politics was currently a more optimistic force for opposition than was culture. "Even what is begun with the best intentions turns out to be detrimental," he concluded; "—support of art by banks promotes bank-type art, and so on. So one is obliged to be opposed to society as a whole; one assumes a radical political stance, for cultural reasons." [117]

Rosenberg's restless mind embraced many areas of thought. He saw art as event, politics and discussion as event, and criticism as event—so that art criticism and political criticism were nearly the same thing, were active processes, and were similar to his outgoing declamatory style. Life and thought were partly a show, partly to be marketed—as Bell and Hook had complained of his radicalism. But all this made him attractive to readers and observers, and it gave him an influence that satisfied his "power-stir." Rosenberg's humor and dissenting outlook were never more apparent than in his evaluation of the literature of ex-Communist repentance in the 1940s and 1950s.

Confession as a Political Weapon

In the opinion of the dissenters in the New York group, the literature of ex-Communist confession and disillusionment seemed to go beyond threatening the independence of the intellectual. They felt that part of the harmful function of the ex-Communist lamentations was also to suppress the political left in America. Ex-radical penitence, they believed, had the function of enforcing conformity and undermining leftism at the same time. [118]

In the 1950s, both dissenters and affirmers hoped to discover a way to oppose ideology—in the name of pragmatism—without destroying the political left. Certainly those who still considered themselves leftists could not repudiate ideology as thoroughly as the centrists in the group, since a world without ideology seemed a world without promise of anything beyond the status quo. So the task for the left wing of the New York group was to carve out a respectable position somewhere between rejecting Communist ideological absolutism and accepting a conservative pragmatic world without any ideology whatever. For the dissenters, the years after World War II were a time of searching through the rubble of past political visions to identify what constituted good, as opposed to dangerous, ideology.

Leslie Fiedler's celebration of ex-Communist confessions, "Hiss, Chambers, and the Age of Innocence" (1950), was considered by the dissenters to be not only an endorsement of intellectual conformity but also an unveiled attack on the left and the idea of radicalism. In Fiedler's assessment, Chambers was a hero and Hiss a coward and a dangerous political fool. That interpretation, by itself, was not at odds with the outlook of anyone else in the New York group. Where Fiedler parted company with the dissenters was in his indictment of the liberal left in America for its "moral" complicity in Hiss's guilt. Fiedler barely had enough breath to list all the faults of the liberals, one of whose worst sins was their failure to appreciate the role of the ex-Communist penitents. "All the world distrusts a convert," Fiedler scolded, "but no part of it does so more heartily than the liberals." And the liberals, all of them, were living in a fantasy world. Hiss, Acheson, and Eleanor Roosevelt, like all liberals, shared a "lack of realism" that resulted from an outlook "in which liberals, conservatives (and even radicals) are assumed to share the same moral values." Those on the liberal left were simpletons who did not make the proper distinctions, which led them to conclude that "Communists are 'left,' and everyone knows that only the 'right' is bad." [119] The liberal left, according to Fiedler's account, ignored the mistakes of everyone left of center, which, in the case of the Communists, produced a dangerous travesty.

The dissenters might have been able to go even this far with Fiedler, as they had filed their own brief against the fellow-traveling part of the liberal community, whom they despised as dangerous and intellectually traitorous. But he was more imprecise than those liberals he accused of imprecision, since in condemning the liberal fellow travelers he expanded his attack, in his pirouetting enthusiasm, to the entire left of center. "In the end he failed all liberals," Fiedler charged Hiss, "all who had, in some sense and at some time, shared his illusions (and who that calls himself a liberal is exempt?)." This challenge—"and who that calls himself a liberal is exempt?"—infuriated Harold Rosenberg and prompted him to dust off his intellectual artillery and aim it at Fiedler. [120]

Fiedler was not finished. He challenged leftists one more time before ending his essay. "American liberalism has been reluctant to leave the garden of its illusion," he announced sadly, hat in hand, standing over the grave he had just dug for the left, "but it can dally no longer: the age of innocence is dead." Come, we must be men, all of us, shouldering our responsibility—part of which is a manly soul-clearing confession, on our knees, weeping only softly. "The confession in itself is nothing, but without the confession there can be no understanding, and . . . we will not be able to move forward from a liberalism of innocence to a liberalism of responsibility." [121]

Despite Fiedler's pose as the lone prophet uttering the painful truth to a deaf intellectual community, he was shrewd enough to have thrown his fortunes in with that majority of the New York group who were affirmers. He had so much company at his lonely lectern, in fact, that he had to shout to be heard above the others.

As a leading affirmer, Hook agreed with Fiedler about the beneficial effect of repentance, yet he was not eager to see the ex-Communist confessions do serious damage to the democratic left. Looking at the varied group of ex-Communists in America, Hook separated them into two camps: those like the New York intellectuals, who believed that Communism was bad but that the liberal left, on the whole, was good; and those like Chambers, who believed that because Communism was bad, everything to the left of center was also bad. [122]

Dissenters such as Rosenberg disagreed with Hook and insisted on making a finer distinction, finding three camps of ex-Communists instead of two. Rosenberg agreed with Hook about the Chambers school, but divided the New York group into two camps. There were those affirming centrist "ex-radicals" who did not agree with Chambers that everything left of center was to be despised equally, but who had departed from their former radicalism enough to wonder, amid the lamentations and confessions of the ex-Communists, whether much on the left was worth saving. And there were the dissenters who opposed the Communists but felt there was something in the radical tradition worth preserving—something that was being undermined by the anti-leftist confessions. Hook did not notice the split between affirmers and dissenters that Rosenberg detected on this issue, or else he chose not to comment on it. In Hook's eyes, the New York group carried on a unified fight against that party of ex-Communists who were mistaken.

Despite the admiration Hook felt for Chambers on many counts—courage, intelligence, refusal to remain a Communist—Hook charged him with being monumentally wrong. He found unpalatable Chambers's portrayal of the New Deal as "a social revolutionary movement," when in fact it was "an eclectic, unorganized, popular reaction to the intolerable evils of an unstabilized capitalism." The Communists infiltrated the New Deal not because New Dealers were operating a conspiracy, Hook believed, but because of the government's naïveté and "stupidity." Chambers, absolutist that he was, did not make distinctions. "He recklessly lumps Socialists, progressives, liberals and men of goodwill together with the Communists," Hook complained.

Worse, according to Hook, Chambers now rejected as leftists all those liberals who had long been fighting the anti-Communist battle Chambers currently was waging. This was the least excusable of Chambers's crimes, the least pardonable in the eyes of the New York group. Now Chambers wrote with horror about the piercing screams of the victims of Communism, but he was "silent about the fact that the truth about the Moscow trials to whose victims' screams he was originally deaf was first proclaimed by liberals and humanists like John Dewey"—those liberals Chambers now condemned in the same breath with the Communists. "While Chambers still worked for Stalin's underground, it was *they* who sought to arouse the world to the painful knowledge he is now frantically urging on it."

Chambers's memory was short, and his ingratitude large. Now he censured liberals for being man-centered and godless, conveniently forgetting that "in his hour of flight, need and political repentance, it was to the party of Man that he turned for aid first of all." Now Chambers stood sanctimoniously on the political right and criticized everyone to the left of center and everything more secular than Christianity. But, as Hook took pleasure in reminding Chambers, "One would have thought it obvious that Franco, Hitler and Mussolini, and other dictators with religious faith or support, have more in common with Stalin and the Politburo than either group has with the liberals and humanists Chambers condemns." [123]

Though Hook was an ally of the dissenters in their attempt to prevent the left from being demolished in the era of confessions, they viewed him with ambivalence. Like the rest of the *Commentary* majority, Hook was far closer to the *Dissent* faction than he was to Chambers, but the dissenters saw Hook as a friend in theory rather than in practice. The problem with Hook, for the dissenters, was that he defended the theoretical privilege or "right" of the radical left to exist, rather than joining them in an advocacy of a real leftist vision.

The most committed supporters of the left against the attacks of the ex-Communists were Irving Howe and Harold Rosenberg. Like Hook, Howe scorned Chambers's labeling of everyone to the left of center as Communist. "Socialists," in Chambers's story, Howe wrote angrily, "ultimately, were allies of Communism, even if, in mere fact, they perished resisting it; liberals were socialists in disguise, sapped by Marxism." Howe's anger was increased by the fact that the independent left had undergone repression from those like Chambers when Chambers was a Communist, yet that left was still undergoing repression from Chambers and his type now that Chambers had switched uniforms and was an ex-

Communist. The New York group had been damned twice by Chambers as he catapulted across the political spectrum. Chambers failed to realize that the anticommunist left was not Communist, and that it had long been carrying on Chambers's own current fight. "These delicate designations," Howe complained bitterly of Chambers's portrayal, "prompt one to remind Chambers that a good many 'left-wing intellectuals' of one or another feather—those who truly deserved to be called 'left' and 'intellectual'—fought a minority battle against Stalinism at a time when *both* he and Hiss were at the service of Messrs. Yagoda and Yezhov." [124]

Central to the defense of the left against the pressures of Chambers and his school of ex-Communism was an assessment of Stalin's role and responsibility in the course of Soviet Communism. If Stalin was not uniquely culpable, if Communism would have become totalitarian without him, then the entire project of the left was merely an exercise that inevitably led to oppression. If, however, Stalin was entirely to blame, if he derailed the Great Experiment, then the logic of the left was acquitted of furthering an entirely preordained totalitarian course. Chambers felt that liberalism, secularism, and the man-centered universe led to the New Deal welfare state, which in turn led to socialism, which was linked to Communism. The New Deal was a fatal first step. Dangerous leftism all started as liberalism and atheism, progressed to Marxism, and then proceeded unwaveringly to Leninism, Stalinism, purges, oppression, and totalitarianism. The New York intellectuals thought Chambers's vision of history was madness. Even the affirmers, most of whom had all but abandoned their former radicalism, thought Chambers's view of the left was fanatical.

There was obviously a great deal at stake (future politics, ideas, self-respect, influence, intellectual power) for those involved in the struggle over the correct interpretation of recent history—particularly about whether a predominance of leftism, liberalism, or conservatism had led to the totalitarianism of the previous decades. Murray Hausknecht felt that some ex-Communists and their supporters were trying, through their interpretation of liberalism and by their penitence, to remove the latitude and ambiguity in social values necessary not only for independent intellectuals to exist, but also for the left to remain viable. Many ex-Communists, according to Hausknecht, felt that "this ambiguity which seemingly gives a foothold to hostile ideologies must be eliminated." That, according to Hausknecht, was the function of Whittaker Chambers. [125]

Rosenberg agreed with Hausknecht and thought Fiedler as dangerous as Chambers to the liberal left. Why, he asked, was Fiedler's criticism launched in the name of liberalism? "I, too, believed that Hiss was guilty, but so had the jury, he was in jail; so why these profound evocations of his perfidy, and of Chambers' ordeal and triumph, by a 'liberal'?" As Robert Hatch had said of *The God That Failed*: "it is evidence in a trial that has long since ended." [126] The trials were already finished and the case closed before the penitents began their lamentations and hosannas.

Fiedler, Rosenberg concluded, had usurped the name *liberal* for himself, though he was a centrist conservative who opposed the left—in the same way that Communist fellow travelers had also misappropriated the term. Now Fiedler condemned all liberals to share "the guilt for Stalin's crimes through the fact alone of having held liberal or radical opinions, *even anti-Communist ones!* For Fiedler *all* liberals are contaminated by the past, if by nothing else than through having spoken the code language of intellectuals." Like Chambers, Fiedler failed to make crucial intellectual distinctions. But Rosenberg would not accept the guilt that Fiedler pushed his way. "To his question, 'Who is exempt?'" retorted Rosenberg, "I raise my right hand and reply that I never shared anything with Mr. Hiss, including automobiles or typewriters; certainly not illusions. . . . Here I insist that it was Chambers who shared things with Hiss, not 'all liberals.'" By lumping together everyone to the left of center with the Communists, as Chambers had done, Fiedler had committed "slander ex-Communist style." Had Hiss fallen to his knees and confessed for "all liberals," as Fiedler recommended, Rosenberg concluded that the judge should have tacked "an additional five years" to his sentence. [127]

In sum, Fiedler was wrong on three points, according to Rosenberg. First, liberalism was not responsible for the crimes of Communism, for one could find no way in which "a belief in freedom, equality, individuality" would lead anyone to support Communist oppression. Second, the liberal left was not to be equated with fellow-travelers, the latter of whom Rosenberg believed to be truly guilty. The fellow travelers were "scoundrels" who had failed to be "open-minded" and had not maintained the proper function of intellectuals. Third, and by far the most important, Fiedler neglected to credit the independent left, those anti-Stalinist intellectuals in the New York group and elsewhere, for their pivotal and successful fight against Communism during the previous two decades.

The reason that the anti-Stalinist New York intellectuals had been excluded from the story by Chambers, Fiedler, and others, Rosenberg charged, was that these latter detested the forces of independent radicalism more than anything else. Chambers's hatred derived from his absolutism. In Fiedler's case, who could tell? "Like their master in Moscow," Rosenberg wrote defiantly, "the Communist intellectuals in America detested above all, not capitalism nor even fascism, to both of which the switching Party line taught them to accommodate themselves—their one hatred which knew no amelioration was toward the independent radical." Just as the Soviet Stalinists had erased the anti-Stalinists from their official version of history, so in America, Rosenberg argued, the Stalinists (and, as in the case of Fiedler, some liberals) were attempting to excise the anti-Stalinist left. "To the antipathy officially demanded by the Party toward its foes on the Left, the sordid Leftish mass added its own spite toward the outsiders who undermined their revolutionary conceit." [128] So, according to Rosenberg, it was the New York group—the Trotskyists, the independent radicals—who were the most abhorrent to the Communists and ex-Communists alike.

All of this led Rosenberg to conclude that the ex-Communist confessions were useless, of no value whatever except to attack the left. All the ex-Communist confessions were unneeded, Rosenberg felt, because the anti-Stalinist New York group had already defeated Communism in America years before. In fact, "Communism in the United States had been rather decisively defeated as an intellectual current long before a single ex-Communist had voided his memory from the witness stand," Rosenberg wrote with pride. "The Communist who 'passed' into an Ex is himself, very often, the product of this criticism." [129] Chambers, in other words, was converted by the anti-Stalinist New York intellectuals, not by God, to ex-Communism.

Thus three themes dominated the New York intellectuals' responses to the canon of ex-Communist repentance literature. First, they worried about the faith and absolutism that they saw among the missionary ex-Communist confessors, and the prospect of that continued dogmatism fueled their anti-ideological outlook and reinforced their pragmatism. Second, they perceived in these confessions a threat from Communism and ex-Communism to the role of the intellectual, and it prompted them to split ranks on which of the threats was a greater danger. The affirmers thought the confessions were the best defense against the anti-intellectualism of Communism. The dissenters felt that the confessions themselves were an even more dangerous threat to intellectual independence. Third, the affirmers felt that the confessions represented the honesty and integrity necessary to keep the intellectual project healthy in America, while the dissenters thought the confessions had the potential to repress the latitude necessary for intellectual dissent, and to repress and undermine the already shaky foundation of the intellectual left in America. The dissenters suspected many of the affirmers of supporting the confessions in order to rid the country of the left that the affirmers had since abandoned.

Throughout their debates, one sees again that the New York group was more committed to intellectualism than politics, especially radical politics. Although the affirming majority was not particularly concerned about whether the confessions would be used as sticks to beat the political left, virtually all members of the group did care strongly about the effects of the repentance movement on the intellectual's function—even though they disagreed about those effects. As they had in their opposition to the Waldorf Conference, they gave their intellectual identities and values precedence over their political identities, especially over their old commitment to political radicalism.

The polemics over political ideology and absolutism in the decade after the war exposed raw and sensitive nerves. It had been painful for the New York intellectuals to fight excessive ideology, fellow traveling, and irresponsible leftism at the Waldorf Conference, although they did so with a grim enthusiasm. It had been difficult to live with the ongoing tensions between affirmers and dissenters over issues of political conformism, proper anticommunism, and appropriate levels of dissent against their own culture. It had been hard for them in the decade after the war to reexamine their own past in light of the new literature of repentance, and to continue to wage the battle against inflexibility and ideology.

In the bitter morning light at mid-century, the New York group became increasingly ready to turn its intelligence and energy away from the fatiguing political arena and toward new and less painful problems. They discovered that cultural issues would allow them to exercise their analytical intellectual function without having to focus on the discouraging aftermath of the recent European crises. The topic of cultural issues, particularly criticism of mass culture, was one on which most members of the group agreed—it united affirmers and dissenters more than almost any other issue. Cultural issues, in the painful gray dawn, were easier to face than political issues, and cultural criticism allowed members of the group to write about political concerns without really seeming to do so.

Sidney Hook and John Dewey in a photo taken by Hook's son in 1949. Hook wrote his doctoral dissertation under Dewey at Columbia University in the late 1920s, and in the 1930s and 1940s the two men joined to oppose totalitarianism and absolutism. Courtesy of Ernest B. Hook.

Freda Kirchwey and some of the editorial staff of the *Nation* in the mid-1940s. A constant antagonist of the New York intellectuals, who thought her too sympathetic to the Soviet Union, Kirchwey argued with Sidney Hook and Dwight Macdonald about their criticism of the Waldorf Conference. From the left: associate editor Keith Hutchison, managing editor J. King Gordon, drama critic Joseph Wood Krutch, editor and publisher Freda Kirchwey, associate editor Maxwell Stewart, and Washington editor I. F. Stone. Courtesy of the Schlesinger Library, Radcliffe College.

Harlow Shapley (third from right) in June 1945 as Harvard's representative at the 220th anniversary of the Academy of Sciences in Moscow. An adversary of the New York intellectuals during the Waldorf Conference, which he chaired, Shapley was a professor of astronomy at Harvard, director of the Harvard Observatory from 1921 to 1952, and president of the American Academy of Arts and Sciences from 1939 to 1944. Shapley was active in organizations on the political left, and many observers saw him as a man of peace who suggested cooperation in science and culture with the Soviet Union. The New York intellectuals, however, viewed Shapley as an irresponsible fellow traveler who unwittingly aided Stalinist totalitarianism. Courtesy of the Harvard University Archives.

At a gathering in 1947 are, from left to right, Bowden Broadwater (Mary Mc-
Carthy's husband at the time), Lionel Abel (standing), Elizabeth Hardwick (later
associated with the *New York Review of Books*), Miriam Chiaromonte, Nicola
Chiaromonte (an editor of the Italian *Tempo Presente*), Mary McCarthy, and
John Berryman; sitting in front are Dwight Macdonald and Kevin McCarthy
(Mary's brother). Courtesy of Vassar College Library.

At his office at the University of Chicago, sociologist David Riesman (right) with Reuel Denney in about 1950. An affiliate of the New York group, Riesman learned of Nathan Glazer's work by reading *Commentary* and then collaborated with Glazer and Denney on *The Lonely Crowd*, and with Glazer on *Faces in the Crowd*. Courtesy of David Riesman.

Sidney Hook (at microphone) addressing the opening meeting of the Congress for Cultural Freedom in Berlin in 1950, standing before the Berlin Philharmonic Orchestra. At the speakers' table are some of the European associates of the New York intellectuals: Ignazio Silone (fifth from the left), Arthur Koestler (third from the right, in a white shirt), and Melvin Lasky (far right). Courtesy of Ernest B. Hook.

In Austria in 1953, teaching at the Salzburg Seminar in American Studies, are Daniel Bell (far left) and Seymour Martin Lipset (next left) with students. Courtesy of Daniel Bell.

While in England on a graduate fellowship at Cambridge University in the early 1950s, Norman Podhoretz (right) visited Irving Kristol at the *Encounter* office. Courtesy of Daniel Bell.

French intellectual Raymond Aron (left), whose *The Opium of the Intellectuals* was an influential treatise against communist ideology. Courtesy of Daniel Bell.

Harold Rosenberg, critic of art and culture for the New York group's publications, and later for the *New Yorker*. Courtesy of the University of Chicago Press.

Murray Hausknecht in a photo taken by a friend in 1955. Hausknecht, a sociologist who became a contributing editor of *Dissent* in 1957, thought that the literature of ex-Communist repentance encouraged intellectual conformity and discouraged political radicalism. Courtesy of Murray Hausknecht.

Sidney Hook, with Seymour Martin Lipset behind him, at the Future of Freedom conference held by the Congress for Cultural Freedom in Milan in September 1955. It was at this conference that the phrase "end of ideology" began to gain prominence. Courtesy of Daniel Bell.

English poet Stephen Spender at the Milan conference. A contributor to *The God That Failed*, Spender was from 1953 to 1965 an editor of *Encounter*, a magazine published in London by the Congress for Cultural Freedom. Courtesy of Daniel Bell.

Kitty Galbraith and Arthur Schlesinger, Jr., at the Milan conference. Courtesy of Daniel Bell.

Melvin Lasky at the Milan conference. Lasky was an editor for the *New Leader* in the early 1940s, one of the founders of the Congress for Cultural Freedom, and an editor of *Encounter* from 1958 until the mid-1960s. Courtesy of Daniel Bell.

Hannah Arendt, leading theorist on the origins of totalitarianism, at the Milan conference. Courtesy of Daniel Bell.

In front of a Congress for Cultural Freedom bus at the Milan conference are Miriam Chiaromonte, Czeslaw Milosz, and Mary McCarthy. Courtesy of Daniel Bell.

Daniel Bell in Milan in 1955. Courtesy of Daniel Bell.

Seymour Martin Lipset and Will Herberg at Daniel Bell's summer house in New Hampshire in 1954. Courtesy of Daniel Bell.

Daniel Bell and Irving Kristol share an umbrella in Rome in the mid-1950s. In 1965 the two founded *The Public Interest*, which they co-edited. In 1969 a special issue of the magazine, devoted to an evaluation of student radicalism, was published as *Confrontation*. Courtesy of Daniel Bell.

Dennis Wrong, sociologist and contributor to *Dissent* and *Commentary*, at work in his office at Brown University in May 1957. Courtesy of Dennis Wrong.

Sidney Hook reading galleys at home in Brooklyn in
1958 or 1959. Courtesy of Ernest B. Hook.

Edward Shils at work at the Center for Advanced Study in the Behavioral Sciences at Stanford University, in 1958–59. Courtesy of Daniel Bell.

Daniel Bell and Edward Shils at the Center for Advanced Study in the Behavioral Sciences at Stanford University, in 1958–59. Courtesy of Daniel Bell.

Dennis Wrong in the early 1960s on Central Park West in New York. Courtesy of Dennis Wrong.

Dwight Macdonald (right) with Norman and Adele Mailer. Mailer addressed the Waldorf Conference, was on the editorial board of *Dissent* and contributed occasional articles, and marched with Macdonald and Robert Lowell on the Pentagon on October 21, 1967, a demonstration that became the subject of his *Armies of the Night*. One of the founders of the *Village Voice*, Mailer remained more sympathetic to the Beats and counterculture than did most other New York intellectuals. Courtesy of Gloria Macdonald.

Historian Richard Hofstadter was working in his Columbia University office in Hamilton Hall on April 23, 1968, when protesters filled the building and later occupied it. Hofstadter opposed the actions of the New Left on campuses in the 1960s. Dwight W. Webb, courtesy of Alfred A. Knopf, Inc.

Dwight Macdonald addressing a crowd of protesters in early 1970, probably at Hofstra University, where he was teaching for the year. Although Macdonald disapproved of some of the students' tactics, he was one of the New York intellectuals who supported the young radicals. Courtesy of Gloria Macdonald.

Dwight Macdonald in his studio in East Hampton, Long Island. Courtesy of Gloria Macdonald.

Literary and cultural critic Diana Trilling reviewed books for the *Nation* in the 1940s, was active in the American Committee for Cultural Freedom in the 1950s, and frequently contributed articles to *Commentary* and *Partisan Review*. Courtesy of Tom Victor and Harcourt, Brace, Jovanovich, Inc.

Sociologist Nathan Glazer in 1976 in his office at Harvard University. Glazer was a member of the editorial staff of *Commentary* from its founding in 1945 until 1954. He was teaching at the University of California at Berkeley during the height of the student protests, and in the 1960s he wrote essays critical of the excesses of student radicalism. Courtesy of the Harvard University News Office.

The member of the New York group most active on the intellectual left after World War II was literary critic Irving Howe. In addition to attending conferences, teaching at the City University of New York, and contributing to an array of periodicals, Howe helped found *Dissent* in 1954 and served as its most prominent editor. Courtesy of Irving Howe, *The American Newness* (Harvard University Press, 1986).

Midge Decter, executive director of the Committee for the Free World, an organization that in the 1980s took exception to viewpoints it considered excessively critical of America or insufficiently vigilant about the dangers of totalitarianism. Courtesy of Midge Decter.

Sidney Hook giving the Jefferson Lectures at the National Endowment for the Humanities in 1984. Courtesy of Ernest B. Hook.

Lewis Coser in his office at the
State University of New York at
Stony Brook in 1986. A sociologist
and one of the founders of *Dissent*, Coser was one of the New
York intellectuals who maintained
a radical outlook throughout his
career. Courtesy of Joan Powers.

At the Second Thoughts Conference in Washington, D.C., in 1987, disillusioned
former New Leftists expressed repentance, as some of the ex-radicals of the preceding generation had done in the decade after World War II. Several of the
New York intellectuals attended to encourage or monitor the metamorphosis. At
the dais are, from left to right: Irving Kristol, Nathan Glazer, Norman Podhoretz, Hilton Kramer, and William Phillips. Courtesy of Rich Lipski and the
Washington Post.

4   Mass Culture and the Intellectual

The discouragement of painful political and ideological choices in the Cold War of the 1940s and 1950s was partly responsible for the New York group's increasing enthusiasm for matters of culture rather than politics. Yet, as one would expect from a collection of social and cultural critics, they had already been deeply entangled in cultural issues throughout their careers. The central and most sustained of these issues was the problem of mass culture. Nearly all of them were hostile to it (although Sidney Hook and sociologists Edward Shils and David Riesman defended its right to exist), and their antagonism tapped their imaginations so deeply that their energies exploded in a burst of rhetoric that lasted for twenty years. The criticism of mass culture revealed their overall outlook so well because it struck close to the heart of their intellectual identities and their conception of their own mission and function.[1]

By what they alternately called *mass culture*, *popular culture*, or *kitsch*, the New York intellectuals meant television, radio, Hollywood movies, mass-market paperback books, most advertising, and other mass-produced goods and art. Nearly all the writers in the controversy took their turn defining mass culture. Art critic Clement Greenberg, who drew up the indictment in the group's heresy trial of kitsch, was representative of their outlook. Kitsch was "mechanical" and worked from "formulas." It was unreal, a "vicarious experience" that like a bored wife had to have "faked sensations."[2] It was also mass produced for profit.

The concept of "mass" had never been congenial to the group; after all, mass democracy had unnerved them. At best, in their early years in the 1930s, they had been willing to tolerate gingerly other socialists' enthusiasm for mass organizations, mass movements, mass meetings, mass protests, and mass uprisings. They had never, however, embraced the "massification" that impinged on their own intellectual roles: mass culture, mass taste, mass media, or mass opinion. The idea of "popular" was hardly better to them. From the beginning they couched their opposition in that strain of leftist thought that denounced as demagogic those who encouraged popular prejudices, or who allowed popular or populist outlooks to prevail over correct socialist values.[3]

What came to be known as *middlebrow culture* also was despised by the group. Middlebrow culture was a pretender to serious culture, and included magazines such as *Harper's* or the *New Yorker*, serious but inadequate television and movies, book clubs, and other mainstream culture for a general educated audience. High culture was serious art and thought, and included little magazines and journals, art films, avant-garde or particularly serious painting, and novelists and critics who did not cater to the public. Some critics have argued that the assault on the middlebrow was carried to the American literary canon, where previously canonized middlebrow and popular works were replaced by more complex "writers without audiences."[4]

Because middlebrow culture, like the *Atlantic*, for example, was often mistaken for high culture, the highbrows considered it much more subversive and detestable than unadulterated mass culture. Rather than being pleased at an intellectual "trickle-down" of their thoughts into the middlebrow media, many of the New York intellectuals resented seeing their ideas admired in the glossy magazines under someone else's better-paid byline. Middlebrow culture, according to Dwight Macdonald, was not mass culture made better, but high culture made worse. He identified "Midcult" as Norman Rockwell, the Revised Standard Version of the Bible, *Harper's*, the *Atlantic*, the *New Yorker*, the Book of the Month Club, *Readers' Digest*, and the Luce publications, among other insufficiently intellectual ventures.

Macdonald, however, did not stop with such obvious offenders. His investigation found surreptitious middlebrowism among the intellectuals themselves. "Academicism," he warned, was "Midcult's historical predecessor" because it too opposed the avant-garde; academicism, then, was really only "kitsch for the elite."[5] Even the literati must have feared for their reputations when they read Macdonald, who seemed able, like a congressional investigator, to sniff out heresy among the faithful, to uncover intellectual and artistic spinelessness and treason. Even the realms of high culture harbored their Alger Hisses.

Observers must have chuckled when Harold Rosenberg in turn found Macdonald himself to be sympathetic to mass culture and pointed out his guilt—showing that even those searching out heresy might yet be harboring a deadly thimbleful of treason. Not to be outdone, Daniel Bell later detected that Rosenberg was actually the one who had "undercut" the "highbrows" by introducing the overly democratic and insufficiently cerebral concept of "action painting."[6] The process need never stop.

Radical Romanticism and the Historical View

The most interesting aspects of the mass culture debate concerned the quality of past culture (the reality or myth of that quality) and whether ordinary individuals had the potential to evolve to a higher cultural level.

Many of those who criticized mass culture believed that the common person in America inherently had a high cultural potential and, if allowed to grow and evolve unimpeded, he would aspire to a higher level than mass culture. The New York group's early Marxism provided them with confidence in the potential of the population as a whole, whom they believed to be capable of nobility, virtue, and intelligence—unless otherwise kept down by an oppressive society. The reason that most people in America did not want high culture, their argument went, was that they had been taught to want mass culture; they had been trivialized and debased by advertisers, cultural profiteers, and artistic gruel until, in their lobotomized condition, their only choice was mass culture. "Before man can transcend himself he is being dehumanized," Bernard Rosenberg explained. "Before he can elevate his mind, it is being deadened."[7]

Allied to this outlook was a highbrow conviction that low culture in the past had possessed an integrity, a creativity, a genuineness of expression that contemporary mass culture could not match. Greenberg suggested that it was different before industrialism. "In societies below a certain level of economic development," he told his fellow intellectuals, "everybody works; and where this is so, work and culture tend to be fused into a single functional complex. Art, lore and religion then become barely distinguishable, in either intention or practice, from the techniques of production, healing and even war." Modern society began to separate these processes from each other, but, since under industrialism everyone must work, perhaps work could again unify life and culture.[8]

Between that storied and golden past and the cultural infirmity of the present stood the Industrial Revolution. Greenberg, Macdonald, and Bernard Rosenberg all blamed industrialization for having reduced a formerly proud folk culture to the squalid and demeaning mass culture of the twentieth century. Rosenberg reported that "modern technology is the necessary and sufficient cause of mass culture. Neither national character nor the economic arrangement nor the political system has any final bearing on this question. All that really matters is the most recent industrial revolution." [9]

Ironically, the New York intellectuals favored an artistic modernism that often employed the austere, functional, and technological aspects of industrialism in its architecture and design. Modernist painting also rejected the ornamentation that was part of earlier folk traditions. That is, modernists were antagonistic to kitsch partly because it romanticized the past.

The foregoing interpretation of the history of folk and mass culture put forth by the critics of kitsch was too unpalatable to be swallowed by the entire intellectual community. Edward Shils argued that it was simply an ideological stance in a political struggle among cultural critics. He believed the highbrows had created a historical myth of preindustrialism that was merely a convenient usable past to be employed toward the wrong ideological ends. It was the product of ostensible radicals in politics who were elitist modernists in culture. Shils also nurtured ideological goals, of course, but at least in the process of his argument he unmasked the objective pretensions of all those engaged in the debate.

The vehicle for Shils's attack was a review of Bernard Rosenberg and David Manning White's *Mass Culture: The Popular Arts in America* (1957). The highbrow position championed by those such as Macdonald, Howe, and Bernard Rosenberg, according to Shils, was really only a Marxist radicalism that in its frustration had turned romantic and utopian. Earlier in their careers these radicals thought the working classes could evolve into cultural intellectuals, but after World War II they found that workers were more eager to waste their time "in self-indulgent and foolish pleasures." The intellectuals had been jilted by the working class, and their "preoccupation with mass culture" was really "the obsessiveness of the disappointed lover." The radicals were venting their political frustrations in the cultural arena by employing a "romanticism dressed up in the language of sociology, psychoanalysis and existentialism." Their nostalgic picture of preindustrial life could be traced back "to the early writings of Marx and to German sociological romanticism." [10]

In fact, Shils continued, it was part of a larger romantic impulse that embraced such diverse viewpoints as Roman Catholic romanticism, the Southern Agrarians, and the French Monarchists. What bound the highbrow radicals to this larger orientation was "their dislike of urban society and of bourgeois individualism and hedonism. They were all ideologists, hostile to human beings as they are, and this they share with Marxism." [11]

Shils further accused the radical cultural critics in the group, Macdonald specifically, of having been indoctrinated by the romantic social theory of the Frankfurt School neo-Marxists—Leo Lowenthal, T. W. Adorno, Max Horkheimer, and others. Actually, the influence of the Frankfurt School on the New York group's cultural opinions was minor. In the late 1940s and 1950s the Frankfurt group wrote criticisms of mass culture using the same arguments that the New York group employed, and several of these essays were reprinted by Rosenberg and White in *Mass Culture*.[12] The New York intellectuals, however, had formed their views on mass culture before they read the Frankfurt neo-Marxists on the subject. "I admired the Horkheimer group's work and had some slight contact with them, but their influence was not major," Macdonald wrote in reply to Shils's allegation. He reminded Shils that "before even I had been exposed to Marxism, I was writing about topics like Hollywood and the popular press, and in much the same terms as I did later (as a Marxist of sorts) and as I would today (as a non-Marxist)."[13]

By Shils's account, their intellectual romanticism led the highbrows to construct faulty history. They portrayed the preindustrial peasantry and working classes as producing a strong and worthwhile folk culture, and the upper classes as producing a consistently admirable high culture. Shils disagreed. It was only "ignorance and prejudice, impelled by a passionate and permeative revulsion against their own age and their own society" that motivated the contemporary highbrows to assume that the preindustrial gentry read anything but "worthless" books. As he saw it, contemporary mass culture was "now less damaging to the lower classes than the dismal and harsh existence of earlier centuries had ever been." Where before there had been "bear-baiting, cock-fighting, drunkenness," and public hangings for cultural entertainment, there was currently at least television, inexpensive novels, and the music and art of mass culture.[14]

Finally, the romantic impulse, according to Shils, led the intellectuals to focus their hostility incorrectly on the Industrial Revolution, whose impact was far more beneficial to all classes of society than the high-culture camp would admit. As young adults, the highbrows had followed Marx's economic criticism of capitalist society, focusing as it did on the Industrial Revolution. But these same radicals, chastened in the intervening years and no longer following Marx's economic visions, now formulated their radical criticisms in the cultural arena instead—yet they still kept the Marxist centerpiece of the Industrial Revolution in their analysis.[15]

Although he did not enter the public debate, Alfred Kazin realized that he himself had been hostile to mass culture in precisely the way Shils described. "All that stuff about 'popular education,' army discussion groups, what the peepul are saying & doing," Kazin admitted in his journal, "—all that came from my typical ex-leftist intellectual's desire to do a post-mortem on the proletariat itself, by way of an annihilation of 'mass culture.'" Kazin thought "Shils was right" when he wrote "that the ex-Marxists adore the subject, 'mass culture,' because it gives them a chance to show that the people were wrong, not themselves." [16]

Those high-culture radicals whom Shils attacked were unwilling to let the issue rest. Macdonald (who, in his article in *Mass Culture*, had dissociated himself from both the conservatives and the "Marxian radicals" in the high-culture camp) eagerly responded to Shils on the matter of whether the Industrial Revolution actually had caused a cultural impoverishment. Macdonald believed that "mass culture is a phenomenon unique to the last two centuries," and concluded that Shils's essay was merely "a brisk, knowing and philistine defense of an untenable, though widely held, position on the subject." [17]

Lewis Coser in *Dissent* also wrote a spirited criticism of Shils's article. He portrayed Shils as one who "shares in that contempt for the multitude" that characterized the new postwar conservative impulse. Elitists such as Shils saw a large "gulf between the sodden masses and the cultured elite," so what difference did it make to them whether mass culture was improving or deteriorating?[18]

Besides, even if the highbrows were occasionally romantic, Coser asked, "does that in any way lessen the power of the criticism they make of the present?" If they looked with favor on the "vitality" of folk culture, that did not mean they thought it was possible to return to such a period. "All these elementary points are obscured in Professor Shils's anxious concern to defend the present cultural situation," he complained. Satisfied as he was with America and its culture, Shils "triumphantly assumed that the ideas he is analyzing can only have grown up on the compost of radical alienation." Coser lampooned Shils as "a kind of neo-Burkean conservative gentleman, a moderate, urbane, relaxed and cultivated commentator upon the fads and foibles of impassioned radicals and 'philanthropic liberals,'" an antagonist of the dissenters in both politics and culture.[19]

Some of the New York intellectuals, such as Bernard Rosenberg, stood by their criticism of mass culture for decades. Others became more interested in popular culture during the 1960s; Macdonald wrote for the "middlebrow" *New Yorker* beginning in the 1950s and for *Esquire* in the 1960s. Harold Rosenberg in the 1960s began to write for the *New Yorker* as well. Later Coser also softened and, like Kazin, felt that the attack on mass culture was the intellectuals' compensation for the lost working class, for the working class having failed them by not turning out as revolutionary and noble as the radical intellectuals had hoped.[20]

The critique of mass culture was argued from several angles. In Greenberg's rhetoric were remnants of Marxist philosophy that made his criticism sound like an opposition to false consciousness. Macdonald and Harold Rosenberg sometimes framed their hostility to mass culture as though their real target was the middlebrow patriotic Americanism of the Brooks-MacLeish thesis. Bernard Rosenberg and William Phillips condemned popular culture for having polluted both the American people and high culture. Among most of the New York intellectuals, all of these arguments combined in their animosity to mass culture.

The notion held by radical intellectuals that preindustrial culture was superior, and that the mass of common individuals if unimpeded by commercial mass culture would naturally evolve and ascend to the point where they would choose high culture themselves, was bound to fail and disappoint. This hope was too optimistic and utopian, not only about the American character, but about the cultural desires of people generally. Given a choice, many people prefer mass culture. "In fact," sociologist Herbert Gans pointed out in the mid-seventies, "the attempt of communist governments, especially in Eastern Europe, to discourage popular culture and to promote an official high culture have not been successful, and they have had to give in to the public demand for domestic versions of Western popular culture."[21]

It is no coincidence that the New York group in the 1950s began increasingly to admire Tocqueville while at the same time many of them became actively engaged in the criticism of mass culture. Tocqueville worried that democratic society would produce a mass within which individual freedom and independent thought would be oppressed. Like him, the New York group began to worry that a widespread cultural egalitarianism would destroy both human and intellectual qualities. As they sought to promote their definition of the proper intellectual they became increasingly aware that what was necessary for a happy society was also mandatory for the intellectuals' function: individual choice and freedom. The lesson that the highbrows told in the history of mass culture they constructed was that the preindustrial past had been a time when individuals could be creative and independently expressive. Industrial America, by contrast, was characterized by the destruction of the individual's critical and expressive capacities.

It mattered little whether pre-industrial culture was as rosy as the highbrows saw it or as bad as Shils thought. The real question was not the reality of the past, but rather the ways that intellectuals should think about culture. The important factor was not that one part of the group thought there was more individual choice, creativity, expressive freedom, and cultural integrity in the past, while another part thought there was more in the present. The consequential point was that both parts of the group agreed on the important values to argue about: that the values of individual choice, creativity, expressive freedom, and cultural integrity were essential to preserve and encourage in culture—especially in the wake of a period, such as the 1930s and 1940s, that had seen a severe threat to intellectual freedom from the ideological left and right. They identified these values as important components of their definition of an intellectual, as part of the arsenal needed to perform the proper function of a social and cultural critic.

The mass culture debate began in 1939 with Clement Greenberg's seminal article on kitsch, the first of his career. Perhaps an art critic was destined to be the first to sound the alarm against popular tastes.

Clement Greenberg

Like Harold Rosenberg, Clement Greenberg was an art critic whose interests ranged broadly into social and political areas. Although art criticism was his specialty, in the 1940s and 1950s he was an editor of *Partisan Review*, the *Contemporary Jewish Record*, and then *Commentary*. He was a participant in that generalist intellectual journalism that was so central to the New York group's conception of itself.

Born in 1909 in New York, Greenberg was a member of the group's first generation. His parents were Lithuanian Jews who had immigrated to the United States at the turn of the century and, like so many other parents of the New York intellectuals, they were socialists. When the young Greenberg was five years old his family moved from the Bronx to Norfolk, Virginia, where his father had a clothing store. Six years later, in 1920, the family returned to New York and his father worked in metal manufacturing.[22]

After graduating from Syracuse University in 1930, Greenberg worked in various capacities for the next decade. For a few years he lived at home in Brooklyn, studied languages and literature, and wrote poetry and short stories. Then he worked around the country in 1933 and 1934 for his father in the wholesale dry-goods business, a project he called "an abortive left-handed venture." Next he translated from German to English for Knight Publications. In 1936 he became a clerk at the U.S. Civil Service Commission, and in 1937 he started work at the U.S. Customs Service in New York (Department of Wines and Liquors), where he remained until 1942.[23]

Like Nathaniel Hawthorne, it was during his period at the Customs

Service that Greenberg began to write seriously. "Until then I had been making desultory efforts to write," he recalled, "but now I began in earnest, in my office-time leisure—of which I had plenty—and fairly soon I began to get printed." During this time he began hovering at the edge of the art scene in New York. As he remembered it, "the WPA art project and the Hofmann school" overlapped on Eighth Street in the Village in those years, and he was an "outsider" there trying to absorb as much as he could.[24]

Greenberg was a "precocious draftsman" who had drawn constantly from the age of four. At sixteen he had enrolled in life-drawing classes at the Art Students League. In 1938 and 1939 he was "just beginning to see abstract art," and he was impressed by four lectures given by Hans Hofmann, whom he considered to be a high-quality painter. During these final two years of the decade he began to draw from live models again, this time for free with Igor Pantukhov through the WPA at a location in Chelsea.[25]

In 1939 Greenberg sent a letter to the editor of *Partisan Review* for publication. When Macdonald read it he realized that it was too important to print as a letter; he sent it back to Greenberg and encouraged him to expand it into an article. Later that year it ran in the magazine as "Avant-Garde and Kitsch," the opening volley in *Partisan's* fusillade against mass culture. An article Greenberg published in the magazine the following winter he credited to the "inspiration" of Hans Hofmann.[26]

From 1940 to 1943 Greenberg was an editor for *Partisan Review*. William Phillips thought he had an "enormous confidence and will" and a "strong character." But although he had an "assertive personality," he also had "a polite, almost stammering manner" that was mistaken by some, such as Delmore Schwartz, for "pomposity." William Barrett considered it only a slow, deliberate style of speech among a crowd of fast talkers.[27]

During World War II Greenberg joined Macdonald in opposing the interventionist sympathies of the other *Partisan* editors. He left the magazine shortly after Macdonald in 1943. "It wasn't because of anything like a political disagreement that I left *PR*," Greenberg later reported. "It was because of my discomfort, not with my fellow-editors, but with the job." In 1944 he became the managing editor of the *Contemporary Jewish Record*, which folded that same year. When it began as *Commentary* in 1945 with a different focus, he returned as an editor.[28]

In the forties Greenberg continued to write art criticism for *Partisan Review* and the *Nation*. He felt that most people did not understand his writing, and he complained that no one in New York read or appreciated his criticism except his friends—who read it only because they liked him.

The *Nation*, he wrote to a friend, thought he was too complex for its readers.[29] Literature was one of his other interests, and he later pointed out that "when I began to write it was mainly on literature."[30] Although that overstates the case, in the 1940s he did mix his frequent reviews of art exhibitions for the *Nation* with occasional book reviews on several subjects. For various magazines he reviewed Ernst Cassirer's philosophical *Essay on Man*, Kenneth Burke's *The Philosophy of Literary Form*, a book on Rosa Luxemburg, and poetry by Bertolt Brecht, John Wheelwright, Marianne Moore, and Robinson Jeffers.

Naturally, his intellectually generalist orientation on culture was influenced by others in the New York group—such as Meyer Schapiro on art and Lionel Trilling on literature. Indeed their influence was clear enough in his outlook and writing that the person Greenberg replaced at the *Nation* referred to him rather uncharitably as "Lionel Schapiro."[31] A selection of representative essays, *Art and Culture* (1961), was later supplemented by the two-volume *Clement Greenberg: Collected Essays and Criticism* (1986).

Like Harold Rosenberg, Greenberg was an influential supporter of Abstract Expressionist painting. Both of these critics saw the artist, in the late thirties and forties, as a heroic individualist. Greenberg's view was derived from Leon Trotsky, who had written in *Partisan Review* in 1939 that "the struggle for revolutionary ideas in art must begin once again with the struggle for artistic *truth*, not in terms of any single school, but in terms of *the immutable faith of the artist in his own inner self*. Without this there is no art."[32] In the wake of the Communist Party domination of culture, against which Rahv and Phillips had earlier reacted by closing down the original *Partisan Review*, the New York group leaned strongly toward individual expression in art. Their modernism, in both literature and painting, subscribed to this individualism. The individual, with a proper socialist conscience, was the new revolutionary.

Greenberg and Rosenberg both invested the Abstract Expressionists with the revolutionary responsibility to oppose mass thinking and bring about the socialist revolution through individualistic art. Greenberg's "Avant-Garde and Kitsch" explicitly argued that an individualistic art had to be the future of a successful culture. Rosenberg's "The Herd of Independent Minds" later made the same point. But the stress on an art without social or "party" baggage meant a slow and surreptitious return to the ideal of "art for art's sake" of the Dadaists and the Lost Generation. It suggested that art could not safely depict anything except itself. Ironically, the individualistic political responsibility Greenberg and Rosenberg placed on the Abstract Expressionists was to result in the depoliticizing of the medium.[33]

Greenberg's individualistic modernism, of course, was tied closely to the geometry and utility of industrialism and technology. His career has been described as a movement from radicalism, from leftist party-art, to a position of Marxist technological determinism and modernist vanguard elitism. His movement from radicalism to modernism, according to this view, was an attempt "to reconcile art with industrial society."[34] Greenberg began to see the critic's relationship to the artist in the sort of industrial terms that usually apply between an administrator and a worker. A painter was to paint whatever he was told was needed, and Greenberg and his fellow critics, wearing the managerial gowns of the new urban industrial society, were now the "aesthetic engineers" who gave those orders. The painter-proles were to paint sensations and textures, and Greenberg and the managerial class of critics would provide the meanings and interpretations for the final products before they were shipped from the loading dock to the public. As this view has it, Greenberg's work undermined both radical art and a radically nontechnological society.

Yet his advocacy of modern art and urban industrial society hardly seems so subversive of radicalism—since most radicals of his generation were just as sympathetic to modernism and technology. Further, his provision of a meaning and codification for art should not be taken as evidence of his support for capitalism or the status quo, but rather should be seen as his badge as an intellectual. Greenberg, like others in the New York group in the age of criticism, found it was his function as an intellectual to provide meaning and interpret culture.

According to Daniel Bell, on cultural topics there was a split in the group between those literary critics such as Trilling, Kazin, and Howe who stressed moral and political contexts and ideas, and those art critics such as Greenberg, Rosenberg, and Meyer Schapiro who were formalists and did not emphasize social contexts.[35] It is true that the technological modernist sympathies of Greenberg were somewhat formalistic, yet the art critics, Rosenberg especially, had strong moral, political and social components to their writing. As for the literary critics, they too were prominent supporters of cultural modernism, and the authors they embraced—Joyce, Eliot, James, and others—were close enough to the canon endorsed by such formalist intellectuals as the New Critics that the latter often appeared in *Partisan Review*. The modernist writers that Howe respected were scarcely less formalistic than the painters admired by Greenberg, Rosenberg, and Schapiro.

As an art critic, Greenberg encouraged Jackson Pollock and others in their abstraction and helped interpret them to America. His appreciation for art had both a theoretical and a nontheoretical side. He demonstrated an appreciation for an intuitive response to art, and as early as 1943 had drawn a parallel to Kant's respect for the intuitive. Although this was at odds with the group's rationalist and antiromantic impulse, some members of the group were tempted by the intuitive. (Bell also claimed to be a Kantian rather than an empiricist.) But Greenberg downplayed the theoretical. He wrote that he did not follow a prescription to art, and that his "only criterion, ultimately," was whether "I enjoy it enough." That was why he liked Pollock. If he enjoyed Pollock "more than any other contemporary American painter," it was "because Pollock seems to me to paint better than his contemporaries." [36]

The direct apprehension of a painting was a crucial experience for Greenberg. William Barrett thought of him as an art critic who, unlike Rosenberg or Schapiro, "could be stopped in his tracks by the sheer visual impact of a painting, and let it work on him in silence." Comprehension rested in the act of viewing, not in analytic reviewing. "Doesn't one find so many times," Greenberg asked, "that the 'full meaning' of a picture— i.e., its aesthetic fact—is, at any given visit to it, most fully revealed at the first fresh glance? And that this 'meaning' fades progressively as continued examination destroys the unity of impression?" [37]

When Rosenberg entered the field of art criticism he was a flashier writer and thinker than Greenberg, coining the term "Action Painting" for the new style and championing Willem de Kooning rather than Pollock. The longstanding professional rivalry between the two, however, dated back to Greenberg's tenure as an editor at *Partisan Review* in 1942. At the time both were writing poetry and both were actively interested in poetry and art. Greenberg had written an introduction to a collection of poems in the magazine, and Rosenberg wrote a letter to the editor criticizing his handling of the project. Greenberg wrote a terse reply: "Mr. Rosenberg seems to read my stuff rather closely." [38]

In 1954 Greenberg returned the favor. James Laughlin wrote asking whether he thought *Perspectives* should run an article by Rosenberg on the new painting. Greenberg blanched. No, the Rosenberg essay would not suffice, he wrote in reply. Why would Laughlin want to print a piece on the new art by someone whose ignorance of it had made him antagonistic to it? The problem, he explained to Laughlin, was that Rosenberg's "The American Action Painters" was not an attack on the new art, which could always be sustained, but a destructive misunderstanding. It allowed the audience to assuage their anxiety about not understanding the new art by saying that it was action instead of painting, and therefore not a matter for rational understanding. Greenberg denied that his comments on Rosenberg's piece were the result of competition with him, although he admitted he felt competitive. He claimed he would have been jealous if Rosenberg's essay had been more intelligent and perceptive. [39]

Greenberg was also known by his friends as an art critic who could use his fists as well as his mind. He had a falling out with Macdonald in the 1940s, for example, because Greenberg had slugged Lionel Abel. Decades later Greenberg still felt "remorse about the Abel incident." [40] On another occasion he walked up to Willem de Kooning in Dillon's and asked him, "Why do you tell people that I got my ideas from you?" Seated at the bar, de Kooning realized Greenberg was going to punch him, so he beat him to it and slugged Greenberg in the face. The two were separated. Greenberg later said the story about his fight with de Kooning, told by Lionel Abel, was inaccurate, but maintained that it was "too sordid to bear retelling." [41] Greenberg had the good sense never to swing at Rosenberg, who stood taller and was heavier than he. After an argument about art with Rosenberg, Greenberg is alleged to have promised, "I'm not going to tangle with that guy, he's too big." Although some of the New York group disliked Greenberg's behavior, Hannah Arendt defended him like a "mother hen," and claimed that he showed a sense of moral honor that intellectuals often ignored. [42]

In 1948, in keeping with the ideological changes in the group after the war, Greenberg was calling himself an "ex- or disabused Marxist." By the early 1950s, since the Abstract Expressionist painters had not created the revolution that Greenberg assigned them fifteen years earlier, he faced a decision. He could renounce the painters since they had failed in their important cultural mission, or he could support the painters and instead repudiate the revolution he had so desired. Less radical now, he shrugged and chose to let his revolutionary ideals fade. He remained at *Commentary* until 1957, and there he helped younger members of the group such as Irving Howe get published in the magazine. Like the rest of its staff of affirmers, he stopped fighting the mainstream. [43]

When Norman Podhoretz first began to work for *Commentary* in the middle 1950s, Greenberg was still as critical of mass culture as he had been in 1939 when he wrote "Avant-Garde and Kitsch." At the magazine's offices on West Thirty-third Street between Fifth and Sixth Avenues, right off Herald Square, Greenberg, Nathan Glazer, and Robert Warshow sat near each other in cubicles. [44] When Podhoretz first met Greenberg, he was shocked to hear the famous art critic "contemptuously" refer to *Commentary* "as a middlebrow magazine." Podhoretz did not understand; the magazine was highbrow in his own estimation. As time passed, however, he felt that what Greenberg meant was that its head editor, Elliot Cohen, believed in "popularization at a very high level." *Commentary* had a slightly wider audience than the inbred readership of *Partisan Review*. [45]

After almost two decades as an editor, first of *Partisan Review* and then

Commentary, Greenberg, in addition to being a critic of painting, maintained his active interest in the criticism of mass culture. The evidence of his continued hostility to popular taste was his disparagement of his own magazine for wandering into the shame of middlebrowism.

Antiromantic and Antitotalitarian

The New York group rejected romanticism as strongly as they opposed absolutism, and in their opinion the two evils were interconnected. This antiromantic strain surfaced clearly in their antagonism to mass culture. Greenberg, for example, discerned precisely the date when the long slide down the hill of culture into degeneration had begun. It was the English Romantic poets, their gaze fixed on the clouds rather than on the trail ahead of them, whose feet had slipped on the rocky path leading toward the summit of culture, and whose slide, like Adam's, had taken the rest of humanity with them. "Indeed," he reported, "the Romantics can be considered the original sinners whose guilt kitsch inherited. They showed kitsch how." [46]

It was no accident that Greenberg chose to accuse a collection of romantic and intuitive writers of causing the fall, for as the group saw it, mass culture could be absolutist like communism, ideology, or faith: it was so all-pervasive that people failed to realize they were encompassed by it. Therefore it offered no real alternatives, no genuine escape, and forever undermined the possibility of free choice in culture—as communism ruled out the possibility of democratic free choice in the future.

The *Partisan Review* editors explicitly tied the issue of mass culture to their opposition to the Soviet Union in the magazine's preface to the "Our Country and Our Culture" symposium in 1952. The editors quoted Ortega y Gasset's criticism of mass culture with an undisguised admiration but could not fully embrace it because, so long as Soviet totalitarianism threatened intellectuals and others in the world, some democracy—in this case even the cultural democracy represented by letting the common people choose their own aesthetic sustenance—had to be tolerated as a barrier to that Communist threat. [47]

The antitotalitarian ideals that permeated the group's criticism of mass culture were more than mere anticommunism. The group also shared Tocqueville's fear that an undifferentiated mass of individuals, fueled by an overly enthusiastic democratic or egalitarian impulse, would create a soft, faceless, benignly suffocating totalitarianism. Bernard Rosenberg, who bridled at the "implication that you are undemocratic if you criticize mass culture," worried "that we may establish totalitarianism in the

United States without concentration camps through the use of mass media, which are perfectly neutral in themselves." He admitted that little could be done to counter totalitarianism and mass culture other than to study them. That course of action might be futile, but, Rosenberg asked in a memorable phrase, "would any man who cherishes his sanity withdraw from the battle against kitsch and Khrushchev for that reason?"[48]

In the struggle against kitsch and Khrushchev, against mass culture and communism, the affirmers and the dissenters were bound together by their shared commitment to intellectual values. Antitotalitarianism was essential to protect the intellectual vocation in the postwar world. Though he was only a marginal associate of the New York group, Edward Shils shared their concern about the function of the intellectual in a free society.

Edward Shils

Even at the tender age of five, Edward Shils was slightly more conservative than those around him. One autumn evening in Philadelphia in 1916, the young Shils took a piece of chalk and at the corner of Oxford and Twelfth wrote "Vote for Wilson." Already he provoked others with his opinions. "For this," Shils recalled, "I received a blow from my slightly older brother who, with my father, was a partisan of Debs in that election."[49]

Shils was born in 1911 and, like fellow sociologist David Riesman, was raised in Philadelphia. Although he was not a central member of the group, like some of their European associates he occasionally was associated with one of the group's organizations or conferences and wrote for their publications (especially *Commentary*) on subjects such as anticommunism, mass culture, ideology, the breakdown of tradition and authority, the New Left, and the function of intellectuals.[50]

Although he never embraced the label himself, Shils was often thought of as a "structural functionalist" sociologist who followed in the line of Talcott Parsons, with whom he collaborated.[51] The functionalists believed that social cohesion was achieved by common values cementing society together. Those norms and values defined society and united various elements into a community that shared common goals and principles. This outlook can be thought of as a "consensus" view of society, stressing the values that unite it—in contrast to a "conflict" approach.[52]

The rest of the sociologists in or around the New York group—Bell, Coser, Glazer, Bernard Rosenberg, Murray Hausknecht, Seymour Martin Lipset, Dennis Wrong, and David Riesman—were more distant than Shils from Parsonian structural functionalism. Almost all these sociologists earned their doctorates at Columbia and studied under Robert Merton, and, although Merton advocated functional analysis, he rejected the Parsonian assumption of social cohesion based on shared values that was the basis for the more all-inclusive theory of structural functionalism. Especially the dissenters who were sociologists—Coser, Bernard Rosenberg, Hausknecht, and Wrong—owed more to concepts of conflict derived from Marx, Weber, and, especially in Coser's case, Simmel than to any version of functionalism or Parsons.

Although Shils was more of a structural functionalist than others in the group, and was sometimes labeled a "consensus sociologist" by more radical sociologists, his social theory combined both the consensus and conflict outlooks. The central image that reflected his dual view was his proposition that societies contain a center and a periphery. The center is that ruling or dominant portion of society that exercises cultural and political authority or power, and the periphery is that remaining part of society that is culturally and politically subordinate. Shils saw both consensus and conflict at play in the interchange between center and periphery. There is a consensus on values, usually articulated and enforced by the center, but agreed upon by the periphery partly because all persons want a well-defined and understandable society. But there is also conflict between the center and the periphery, largely due to competing self-interests.[53] He outlined this view in *Center and Periphery* (1975), which also includes essays on the values that bind society: the personal, the sacred, civility, ritual and crisis, and tradition.

According to some accounts, this picture of an ordered society was constructed to show that ideology was unnecessary, and that both agreement and disagreement existed in balance in the relations between various sectors of a population. But like the rest of the group, Shils, while opposing ideology, remained politically engaged and ideological himself. His *Torment of Secrecy: The Background and Consequences of American Security Policy* (1956), a response to McCarthyism at home and hostility to intellectual freedom abroad, was not free from political subjectivity. Some of his critics argued that he had "always been overtly, and often aggressively, politically committed" as "a high-level ideologist . . . of 'pluralism' and 'civility,' and the rest of the liberal, Cold War package of the fifties and early sixties."[54] That sense of political engagement in his cultural studies, of course, was part of the common ground Shils shared with the New York group. His frequent essays on intellectuals, ideology, mass society, and civility were published as *The Intellectuals and the Powers* (1972).

Like the New York intellectuals, Shils at times worked as an intellectual generalist. In *The Constitution of Society* (1982) he mentioned his own examination of literary history, "of how literary men gained their livelihood and of the attitude of literary men of the eighteenth and nineteenth centuries towards their own society and towards reforming and revolutionary movements." [55]

Nonetheless, Shils was at each step in his career more conservative than the rest of the group. He "always disliked the sickly watery socialistically inclined liberalism of the *Nation* and the *New Republic* of the late 20's and 30's." He objected from the first to the outlook that the Soviet Union was always right and the United States always wrong, and "saw through fellow-traveling from the beginning in the 30's." Although he claimed "some sympathy with social democrats," they were acceptable only so long as they were ignorant workmen unable to discern the truth for themselves. "I thought it much less admirable for educated persons," he admitted, "who should have known better, to espouse those views." In the 1930s he was "marginally amicable with a number of Trotskyites" because of their anti-Stalinism and their intelligence and taste in matters of culture, in addition to their being "a lively and warm-hearted lot." Already in the 1930s Shils was suspicious of the gemeinschaft criticism of contemporary society, and the view that society had to be bound by an ideology. He was also convinced from this point on that revolutionary thinkers of the left and the right used different "formal properties" of thought from "moderate, liberal, and conservative intellectuals." [56]

Shils knew some of the New York intellectuals before the war and met others throughout the 1940s. Lionel Abel remembered walking with Shils in April 1940 in Chicago at the "outset" of Shils's career. They walked up and down the Midway, "arguing about the war," in agreement that the Trotskyist political line of nonintervention was "ridiculous," wondering together whether there was any way to stop Hitler without American involvement. After the war, Daniel Bell from 1945 to 1948 joined Shils and Riesman at the University of Chicago and together they, along with several others, taught a social science course. [57] When Bell left in 1948 he was replaced by Lewis Coser, and later Harold Rosenberg joined Shils as a member of the Committee on Social Thought. So through the University of Chicago Shils came into a working relationship with several members of the group, and in the fifties he was associated with additional members in the Congress for Cultural Freedom.

In the decade after the war Shils began to be much more interested in studying the function and outlook of the intellectual, and in the summer of 1949 he began teaching and writing about intellectuals. Ideology was not such an important attachment to society, he decided, that it could not be replaced by what he called "civility," that is, "a relatively unintense attachment to society as a whole" which "did not demand a monopoly of the individual's loyalty or of his capacity for attachments." Shils wanted less passionate and less ideological social attachments, and he became identified with the end-of-ideology movement. He thought the criticism of mass society in the 1950s "rather odious" because it came from "snobbish radicals, some of them with aristocratic pretensions mixed with a hypocritical egalitarianism of Marxist inspiration." The radicalism of those critics bothered him more than their aristocratic pretensions, which he never found reason to criticize in T. S. Eliot or others. Shils thought that C. Wright Mills and other postwar radicals were fooling themselves that intellectuals were powerless—Mills's experience in leading disaffected youth disproved that.[58]

At the Congress for Cultural Freedom in Berlin in 1960, Shils argued publicly with William Phillips. As Phillips recalled the event, Shils gave a speech supporting mass culture. When Phillips got up to contradict his position, "Shils kept interrupting me to point out my errors, until I finally asked whether he was going to let me talk, to which he said no." Phillips was outraged. "I pompously announced I was walking out of the meeting and would call a press conference to publicize not being able to speak." His brief walkout was joined by Mary McCarthy and Robert Oppenheimer, but before long all of them were lured back into the conference.[59]

The radicals had characterized him as "reactionary," Shils noted, ever since the period of McCarthyism in the early 1950s. Of the sixties he confided to his readers, "I abominated the 'black power' fantasy and the 'student revolution' and most of the radical manifestations of the decade which followed the Free Speech Movement. I found the patronage of revolution by *Esquire* and the *New York Review of Books* ridiculous." Although, as Daniel Bell wrote, Shils believed that the intellectual was the moral guardian of society whose function was to "maintain the continuity of tradition" and to remain "above political battle," Shils's hostility to radical blacks and students contradicted that Olympian neutrality. Shils saw himself as a liberal of the Chicago school (Frank Knight, Milton Friedman), although one may question the usefulness of calling classical liberals "liberal" in the mid-twentieth century. His dean at Peterhouse, Cambridge, introduced him once as "the only Tory sociologist in the world," a term that Shils conceded might well fit him.[60]

In his Tory (rather than liberal) conservatism and his wish to remain neutral in political battles, Shils diverged from the brand of liberal conservatism that the New York intellectuals slowly developed in the postwar period. But in a statement that could serve for the New York group as a whole, Shils maintained that his politics were determined by his intellectual pursuits rather than vice versa. "My preferences for certain political arrangements," he concluded, "did not lead to my sociological views; up to a point it has been the other way around." [61]

Cultural Pluralism or Elitism?

The New York intellectuals' criticism of mass culture underlined the tensions between the intellectual's task of maintaining standards and the liberal left's desire to encourage a healthy cultural diversity. It raised intriguing questions. Could intellectuals endorse aesthetic populism, or were they by definition elitists? Could an intellectual be a political democrat without being a cultural democrat?

Macdonald was representative of the group's high-culture elitism. He lamented the fact that although at one time folk art was the province of "the common people" and high culture was the domain of "the aristocracy," the blurring of the social order, beneficial politically, "has had unfortunate results culturally." It was a shame, thought Macdonald, that whereas formerly high culture could "address itself only to the *cognoscenti,* now it must take the *ignoscenti* into account even when it turns its back on them." He hoped for the development of "a clearly defined cultural elite here" so that the masses could settle into their kitsch and "the classes" could relax with their high culture. [62]

The elitism in their outlook was not a socioeconomic sort dependent on upper-class privileges, of course, but rather an intellectual elitism—a Jeffersonian aristocracy of talent, ability, intelligence, and critical acuity. They were worried about maintaining the intellectual vocation and its values. Further, they were the elite as the vanguard, the principled, minority, avant-garde intellectual cadre—as well as elite in the sense of being the elect or chosen. [63] But all these types of elitism had some connection: they were ways of conserving power for one group, and they resulted in a patronizing condescension toward the lower orders of society.

Hook later charged that the group did not have the courage to admit its elitism at the time, but he felt that in retrospect it was obvious. Although less elitist than the others, Hook felt a similar animus against popularizing science, and he believed that standards had to be maintained within disciplines, a view he attributed to Jefferson and Dewey. [64]

Although all of the group professed to support cultural and aesthetic pluralism, only a few such as Hook and Riesman were willing to support the implications. Aesthetic pluralism can be thought of as a system that allows various blocks of the population to have their own cultural standards, a sort of free-market democracy of choice.[65] Here each person would develop and follow his or her own aesthetic taste, and in effect it would allow the common person to be the arbiter of cultural good and bad. The result would be a culture in which the majority ruled and the community average dominated. To most of the New York intellectuals, however, this prospect produced a vision of a crowd of the uncultured putting its dirty hands on the intelligentsia's work.

An interesting challenge to the idea of aesthetic pluralism was launched by William Phillips, who thought the concept in this context was fraudulent. "It seems to me," Phillips suggested, "the notion of pluralism in culture is highly questionable." Of course if one only meant by it that "people have a legal right to their opinions," then nobody would challenge this first amendment right. But Phillips said that the concept implied more. It conjured memories for him of students of his who had proposed that if Germans had wanted fascism and the Russians wanted Communism, they should have it. Yet even if the German or Russian people wanted precisely that, Phillips pointed out, those like Hook would still be opposed to their right to have it. How could someone such as Hook, Phillips wanted to know, pretend that he could support cultural pluralism when in fact his value system made that support impossible? "It seems to me," Phillips concluded, "that the whole question of pluralism is basically a cloak to conceal our values."[66]

Phillips's argument implied that since we fight for what we believe anyway, pluralism is only a convenient ruse that allows us to feel better about our intentions. It allows us to avoid asking ourselves the necessary questions. Could one be a pluralist and yet fight for what one believed? Could one be a pluralist such as Hook claimed to be and yet oppose the right of nations to choose totalitarianism? That is, could one still be a pluralist if one opposed the results of a pluralistic decision-making process? Hook felt he resolved this political contradiction by arguing that since pluralism is a structural process, then in order to maintain a pluralist outlook one could allow decisions or outcomes of any type except those that prevent pluralism itself from being a continuing option. But, Hook believed, contrary to what the New York group feared, the existence of mass culture did not prevent continuing options in the cultural realm and therefore should not have been opposed by real pluralists who cared about diversity.

Faced with a contradiction between their ostensibly democratic political orientation and their undemocratic views of the proper cultural order, some members of the group felt uneasy. Of course none of them would have seriously argued with the *right* of mass culture to exist. Like Stalinists, proponents of mass culture had a formal right to speak their opinions freely, but responsible intellectuals also had a duty to combat those pernicious ideas. The group had a history of allowing people to say or choose what they wanted (within limits, as Hook believed), but then subjecting those people to tough intellectual criticism for the incorrect choices they made. Was that so repressive? What was an intellectual's responsibility if not to serve as a critic? The group did not envision censoring mass culture out of existence, but rather wanted to attack it with their criticism and dominate it with the force of high culture until it was powerless.

Further evidence of Hook's disagreement with the others about the intellectual's responsibility to culture surfaced at a late 1950s *Daedalus* conference on the subject in the Poconos that many of them attended. There some members of the group worried that mass culture would fatally undermine serious culture. Few of them would have contradicted sociologist Ernest van den Haag when he suggested that television productions of the Grimms' tales would divert interest from the superior written originals. But Hook wondered why. Yes, the written tales were better, Hook admitted, but if one were interested in Grimm why would a poor television version deter a person from reading the book? The same with Shakespeare on television: why would it lessen our interest in the plays? "After all, a good deal of popular science is just superstition. But would anyone say that the dissemination of popular science today has undermined work in pure science?" [67]

Hook was the only central member of the New York intellectuals to speak in defense of mass culture, although Shils and Riesman, both associates of the group, also did. The conservative Shils defended mass culture because he thought the lower orders ought to have what they wanted, and he also thought that those in the group who criticized mass culture were merely exercising a romantic radicalism that he personally opposed. Riesman's reasons for defending mass culture were more similar to Hook's. The liberal Riesman argued in *Partisan Review* that mass culture was actually much more diverse and lively than intellectuals had the courage to admit. [68]

Neither Hook nor Riesman praised the qualities of mass culture, but both defended the freedom of fellow citizens to choose it. At the Poconos conference Hook raised the issue of cultural democracy and its relation to the criticism of mass culture. "I confess that as a democrat I have no desire to impose my judgments of values and my taste upon other people in the community," he told his fellow participants, "and I certainly would resent it if they tried to impose their tastes and value judgments upon me."[69]

It seems paradoxical that Hook, the most intransigent of the group on matters of anticommunism, was its most flexible on cultural matters. How was it that he had no desire to impose his cultural values on the community but did not hesitate to impose his political values on others? Actually, he was more consistent than he appears. In both the political and cultural spheres Hook was committed to the principles of pluralism, diversity, free choice, and self-determination. His strident anticommunism sought to protect pluralism in the political arena, despite the fact that in the execution of his anticommunist impulse he often bordered on an absolutist orientation. In the cultural realm Hook defended the pluralist principle by arguing that more than one cultural taste-level had a right to exist.

The quandary for the rest of the New York intellectuals was that they believed in diversity and pluralism and wanted the cultural freedom that pluralism produced, yet they wanted to institute high culture as well. As we have seen, one of their strongest reasons for opposing mass culture was that its all-encompassing soft totalitarianism defeated pluralism—yet they failed to acknowledge that a unilateral imposition of high culture would also destroy cultural pluralism. Obviously, in making these trade-offs members of the group had to decide individually how they would define cultural repression. High culture can repress pluralism by unifying culture vertically; mass culture can repress pluralism by unifying culture horizontally. Hook and Riesman objected more to the vertical repression accompanying high culture, and most of the others feared the horizontal repression accompanying mass culture.

There certainly appeared to be a contradiction between the group's support for political democracy and opposition to cultural democracy. An observer might even wonder whether it is possible for a person to be a political democrat without also being an aesthetic democrat. For the New York group, whose intellectual identities were of primary importance to them, the problem was difficult: in a society in which not all individuals had the same level of cultural discrimination, could a cultural democracy be allowed to rule? If an aesthetic free market was allowed to determine culture, then what would be the outcome for intellectual culture, the intellectual vocation and values, and the intellectuals themselves? If it was not permitted to rule, then there was a very tenuous relation between political democracy and cultural democracy that permitted a person to support the former but not the latter.

So was there a contradiction between the political and cultural outlooks of the New York intellectuals? Obviously for some of those such as Hook and Riesman, who spoke out for cultural democracy, there was little contradiction. But what of the much larger part of the group who opposed mass culture? Insofar as their political rhetoric was democratic we might assume that their undemocratic cultural position was in conflict with it.

However, socialists and liberals have had different conceptions of democracy, as Raymond Williams has noted. "In the socialist tradition," he pointed out, "democracy continued to mean *popular power*: a state in which the interests of the majority of the people were paramount and in which these interests were practically exercised and controlled by the majority." This, as we know, has been the theory rather than the reality of socialist states. "In the liberal tradition," Williams continued, "democracy meant open election of representatives and certain conditions (democratic rights, such as free speech) which maintained the openness of election and political argument. These two conceptions, in their extreme forms, now confront each other as enemies."[70] Although this last assertion is stated too dramatically (Williams after all, began as a drama critic), it does remind us that socialism in rhetoric has been tied more to direct democracy and liberalism has been tied to representative democracy, and that there is indeed a tension between them. Those who criticized mass culture thought they were being perfectly democratic—as they defined the term.

These critics from their earliest radical days in the 1930s had always leaned more toward liberal representative democracy than toward socialist or populist direct democracy—so it had never been particularly inconsistent for them to propose cultural leadership by intellectual elites. As intellectuals at heart, they always felt it better to have the masses led by the more talented and perceptive—and the group made this choice in both politics and culture. That appreciation for a vital distance from the people was what underlined the group's identities as intellectuals and fueled their commitment to liberal representative processes.

In other words, if one thinks of them as enthusiastic democrats in the postwar period, then their cultural outlook was contradictory. The apparent contradiction between their political and cultural views, however, shows that their political position had never been enthusiastically democratic. Politically, they were afraid of the masses. Theirs had always been an intellectual political position, left of center in the 1930s and then increasingly more centrist in the postwar period. It was a theoretical outlook, based on words rather than deeds (and even then, not particularly democratic words), and that approach was consistent with their cultural position of intellectual predominance and opposition to cultural democracy. For all their ostensible attachment to labor in their early days, they never really had their hearts with the cultural or aesthetic (and often political) choices of the masses.

Their early fear of cultural equality presaged these same explicit impulses in their outlook in the decades following the mid-1960s. The New York intellectuals had possessed little enough political and cultural faith in the people in the 1930s. By the 1950s that feeling had evolved into Jeffersonian meritocratic sympathies. In the 1960s and 1970s that meritocratic impulse emerged more explicitly in the struggles over affirmative action.

In establishing their relationship to mass culture, the former socialist intellectuals in the group were forced to ask themselves what it meant to be either "left" or "right" with respect to culture generally. Obviously it was easier to determine left or right politically than culturally. But, admitting those difficulties, one found a situation in the 1950s where dissenters such as Macdonald and Howe, on the political left, were considerably more elitist (and perhaps more conservative) in culture than were affirmers such as Hook and Riesman, who by many measures were to their political right. Because it is difficult to establish a meaningful spectrum of left and right in the cultural realm, it is easier to talk of a democratic-to-undemocratic spectrum. In this case it seems that Hook and Riesman were more democratic, pluralistic, and tolerant in their cultural orientation than were the radicals who constituted much of the high culture camp.

Is this unfair to the New York intellectuals? Does it really contradict their pluralist outlook for them to believe that mass culture is inadequate and criticize it accordingly? Just because they believe in free choice, does that mean they have to believe all choices are equally good? Does it mean that they can no longer be polemical critics and get involved in voicing their own opinions on the subject? Were they not, in both politics and culture, allowing free choice but then fighting for their side? Was it really so different from what they did during other battles during their careers? What is so repressive or elitist about that? In response one might say that there is nothing terribly repressive about it, but it is elitist and not very sympathetic to aesthetic free choice or the cultural self-determination of the individual. Again, perhaps that is an elitism that intellectuals cannot avoid.

Would tolerance in cultural matters produce such an abandonment of intellectual standards that one would cease to be an intellectual in any meaningful sense of the term? Perhaps intellectuals should maintain their own standards and proclaim them, but realize that this carries no responsibility to impose these standards on others. One can be an intellectual while still encouraging nonintellectual culture. Like Hook or Riesman, an intellectual can maintain high standards in a discipline, appreciate high culture, and still recognize that other people have a right to choose the level of culture they want to enjoy. Hook and Riesman, of course, were closer to Jeffersonians than to cultural populists, but their sympathy for a proliferation of "taste cultures" showed that the intellectual function and cultural tolerance could be combined.

Yet part of the contradiction between the group's view of politics and culture on this issue is that, while they became Madisonians in politics in the forties, this critical crossing took them longer in the cultural realm. Politically, by midcentury their tragic view had won out over an idealistic view of mankind's inherent goodness, and the focus instead was on guarding against the worst. But in matters of culture, which as intellectuals was always centrally important to them, it was harder for them to abandon their hope. As Shils pointed out, they maintained an idealistic and romantic view of the masses, and assumed that an unoppressed populace would rise and demand high culture. In the 1960s, as time passed and mass culture became more formidable, the group's tragic view caught up with them culturally and they began to expect less from their fellow citizens. The criticism of mass culture no longer seemed the achievable and vital holy crusade it once had.

Younger Leftists and Mass Culture

The New York intellectuals, of course, were not the only American critics to address the difficult problems of mass culture in the postwar period. Increasingly, as the forties and fifties gave way to the sixties and seventies, a younger generation took up the question of mass culture in different terms.

In the late 1950s and early 1960s, when the rumblings of a political split could be detected between the Old and the New Left, a division was also underway in cultural analysis. The younger generation was not unified in its outlook about mass culture, or culture generally, although there were a few assumptions shared by some of the most prominent approaches.

The young and mostly academic cultural radicals, from the 1960s through the 1980s, owed an intellectual debt to several sources.[71] One influence was Antonio Gramsci, the Italian Marxist whose work was translated and became more widely available in the 1950s. Gramsci's influence led his followers to examine the "hegemony" of one part of culture over another—the control that the dominant group's values assert over the subcultures' outlook.

Another influence on the younger generation was the British Marxist Raymond Williams, a cultural critic who was himself influenced by Gramsci. Beginning in the mid-1950s, Williams began to expand his definition of culture beyond aesthetic developments to encompass the additional senses of culture as an entire way of life (as the philosopher Johann Herder had suggested), and as "the works and practices" of intellectual and artistic activity.[72] This latter definition suggested that critics need to investigate the specific practices and relationships of cultural practices, and study the effect of cultural institutions on the production and consumption of culture—on dominant and peripheral groups within a culture, and how their values are included or excluded from cultural material.

Therefore, in Williams's opinion, the earlier criticism of mass culture had been ineffectively cast. Even the word *mass* was so broad and meaningless that its "merely descriptive and assumptive use is a way of avoiding the true sociology of communications." If pursued correctly, the investigation would involve "the whole contentious problem of the real social relations within which modern communications systems operate." He proposed that "we should look not for the components of a product but for the conditions of a practice" and when we view cultural works "we should find ourselves attending first to the reality of their practice and the conditions of the practice as it was then executed." Those "undifferentiated and blocking concepts," such as the term *mass*, "need to be replaced by the motivating and specifying terms of hegemony." Instead of employing easy terms of derision, critics should pursue the "complex sociology of actual audiences, and of the real conditions of reception and response in these highly variable systems."[73]

Williams's broader definition of culture was seminal in the new academic and leftist redefinition of that concept in the 1970s and 1980s. This approach was consistent with a new focus in the humanities and social sciences on the details, persons, traditions, and beliefs at the bottom rather than the top of society: a more anthropological outlook. An approach from the bottom of culture placed more worth, of course, on popular traditions and culture—on mass culture.[74] Although the New York intellectuals had an integrated view of culture, derived from their earlier Marxism, they did not share Williams's conception of culture as a whole way of life and its practices, and the anthropological view of culture was not yet current at the time that they were criticizing mass culture. By the

1950s the New York group might have resisted defining culture as an entire fabric of life anyway, since by then most of them would not have wanted to be forced to indict all of American culture along with its mass culture.

A parallel development that shaped the younger cultural critics was the growth of the new social history in the early 1960s, particularly E. P. Thompson's *The Making of the English Working Class* (1963). Thompson's work, like that of Herbert Gutman in America, studied the formation, development, and behavior of a subordinate class or subculture. Rather than merely documenting the oppression of the working class and showing how the dominant ideology of society ruled the subordinate class, Thompson described how the working class developed its own independent culture and defended itself from the hegemonic power of the dominant ideology. He illustrated how the subordinate class influenced the dominant outlook, as well as the reverse—and so gave the working class greater control over the development of their own important culture. Thompson and those who followed him looked at belief and ritual systems and their transference, studied the continuities and patterns of life and work, and illustrated the development of class and subculture consciousness. With an emphasis on belief systems, practices, localisms, and unwritten traditions, the new social history, like Williams's cultural criticism, was an anthropological investigation from the bottom up.[75]

In Britain this culturally anthropological Marxist view, bred by Gramsci, Williams, and Thompson, was established by Richard Hoggart and Stuart Hall at the University of Birmingham under the name *cultural studies*. It was driven by many of the same culturally radical concerns that powered the New Left. In contrast to the New York intellectuals and some of the Frankfurt School, most of whom had criticized mass culture as pernicious, the cultural studies group defined itself, in part, as "primarily concerned with 'neglected' materials drawn from popular culture and the mass media, which . . . provided important evidence of the new stresses and directions of contemporary culture." Instead of being repelled by popular culture, the cultural studies scholars saw the concept of popular as "the ground of common sense in which more developed and organized 'philosophies' intervene," and they pursued the popular "as the stake in the struggle for hegemony and consent," in which different class practices betrayed themselves.[76]

During the 1970s and 1980s, through the influence of literary and cultural studies from Britain, some of the cultural studies approach filtered into the outlooks of the younger members of the American university community, and it provided a popular Marxist-anthropological alternative to the New York group's more "old-fashioned" Marxist rejection of mass culture. The younger academic generation (particularly in literature and philosophy, but also in history) was further stimulated by French structuralist anthropology and linguistic radicalism, and the result was a postmodernism with an appreciation of popular culture as material containing signs, symbols, and metaphors that reflected society's fundamental beliefs. Stuart Hall observed, in the structuralist approach, a similar broadening of the concept of culture to that proposed by Williams and Thompson. In the early 1970s, the American anthropologist Clifford Geertz was a further influence encouraging an investigation of "texts" and traditions for the symbols and signs they revealed.[77]

Some members of the younger academic crowd went so far as to voice skepticism about the authority of all existing culture, a view that unsettled those who were closer to the New York intellectuals' outlook. Historian John Diggins and *Dissent* coeditor Michael Walzer, for example, worried about the influence of postmodernist linguistic radicalism on social criticism. "In literary studies, according to some observers," Diggins explained in 1987, "critical theory has shifted the task of interpretation from establishing meaning to celebrating its absence and the presence of nothingness—save the tyranny of language that structures all thought." Language, created by the dominant among the cultural classes, was a form of oppression. Not just the language of mass culture, but all language was a conspiracy against freedom of thought and action. "History," Diggins complained, "was once seen as the story of man's rise to the challenge of freedom and its responsibilities; now it is interpreted as his unconscious submission to the structures of power and the alleged pacification of discourse." Similarly, the critic Giles Gunn wrote that the "New New Critics" displayed a "hermeneutics of suspicion," while critics like the New York intellectuals employed a "hermeneutics of restoration."[78]

Susan Sontag and Christopher Lasch were members of the younger generation who differed with the New York group's view of mass culture, but who served as a bridge between them and the younger, more anthropologically oriented academic critics. Both emerged in the 1960s as critics of the New York intellectuals who were sympathetic to the group's original "leftist" values, but who thought their approach needed significant revision. Both contributed essays to *Partisan Review*, but neither shared enough of the group's outlook to function as a member.

That many observers, apparently including some of the New York intellectuals themselves, considered Sontag part of the group was curious. Early in her career, in her essay "Against Interpretation," she expressly rejected the tenets that underlay their cultural outlook. There she argued for the celebration of form over content, for a greater formalism consistent with the structuralism of Roland Barthes. "What is needed, first," she counseled, "is more attention to form in art." Interpretive criticism, she insisted, was oppressive and dominating: "It is to turn *the* world into *this* world." Interpretation established meaning, and established meanings were an oppressive tool used to emasculate art and preserve hegemony. Therefore criticism should get out of the way of art and thought, strive for "transparence," seek to become clear rather than meaningful.[79]

Sontag was influenced both by her own postmodernist generation and by the New York group's more historical and contextual Old Left orientation—and she leaned toward the former. Her "Notes on 'Camp,'" in *Partisan Review* in 1964, illustrated her difference with the group's attitude toward popular culture. Camp has its good points, she maintained, one of which is that it is defined largely by its style, and therefore it underscores form rather than content and resists the corrosive effects of interpretation. Not all popular or mass culture was bad; even kitsch had its place for the serious observer. "Many examples of Camp," she instructed her *Partisan* readers, "are things which, from a 'serious' point of view, are either bad art or kitsch."[80] Still they had merit, and she had some affection for camp—even though (or perhaps because) its very definition was art that had failed in its seriousness.

Still, despite herself, Sontag shared a hint of the New York group's elitism about high art. After all, camp was funny to her because, in a patronizing way, she could smirk at its failure to be what it had tried to be. To her a bad lamp was a "lamp." But the effects of the anthropological view of culture she shared with her generation prompted her to find in popular culture a record of life from the bottom up. She could sift through the artistic junkpile, stifle her laugh to a soft breath, and find out how the less culturally adept had gotten by these past few decades and what they believed. She gave more credit to popular culture than the New York group had, but even while she promoted it she joined in their condescending outlook.

Another young critic on the left who began to make his mark in the 1960s was Christopher Lasch. As a historian he was critical of both the New Left and the Old Left, and in the following decades he tried to walk an independent line between the two.[81] A graduate student of Richard Hofstadter's, Lasch was influenced by the psychological and sociological theory afoot at Columbia University in the 1950s that prompted Hofstadter to investigate the "paranoid style" in America, and to hypothesize status revolutions, resentments, and inner turmoils in the American population. In the 1960s and 1970s Lasch was also affected by the Freudianism of Philip Rieff and others, and he became increasingly interested in what he, Jackson Lears, and other historians and critics called the "therapeutic culture."[82]

Characteristically those writers interested in the therapeutic culture have been opposed to modernism and what it has wrought in America. To say that they were antimodernist is not to suggest that they were opposed to the modernist movement in literature, painting, and architecture, but rather against modernization, modernity, and the social and cultural effects that transformation brought about. Modernization refers to the institutional developments that accompany industrialization, bureaucratization, corporatization, rationalization, and the increased organization of life.[83] As such, this antimodernism need not be specifically anticapitalist, a point that many antimodernists have been too soft-headed to realize.

In his antimodernism, Lasch has celebrated folk culture, kinship, community, myth, family, and preindustrial tradition, and suggested those values as a shelter from the modernization of the twentieth century. As he realized, that put him at odds with the New York intellectuals, who were quite happy to see the country industrialized and modernized so long as the benefits were shared equitably.[84] Although Lasch was sympathetic enough to the group that he served as a consulting editor for *Partisan Review* in the 1970s and 1980s, there was a tension between his leftist antimodernism and their leftist promodernism.

Lasch shared the New York group's hostility to mass culture, but found its criticisms of popular culture flawed beyond repair. He felt that part of the problem was that the group had not understood mass culture, had based its views on the assumption that class structures no longer existed, and had allowed their argument to become an undemocratic "satire against popular taste." Further, the group had mistakenly thought that only the highbrows opposed mass culture and had failed to notice that "a real popular culture" and folk culture in America had successfully resisted modernization and mass culture. This remnant that had survived from the pre-industrial golden age was cause for optimism.[85] Lasch's fondest hope was that the leftist folk culture that he had discovered in the American population would be recognized by other critics as well—discovered with the techniques of the new anthropological criticism and social history—and that this small nugget of true and honest folk culture would rise up and throw off the oppressing yoke of modernism, capitalism, and mass culture.

Although he had differences with the New York group, in the early 1980s Lasch crept closer to their criticism of mass culture and began to echo some of their earlier denunciations. Because mass marketing narrowed the range of consumer choices and competing products became indistinguishable, democracy, he insisted, could not be confused with the free flow of consumer goods. He announced that most leftists felt that mere representative institutions were no longer sufficient to "assure a democratic way of life," and so those radicals were opposed to a "minimalist conception of democracy." [86] Culture, for his portion of the left, in other words, was too precious to be chosen by its individual consumers. Instead his view of leftist culture, reminiscent of Herbert Marcuse's opposition to tolerance, was that some choices were too important not to be decided by enlightened leaders who were better informed of what is best. Lasch in the seventies and eighties, like those in the New York group who criticized mass culture earlier, was unwilling to recognize the lessons that socialists should have learned in the 1930s: that individuals themselves know best what cultural values they should adopt. That approach betrayed an intellectual and social intrusiveness that some parts of the left shared with many nonlibertarian conservatives.

In the arguments of those who supported mass culture, such as Hook and Riesman, Lasch saw a serious mistake. He found that "when it comes to discussions of mass culture, the familiar effects of mass marketing—consolidation of financial power, standardization of products, declining craftsmanship—disappear in a cloud of populist rhetoric." Intellectuals, even leftist intellectuals such as Lasch, rarely appreciate populist rhetoric. "The most remarkable feature of the mass-culture debate," he complained, "is that so many people on the Left, eager to acquit themselves of the suspicion of elitism, resort to a kind of free-enterprise ideology in defending mass culture that they would quickly repudiate if others advanced it as an argument, say, against government regulation of industry." [87]

It was astonishing that Lasch could not see the vital difference between the necessity of the free market in the realm of ideas and its place in industrial life. That he could even compare the desirability of unfettered culture to unfettered industry was an unsettling indication of how little the younger generation had learned from the mistakes of socialism in the preceding century. Lasch would have done well to listen to his father-in-law, the historian Henry Steele Commager, who believed that "the only free enterprise that counts, in the long run, is intellectual enterprise, for if that dries up all individual enterprise dries up." [88] The answer to Lasch's complaint about those who employed a "free-enterprise ideology in defending mass culture" was that it is essential above all else to keep an open market in the realm of ideas and culture, including mass culture.

The regulation of industry can have debatable effects, which intelligent and honest people can disagree on, but the regulation of culture and ideas can have nothing but the most fatal results.

Overall, the cultural outlook of the New York intellectuals had little effect on the academic revolution in cultural studies, history, and literature that began in the universities and esoteric radical linguistic journals in the mid-1960s. The group's criticism of mass culture did, however, have some effect on the cultural analysis and rhetoric of those younger radicals who felt some tie with Old Left values. In this respect Lasch shared more with the New York intellectuals than Sontag did, since he tried to revise their rejection of mass culture by proposing an antimodernist rationale, while she was more given to cultural formalism, to attacking intellectual interpretation, and to celebrating popular culture.

More importantly, while the New York intellectuals' orientation toward mass culture illuminates the rest of their critical outlook, it was but a small part of their cultural vision. The more significant and enduring part of their cultural work consists of their contributions to moral, economic, and historical criticism, to the generalist tradition of writers as diverse as Edmund Wilson and Joseph Schumpeter. This legacy has remained an important alternative to the cultural formalism of the last half of the twentieth century, and it informs the developing "new historicism" in criticism in the late 1980s.

Unsettling Transformations

Part of the New York group's concern about the proper balance of individualism and community within culture was conditioned by the changing status of intellectuals in the postwar period. As their own social and professional status improved, they wondered whether they and the intellectual community at large were losing the detachment necessary to perform their analytical cultural function.

Herbert Gans has argued that the criticism of mass culture in postwar America "has appeared when intellectuals have lost power and the status that goes with power, and it has virtually disappeared when intellectuals have gained power and status." According to him, the critique was most energetic during the late 1940s and 1950s, because in the period of affluence the intellectuals' position fell relative to the rest of society. Their hostility to mass culture died during the 1960s, in Gans's opinion, because intellectual status rose during the Kennedy and Johnson administrations. "Such pessimism is not unusual among downwardly mobile groups," he concluded, "for they exaggerate their own loss of influence into a theory of overall social deterioration." [89]

Although he confused the direction of their status change, Gans was right that part of the cause of the mass culture criticism was the changing position of the intellectual at mid-century. Instead of declining, as he suggested, the status of the New York intellectuals between the mid-1930s and the mid-1950s shot upward so quickly that it surprised even them. In the 1930s many of them were poor second-generation immigrants whose aspirations could find an outlet only in their own small magazines, because as Jewish outsiders to American culture they were denied university positions. Some worked for the WPA or other New Deal agencies, many lived cheaply in the Village, and most of them were unknown outside their own small circle.

By the early 1950s all that had changed. They now held faculty positions at universities such as Brandeis, New York University, Berkeley, and Columbia. Those who lived in New York resided in the nicer buildings of the Village or the Upper West Side. Their magazines and personal reputations already had climbed, in many cases, to the top of the intellectual ladder. Their power had risen quickly, but it had unsettled them—for what did it mean for their roles as intellectuals? Could one be a useful intellectual from within the walls of power, or was it necessary to be detached, a member of a lost generation in perpetual self-exile from the culture? This disorientation made them especially eager to assert their intellectual and individual primacy within the culture, and it helped fuel their criticism of mass culture.

In order to retain their positions as intellectuals in the face of growing competition from mass culture, the group sometimes acted and sounded like a professional organization intent on upholding the correct vocational standards. Greenberg and Macdonald complained that one of the problems with kitsch was, in Greenberg's words, that it "predigests art for the spectator and spares him effort."[90] They resented people experiencing art easily because, in effect, that rendered intellectuals useless. If one could experience culture without trouble, there was no need to employ an intellectual to interpret it for you. To experience real art, the group felt, one should have to do it the hard way—to earn one's intellectual union card or else call in a journeyman in good standing.

Their attack on middlebrow culture was thus in part an extension of their attempt to maintain their central position as recognized intellectuals in a period of transformation. Part of their bluster against middlebrow magazines, hack writers, "phoney Avantgardism," and "sophisticated kitsch" was only the aggravated barking of the watchdogs of intellectual culture straining against their leashes to protect their territory from the unqualified invaders. If the group acted like a professional organization that fixed standards and certified the qualified, it was because they hoped to offset the diluting effects of the postwar expansion of the intellectual ranks. The infusion of movie directors, television critics, and other new intellectual categories created by technical and demographic changes seemed to threaten intellectual standards and the New York group's position.

This is also why the avant-garde was so important to them in the years before the early 1960s. The only way that the New York group's elite cultural status could prevail was by an avant-garde culture of modernism in which the intellectuals could constantly change the form and requirements of high art (a tradition of the new), therefore making it unable to be easily reproduced by those not in the inner circle. That way they kept culture, at least high culture, for themselves. In a period of growing mass media where forms could be copied quickly, this avant-garde was especially important. At a time of high technical mastery by society at large, a static or slowly changing art would allow the middle and lower levels of society also to turn out work that was nearly indistinguishable from high art. To keep a secure intellectual and artistic status in a period of easy imitation, the forces of high culture had to depend on an avant-garde that continually and rapidly changed its art and ideas.

The New York group's effort was not what the younger critics would have called a struggle against a dominant and hegemonic mass culture, since the group's high-culture perspective was neither a radical alternative nor a challenge from a dominated subculture. Rather, the New York intellectuals wanted to empower their own version of the dominant culture. In the terms used by Stuart Hall and his cultural studies colleagues to describe other middle-class countercultures, the group's criticism of mass culture was an altercation *"within* the dominant culture" instead of *"against* the dominant culture," an encounter adaptive to the system as a whole. In this view, "because they inhabit a dominant culture (albeit in a negative way) they are strategically placed (in ways which working-class subcultures are *not*) to generalise an internal contradiction for the society as a whole." Therefore, Hall suggested about these uprisings, "by extending and developing their 'practical critique' of the dominant culture from a privileged position inside it, they have come to inhabit, embody and express many of the contradictions of the system itself." [91]

What internal contradictions of the larger culture did the group represent in this confrontation? The most obvious was the split within the group itself over whether subcultures should be able to choose their own aesthetic pleasures without condescension. A more important incongruity was that most of the group wanted to control the cultural process (as intellectuals perhaps must) but at the same time wanted to maintain the illusion that individuals and taste cultures choose their own cultural products. The New York intellectuals, like much of American society, wanted to maintain power for themselves (in this case as cultural arbiters) but maintain the rhetoric of a decentralized and egalitarian system.

Here again, the New York group's allegiance to their intellectual identities was stronger than their commitment to their political identities— as was the case at the Waldorf Conference and in their responses to the repentance literature. Instead of focusing on mass culture as a problem of capitalist politics and economics (a point they raised in their portrayal of mass culture as commodification), they described it as a dangerous undermining of free intellectual culture. Instead of supporting the working class, their ostensible political ally, in its choice of mass culture, the group chose to break with it over the importance of correct intellectual culture.

Contrary to the New York intellectuals' interpretation of their own political journey, their perennial cultural elitism and undemocratic attitude toward mass culture indicate the extent to which their increasing conservatism did not arise out of the conflicts of the 1960s, but had been a part of their larger orientation as intellectuals since the 1930s. Their form of liberal conservatism, that is, grew naturally and gradually from the 1930s to the 1980s.

It is not that the New York intellectuals were full-blown conservatives in the 1930s, but that their outlook was a leftist elitism—a leftist conservatism, we might say—that slowly evolved into the neoconservatism increasingly apparent in the group in the 1970s and 1980s.[92] Their example should make us question what we mean when we call a group "leftist" or "radical." It should prompt us at the very least to remember that there are many varieties of leftism, not all of them equally committed to the promotion of free choice and tolerance in all areas, and not all of them enamored with the common person in culture and politics.

Beginning in the 1950s, it was not only mass culture that irritated the New York intellectuals, but also the increasingly countercultural orientation of the young. As the fifties slowly evolved into the sixties, this new antagonism supplanted the group's hostilities to mass culture, and many of them became increasingly uneasy about their former position. Indeed, by the 1980s their battle over mass culture had so completely disappeared from their memories that they omitted it from their autobiographies and decided to let their new outlook be the face they presented to posterity. Considering the amount of energy they spent on that issue, it is a striking omission.

5   The New York Group and the New Left

By the early 1960s the New York group considered the threat of mass culture much less dangerous than the radical impulses of the young. It had now been ten or fifteen years since the group had sublimated its interest in political issues beneath the rhetoric of cultural analysis—in order to take a rest from fatiguing Cold War political battles. In the early 1960s politics did not seem as futile and desperate as it had in the gray dawn of the nuclear age and the bitter postwar peace. Rejuvenated, the group became more enthusiastic about political and ideological conflict with other parts of the intellectual community.

The contention between the Old Left and the New Left was partly generational. It was also an extension of the New York group's continuing struggle over what constituted responsible intellectual culture in the postwar period. Further, it was a disagreement about what it meant to be a leftist and what was required of a radical intellectual. It was a dispute within the family of the left, although even the dissenters were now closer to liberalism than to the socialist left. Yet many of them still felt themselves at least nominally tied to radicalism, even if only in the sense, as Sidney Hook had once said, that modern biologists are still Darwinian. As in all family arguments there was a mixture of intense likes and dislikes, admiration and disgust, rivalry, parental condescension and youthful bravado, some common outlooks and goals, some common backgrounds, frequent disagreements about means and ends, and debates about what constituted a desirable future.

The Beats

The New York intellectuals' antagonism toward the New Left in the 1960s was foreshadowed in their response to the Beats in the 1950s. A literary

186

and cultural movement, the Beats jumped from the campuses of Columbia and Reed College and surfaced in San Francisco and New York with the novels, poetry, and antics of Jack Kerouac, Allen Ginsberg, Gary Snyder, Philip Whalen, Lew Welch, Gregory Corso, and Lawrence Ferlinghetti, among others. The early formation of the group was fostered by San Francisco poet Kenneth Rexroth, who, according to Gary Snyder, was "a catalytic figure for all of us," and whose house, "literally, was the place that we met."[1]

The Beats represented a romantic literary tendency, similar in some respects to the transcendentalist vision of nineteenth-century American writers such as Thoreau and Whitman—the latter of whom they self-consciously claimed as a forefather. The Beats carried on many of the earlier romantic commitments to nature, intuition, transcendental consciousness, and anti-industrialism. There was a diversity among the Beat visions, from the focus of Kerouac and Ginsberg on the street life of drugs, poverty, and the lower orders of the disenfranchised "beat" (beaten) people, to the focus of Gary Snyder on nature, simplicity, and Oriental thought. Snyder later affirmed that, despite their diversity, in the 1950s the Beats "did embody a criticism and a vision which we shared in various ways," but he admitted that they were not very political. In the 1960s they drew closer to one another through a fascination with Eastern religion, and in the 1970s their common bond included a "powerful environmental concern, critique of the industrial state, and an essentially shared poetics."[2]

As an artistic perspective, Beat writings and pronouncements were bound to draw the attention of the New York intellectuals, as many in the *Partisan Review* crowd were literary critics. Norman Mailer was the only member of the group who was sympathetic to the Beats; the others varied in the level of their hostility. It was not an accident that the novelist in the circle was the most sympathetic to the nonrationalist bohemians. Nor was it surprising that Mailer, who always showed enthusiasm for the outrageous, the new, and the spectacular, was the New York intellectual whose imagination the Beats most easily engaged.

In 1957 *Dissent* published Mailer's "The White Negro: Superficial Reflections on the Hipster." His article addressed the street manifestation rather than the literature of the Beat and hip—although the two were closely connected. As one of the three original founders of the *Village Voice* in New York in 1955, Mailer had become acquainted with the hip movement on the street in Greenwich Village. He contributed $15,000 to the *Voice* during its first year and wrote a column called "The Hip and the Square." When he gave up his column and his close association with the paper he complained that the other two founders wanted it to be "more Square—I wish it to be more Hip."[3]

The Beats stressed spontaneity in their written language, reflecting the importance they placed on chance occurrence in life, on intuition and action rather than critical thought and orderly design, and on the primacy of the event. Mailer approved. In his opinion "the language of Hip which evolved was an artful language," one that was "a pictorial language, but pictorial like non-objective art." It was a style that worked abstractly rather than a written approach that conveyed meaning precisely and directly. "Hip is the language of energy," Mailer said of the new tendency, and "Movement is always to be preferred to inaction."[4]

The year after Mailer's essay appeared, Norman Podhoretz took to the pages of *Partisan Review* to ridicule and dismiss the new bohemian writers. As artists, he wrote, the Beats were failures. Their "bop language" showed "contempt for coherent, rational discourse which, being a product of the mind, is in their view a form of death." A Beat author showed his "true intellectuality" by speaking "with his tongue tied" and making "noises that come out of his soul." This inarticulateness, Podhoretz complained, was paraded as spontaneity. Kerouac and the Beats thought spontaneity was writing whatever first invaded the writer's head. The Beats wanted the "first words" instead of the "right words"; they wanted words reflecting "emotion" rather than thinking. Podhoretz concluded that the bohemians' worship of spontaneity was "a cover for hostility to intelligence."[5]

The New York group was eager to resist any new challenge to their own rational critical approach to literature, and they left no question that the Beats represented a danger. Podhoretz warned of the degeneration of standards and explained that "the Beat boys make their own rules for literature, defining carelessness as spontaneity, incoherence as clarity, drunkenness as vitality, and inarticulateness as eloquence. Control is 'chicken' and subtlety is 'crap,' both in the street-gang and among the Beats." Paul Goodman, hardly the most committed rationalist of the New York intellectuals, concluded that "the paucity of its vocabulary and syntax is for the Beats essentially expressive of withdrawal from the standard civilization and its learning."[6]

An even greater threat was that the worship of spontaneity apparently had led the Beats and hipsters to a fascination with violence. That prospect did not bother Mailer, although it alarmed others in the group. The hipster, Mailer counseled, felt "the desire to murder and the desire to create," and was "a philosophical psychopath." He calmly assured his readers that the hipster-psychopath commits "murders—if he has the courage—out of a necessity to purge his violence, for if he cannot empty his hatred then he cannot love." Murder was not a cowardly act, Mailer reasoned: a "courage of a sort is necessary, for one murders not only a weak fifty-year old man but an institution as well." The hipster was thus "daring the unknown." And hipsters were not without feeling. "At bottom," Mailer reassured his audience, "the drama of the psychopath is that he seeks love." [7]

Mailer's fellow New York intellectuals were not so enthusiastic about the benefits of violence. In the summer of 1957 Alfred Kazin noted in his journal that Kerouac's *On the Road* was disturbing in its "romantic incoherence, the *longing* for violence, the gravitation towards the underworld." Kazin found "depressing" the novel's "wilful hardness" reminiscent of Hemingway, and "the masturbatory intoxication on violence!" [8]

Podhoretz went a step further and wondered whether romanticism naturally led to violence. He explained that "whenever I hear anyone talking about instinct and being and the secrets of human energy, I get nervous; next thing you know he'll be saying that violence is just fine." He then accused the Beat authors of harboring a wish to kill intellectuals. He heard "a suppressed cry" in the books of Ginsberg and Kerouac: "Kill the intellectuals who can talk coherently, kill the people who can sit still for five minutes at a time, kill those incomprehensible characters who are capable of getting seriously involved with a woman, a job, a cause." [9] For those who were puzzled by Podhoretz's interpretive zeal, he did not bother to document the evidence of violence and death he found in Beat literature.

The Beats were mystified and alarmed by such intemperate characterizations of them and their work. Ginsberg thought that a "Frankenstein image" of the Beats was being produced "by everything from [the] Congress for Cultural Freedom, [to] *Encounter* magazine, through *Partisan Review*." He considered it "a sort of yellow press image of what was originally a sort of ethereal and angelic perception of America, and the world, and the nature of the mind." How could Podhoretz, in his paranoia of anyone who did not subscribe precisely to his ordered bourgeois outlook, mistake an angelic vision for a violent mob that wanted to kill intellectuals? "I realized early," Ginsberg reflected, "that if they were going to do that to us who were relatively innocent—just a bunch of poets—if they were going to make us out to be monsters, then they must have been making the whole universe out to be a monster all along, like from the Communists to the radicals to the anarchists to the Human Being in America." [10]

The New York group also faulted the Beats for an irrationalist anti-intellectualism. Mailer sympathetically described a revolution that confirmed many of Podhoretz's darkest misgivings about the Beats. The hipster, according to Mailer, may represent "the first wind of a second revolution in this century . . . backward toward being and the secrets of human energy . . . backward to the nihilism of creative adventurers." If the century's first revolution was "an expression of the scientific narcissism we inherited from the nineteenth century, a revolution motivated by the rational mania that consciousness could stifle instinct and marshall it into productive formations, the second revolution . . . would have consciousness subjugated to instinct." [11]

Podhoretz, however, did not share Mailer's sympathy for instinct, and he suspected that the Beats' hostility to intellectual culture was not of a mild, restrained sort. "The plain truth," he explained to his readers, "is that the primitivism of the Beat Generation serves first of all as a cover for an anti-intellectualism so bitter that it makes the ordinary American's hatred of the egghead seem positively benign." The Beats, in his view, were not simply members of the intellectual community with whom the New York group had disagreements. They were so far out of the intellectual community and so threateningly antagonistic to it that the normal provincial American stood between the Beats and the intellectuals. The intellectuals therefore had to repel the hipsters' attack.

Podhoretz was not alone in his criticism of Beat anti-intellectualism. "The new Bohemia's inferiority shows up clearly in its lack of intellectual content," Ned Polsky complained to Mailer in *Dissent*. "Most hipsters scarcely read at all," and the "pseudo-profundities" of jazz were all they would discuss seriously. Even Paul Goodman accused the Beats of committing themselves to "voluntary ignorance" to match their vows of "voluntary poverty." He was discouraged that "they don't know anything, neither literature nor politics." [12]

The group's antagonism to Beat anti-intellectualism struck many of the same chords as their criticism of mass culture and kitsch. Although the Beats also criticized mass culture, their analysis was not intellectual enough for the New York group. Further, the group feared that the Beats, like mass culture, would lower overall cultural standards. Both tendencies represented an intellectual degeneration. The Beats were a form of romantic kitsch for those who were too young or too unsophisticated for intellectual culture.

The worst that could happen, of course, would be for the relatively isolated and ignored Beat culture to penetrate mass culture and combine in a monstrous hybrid—and then be disseminated into widespread prominence through the media of mass culture. Then the New York group would have the greatest dangers of their two adversaries—mass culture and the Beats—combined in one. That was precisely what they would later believe happened in the 1960s. Mass culture and the Beat outlook combined to produce a mongrel countercultural kitsch that represented the dangers of irrationality. The task for rational intellectuals became that much more desperate.

Finally, perhaps most discouraging to the New York intellectuals was that the Beats did not appear to represent real radicalism at all, and what little radicalism—as opposed to style—they displayed looked as though it drew from the political right rather than the left. Kazin worried that the Beats' antiestablishment stance was merely a criminal posture. "The criminal *is* the *protester*," Kazin wrote with discouragement in his journal. "The real question here is: are they doing anything more than 'protesting'? Is there anything more than a striking of attitudes?" [13]

Irving Howe believed the Beats' radicalism was thoroughly part of the middle-class society they tried to oppose. They had "no clear sense" of problems, no agenda, no defined "principle" of opposition, and their incoherence reflected the confused society that troubled them. They had fallen into the trap of rebellion in a mass society. "In their contempt for mind," he reported, "they are at one with the middle class suburbia they think they scorn." They had no program, only dreams, but they were unable to "dream themselves out of the shapeless nightmare of California"—a particularly gruesome condition for a New York intellectual to ponder. Dreams had been substituted for radical intelligence, and in consequence they had been unable to shake the middle-class vision; instead "they sing out an eternal fantasy of the shopkeeper." That is why it was so difficult to be anti-intellectual and a radical at the same time, "for if you shun consciousness as if it were a plague, then a predicament may ravage you but you cannot cope with it." [14]

Yet when the bohemian writers did venture a political statement it was likely to arouse the anger of the New York intellectuals. Comments by the 1950s Beats foreshadowed the later New Left disagreement with the New York group over communism. "Poets," Kenneth Rexroth announced, "are coming to San Francisco for the same reasons that Hungarians have been going to Austria recently." Even Delmore Schwartz, who was not particularly possessed by Cold War animosities, could not let that comment pass. In a lecture at the Library of Congress in 1958 entitled "The Present State of Poetry," Schwartz lamented that the San Francisco poets (whom he called the San Francisco Howlers) failed to "recognize the difference between the Red Army and the *Kenyon Review* critics, between Nikita Khrushchev and John Crowe Ransom, or between the political commissars of a police state and the tyrants who write advertising copy on Madison Avenue." [15]

The New York group was ever vigilant about those who made unacceptable statements about Stalinism, even if that treason issued from the mouths of young, apolitical poets who knew no better. The utterances of irresponsible leftism, even if spoken softly in confusion, could damage a country if left unopposed. Gary Snyder admitted that the Beats were unschooled in politics and wandered into unfamiliar territory, but, unlike Podhoretz or Schwartz, at least Kenneth Rexroth gave them some friendly counsel.

According to Snyder, Rexroth "provided for some of us a very valuable bridge between floundering in Stalinism/anti-Stalinism at a time when the *Partisan Review* was talking about the failure of intellectual America." During the 1950s, Snyder remembered, Rexroth "was a very valuable aid and bridge and teacher in helping me, and I think some others, retain our radical vision and radical perspective without falling into the either/or of American capitalism or Stalinism." To escape the forced choice of capitalism or Stalinism, the Beats followed Rexroth into anarchism, and Snyder felt that "anarchism as a credible and viable position was one of Rexroth's greatest contributions for us, intellectually."[16]

Podhoretz, however, worried about the "populism" of their work, and feared that "the Beat rebellion comes, if it can be interpreted politically at all, from the right, not the left." The Beats expressed "a kind of know-nothing populist sentiment" that was fascinated with the lower orders of society. Allen Ginsberg did not agree. Again, Ginsberg saw the Beat populist vision as angelic and spiritual, rather than destructive and violent. Ginsberg connected "our own struggle back to the tradition that was immediately contactible in the Populist good heart of William Carlos Williams" and Walt Whitman. How could that be destructive? How could that be considered right or left?

Yet Podhoretz interpreted the Beat tradition differently. Whereas the earlier bohemianism of the 1930s had been against American provincialism and for European modernism, the Beats of the 1950s were "hostile to civilization" altogether.[17] Like others in the *Commentary* circle, Podhoretz believed that there had to be some affirmation in a radical outlook. That the Beats affirmed many spiritual and communal values was not enough for Podhoretz. Further, he never made clear why the Beat populism was tied to the right rather than the left. As with others in the New York group, his antiruralism and fear of the masses prompted him to interpret all populism as a dangerous impulse from the right.

One of the factors that compounded their hostility to the Beats' radicalism was that the group accepted middle-class values while the young bohemians rejected them.[18] The New York intellectuals, for all their talk of socialism, believed strongly in the values of the bourgeoisie: respectability, order, civility, process, rationality, system, coherence, virtue. They found problems with the political, social, and economic order of mid-twentieth-century America—some problems large enough to require democratic socialist solutions. Yet, except for some redistribution of economic and political power, most of the system was workable. They wanted to leave the system intact, or at least its underlying values, and merely tinker with its gears.

The New York intellectuals were children of immigrants whose socialism, as much as anything else, was to serve as a lever with which to boost themselves into middle-class life. Those of them who were radical at all supported a bourgeois socialism. For many of them, their adolescence and college years came during the Depression. They were bound to clash with those who graduated from college after World War II and who discarded middle-class values in favor of bohemian culture.

One has only to read the work of Norman Podhoretz to catch a sense of some of the group's middle-class yearnings. In 1957 he upbraided his generation for being so conservative, timid, and responsible, but despite his bravado he subscribed firmly to their outlook. Like his contemporaries, he celebrated early maturity, early marriage, family, a steady job—all of the values the Beats ridiculed. "In that period of my life," Podhoretz later remembered, "there was nothing that appealed to me less than the idea of refusing to grow up and settle down—which . . . was what Kerouac and Ginsberg and their friends stood for—and nothing that I wanted more than to take my rightful place as an adult among other adults."[19] One could hardly find another statement so completely at odds with the young bohemian outlook.

It is not surprising that the two different visions of radicalism clashed. The Beats were romantic, intuitive, nonpolitical, irrational, antibourgeois, and anti-intellectual. Members of the New York group were rationalist intellectuals, pragmatic and programmatic liberals or liberal leftists who took seriously politics and radicalism—or at least other people's statements about radicalism. They had never liked visionaries, and so they refused to consider the Beats true intellectuals or radicals—any more than they had granted that status to the Communists in their earlier battles. For Norman Podhoretz, as for many of his colleagues, the Beats represented the same mix of dangerous tendencies they would later find in the counterculture and the New Left.

Norman Podhoretz

Although it is doubtful that Norman Podhoretz ever subscribed strongly to the values of the left even in his youth, his rhetoric and public stance moved from a moderate position in the 1950s to an aggressively conservative position in the 1970s. That is, during the student unrest he crossed the political paths of most of the New York intellectuals and afterward stood to their right.

Born in Brooklyn on January 16, 1930, the son of a milkman, Podhoretz was twenty-seven years younger than first-generation Sidney Hook and ten years younger than second-generation Irving Howe. His third-generation cohort of New York intellectuals included Michael Walzer, Susan Sontag, Steven Marcus, and others who were in college in the late 1940s and early 1950s.[20]

A bright youth in the Brownsville section of Brooklyn, Podhoretz "had literary ambitions even as a small boy." Partly because of the tutelage of a high school teacher who convinced him that he did not want to continue being "a filthy little slum child," he went on to study at the Seminary College of the Jewish Theological Seminary and at Columbia College, to which he had won a scholarship.[21] He took with him into adulthood the cultural ambitions encouraged by that teacher.

Fellow undergraduates in the Columbia English department included Allen Ginsberg and future New York intellectuals Jason Epstein and Steven Marcus. Kerouac, formerly a Columbia student, visited Ginsberg at the college while Podhoretz was there. Indeed, if Podhoretz had not altered his earlier dream of being a poet he might have run with the same crowd as Ginsberg and Kerouac and might have grown much closer to the Beat outlook he later hated so much.

While in college the young Podhoretz found more than literary influence. In his senior year, as a twenty-year-old, he read the newly published *The God That Failed*, which left him "dazzled and exhilarated." That book ushered him into the anti-Communist outlook of the New York group. Books that further cemented his antitotalitarianism were Hannah Arendt's *The Origins of Totalitarianism* and Whittaker Chambers's *Witness*.[22] His mentor at Columbia, Lionel Trilling, years earlier had published *The Middle of the Journey*, and the young protégé surely had little trouble understanding what political orientation was expected of ambitious boys who sought to join Trilling's group of critics.

F. W. Dupee, one of the original six editors of the revived *Partisan Review* in 1937, was, like Trilling, on the Columbia English faculty. Podhoretz took courses from both of them, but came under the special care of Trilling. With the example of Trilling and Dupee immediately before him, he decided that becoming a literary critic was a much better career than being a poet.[23] As ambitious as he was talented, he saw that prestige could be gained as a man of letters.

Indeed, ambition was at the core of Podhoretz's life, and his open thirst to achieve success shaped his career more plainly than most. He was receptive to his high school teacher's advice to use his ambition to vault out of the Brownsville slum, and he undertook the long "journey from Brooklyn to Manhattan," the goal that glittered before him like a jewel.[24] He rejected Beat bohemianism to marry young, have a family, and join society. Throughout his life his urge to "make it" stamped its influence on his ideas and career.

Following Columbia, graduate study on a fellowship to Cambridge University, and two years in the army, Podhoretz began to write book reviews and position himself as a literary critic. He remarked later that "among our most talented literary intellectuals (including just about everyone I know) reviewing is regarded as a job for young men on the make; you serve an apprenticeship as a reviewer and then you move on to bigger and more ambitious things."[25]

Reviewing, editing, and writing nonfiction essays were the avenues taken by the young Podhoretz, and he was not modest about the worth of those particular undertakings. Critic Robert Brustein accused him of claiming an intellectual impact for those callings superior to that of a novelist. "Behind it," Brustein wrote of Podhoretz's declaration, "one can detect an effort to capture for the journalist some of the novelist's prestige." Brustein saw a young man on the make, one who wanted to assure the world of the height he was achieving. "There is something poignant about this writer's effort to elevate whatever profession he happens to be pursuing at the moment, but there is something solipsistic about it too," Brustein noted critically. "I am certain that if Mr. Podhoretz ever went into the plumbing business, we would soon have an essay on how the toilet bowl is replacing the book."[26]

Much of Podhoretz's literary criticism was intelligent, brave, and provocative. He was particularly good at judging and commenting on generational trends, although the explicitly literary element of his work did not rank with that of the best of the New York group. Some of his earliest pieces seemed derivative; his essay on Faulkner, for example, largely restates Kazin's insights in *On Native Grounds*.[27] Podhoretz's essays were collected in *Doings and Undoings* (1964), after which he went on to ventures other than literary criticism. The few argumentative literary pieces he wrote in the following twenty years were issued as *The Bloody Crossroads: Where Literature and Politics Meet* (1986).

After an apprenticeship of reviewing books for *Partisan Review*, the *New Yorker*, and *Commentary*, Podhoretz served as an editor at *Commentary* from 1955 to 1958. With Jason Epstein he was involved in book publishing for two years, and then in 1960 he became editor-in-chief of *Commentary*. When Podhoretz took control of the magazine he was generally perceived as moving it politically to the left. Often cited as evidence was his publication of chapters of Paul Goodman's *Growing Up Absurd* and Podhoretz's early opposition to American involvement in Vietnam. But at least since the late 1950s when he wrote his attack on the Beats, he had harbored a strong animus against the values of the counterculture. When the New Left appeared in the early 1960s, some thought Podhoretz was initially sympathetic to it, as he printed Staughton Lynd, a young American historian at Yale associated with the New Left. But his admiration of Lynd was brief.

He initially liked Lynd, who had written an "evenhanded, almost neutralist" article for *Commentary* titled "How the Cold War Began." But some of Podhoretz's friends began to whisper that Lynd was soft on the Soviets, and the *Commentary* editor found himself having to defend his decision to publish the article. To gauge Lynd's real outlook, he invited Lynd to his apartment one evening and they talked until nearly dawn. Podhoretz concluded that Lynd was more sympathetic to China than to the Soviet Union, and was "more benevolent" toward Communism and "more hostile" toward America than he had suspected.[28] Lynd stopped appearing in *Commentary*. It was not in Podhoretz to appreciate the New Left; his values clashed too clearly with theirs. Any nudging of *Commentary* to the left (if that took place at all) was brief and evanescent.

Three years after he began as editor of *Commentary*, Podhoretz printed "My Negro Problem—and Ours," one of his most celebrated articles. Although it drew mixed and some bitter reaction, most who read it agreed that it was a brave attempt to be honest about how white liberal intellectuals felt about blacks. It was partly a response to articles that James Baldwin had printed in which he talked about the black hatred of whites. Podhoretz countered by remembering his youth in Brooklyn. There, he wrote, Jews thought blacks were better off than they because blacks were better athletes, stronger, could be more lawless and erotic, and had little family supervision. Blacks also had punished him physically, so he had hated them—and still disliked them in 1963. As Nat Hentoff pointed out in the *Nation* at the time, there seemed to be a consistency of hatred in Podhoretz that was turned against unlikely victims—the Beats or blacks—who were not particularly threatening.[29]

Race relations were a two-way street, Podhoretz felt. Yes, blacks were invisible to whites, but whites were also faceless to blacks. Some of his critics thought this unfairly made blacks bear the burden of the hatred they received, and many thought him blind for not understanding how blacks could see in any white a potential oppressor. Interestingly, Podhoretz also suggested that ethnicity and race should be eliminated—that there should be no more Jews nor blacks, and that through intermarriage a solution would be found to racism.[30] It was a brave proposal from the editor of a Jewish magazine, and one that he soon stifled.

Podhoretz was an early, though not radical, critic of the Vietnam War, and as late as 1969 he was still involved enough to give a Moratorium Day speech in which he urged "an immediate withdrawal" by the United States. Two years later he found himself ambivalent about Nixon's plan of disengagement in stages, and said it was "not the policy I would have wanted him to follow." Although the president's policy had the benefit of discouraging a Communist takeover of South Vietnam, Podhoretz said there were reasons for thinking it would not occur in any case. He supported Nixon's withdrawal "provided that policy did not entail continued American military participation in the war, whether on the ground or in the air." The bombing of Vietnam, Laos, and Cambodia, he felt, was "so disproportionate in its destructiveness to any conceivable objective" that it should be stopped.

Actually Podhoretz went even further. Although he did not want to see an "unambiguous American defeat," he confided that "I now find myself—and here is the main source of my own embarrassment in writing about Vietnam—unhappily moving to the side of those who would prefer just such an American defeat to a 'Vietnamization' of the war which calls for the indefinite and unlimited bombardment by American pilots in American planes of every country in that already devastated region." (Less than a decade after this article, his foreign policy views were so strident that these earlier words were surely an even greater "embarrassment.") During the antiwar protests of the first Nixon administration, Podhoretz recommended "a complete American withdrawal—from the air as well as the ground," for U.S. forces.[31]

If in the 1960s his views on Vietnam were opposed to administration policy, he shared Nixon's hostility toward the counterculture. Podhoretz's outlook was not unusual for the New York group, but the strength of his animosity toward the young was unique. Rather than idealistic, he found the counterculture selfish and smug. He thought those critics sympathetic to the cultural radicals, such as Susan Sontag and Leslie Fiedler, were guilty of supporting "junky and trashy fashions in the service of the revolution in sensibility which goes hand in hand with the revolution against the American political system and the American social order."[32]

William Phillips, who continued to edit *Partisan Review*, recalled an argument with Podhoretz over the counterculture. "Norman was putting down the younger writers as a group, insisting, among other things, that they were lazy and spoiled," Phillips remembered. The *Partisan* editor had disagreed: the young were almost too busy and energetic. To smooth over their disagreement, Phillips then tried to create a common generational bond with Podhoretz, telling him that together they faced a new generation, "a new world, which will sweep away those of us who belong to the old world." Podhoretz, alarmed and intransigent, retorted hotly that he would never allow himself to be pushed aside by young radicals.

Phillips was surprised at the outburst. "It struck me at the time as a very vivid and disturbing example of the conservative impulse to preserve the old order against the new barbarians, to preserve moral values, aesthetic standards, and social order." With Podhoretz taking such an extreme position against the counterculture, Phillips pointed out, the young responded to him in kind, and "It became a holy war on both sides." [33]

A person with Podhoretz's unremitting drive for bourgeois success could never be sympathetic to bohemianism. In 1967, at the first full flush of the counterculture, Podhoretz published *Making It*, the autobiography of a brash thirty-five-year-old who celebrated his ascendance to a position of cultural power. The book's subtheme was the American ambivalence toward success, which, like sex, it both craved and hid. Trilling advised him not to publish it. He did, and it was reviewed mercilessly. Actually it was the best early book on the genesis of the New York intellectuals, and, had he been more modest about his own ambition and success, *Making It* would have achieved a justified acclaim.

Yet a celebration of himself and his lifestyle was too large a part of the book to be ignored. Like Mailer's *Advertisements for Myself*, the very title *Making It* announced the sense of notoriety both writers sought. It was no surprise that Mailer was one of his favorite writers. As one of Podhoretz's own critics charged, "inevitably, Mailer's depressing development—his theatrical strutting and fretting—is described by Podhoretz as an 'exemplary career,'" because "the pursuit of success" was central to both of them. "Actually, Mr. Podhoretz's concern with the 'pursuit of success' has nothing whatever to do with the writing of fiction; it is simply a self-conscious idea about the writer's *role*." [34]

Podhoretz did not write much in the year or two following *Making It*, but during that time he apparently decided that the world was threatening his plans for success. How could he succeed as a champion of middle-class values if the bohemian counterculture prevailed instead? How could he rise to the top of world power with his nation if America was defeated in Vietnam? How could he hold up his head as an international intellectual if American power was second to the Soviets', or if America could not exercise its will in the Third World? How could he feel as though he had made it if the Jewish intellectual community had not made it, and how could Jewish intellectuals be said to have succeeded if they demonstrated self-hatred in their criticism of Israel and America? How could he feel good about making it in America if his fellow citizens criticized American domestic policies and attitudes? Podhoretz realized that to really make it, to achieve genuinely meaningful success, he would have to mount a campaign against the detractors of his way of life.

In June 1970, Podhoretz initiated a monthly column in *Commentary* in which he undertook the first struggles in this campaign. In his first column he criticized the Jewish intellectuals associated with the *New York Review of Books* for their radicalism and questioning of America, which amounted to American self-hatred and Jewish self-hatred. In later columns he denounced such opponents as the counterculture, the adversary culture, the American Civil Liberties Union, and George McGovern and the New Politics.[35]

In his column Podhoretz also reflected about the reason for his new conservatism. He reminded his readers that he had been "one of the people who participated rather actively in the movement of those days [the early 1960s] to revive the dormant spirit of radical social criticism within the American intellectual community." Podhoretz admitted that by the end of the 1960s, however, he had lost his sympathy for the left because of "the barbaric hostility to freedom of thought which by the late 60's had become one of the hallmarks of this ethos."

Moreover, the left thought that the world's problems could be resolved by political means. Podhoretz reported that he once agreed, but lost that hope in the course of the 1960s. He and the other affirmers in the New York group (who in this campaign constituted the first ranks of what by the mid-1970s became known as neoconservatism) thought that it had "become more important to insist once again on the freedom of large areas of human experience from the power of politics, whether benevolent or malign, than to acquiesce in the surly tyranny of the activist temper in its presently dominant forms. It is in this sense that we consider ourselves deradicalized."[36]

This particular movement away from politics was conservative, as Podhoretz himself admitted. It warned against the unintended consequences of reform, and suggested not only that liberals should stop their activist programs but that since politics was not the correct arena in which to solve social problems, each person should be left to solve problems individually. The conservative implications of that outlook were obvious, since it was skeptical of organized social change.

In the following years his foreign policy views became the strident outlook of one who wanted to be assured that his country was making it successfully. He worried that American intellectuals cared only about making the world safe for communism. He fretted about a "final collapse of an American resolve to resist the forward surge of Soviet imperialism" which would produce "the Finlandization of America."[37] Podhoretz, by the 1970s, had become the Sidney Hook of the third generation, a Johnny-one-note who lacked Hook's intellectual power.

Increasingly *Commentary* and Podhoretz reversed their earlier opposition to the Vietnam War, and reinterpreted it as a brave and necessary defense against international Communism, a war that was undermined by the weak and self-hating critics of America. Podhoretz worked himself into an anti-Communist passion. Even *The God That Failed*—the book that had initiated the young Podhoretz into the New York group's anti-Communism—now seemed weak and tepid broth. Though it might have been sufficient for its period, Podhoretz now advised that "the kind of anti-Communism legitimized in *The God That Failed* was shot through with too many reservations and qualifications to stand firm against the pressures of the years ahead."[38] Sterner stuff would be needed, and Podhoretz would provide it.

If Podhoretz had merely promoted his neoconservative opinions he would not have been so provocative to the rest of the intellectual community. As it was, he infuriated those who disagreed with him by rewriting history through a strongly neoconservative filter. He not only recast the Vietnam War as a noble and necessary affair, and admonished *The God That Failed* for its weak anti-Communism, but also tried to resuscitate George Orwell as an eighties neoconservative. "Normally, to speculate on what a dead man might have said about events he never lived to see is a frivolous enterprise," Podhoretz admitted. Nonetheless he pressed to his conclusion that had Orwell survived into the 1980s he would have opposed the nuclear freeze and the no-first-use pledge, would have rejected the possibility of a verifiable disarmament agreement with the Soviets, and would have turned his back on democratic socialism. Podhoretz was convinced that "if Orwell were alive today, he would be taking his stand with the neoconservatives and against the Left." A subsequent storm of protest and ridicule from the left did not faze him.[39]

Part of Podhoretz's move to the right was brought about by his position of leadership in the American Jewish community. Although he had always been antagonistic to cultural radicalism, his shift to political conservatism coincided with the Arab-Israeli war of 1967. Podhoretz had always been concerned with making it himself, but after the Six-Day War he tied his own success more closely to that of Jews in America and Israel.

By the early 1970s he had already decided that "publications of the ideological Right" were less anti-Semitic than "publications of the Left like the *Village Voice*," which apologized for anti-Semitism. Although he denied suggesting that Jews "join the ideological Right," he did propose that "Jews should recognize the ideology of the radical Left for what it is: an enemy of liberal values and a threat to the Jewish position." And although he was fighting the left "in the name of liberal values, not in the name of Judaism," he was "fighting the fight for Jewish security in America as well." [40]

Even his distaste for McGovern and the New Politics was interwoven with his concern for his own success and for the Jewish position in society. McGovern and the New Politics, in Podhoretz's opinion, were an extension of that countercultural hostility to middle-class values, and Podhoretz discovered that, like him, the Jewish community saw "in that antagonism not only a denigration of them, of their achievements and their aspirations, but a threat to their future position." [41] One insult he would not accept against himself or Jews was a threat to their achievement, aspiration, or future position. In America the right to make it, however one defined that, was a right he valued dearly.

Robert Brustein had not been the only observer to remark on Podhoretz's will to succeed; reviews of *Making It* had made sure of that. Yet, well into the 1980s those observations were still being posted. Christopher Hitchens of *The Nation* referred to him as the "sort of well-heeled power worshiper who passes for an intellectual these days." [42] Conor Cruise O'Brien also discovered that impulse in him. Podhoretz only admired those who had succeeded in throwing their weight around, O'Brien suggested, and if Henry Kissinger had not made it among the powerful then his memoirs of those years would not have achieved literary greatness in Podhoretz's estimation.

Neoconservatives like Podhoretz wanted to get close to power, according to O'Brien, but as zealots and ideologues they would never be employed by those in power, because they were not flexible enough. Neither would Podhoretz be an important American writer who would be long remembered, O'Brien predicted, because he wrote too quickly, urgently, and politically, as though he had a bus to catch—the bus of political power. Since his essays would be forgotten, Podhoretz would make it neither as a writer nor as a politician. Therefore, referring to Podhoretz's book *The Bloody Crossroads: Where Literature and Politics Meet*, O'Brien declared that the *Commentary* editor "is not so much an authority on 'the bloody crossroads' as another of the romantic and power-infatuated victims with whom that crossroads is bestrewn." [43]

Three of Podhoretz's characteristics are particularly prominent. First, he was ambitious, so he wanted everything he was associated with to be dominant: American power, middle-class values, the American Jewish community, Israel, and neoconservatism. Second, after Israel's 1967 war he came to feel a justifiable concern for the welfare of Israel and for American Jews. After all, he was editor of the most prominent American Jewish publication. Those concerns increased his desire to see American power not only be strong enough to protect its interests but be dominant.

Third, *Commentary* has been the central publication of the affirmers in the New York group, and like many other affirmers Podhoretz did not make precise distinctions between justifiable and unjustifiable criticisms of America. He did not distinguish between criticism of American culture and anti-Americanism, between Jewish criticism of Zionism and Jewish self-hatred, between criticism of American domestic inequalities and an abhorrence of all American institutions.

The antagonisms fostered by the New York group's polemical style and outlook sometimes created a kind of holy warrior mentality. Podhoretz and Hook are the clearest examples of writers so intent on their struggle against absolutism, holism, and extremism in the world that they tended to overlook those tendencies in their own work.

The Proper Order of the Intellectual Community

The rise of the New Left and the campus disorders in the 1960s compelled members of the New York group once again to argue their definition of what constituted acceptable limits of speech and action within the intellectual community. The student uprisings struck at the heart of the group's value system, since the university was nearly a sacred institution to them. Even more than their small magazines, the university was an institution that protected open inquiry and the free dissemination of ideas. It was a microcosm of the group's ideal state: open, free, stable, independent, inquiring, diverse, and a repository for high culture. As the group looked to America to defend the world against the Soviet Union, so they looked to the university to defend America against the more dangerously irrational elements in domestic culture and politics.

As in their former campaigns, the conflict with the students created disagreement among the New York intellectuals about how strongly to fight their opponents, and by what means. Members of the group needed to decide whether the police should be called, or if intellectuals should control their own house instead. They had to determine where authority should reside in the university community. If democracy and majority rule were good enough for Sidney Hook in all other aspects of American society and culture, for example, was it acceptable in the university? If so, how would a professor run a class or a department? The group had to decide whether there should be a hierarchy of authority in the university, which suggested that some groups had different interests, or if instead there existed a common interest among all groups. Further, what rights did the forces of free scholarly inquiry and a neutralist disengagement have—as opposed to student demands for political advocacy from the faculty and administration? Was advocacy dangerous to the intellectual community as a whole, or just to teachers?

Most of the New York intellectuals were interested in the first stirrings of the political New Left, particularly since American campuses had not seen any significant student radicalism in several decades.[44] The dissenters followed the new developments most closely—as Howe, Coser, and others around *Dissent* had hopefully monitored the failing pulse of the American left throughout the 1950s. Yet even many affirmers in the group became engaged with the young radicals at the beginning.

In 1962 *Commentary* was sent a copy of the Port Huron Statement, the opening manifesto of the New Left, but Podhoretz declined to publish it. The manifesto asked that "the individual share in those social decisions determining the quality and direction of his life" and that "society be organized to encourage independence in men and provide the media for their common participation." But the document, drafted by Tom Hayden, went beyond issues of individual participation in political and economic processes and crossed into a transcendental rhetoric about human possibility that was reminiscent of the Beats—thereby tying the young political movement to the cultural radicalism that had preceded it. The charter announced the young radicals' belief that "men have unrealized potential for self-cultivation, self-direction, self-understanding, and creativity," and urged individuals to find "a meaning in life that is personally authentic." Work, the young radicals thought, "should involve incentives worthier than money or survival."[45]

Podhoretz later regretted his decision not to publish the document. He reflected that since it "almost immediately achieved the status of a historic document, the decision I made against running it, at least in a shortened version, might easily be considered the worst judgment of my entire editorial career. . . . Nevertheless, historic or not, the Port Huron Statement simply was not on its intellectual merits worth publishing." Although he rejected the manifesto because he considered it cliched and derivative, he and others in the *Commentary* circle were not hostile to its message. Fellow affirmer Nathan Glazer later even called the declaration "a model of humanistic radicalism."[46]

Dissent took a more active interest in the early New Left. In the spring issue of 1962 the editors published a long symposium, "The Young Radicals," consisting of statements by young leftists. Later that same year the Students for a Democratic Society (SDS) paid a visit to the *Dissent* offices. Both undertakings produced signs of the disagreements and antagonisms that would hinder relations between the two groups throughout the next decade.

Michael Walzer, a former student of Howe's at Brandeis and a young writer already associated with *Dissent*, led "The Young Radicals" symposium. He asked his fellow contributors what made them radicals and how they were different from the older generation of leftists. They produced no unified answer, although most of them were softer on the Cold War than the Old Left and some were more "existential." Staughton Lynd, for example, rejected the term *socialism* as meaningless to young radicals, and wanted "a new atmosphere in human relationships, a new creativity in daily life." Although he thought long-term goals and strategies were "fatal defects," he also wanted to avoid an "intellectual shallowness." He felt some kinship with Third World revolutions, a position for which the New York group had little sympathy.[47]

As *Dissent*'s designated representative of the Old Left, Lewis Coser responded with some apprehension. He worried that there was no longer a sense of continuity on the left among the young, that there was too little concern for democracy and for analytical criticism and too much interest in romantic Third World revolutions. The new radicalism was too "visceral," the same complaint the New York group had lodged against the Beats.[48]

When later that year SDS visited the *Dissent* offices for a talk, it did not go well. In attendance for the magazine were Irving Howe, Michael Harrington, Murray Hausknecht, Bernard Rosenberg, Stanley Plastrik, and Emanuel Geltman. Among the visitors were Tom Hayden, Todd Gitlin, and Carl Oglesby. During the discussion Howe objected to SDS's use of the term *participatory democracy* because it seemed to undermine the value of representative democracy and was reminiscent of the Stalinists' rejection of "mere" bourgeois democracy.

There was also an unmistakable generational conflict at the meeting, and Howe later admitted that the *Dissent* editors "mishandled the meeting badly. Unable to contain our impatience with SDS susceptibility to chauvinistic dictators like Castro, several *Dissent* people, I among them, went off on long windy speeches." But the fault was not all Howe's; he found Hayden "rigid" and "fanatical," a nascent "commissar."[49] Hausknecht got the impression that the young radicals regarded the magazine's editors as people who had nothing to say to them, as old fogies from the archives of the Old Left. That, according to him, was traumatic for the dissenters. Hausknecht found their talk of participatory democracy and the other ideas in the Port Huron Statement partly appealing, partly empty rhetoric.[50]

Two years later a series of campus disorders across the nation directly set the young radicals against the New York group, most of whom were defending their cherished institution, the university, as faculty members. The first clash was at Berkeley in 1964. Among the prominent New York intellectuals on the faculty at the time were Nathan Glazer, Seymour Martin Lipset, Philip Selznick, and Lewis Feuer. Sides were drawn, with Glazer, Lipset, and Feuer critical of the New Left, and Selznick more sympathetic to the young radicals.[51] What Glazer wrote soon after a tense Academic Senate meeting could have been said about the Berkeley experience as a whole for the New York group: "Afterward men who had been friends for years but had taken opposite sides approached each other with hesitation, and felt it necessary to reaffirm their friendship, so deeply had their emotions become involved."[52]

Four years later, in April 1968, the protests struck closer to home when students occupied Columbia University. Daniel Bell, Richard Hofstadter, Lionel Trilling, and F. W. Dupee were faculty members, and many others in the group resided in Manhattan or within commuting distance. The original issue was student opposition to the presence of the Institute of Defense Analysis (IDA) on campus. Columbia was affiliated with the IDA, as were such leading universities as Berkeley, Chicago, Stanford, and Princeton. Under student pressure Columbia cut its ties with the IDA, although Grayson Kirk, Columbia's president, remained a member of the IDA board of directors.

Although the students demanded that Kirk resign, the IDA issue did not sufficiently provoke the student ranks, so SDS leaders added to the fire the issue of the controversial new gym that was to be built in Morningside Park. Despite a neighborhood poll of Harlem to the contrary, the student leaders claimed that the gym was an infringement on Harlem and excluded its residents.[53]

On Tuesday, April 23, demonstrators gathered at the sundial at the center of campus at noon. They pushed their way up the stairs to Low Library, the main administration building, where they hoped to confront President Kirk. The crowd was turned back by counter-demonstrators. Led by SDS president Mark Rudd, a Columbia student, the demonstrators then marched to the gym site, tore down a fence, held a brief rally, and finally returned to campus. They then decided to occupy Hamilton Hall, the building where the undergraduate college administration and some faculty offices were housed.

Richard Hofstadter was leaving campus when he saw the demonstrators returning from the gym to the sundial. He followed the marchers into Hamilton Hall, as "it seemed to me to have the makings of another sit-in." Hofstadter went to his office in Hamilton as the students gathered on the main floor. When he left around three-thirty in the afternoon he did not think the students would take over the building.[54] They did.

That first night of occupation, Lionel Trilling, a member of the Executive Committee of the Faculty, attended emergency meetings on campus. Diana Trilling stayed at home waiting for him, "playing Canfield, an unopened book on my lap, the unceasing campus radio at my side, straining for the unfamiliar sound on the street beneath my shaded windows, the tramp or rush or scuffle of invasion."[55]

The next morning, Wednesday, a few of the faculty met in Philosophy Hall and formed an ad hoc committee to mediate between the students and the administration. Daniel Bell had been out of town when the seizure of Hamilton Hall occurred, but when he returned on Saturday he joined the steering committee of the faculty ad hoc committee.[56]

Hofstadter occasionally attended the faculty committee's meetings, although he never spoke. He considered himself "one of the more conservative members" of the committee. "I generally tended to go there only when one of my friends called up and felt an important issue was coming to the floor, and when it was suggested people of my tendency, so to speak, were needed, because senior faculty were drifting out of the committee and it tended to become . . . relatively heavily weighted towards marginal and junior faculty. A lot of us were concerned about its non-representative character."

As the week wore on, Hofstadter thought the committee felt within itself "an increasing spirit of animosity, an increasing factionalism between right and left."[57] One of the main points of contention was whether or not to call in the police to remove the students from Hamilton Hall. Bell and many others on the committee thought that if police were called in, the student body would be "radicalized" and the SDS would have gained a victory. Some of the students, Bell thought, might be persuaded through negotiation to leave Hamilton Hall.[58] Bell was never sympathetic to the New Left's program or tactics, and the difference between him and others like Hook, Hofstadter, and Diana Trilling was not in softness toward the aims of the young radicals. Instead, while opposing the student movement, Bell thought that the young should not be clubbed by police called by the faculty. The university should run itself, maintain a model of cool rationality for the young to observe and follow, and attempt peace through discourse and negotiation. Proper tactics, he thought, were equally important for both faculty and students to observe.

Hofstadter reported that, unlike Bell, he "did not sign a faculty pledge which was circulated at that time . . . not to teach if police were brought to evacuate students from buildings." He was discouraged that the faculty, "toward the end of the week, were beginning to forget that force had been introduced on the campus by the seizure of the buildings by the students, and were thinking only of the force that might come if the police came." [59]

Bell and others on the ad hoc committee, Hofstadter remembered, "even at the end felt that not all the possibilities of negotiation had been exhausted at the time the police were called, and I suppose that a lot of people in the faculty would have strung the situation out further." But Hofstadter had lost his patience. Nor did Diana Trilling have Bell's patience for negotiation with the students. She applauded the administration when it "bypassed the faculty in calling the police because it believed—rightly, I think—that the faculty was making matters worse by delaying the police confrontation." [60]

Sidney Hook also disagreed with Bell's stance, and even years later maintained that his friend lacked a fighting spirit. Hook argued that Bell's "dissident faculty group" had "encouraged student intransigence by seeking to mediate between the rampaging students and their victims." That Bell believed "under no circumstances should the police be called to keep the peace on the campus" was for Hook "the acme of foolishness, an invitation to student storm troopers of any ideology to run riot." At times, Hook advised, "even a pacific-minded right-wing Social Democrat should call the police." [61]

Hook posed the issue as one of intellectual appeasement: whether or not intellectuals would protect the territory of free thought. If a university official, Hook concluded, "is willing to permit himself to be manhandled by students and publicly humiliated when he capitulates to their lawlessness . . . he has been guilty of intellectual treason." [62] Bell saw it differently. One could not simply assert authority in a community and thereby regain it; one had to earn it by "going in and arguing" with the adversary in a "full debate," and then changing what needed to be changed. He felt that "repressive force is self-defeating. The Columbia administrators may have known about Berkeley and Wisconsin, but they did not show it." [63]

Dwight Macdonald, however, was exhilarated by the Columbia uprising—for which he earned the disdain of the rest of the group. Friday, two days after Hamilton Hall had been seized, a giddy Macdonald headed to

Morningside Heights from his Upper East Side apartment, "egged on" by his wife and F. W. Dupee, the latter of whom had told Macdonald on the phone: "You must come up right away, Dwight. It's a revolution! You may never get another chance to see one."

Macdonald concluded that his friend Dupee was right. "I've never been in or even near a revolution before," Macdonald admitted breathlessly. "I guess I like them. There was an atmosphere of exhilaration, excitement— pleasant, friendly, almost joyous excitement. . . . Everybody was talking to everybody else those days, one sign of a revolution." While he was there he visited two of the student "communes" in occupied buildings and had a grand time.[64]

The spectacle of an effervescent Dwight Macdonald enjoying himself on her campus in the midst of the insulting students was too much for Diana Trilling to take. "The militant Harlem leaders," she wrote with disgust, "had at least a demonstrable political motive based in the genuine grievances of their race and class: could one say as much for the white tourists, for—say—Robert Lowell, Dwight Macdonald, Paul Goodman?" Bell was sympathetic to her revulsion, and wrote with disapproval of the many "members of the New York literary 'establishment,' who were ec- static at having a real revolution on their doorstep. Norman Mailer threw a large fund-raising party. Dwight Macdonald wrote a 'begging' letter to his friends for money in support of SDS."[65]

Even those New York intellectuals whose campuses did not burst into revolt were antagonistic to the young radicals. Irving Howe, because he was so combative, polemical, and concerned about the condition of the left, found relations especially difficult to maintain. Howe acknowledged that in the 1960s "the 'kids', as the phrase goes, 'got to me.'" He wished later that he had not been "so emotionally entangled in disputes with the New Left," and that he had not "overreacted, becoming at times harsh and strident." Even his fellow dissenters mentioned his demeanor. "Friends began to hint in the kindliest way that I was becoming a little punch-drunk. . . . Couldn't I make my criticisms more temperate?"[66]

David Riesman spent the year at the Center for Behavioral Studies at Stanford in 1968–69, and both Irving Howe and Lewis Coser were there. Riesman recalled that some people at the Center would go to the campus to watch the students confront the police. Howe was one of them. "Irving Howe never went out to lunch with us once, because he was always going down to argue with the bad students," Riesman reported. "He loved that forensic. Coser was much more reserved."[67]

Howe offered a similar story. Each day while he was at the Center he drove to the Stanford campus to lunch with his wife. "One day a group of SDS students led by a fellow named Cohen forms a semi-circle behind us, chanting hostile slogans. They mean to carry the battle against decadent liberalism to the heart of the enemy. This continues day after day. Go elsewhere for lunch? My pride won't allow it." One noon an angry Howe spins to the group following him and shouts at Cohen, "You're going to end up as a *dentist*!" Howe was relieved. "Cohen blanches—the insult is simply too dreadful—and I march off in miniature triumph." [68]

It was not only what Howe said but also what he wrote that disturbed some of his associates. "When 'New Styles in "Leftism"' first appeared," he remembered painfully, "I was the happy recipient of a considerable amount of advice about the inappropriateness of my tone." But, he wondered, "what is the use in telling people who feel strongly about an intellectual matter that they should keep their voices low and sweet?" His defense was that he had come from a polemical tradition that cared more about the pursuit of truth than the pursuit of manners and gentility. The best of the New Left, he assumed, would respond well to serious criticism and prefer "an exchange of ideas" to flattery. [69]

Several of the New York intellectuals believed that the university community as a whole—both students and faculty—had a common interest, and that the university would be gravely threatened if that common interest became divided. Hook thought that a university constituted a "family," albeit with differences of status, function, and authority, "where mother, father, older and younger children accept different tasks and responsibilities." This authority was not based on anything so primitive as "the rule of the majority, but on knowledge," and intellectuals who had earned the right to authority therefore exercised that power. Intellectuals could not rule the university by a show of hands, since democracy did not mean that all minds were equally qualified. "Of course the faculty is not infallible," he concluded, "but because no one is infallible, it does not mean that all are equally qualified to decide." [70] Hook's commitment to democracy did not extend into the area which intellectuals inhabited. It could work outside their camp, in issues of the political and cultural self-determination of the general population, but not inside the university. Within, standards had to prevail or any meaningful sense of intellectualism would be lost.

Bell also worried about the New Left dividing the university. The students were wrong to portray the university as the enemy, he wrote, since in the 1960s the universities had been the source of antiwar pressures on society and had staged teach-ins. Similarly, the university should not treat students as antagonists, and it should deal with disruptions "not by invoking civil force but by rallying an entire community to establish common rules of common procedure." The university ruled by moral rather than civil authority, Bell thought, which was why he disagreed with Hook on proper tactics. "If the university is a community, asking for special loyalty from its members, how," Bell inquired, "can it sanction the clubbing of its students?" He agreed with Hook, though, that the university community must respect a proper hierarchy based on a "definition of areas of rights and powers and responsibilities appropriate to the division of function and place in the university itself." [71]

Glazer wondered whether there was to be no commonly agreed-upon set of rules. "What of the faculty? What of the students?" he asked. "Are all incapable of determining what is proper on a university campus?" Would various sections of the campus be self-ruled? Would each individual be autonomous? Was there no common ground for the organized intellectual community? "Constitutions can be changed," he acknowledged. "But should the constitution of a university include a grant of immunity to any and all forms of action that go by the name of politics?" [72] If not, who would decide what was permissible?

Further, the group felt that one of the most dangerous problems with the New Left's activism on campus was that free scholarship would be threatened by the requirements of political commitment. Even for the New York intellectuals, who mixed political commitments with their scholarship, the New Left transgressed the boundaries of what was acceptable in this regard.

The New York group was not proposing that intellectuals withdraw from society, only that they not be required to perform their analyses for a specific political purpose. They recognized that the difference between an intellectual and a scholar was that an intellectual had a wide curiosity and engagement with the contemporary world and with other disciplines, and that a scholar withdrew to neutral detachment and archival studies. They were among the most enthusiastic supporters of the general intellectual ideal, and were by no means suggesting to their New Left antagonists that those in the university community should withdraw from contemporary concerns. Still, the group did not want the scholarly role sacrificed entirely to intellectual activism.

Far from counseling withdrawal from the political and social world, Irving Howe pointed out that although universities were stocked with "scholars who live in the past and know far more about it than most intellectuals," the real "struggle for the *idea* of the past can be conducted with some hope of success only by those intimately related to the crises of the present: which by definition, so to say, the intellectual is and the scholar, insofar as he remains simply a scholar, is not." Paradoxically, "it is the intellectual who is particularly obligated and in the best position to teach the young the beauty of scholarship." [73] The ideal, as the group saw it, was to have both an engagement with the contemporary world and the freedom from having that engagement place any political or social requirements on their analysis.

Seymour Martin Lipset summarized their case. The political activist, he observed, is expected to be an advocate, "a lawyer, whose obligation is to make the best case possible for his client." Like a lawyer, an activist could be selective with evidence, not presenting contradictory or damaging facts, not addressing all points of view. But scholarship, he reminded the intellectual community, "emphasizes the opposite characteristics." [74] Therefore the roles of scholar and activist undercut each other and could not be pursued simultaneously. The political guidelines imposed by New Left activism reminded the group of requirements demanded of intellectuals by the Communists in previous decades.

The New York group's emphasis on intellectualism against the New Left's ideological activism illustrated aspects of continuity and change in the group's concerns. The members' anti-ideological stand echoed their earlier rejection of party-line requirements in the 1930s and 1940s. But the group also had evolved in thirty years—from political intellectuals and ideological activists at small magazines, to respected scholars at major universities who were increasingly concerned about preserving the proper function and prerogatives of the university and the scholarly role. That proper function, in their opinion, demanded an open and free university without specific political commitments, and an independent and secure scholarly role. Bell was a good example of one who had evolved in this period from a journalistic intellectual to a recognized major scholar.

Daniel Bell

Daniel Bell frequently has been portrayed as a principal contributor in the 1950s and 1960s to the conservatism that manifested itself in the end-of-ideology movement and related impulses, and throughout the 1970s and 1980s he was thought of as a neoconservative. Yet his complex style of thought cannot be so easily categorized, and his independence set him apart from his neoconservative friends. While Norman Podhoretz began as a political moderate and then wobbled to the left and right during the course of the 1960s, Bell's social democratic politics changed very little.

Bell was born Daniel Bolotsky on May 10, 1919, in New York, and he grew up on the Lower East Side. His father died when he was six months old, and his mother worked in a factory. The young Bell spent a large portion of his time in a "day orphanage" because his mother worked into the evenings. "So I had what is today called a deprived, disadvantaged, broken-home background," he explained. "I have an impeccable social origin, as they say, when the revolution comes."[75]

He "came to political awareness in the Depression," Bell remembered, "and joined the Young People's Socialist League in 1932, at the precocious age of thirteen." Within a year he began to be more sympathetic to the Communists because they seemed to be the only alternative to the rising fascism in Europe. But several of his mother's cousins were anarchists who, alarmed at the youngster's tilt toward Communism, gave him pamphlets on the Bolsheviks and the Kronstadt rebellion. Every generation has its Kronstadt, Bell later remarked. "My Kronstadt was Kronstadt." The pamphlets convinced him, and from that point forward he was aggressively anti-Communist. "I moved to the right wing of the socialist party."[76]

The right wing of the socialist party was where his friends found him in the lunchroom debates at City College in the mid-1930s. He had been a member of the Socialist party in 1936, but when the Social Democratic Federation split off from it that year, he went with them. So Bell, beginning in the 1930s, was a social democrat, a more conservative socialist than many of the other young New York intellectuals.

Bell entered City College in 1935, and after three years entered Columbia Law School. Following his first semester he switched from law to sociology. Then after studying sociology for a year and a half full-time, he began work at the *New Leader* in the summer of 1940. As Nathan Glazer pointed out, Bell fit in well at this journalistic forum for social democrats. It was there Bell met Sidney Hook, the social democrat who would be so close to him. After a little more than a year, at the age of twenty-two, Bell became managing editor. During this period he wrote many of the paper's articles "using four or five different names"—including John Donne (before Hemingway used the name) and Andrew Marvell.[77] His early journalism addressed political parties and strategies, Marxist or leftist factional arguments, and economic conditions, but, as a generalist, he also wrote reviews of dance, fiction, and international affairs.[78]

During the early 1940s, as he tried to find new writers for the paper, Bell read a piece by C. Wright Mills in the *American Sociological Review*. He wrote and asked Mills to contribute to the *New Leader*, and the two became good friends. In turn Mills introduced him to Richard Hofstadter in 1942 or 1943.[79]

In 1945 Bell was brought to teach at the University of Chicago by

Maynard Krueger, an economist. "Chicago was to me a great revelation because I got an education there for the first time," he remembered. "I really didn't have an education before that. I had a patchy education, in the sense that I knew a lot from study groups, but it was a floating, undigested mass." Edward Shils had assembled the social science staff, and Bell worked with Shils, Milton Singer, David Riesman, and Barrington Moore, among others. Philip Rieff was a graduate student and a member of a small group to which Bell served as faculty advisor. All of those he worked with seemed to be bright and in their late twenties. "During the war Shils had been active in the area of psychological warfare, and a lot of these people had worked for him. Shils brought some of them back to Chicago, and he was very eager to find the best young people around."[80]

Like fellow sociologists Coser, Mills, Riesman, and Glazer, Bell closely followed Macdonald's *Politics*. While he was in Chicago, however, he went through a period of strained relations with Macdonald. In November 1946, Macdonald sent Bell a harsh letter explaining why he had been unfriendly to Bell on the phone: Bell had not been writing for *Politics*, had failed to answer letters, and his correspondence had none of the friendly intellectual give-and-take Macdonald expected. Instead, as Macdonald explained to him, his letters were "nothing but a lengthy and detailed account of your own little academic busynesses . . . full of complacency and self-satisfaction. . . . Just a smug retailing of your doubtless highpowered activities, in few of which I could take much interest." Because Bell found the academic atmosphere at Chicago so cozy, Macdonald felt "there's not much in common between us any longer." Bell's "greatest weakness" was "careerism," according to Macdonald, and he wrote Bell that "a streak of careerism which has always bothered me about you has widened a lot."[81]

Part of the reason for the hurt feelings was that Bell and Macdonald were traveling different roads. Under the academic influence of teaching, Bell was beginning to approach ideas more as a scholar. Bell was becoming less like Macdonald, who could be giddy and flamboyant about his intellectual journalism, a person who, as Bell once pointed out, had a "habit of wearing the loud pink-and-black striped shirts" of the less restrained.[82] Later, Bell felt that "when I went to Chicago and began contributing to *Commentary*, Dwight became cross with me. After all, *Commentary* was paying for articles—careerism?"[83]

Although he continued as a columnist into the 1950s, by the late 1940s Bell began to drift away from the *New Leader*, because he remained more interested in socialist politics than the paper was. Macdonald, however, felt sure that Bell broke with the magazine over the stridency of its Cold

War rhetoric. "Good for you to break with the *New Leader*," he wrote Bell, "(especially as it was such a personal wrench) over their war-drums beating." He told Bell that "the neurotic intensity with which those circles pursue a hate-Russia policy is making it easier for the black-rightists to push this country still faster toward something damned unpleasant—as in the red purge now projected in govt offices." [84]

After leaving Chicago, Bell returned to New York. For ten years, beginning in 1948, he was labor editor at *Fortune* magazine. He also began teaching in 1952 "as an adjunct lecturer" in General Studies at Columbia. An interdisciplinary faculty seminar on McCarthyism that he taught there with Hofstadter and Seymour Martin Lipset in 1954 yielded *The New American Right* (1955)—a collection of essays on McCarthyism, populism, and the New Right, edited by Bell. The seminar also inspired Hofstadter's interest in the use of sociological perspectives in writing history, which was a perspective prominent in much of his work after that point. [85]

Bell worked for the Congress for Cultural Freedom in Paris in 1956–57, and when he left he decided not to return to *Fortune*. He was asked whether he wanted to edit *Commentary* but said no. A year later he took "a 50% salary cut to go back to Columbia." C. Wright Mills was not happy about Bell returning to the Columbia sociology department, and went to the Dean of the College about it. "At that point," according to Bell, "Dick [Hofstadter] turned against Mills and told him that he would support me, against Mills, and Dick's support, along with that of Lionel Trilling, was decisive." Bell was awarded his doctorate in sociology from Columbia in 1960, and he taught at Columbia for ten years before moving to Harvard. [86]

It is evident that Bell's interests and outlook changed from the 1940s and early 1950s, when he was at the *New Leader* and *Fortune*, to the late 1950s and beyond, when he taught full-time at Columbia and Harvard. In the 1940s he had labored on a "tired" Marxist book called *The Monopoly State*, which he later jettisoned. At that early point in his career he wrote shorter, more political articles, and was more politically engaged. After the late 1950s, while teaching, he found his interests naturally became "more scholarly, reflective, and academic," and the length of his essays increased tenfold. [87]

Like Sidney Hook, Bell could be sharply contentious with those he thought wrongheaded, but, more than Hook, Bell was also a reconciler. Hook, for example, thought that Bell had been too easy on his adversaries in the 1950s (over the issue of how the American Committee for Cultural Freedom would respond to McCarthyism) and 1960s (the students at Columbia). In an otherwise laudatory and affectionate account of Bell and others printed later, Hook told his readers that Bell had "no fighting heart." Hook thought that was demonstrated by Bell's willingness to compromise and mediate with radical students who used improper tactics. Asked about this later, Bell laughed and said that Hook was too much of a fighter, and did not always judiciously choose his battles or his timing— as Bell had warned him on occasion. Bell retorted that contrary to Hook's characterization, he thought of himself as a fighter, but a fighter for moderate positions. He was a "passionate centrist." He had been the one in the ACCF, he maintained, who had told people that if they wanted to be effective they had to discard their sectarian vices. [88]

Elliot Cohen and Hook had been the battlers in the ACCF, according to Bell, and he and Diana Trilling had been the menders, the centrists. The old joke around the group, Hook remembered mirthfully, was that if you were hungry and you had no place to eat you would attack Bell; to settle the argument and make up he would invite you to dinner. "Fighting, real fighting," Hook proclaimed proudly, "is when someone insults you and you kick them in the balls." [89]

Neither Bell nor Hook was among the easiest people to get along with, but in Hook, who was another contentious social democrat, Bell found a friend and teacher. He acknowledged the debt. "In a personal and intellectual sense, I owe most . . . to Sidney Hook, who taught me the appreciation of ideas," Bell wrote in his dedication to *The End of Ideology*. "While never, formally, his student, I learned from him in the more valuable ways of working together in common enterprises and in the informal, albeit argumentative, exchange of ideas."

Rather than relating as editor to contributor, or professor to student, Hook and Bell harmonized as older and younger colleagues in such undertakings as the ACCF, and in their writing they defended similar critical values. "I share most of his intellectual concerns while disagreeing with some of his passions," Bell noted, "but above all I admire his courage, personal and intellectual, which is expressed in his refusal to shirk a fight, however unpopular the cause, or to abandon a friend. He is, as all who have heard him know, one of the great teachers of the generation." [90]

Further, Bell noted that "Sidney was quite realistically a father to me. I had grown up without a father and for a period of time, Sol Levitas and Sidney were, quite openly, fathers to me. But as in Jewish families, one argued a lot with them." He was closest to Hook in the 1950s. In the early 1960s they began to drift apart for more than a decade. "In part, Sidney was dismayed by my turn back to religion and Judaism and the evident sense that I had rejected his and Dewey's naturalism in favor of a Niebuhrian neo-Augustinianism and an Old Testament view of human nature. In part, because I thought Sidney had become, paradoxically for the labels, too conservative."[91]

One of the more intellectually curious of the New York group, Bell's interests have been diverse. In college he was influenced by John Dewey and by Karl Mannheim's *Ideology and Utopia*, and when he taught at Columbia he was affected by the members of the Frankfurt School who were in residence at the Institute for Social Research at Columbia—especially Franz Neumann and Leo Lowenthal (and less so Max Horkheimer and T. W. Adorno, the latter of whom Bell thought "pretentious and somewhat of a fraud"). But over the course of his career the greatest written influence was Max Weber, from whom he understood the relationship of politics to society.[92]

Bell and other sociologists in the group were often accused by members of the New Left of being Parsonian structural functionalists who emphasized a consensus view of society in their sociology. But the Parsonian scheme was too formalized around a system of shared values for those in the *Partisan* circle to accept it. Rather, most of them subscribed to some form of conflict theory or to a view that sociology is attached to history and institutions and evolves with them. A set holistic theory like structural functionalism was as inadequate as a set ideology; neither allowed the dynamic flexibility essential to intellectual analysis.[93]

Of course, members of the New York group were not opposed to interrelatedness, but to "total" systems. After all, one of their signal contributions was to keep alive, in the age of specialization, an intellectual generalism from their Marxist pasts that promoted an interdisciplinary mixing of culture, politics, social science, journalism, and activism. But total and absolute systems—whether ideological utopianism, final solutions, or rigid sociological structures—were unacceptable to them.

Still, Bell and some of his fellow sociologists were criticized by the more radical members of the younger generation for emphasizing consensus instead of division in society. Basing their assumptions on European neo-Marxists such as Antonio Gramsci and Raymond Williams, many of these younger social critics described a society as a field for asymmetrical power relations in which hegemonic groups subtly oppressed subordinate groups; these inequalities were compounded and unconsciously reinforced by language itself.[94]

The consensus label was used primarily for a group of historians in the 1950s such as Hofstadter, Daniel Boorstin, Louis Hartz, and Allan Nevins, who emphasized the American population's agreement rather than disagreement over political and cultural goals. The label at least partly applied to Hofstadter's *American Political Tradition* (1948), as he later admitted, and his *Age of Reform* (1955). But both Hofstadter and Bell were descriptive rather than prescriptive consensus writers, in Hofstadter's terms. That is, rather than prescribing and celebrating an American pragmatic consensus, as Daniel Boorstin did in his *Genius of American Politics* (1953), Hofstadter and Bell described a condition of apparent middle-class dominance and stability but were still somewhat critical or skeptical of it.[95]

Neither Bell nor Hofstadter included a radical vision in their "consensus" books, but those works were less conservative than some of their critics alleged. Indeed, Hofstadter argued that "the idea of consensus is not intrinsically linked to ideological conservatism," but shared as much with Marx as with Tocqueville. Marxist historians, after all, also noticed the middle-class liberal dominance of American society, and therefore "a 'left' consensus interpretation" was also possible. "My own assertion of consensus history in 1948," Hofstadter reported, "had its sources in the Marxism of the 1930's."[96] The same might be said of Bell's *End of Ideology*, which appeared in 1960.

The consensus view, whether prescriptive or descriptive, was part of the larger anti-ideological impulse of the period. Bell's provocatively titled *End of Ideology*, however, made him the target of critics of the anti-ideological outlook. The book was more complex than his critics acknowledged, and his title less celebratory or prescriptive than they assumed.

In publishing *The End of Ideology*, Bell had two agendas. First, in these essays, written over the course of the 1950s, he outlined the anti-absolutism that all the New York intellectuals shared—both affirmers and dissenters. The book argued against a crusading moral absolutism that promoted an all-or-nothing intemperate set of political demands. Instead, Bell made a case for tentative and empirical thinking that allowed for modest compromise instead of total conflict.

Bell's second agenda was to show that between the 1930s and the 1950s America had become a more pluralistic, diverse, and open society, with less economic oppression, class immobility, and civil rights abuses. In order for the affirmers to justify no longer dissenting as strongly from American culture and society as they had in the 1930s, America had to be recast as an example worthy of affirmation in the postwar period. Bell, who associated more with the affirmers than with the dissenters, described this change in American conditions in his book. The documentation of this change continued into the 1980s in the work of most of the neoconservatives—Irving Kristol, Nathan Glazer, Norman Podhoretz, Hilton Kramer, Kenneth Lynn, and contributors to *Commentary* and the *New Criterion*.

Still, Bell's *End of Ideology* was not an uncritical celebration of America. It is true that he argued that America in the 1950s was no longer stratified by immovable classes, that there was no real ruling class, that mass society was still varied and diverse, that there was social mobility, that crime had actually declined, and that the socialist ideas and the socialist example were exhausted in America. Yet he also argued for greater social justice, criticized capitalism for its irresponsible worship of efficiency that resulted in worker alienation and dissatisfaction, and proposed responsible liberal reform on a nonideological basis.

A nonideological reformism, Bell thought, should strive toward social justice through a pragmatic economic and governmental social policy aimed at achieving specific solutions to specific problems. It should reject the more ideologically sweeping proposals that assume a tragic flaw in American society that only a large-scale reorientation could fix definitively. Keynesian countercyclical economic policy and specific adjustments to the welfare state were more attractive to the increasingly pragmatic, experimental, and tentative reform outlook of the New York group.

The End of Ideology reflected the complexities and contradictions that were central to Bell's thought throughout his career. Increasingly after the 1950s he placed importance on religious values in society, yet in his role as a secular intellectual he might be described as an agnostic and skeptic. Profoundly influenced by Kant and the intuition of the spirit, he seemed to contradict that as a social scientist whose rationalist empiricism on many issues resembled Hook's pragmatism. Although Bell constantly affirmed the importance of a strong commitment to moral values in society, he was one of the strongest opponents of moral absolutism. Closer to the affirmers, he still wrote occasionally for *Dissent*. Bell was a thinker who was committed to his view of the intellectual function, an open society, and free politics, but who was skeptical and moderate enough that rarely was he hotly committed to causes. Thus his outlook split on many planes, and contained many apparent contradictions.

Paradox was so central to Bell's thought that some observers have suggested that all of his later work was formed by the contradictions he faced in the 1930s and 1940s. According to one account, the young Bell's desire for socialism in the West even as he saw that planned capitalism was more likely to prevail forced him "to pursue socialist ends through the instrumentalities of the capitalist state." By another account, Bell struggled to reconcile "certain parochial identities such as Hebraism with the universal aspirations embodied in Hellenism" and to face the "contradictions and tensions that emerge when one seeks to temper the radical idea with the conservative impulse." [97] Precisely these sorts of tensions and uncertainties were laced through *The End of Ideology*.

Bell had opposed intellectual absolutism and holism at least since the disillusionment of Kronstadt. His opinions were reinforced by the stories of Communist oppression told by Arthur Koestler, Ignazio Silone, and Manes Sperber, as well as by Max Weber's "Politics as a Vocation." Weber warned about the difficulty of combining a commitment to politics with an allegiance to intellectual freedom and ethics. One had to choose between the "ethic of responsibility" and the "ethic of ultimate ends," and Bell chose responsibility and the path of compromise over the zealous pursuit of ultimate ends. Like Weber, Bell "came to reject any ethical absolutisms." [98]

Bell's realization that absolutisms produced Kronstadts made him "a lifelong Menshevik—the chooser, almost always, of the lesser evil." Further, the various Kronstadts produced by the mass politics of the mid-twentieth century prompted him "to fear the masses in politics and those who would whip up the passions of the mob 'in the name of the people,' as was once done in the name of God." The ethic of responsibility, of compromise, the politics of civility (as with Shils), and the fear of the moral zealot were the concerns that Bell felt governed his intellectual life. Bell lived according to the advice of Max Weber: "He who seeks the salvation of the soul, of his own and of others, should not seek it along the avenue of politics." [99]

Although he was deeply interested in issues of religion and salvation, most of Bell's writings were characterized by a search for realism. His work with Irving Kristol in 1965 to found the *Public Interest* was part of his search for practical solutions. Intended to combat ideological misinformation about social actions and consequences, the journal was devoted to the social scientific analysis of public policy problems. The *Public Interest* served as a forum for social analysis and the sociologists in the group, as *Partisan Review* had served as an outlet for mainly cultural ideas. Along with *Commentary*, the *Public Interest* quickly became recognized as the spiritual home for the social scientific neoconservatism increasingly associated with the New York intellectuals.

Like Trilling, Hook, Niebuhr, Glazer, and others, Bell valued complexity and ambiguity. He was against a "closed system," one governed by "totality" or "integration." His sociology, he reported, was "based on the methodological repudiation of a 'holistic' view of society, be it Marxist or Functionalist." In this respect, he joined Hook in the tradition of William James and John Dewey. Unlike Dewey, however, Bell had a dark side that was skeptical of natural progress, that was more associated with the misgivings of Max Weber, and that showed itself in the occasionally pessimistic tone of the *Public Interest*.

His long-standing opposition to ideological rigidity began in the 1970s to be framed in new terms. The solution to intellectual holism was to break the realms of social reality and social theory into a multiplicity of realms, as he proposed in *The Coming of Post-Industrial Society* (1973) and *The Cultural Contradictions of Capitalism* (1976). "Against these holistic views," Bell instructed his readers, "I have argued that society is better understood as being composed of diverse realms, each obedient to a different 'axial' principle."[100] The realm of the economy is guided by efficiency, the polity is ruled by the principle of equality, and the culture is dominated by self-realization or self-gratification. Since they are "contrary" principles, society has been in a constant state of tension with its beliefs. In Bell's opinion, this accounted for much of the previous century's cultural and intellectual history.[101] His proposal to fracture social thought into various axial principles reflected his dissatisfaction with simplicity and his hesitation to put too much trust in any one area of explanation.

Bell led the way, in the dissolution of unified ideological fields, by announcing that he was "a socialist in economics, a liberal in politics, and a conservative in culture." He was a socialist, he reported, because he believed in a "social minimum," and he believed that the community rather than the individual should be the first priority of economic policy. But because he believed that the individual rather than the group should be the primary actor in society, he considered himself a liberal in politics. Bell also endorsed the liberal beliefs that consenting parties should decide their actions, and that the public and private spheres should remain independent of each other. Finally, he labeled himself a conservative in culture because he respected tradition, supported "reasoned judgments of good and bad about the qualities of a work of art," and defended "authority—in the form of scholarship, teaching, and skilled exegesis."[102] In other words, he defended the authority of intellectuals.

It is unfortunate that Bell has been remembered primarily by the phrase "end of ideology." While there is a strong conservative component in his work, he has been a much more subtle political thinker than many of his critics concede. One of the few affirmers who also wrote for *Dissent*, he later quit his affiliation with the *Public Interest* because he thought that group was getting too conservative. In the mid-1980s he resigned from the board of *Partisan Review* because he disagreed with William Phillips's decision to use, as a centerpiece for a symposium, what Bell considered to be a tainted article by Michael Ledeen. On the fiftieth anniversary of *Partisan Review* he scolded the Committee for the Free World not only for their strident foreign policy views but for their gratuitous attacks on the writings of Michael Walzer and Irving Howe. Thus he spent the 1980s warning the neoconservatives about their excesses.[103]

In many ways Bell served as an opposite to Norman Podhoretz within the group. While Podhoretz increasingly simplified his thought from the 1950s to the 1980s, finding a simpler and more identifiable evil, Bell went from being a partly ideological writer in the 1940s to a more scholarly and complicated thinker in the 1950s and after.[104] Unlike Kristol, Podhoretz, or others who have moved from the left to the right of center, Bell has stayed relatively steady near the center. This situation has given rise to the illusion that he has actually moved back and forth across the middle as the intellectual community shifts around him. It has also prompted the idea in the 1970s and 1980s—when many in the group moved slightly to the right of center—that Bell may have moved slightly to the left. For example, around 1970 this illusion was created when Podhoretz crossed Bell's political path, moving from Bell's left to his right. Although less interested in socialist organizations than he once was, Bell remains in the 1980s the social democrat he has been for most of his life.

Defense Against the Counterculture

By the 1960s most of the New York intellectuals inhabited the liberal center or maintained a respectable democratic socialist dissent. They were former radicals who felt their fortress was being stormed and saw it as their duty to protect society. One reason they had abandoned their earlier radicalism was that their revolutions largely had been won. Stalinism had been discredited, anti-Semitism had declined, modernism had become mainstream, and America was becoming more internationalist in culture. Their country was a leader in protecting free thought—partly because of having followed their advice about the Cold War, or so they liked to think. By the 1960s they genuinely valued liberal politics and liberal society.

Even in its most radical days, though, the New York group had held to the paramount values of rationalism, pluralism, system, temperance, moderation, informed debate, analysis, civility, pragmatism, and reason. So the group saw a threat to liberal society in the counterculture's sympathy for mysticism, irrationalism, ideology, nihilism, the adversary culture, romanticism, emotionalism, moralism, absolutism, and inflexibility. It was against these dangerous heresies that the group attempted to hold the line.

The young radicals' hostility toward authority was especially frightening. The New York intellectuals believed in authority—either from a particular class, an idea, or an institution—and they had supported respect for authority even in their most radical moments. Daniel Bell could sympathize in theory with an opposition to certain types of authority, but he considered a general opposition to authority to be a romantic vision of a nihilistic generation. In his eyes the young radicals were "anti-institutional and even antinomian."[105]

The student radicals dismissed these worries of the New York intellectuals as those of "a new conservatism rather than of liberalism." Singling out the Berkeley faculty members in particular, two graduate students there accused them of valuing "order" above "democratic goals." It was not a new accusation. Young scholars since the late 1950s had noticed the group's fear of the masses and their worry about the decline of authority.[106]

Later, Bell thought his critics were right about himself and others in the group.[107] As he put it in 1972, he realized that both Stalinism and the Holocaust had been "traumatic" experiences that had affected his generation. He and Richard Hofstadter, troubled by these events, had "long conversations" that revealed "what might be called a fear of mass action, a fear of the sort of thing that emerged to some extent in his whole interest in Populism. What happens when a mass gets out of hand and becomes a mob? And therefore there was a great suspicion and fear of mass action of a particular kind, and fear of those situations which in a sense tear down the very fragile bonds of society." He noted that Niebuhr, Arendt, Riesman, and many others in the group shared those fears.[108] "And in this sense," Bell admitted, "we all became somewhat conservative."[109]

Bell saw in Hofstadter and others that their "fear of mass action" was the same fear they would have "if anarchy were let loose, so to speak, in the world." At Columbia in 1968 that fear "came home, in a very direct immediate way." The student unrest, Bell felt, "in a sense fulfilled—confirmed all [Hofstadter's] worst forebodings."

Part of the origin of this fear of mass action was grounded in recent history. Jews of the New York group's generation had been victimized by mass uprisings in Europe, and the Soviet Union, and they had feared anti-Semitism at home in Father Coughlin's following.[110] Their generation, Bell noted, had "this fear in a sense of the nihilistic elements which lie deep in human nature." In addition, Bell maintained, the Jewish element in this fear went even deeper. There was "a fear of the animal" in Jewish life, he noted. "There's a great sense, you know, that man is a raging beast, and it's only a kind of tough-minded law which holds him down, which is why in Judaism you always have the symbol of the Torah, essentially of the law, as against any other precepts of this kind." Therefore, among both the affirmers and the dissenters, there was a desire for authority, reason, and law, against what they feared was an uncontrollable passion in the students.

As early as three years before the Berkeley protests, Lionel Trilling was worried about the values professors were teaching their students. In their required courses students studied modernism, which had been imported to America with the enthusiastic help of *Partisan Review* and the New York intellectuals. Yet in that modern literature Trilling found "the disenchantment of our culture with culture itself," and discovered a "bitter line of hostility to civilization which runs through it." The literature itself should not be discarded, but he thought professors should hesitate before passing it along to the uninitiated. "My doubts do not refer to the value of the literature itself," he assured the intelligentsia, "only to the educational propriety of its being studied in college." [111] Why a sympathy for modernist literature had not fatally harmed his own generation, he did not say. Four years later, in 1965, Trilling surveyed the subject again, and found that an "adversary culture" had formed among the young, as he had predicted. Again he complained about "the adversary intention, the actually subversive intention, that characterized modern writing," an intention to exalt individual autonomy at the expense of society and culture. [112]

Bell saw an irony in his colleagues' fear of an adversary culture. Rahv, Abel, Howe, and others celebrated modernism, Bell wrote, but were afraid of modernism's natural culmination in the nihilism of the sixties. Yet unlike Trilling, who began to question modernist literature, many others in the group praised the aesthetic of modernism while denouncing the adversary culture it created. [113] For Bell, however, an important distinction separated an adversary culture and the sixties counterculture. An adversary culture was a facet of "serious culture," and was derived "in many respects from the whole modernist temperament." Its animus was to "tear down bourgeois society" and "all restraints on civilization." It articulated "a preoccupation with the abyss and the sense of nothingness that comes from it." In contrast, the counterculture "derives from certain elements of hedonism, particularly in American bourgeois life—the search for pleasure, the search for excitement, the search for sensation—and it is abetted, in many ways by campus culture itself." Adversary culture was a troubling product of high culture, while the counterculture was a self-indulgent offspring of mass culture. [114]

That nihilism, the New York group believed, was accompanied by irrationalism, mysticism, and reverence for the transcendentalism of drug experiences. Another way to phrase it is that they were convinced that the counterculture had a strongly religious and mystical component that could lead to irrational and destructive tendencies. The counterculture was more likely to pursue the avenues of faith, intuition, and sensation than of reason or intellectual analysis.

Even Paul Goodman, who had a less rationalist orientation than many of his fellow critics, found youth in the 1960s to be surprisingly spiritual. "I had imagined that the worldwide student protest had to do with changing political and moral institutions, to which I was sympathetic," he wrote with surprise, "but I now saw that we had to do with a religious crisis of the magnitude of the Reformation in the fifteen-hundreds." To replace their previous dependence upon science and progress, the young had turned to "religious innovation, new sacraments to give life meaning." Although he was sympathetic to these mystical yearnings, Goodman complained that the young brought their religious concerns to the political field. "But [religion] is a poor basis for politics," he told them, "including revolutionary politics." [115]

The need for this religious experience or transcendence, these critics thought, also produced in the counterculture an inflexible moralism, a rigid, visionary self-righteousness. Some of the young, it seemed, could have written a book with a title like *Witness.* Hook, as might be expected, was a leading critic of the counterculture's inflexible true-believers. Complaining that "the student population has become 'moralistic,'" Hook told the young that, instead of being tentative and making careful distinctions, they saw "only right or wrong, good or bad, and no degrees of evil." Forgetting history, they saw a current good as a perennial good, a current evil as a perennial evil. Therefore in any conflict they could see only one way to progress: "the ideal solution." The counterculture's ideological moralism was ill-informed, too simplistic, and predicated on faith rather than experimental analysis. Hook had said nearly the same to Whittaker Chambers fifteen years earlier. [116]

To the charge that they were too simplistic, some in the New Left retorted that complexity was only a veil for conservatism. A devotion to complexity and ambiguity, it is true, often allowed some members of the New York group to argue that attempts at social reform were too simplistic and produced unintended results. It allowed some of them therefore either to shy away from reform or denounce reform as utopian. Disciples of complexity and ambiguity often were identified, with justification, as the inheritors of the end-of-ideology outlook. Those liberals or conservatives who liked the more complicated approach, however, credited the New York intellectuals with providing a successful challenge to simple ideologists and bringing a higher and more intelligent level of debate to political, cultural, and social problems. [117]

To those who admired the New York group for their impatience with simplistic notions, Glazer's advice to the young radicals was welcome. Glazer, who was moving from Berkeley to Harvard at the time, cautioned the counterculture that their insistence "that something fundamental is wrong leads easily to the conclusion that something grand and apocalyptic is required to set it straight." The inverse was also true. If the young wanted a total transformation, some overwhelming evil had to be discovered to justify it.

In an "advanced" society like America, Glazer believed, only a small and diminishing number of problems could be solved "by direct clashes between competing interests," the sort of large and total conflicts that ideologists waged. Currently, "clear evils to fight against are rapidly succeeded by increasingly ambiguous evils, whose causes and solutions are equally unclear." Because "no solution is ever complete or final," Glazer counseled, "there is no alternative to bureaucracies, administrators, and experts." His difference with the young, he reported, was that he saw "no Gordian knot to be cut at a single stroke."[118] His advice? Leave moralism, ideology, and inflexibility behind.

In sum, the New York intellectuals considered the values, methods, and ends of the counterculture to be subversive of a liberal pluralist society. Liberal pluralism was based on humane tolerance, civil freedoms, free and independent critical inquiry, and respect for diversity. Liberal pluralism, in turn, supported and protected the values important to the New York group—not least of which was the freedom to be intellectuals. Although they themselves had criticized that society in the 1930s, in the postwar years they gradually came to be among its most vocal defenders. In the 1960s they were not prepared to stand aside and let it be trampled by an enemy from within.

Part of the problem, as *Dissent* editor Howe saw it, was that the young had not studied liberalism enough to understand the tradition they were rejecting. To the young radicals "liberalism means Clark Kerr, not John Dewey; Max Lerner, not John Stuart Mill; Pat Brown, not George Norris." They did not realize that liberalism provided radicals with "a heritage of civil freedoms, disinterested speculation, humane tolerance."[119] Ignoring the liberal tradition, the young escalated their tactics into a policy of extremism, Howe complained. They brought physical violence to campus, but then objected to police force. They burned government papers and records, but protested when their own offices were invaded.[120] The New Left attacked the liberal society, but cried foul when not protected by it.

There was, of course, a range of liberal opinion within the New York group—from a neoconservative and grudging liberalism on one side (represented by affirmers like Norman Podhoretz) to a liberal socialism on the other side (characterized by dissenters like Irving Howe). But despite these differences, all of the New York intellectuals agreed that the liberal pluralist society was what made America unique, and they felt that when the counterculture rejected liberal pluralism it rejected America. For the young, though, it seemed that they had to reject part of America in order to regain America's genuine promise and potential.

Proper Radicals and Critics

Central to each of the battles the members of the New York group waged against their various antagonists was their attempt to promote a responsible political and intellectual point of view. In these conflicts they constructed their vision of a beneficial politics of dissension. In doing so, they were repeatedly forced to define the proper limits of radicalism, the extent to which leftism had to be mixed with liberalism, and the amount of openness and independence required to sustain a healthy radicalism or intellectualism. Increasingly, as former leftists, they decided that liberal values constituted the heart of proper "radicalism."

At the Waldorf Conference they decided that useful intellectual radicals had to be open, honest, and nonpartisan. Leftists could not misrepresent their ideas or their allegiances. In their response to the literature of repentance, the group found that respectable radicals had to set their own records straight, but avoid patriotic partisanship that could enforce conformity and undermine further dissent in the political community. In their debate over mass culture, the group reaffirmed the intellectual axiom that standards must not be compromised by either radicals or conservatives.

In their conflict with the New Left, they found that a correct and useful leftism was liberal, democratic, moderate, practical, and even technical. The radical impulse had to be tempered by some of the modesty, sobriety, and pragmatism of the *Public Interest*. By the time of Kennedy, Johnson, and Nixon, if not before, liberalism was the true left for the New York group. That outlook was modest rather than dramatic. It avoided excessive anti-Americanism as thoroughly as it refrained from a celebration of America. Proper radicalism was neither authoritarian, irrational, mystical, nihilistic, nor romantic. It was antitotalitarian but not absolutist or extremist in its means. A successful leftism had to have a program. It had to be able to work in a coalition with other enlightened and responsible political forces, and had to avoid factionalism. A worthwhile radicalism had to have virtue, which meant it had to reject violence, minority rule, and excessive civil disobedience in favor of civility, intelligence, rational argument, and reason.

What the group asked of leftists was perfection, because if radicalism could not be perfect it was hardly worth preserving. Yet what they asked of radicals was no more than they asked of intellectuals, which meant it was no more than they expected of themselves.

Harold Rosenberg had said that intellectuals turn answers into questions. Yet in their conflict with the young, the group was antagonistic about the New Left questioning traditional American liberal "answers"— and in that way the New York group defended a form of orthodoxy. By contradicting Rosenberg's definition, did the members of the group disqualify themselves as intellectuals? The paradox can be resolved by noting the group's motives: they defended a liberal orthodoxy out of fear that the romantic, irrationalist, and ideological outlook of the New Left would contradict and undermine liberal society's tolerance for the very practice of questioning. Not all questioning was equally beneficial, in the group's view. Especially bad was a style of questioning that appeared to lead to its own closed system of orthodoxy and that would stifle questioning in the future.

They supported liberalism because they were convinced it would permit intellectuals to continue to oppose orthodoxy—to turn answers into questions—in a way that more passionate ideological visions would not. In their view, they contradicted Rosenberg's dictum in the case of the New Left in order to preserve the right to continue questioning in the future. This, of course, was the same position they had taken against the Communists decades earlier.

Another continuity in the group's outlook was the belief that an intellectual's responsibility was to evaluate and interpret society and culture openly and honestly. As Dennis Wrong phrased it, one had to show a "scrupulous concern for intellectual rigor," and maintain one's "duty as a political intellectual to criticize 'incorrect analysis' by writers" with whom one honestly disagreed.[121] But, as we have seen, dissenters and affirmers disagreed about whether intellectual rigor required a vigorous criticism of one's own culture. The dissenters thought that a large part of the intellectual's function was to maintain intelligent criticism, loyal opposition. In contrast, the affirmers agreed with Irving Kristol, who complained that many intellectuals not only were "critical of the failure of this civilization to realize perfectly the ideals it claims as inspiration" but also extended that to "an adversary posture toward the ideals themselves." Cultural intellectuals, he believed, had "always been assigned the task of, and invariably accepted responsibility for, sustaining and celebrating those values" of the culture.[122] For the affirmers, an intellectual was a sustainer.

Among the values necessary for intellectuals and their magazines was a "commitment to dispassionate inquiry as the ground of understanding," Daniel Bell and Irving Kristol reported. "But also there is the commitment to the idea of rational authority; to the view that opinion is not knowledge, that intellectual qualifications are a condition for judgment, and that some judgments are more worthwhile than others. It is thus a commitment to reason and to its mode of discourse, the mode of civility." Reason—and the process of reason, which included civil discourse—was absolutely central. "We believe," they continued, "that without rational authority and civil discourse, a civilized society—and that is the ultimate model of the university—is impossible." [123] It was this strong attachment to rationality and reason that bound affirmers and dissenters together from the beginning. Despite their serious differences, both sides of the group shared a basic consensus on means (reason, rationality, due process, standards) as well as ends (diversity, openness, freedom, antitotalitarianism).

Repeatedly throughout their careers, members of the New York group decided that their political and cultural beliefs should be predicated on their intellectual role. That is, in progressive stages in the decades after the 1930s, they slowly abandoned any commitment to political leftism that contradicted their vision of what it meant to be free, independent, unbeholden intellectuals. In their conflict with the New Left, as with virtually all of their other decisions at significant crossroads, they chose to support their intellectual identities over their political identities. Although they had long thought of themselves as leftists or radicals, even if moderate liberal leftists, they chose to denounce the first indigenous radical movement that had appeared in decades. Rather than considering it most important to support their heritage of political values at all costs, they found it more essential to endorse their intellectual beliefs. In the end that left the great majority of them neither radicals nor conservatives—but liberal intellectuals. They increasingly saw liberalism and pragmatic intellectualism as symbiotic values, each of those values a vehicle to insure the health of the other.

In the end, the group's struggle with the student left was reminiscent of its campaign against the Waldorf Conference. Sidney Hook, for one, had not altered his rhetoric or his logic since his denunciation of Harlow Shapley and his colleagues twenty years earlier. He was still concerned with intellectual honesty and the freedom of ideas.

The greatest weapon against all adversaries, Hook still thought, was reason. He advised his fellow intellectuals to "assume that most students can respond to ideas and that they are responsible in large measure for their actions. Although it is possible that they may continue to turn a deaf ear to criticisms of their position and a blind eye to ideals continuous with the liberal and humanist tradition from Socrates to John Dewey, the effort must be made until they see reason." Hook might have written exactly the same sentiments about the Waldorf participants two decades earlier. "Whether they see reason or not," he concluded, "what their teachers say and do must exemplify it." [124]

6 The View from the Plaza

As this story began with a conference in New York, so will it end. On February 12 and 13, 1983, the "Our Country and Our Culture" conference was held at the Plaza Hotel, just ten blocks north and a few blocks west of the Waldorf-Astoria. Midge Decter, her husband Norman Podhoretz, and other affirmers in the New York group staged the Plaza meetings to promote a hard-line anti-Communist consensus in politics and to oppose what they considered anti-Americanism in culture. Appropriately, the 1983 conference took its name from the title of the 1952 *Partisan Review* symposium that had marked the beginning of the New York intellectuals' public affirmation of America.

Just as the Waldorf Conference nearly thirty-five years earlier had drawn opponents to its meetings, so now did the Plaza Conference. Again, affirmers and dissenters disagreed about the proper amount of anti-Communism and the correct level of criticism of American culture. Podhoretz and Decter, instead of Sidney Hook, led this meeting of affirmers. Dwight Macdonald, who might have organized the dissenters against this event, had died the previous year. Now it was Alfred Kazin, a dissenter skeptical of the conference's aims, who sat in the audience. The conference leaders had recently formed the Committee for the Free World, an organization that Kazin complained was "the latest and most aggressive of those bodies of former leftist intellectuals, in the tradition of the Congress for Cultural Freedom, which, concentrating on the danger of communism abroad and at home, still consider themselves an avant-garde of sorts." [1]

Several of the conference speakers lamented that American cultural critics were as cold toward their country as the snow that was falling outside. The audience heard them deplore the level of anti-Americanism coursing through the culture during the Reagan decade. Joseph Epstein, editor of the *American Scholar*, worried that "the contemporary literary scene is rife with writers whose chief stock in the trade of ideas is a fairly crude sort of anti-Americanism."[2]

The Plaza weekend was a celebration not only of American culture but also of the undisputed position of cultural influence and leadership the affirmers now believed they held. The Reagan administration was consulting *Commentary* and its editors for foreign policy advice (Jeanne Kirkpatrick was appointed ambassador to the United Nations in part on the strength of her essays in the magazine), and the question became whether Reagan was hard-line enough for *Commentary* rather than vice versa.

Podhoretz told the audience that the neoconservative affirmers were "a political community now. The resonance of what we do is greater than ever. . . . There are more of us around than there were ten years ago. . . . We are the dominant faction within the world of ideas—the most influential—the most powerful. . . . By now the liberal culture has to appease *us*. . . . People like us made Reagan's victory, which had been considered unthinkable."[3]

Kazin was alarmed at the ideological extremism apparent among the more aggressive affirmers. "In summing up the conference," Kazin reported, "Podhoretz assured his audience that 'partisanship is the only way to establish a cause,' that neutrality in intellectual opinion is as absurd and dangerous as neutralism between America and Russia."[4] As the Plaza Conference demonstrated, in the 1980s members of the New York group were still engaged in the concerns that had engaged and divided them since before World War II.

During the same year as the Plaza Conference, Irving Kristol, one of the most intelligent essayists among the affirmers, published his *Reflections of a Neoconservative*. Kristol had become an influential voice during the 1970s and 1980s, writing in the *Wall Street Journal*, *Commentary*, and other publications. One of his important contributions was his argument that corporations should fund ideological ventures that supported a capitalist outlook.

In the introduction to *Reflections*, Kristol provided a brief sketch of how political good and evil have manifested themselves in the world. Like other conservatives of varying stripes, Kristol blamed the French Revolution and celebrated the British Enlightenment. The French Revolution made the mistake of promising happiness, fraternity, and equality, and so it led to Soviet culture, Marxist Third World regimes, unreasonable demands on the welfare state, sex and drugs, and the New Left. In contrast, the British Enlightenment was forged by rationalists who were politically more modest and disciplined, who promised instead a free market, self-interest, and secular civility; therefore it produced Adam Smith, nineteenth-century rationalism, Herbert Hoover, business, and the neoconservatives. Kristol believed his role was to rally the forces of the British Enlightenment—to deny to the undisciplined poor and the rest of the cultural inheritors of the French Revolution the unreasonable demands they made upon the structure of government, and to stop their distortion of responsible liberal culture.[5]

Although the New York intellectuals in the 1930s were themselves mistaken for radical descendants of the French Revolution, they were never comfortable with that outlook. Nearly from the beginning they were attracted to the rationalist and pragmatic strains of the British Enlightenment, partly through the work of the scientific naturalism of John Dewey. Kristol realized this allegiance in most members of the group, and certainly in himself and the liberal capitalist majority of Americans. An important task, as he saw it, was to refurbish the ideology undergirding corporate America, and to make sure that capitalist leaders realized the importance of the ideological fight. Thus his French and British history lesson.

Kristol's devotion to the British Enlightenment is yet another example of the pragmatic impulse in the New York group. During the fifty years from the mid-1930s to the mid-1980s, the New York intellectuals made a critical crossing from ideology and utopianism to pragmatic criticism. Intellectual witnesses, they chronicled their transformation and promoted it in the larger culture, impatient with those who would not join them. Their journey from ideology to liberal rationalism produced a cultural criticism based on tentative truths—which they pursued with conviction and ardor (and sometimes inflexibility and extremism), ignoring the small ironies that catch even the best-intentioned.

They were not a group who wanted to be isolated from what Americans persist in calling "the real world," and as a consequence they were a collection of critics who actually affected the world around them. Although they influenced the project of culture and criticism in the intellectual community—adding a polemical contentiousness, a historical outlook, a moral test for literature, and a Marxist generalism—they also led the charge to find a responsible liberal anti-Communism, a central political problem in postwar America. One may argue over whether their anti-Communism was responsible, but no one can dispute the prominence of their role in making anti-Communism the official ideology of postwar America. During the McCarthy period the New York intellectuals helped set the acceptable parameters of that ideology. Balancing a passionate an-titotalitarianism with the rhetoric of reason, they were as strident in their anti-Communism as it was possible to be without crossing the line from liberalism, such as it was in that frantic period, into reaction and conform-ist oppression.

The group was also directly engaged in face-to-face confrontations with the New Left and student protesters during the 1960s. The New York intellectuals were not hidden in libraries nursing ideas; they were leading and visible members of faculty councils that legislated the out-come of the student rebellion. Often it was they who determined whether police force would be used, whether university policies would be altered, and what sort of radicalism would be tolerated in the centers of American cultural and professional training. On the campuses, as in national policy and public opinion, the New York group exerted a decisive effect on the real world.

The formal political memberships of the group began to change in the wake of the Great Society and the Vietnam War. In the 1970s and 1980s a number of the affirmers began to think of themselves as Republicans rather than Democrats—partly because their views on foreign and do-mestic policy had grown increasingly neoconservative, and partly because of their hostile reaction to the young in the 1960s, many of whom had ended up in the Democratic Party. Still they continued to argue the merits of affirmation and dissent: Could responsible intellectuals affirm patriotic nationalism? Was there too much anti-American dissent in the country? When Podhoretz and *Commentary* led the fight in the 1980s to reinter-pret Vietnam as a noble war, the subtext of their argument was that those who thought otherwise were anti-American radicals—in fact were the same anti-American radicals who had caused the defeat.

In 1987 the Committee for the Free World warned the nation that "never have we been more beset by tempters" such as the "shrewd and formidable" Mikhail Gorbachev. "But most pernicious of all," the Com-mittee cautioned, "is our tendency to blame ourselves for whatever goes wrong in the world. There are people among us, journalists and politi-cians, professors and clergymen, who try to tell us that this tendency reflects a higher moral spirit. We must more than anything else learn not to listen to them."[6]

The hard-line affirmers connected to the Committee for the Free World started the *National Interest* as a forum for their foreign policy views. In the cultural realm the affirmers launched the *New Criterion* to denounce anti-American radicalism and insufficiently optimistic literary critics and novelists. As in the past, magazines representing the dissenters were not as numerous. In addition to *Dissent*, there was the short-lived *Democracy* in the early 1980s, and *Tikkun*, which began in the mid-1980s. *Dissent* remained a small-circulation magazine for several reasons. First, leftist intellectual publications have rarely fared well in America. Second, it did not have the institutional backing and financial support of the more successful *Commentary*. Third, many younger leftists turned away from *Dissent* and toward magazines that dealt with the cultural or academic agendas of the sixties: the cultural studies movement, gender studies, linguistic radicalism, structuralist critiques of popular culture, and material or ethnographic studies.

During the 1970s, the New York group was shocked into reconsidering itself in earnest when several members of the first generation died. After Philip Rahv's death in 1973, some members wrote memorial essays that expressed a nostalgia for the early days of *Partisan Review*, when there were clear evils to fight and the young intellectuals had a passion to fight them. More essays about the group's early years followed the deaths of Lionel Trilling in 1975, Harold Rosenberg in 1978, Dwight Macdonald in 1982, and Sidney Hook and Mary McCarthy in 1989.[7]

In the late 1970s and 1980s, prompted by a sense of their mortality, Alfred Kazin, Norman Podhoretz, Irving Howe, William Barrett, William Phillips, Lionel Abel, Mary McCarthy, and Sidney Hook published their memoirs. During this period, some of the New York intellectuals began to suggest that the group had broken apart over its challenge from the New Left in the 1960s, and several memoirists claimed that the group had long since dispersed. Yet their autobiographies further cemented and represented their closeness to each other—since past and current arguments and hostilities framed those memoirs and underlined the agreement they shared over what constituted the most vital issues. Even in the old days their closeness had rarely been expressed in affection, but instead in the intensity of their disagreements over concerns that they acknowledged were central. Actually, as the Plaza Conference demonstrated, the group remained vigorous and cohesive in the 1970s and 1980s.

But the group's surviving members were scattered around the country in various university communities, and the misconception continued that the group was unraveling. In 1985 in the *New York Times Magazine*, James Atlas stood in mourning, head bowed and hat in hand before what he saw as the passing of an admirable group of cultural critics.[8] Two years later Russell Jacoby's intelligent *The Last Intellectuals* took the case a step further and pronounced the end of the freelance intellectual tradition altogether.[9] Those men and women are gone, he reported, who wrote on issues outside their own field, who wrote for the public in addition to their professional peers, who were involved in contemporary political and social controversies, and who served the broad public function of helping interpret culture to society.

Jacoby described three generations of intellectuals in recent American history. The first consisted of pre-institutional writers like Lewis Mumford and Edmund Wilson, who were perfectly independent freelancers. The second generation, according to Jacoby, consisted largely of members of the New York group, who began as independent freelance writers but in mid-career were lured into the university. They were the last intellectuals, half-crippled by their allegiance to the academy. The third generation, those born in the baby boom after 1940 and largely sympathetic to the New Left, have grown up in a time when the academy and scholarship are the only outlet for writers. The academic outlook, so inherently narrowing, has been fatal to the cultural and intellectual tradition of generalism, which has consequently come to an end. But Jacoby was wrong on one key argument: his contention that universities and other institutions are *inevitably* unable to produce or sustain intellectual generalists.

Jacoby's analysis is the latest in a tradition of jeremiads in America that stretches back at least to Henry Adams's time, with the members of each generation fretting that theirs is the last vestige of the letters tradition and placing the blame on industrialism, capitalism, or specialization. Adams had a hard time leaving the nineteenth century, not to mention the eighteenth, and could not imagine that the intellectual tradition would survive that same journey. It did. Despite Adams's fears, the twentieth century produced Lewis Mumford, Edmund Wilson, the New York group, and others whom Jacoby admires. It also gave us Russell Jacoby. Now it is Jacoby who is having similar trouble leaving the mid-twentieth century behind.

Jacoby, Atlas, and many of the New York intellectuals themselves view institutions as fatal to cultural criticism and the letters tradition because they threaten intellectual independence. They fail to note, however, that the earlier figures they admire never operated without institutions. Magazine editorships are as institutionally confining as academic posts, and many earlier writers like Dwight Macdonald, Harold Rosenberg, and Alfred Kazin jumped at the chance to leave such roles and be "confined" by the university. Institutionalization did not fatally harm the New York group, and future generations of writers will find a way to contribute in an institutional setting. As Harold Rosenberg once noted, "Hasn't the intellectual seen in the perspective of his social group always been in a state of ceasing to be an intellectual?"[10]

There is a need for continued generalism, for those who will write broadly and publicly. It would be a great loss for our culture if Jacoby were correct and the New York group were the last of a long line. The question is whether their example can be reproduced within modern institutions or whether, as Jacoby and others suggest, the institutionalization of the intellectuals will inevitably suffocate that generalist impulse. There is evidence that generalism can exist in the university: the works of such disparate writers as Nathan Glazer, Lewis Coser, Sidney Hook, Noam Chomsky, Lionel Trilling, Garry Wills, Arthur Schlesinger, Jr., Alan Brinkley, and Michael Walzer inside academia have been every bit as broadly cultural and engaged with public issues as the writings of Mary McCarthy, Robert Kuttner, Elizabeth Hardwick, Jason Epstein, Joan Didion, Tom Wolfe, Norman Podhoretz, James Fallows, or Hilton Kramer outside the university.

Jacoby is correct that American universities are not geared toward turning out generalists. Yet within contemporary society there remain some havens for the intellectual. Broad cultural magazines such as those found in the *Partisan Review* orbit, some generalist think tanks, and various interdisciplinary graduate programs are a few of the institutions designed to renew and sustain the tradition of intellectual generalism. Further, in the autumn of their careers, many members of the New York group are trying to foster in the younger generation the broad general concerns that need to be carried on.

Future generations of intellectuals will find or found new outlets for work in the generalist vein. Though we may not again see a group so bound by cultural origins, geography, education, and the institutional affiliations formed by a network of small magazines, the example of the New York group will, in the future, continue to influence American culture and intellectual generalists.

Notes

ABBREVIATIONS

AKJ   Alfred Kazin's journal. The Henry W. and Albert A. Berg Collection, New York Public Library.
DMP   Dwight Macdonald papers. Manuscripts and Archives Division, Yale University Library.
NYT   *New York Times.*

PREFACE

1. Dwight Macdonald, *Memoirs of a Revolutionist* (New York: Farrar, Straus, 1957), p. 27.
2. Randall Jarrell, "The Age of Criticism," *Partisan Review* 19(2):185–201, March–April 1952, p. 187.
3. By *romanticism* I mean those outlooks that depend on such values as intuition or subjectivity; a "sense of liberation from rules and conventional forms"; strong, original, and authentic feelings; or the visionary, "the 'irrational', the 'unconscious' and the 'legendary' or mythical." See Raymond Williams, *Keywords* (New York: Oxford University Press, 1985), pp. 275–76.
4. Neoconservatism has several components. First, it is characterized by a strong anti-Communism. Second, because it depends on the West against the threat of Communism, it is not sympathetic to criticism of America—which it interprets as excessive radicalism, naiveté, or self-hatred. Third, neoconservatism is identified by a fear of the masses and of direct democracy—which distinguishes it from the populism of the New Right. Fourth, it has a history of opposition to mass culture, and this cultural elitism separates it from the more populist right and left. Fifth, it has an appreciation for complexity and ambiguity in the world.

This has led neoconservatives to appreciate "realism" and the tragic view of life in foreign and domestic policy. Sixth, neoconservatives depend on much of twentieth-century liberal philosophy, but are selective about it: they emphasize its meritocratic rather than egalitarian strains, and endorse civil liberties and openness except where government agencies like the CIA are involved. As they have said, they are tired liberals.

5. Dennis Wrong, "The Case of the 'New York Review,'" *Commentary* 50(5):49–63, November 1970, p. 52.

CHAPTER 1

1. *NYT*, March 26, 1949, p. 18.

2. New York *Herald Tribune*, March 26, 1949, pp. 1, 5. *NYT*, March 26, 1949, p. 3; March 27, 1949, p. 45. "Red Visitors Cause Rumpus," *Life* 26:39–43, April 4, 1949, p. 40. Sidney Hook, "The Communist Peace Offensive," *Partisan Review* 51:692–711, double fiftieth anniversary issue, 1984–85, pp. 702–3. I have given greater weight to the contemporary reports of the conference than to later recollections of it by the principals.

3. In this paragraph I have benefited from the perceptive work of Giles Gunn, *The Culture of Criticism and the Criticism of Culture* (New York: Oxford University Press, 1987), pp. 5, 20–25, 36.

4. John Gross, *The Rise and Fall of the Man of Letters* (New York: Macmillan, 1969), shows the importance of reviewing to the tradition in Britain.

5. See Perry Miller, ed., *The Transcendentalists* (Cambridge, Mass.: Harvard, 1950); and Joseph Blau, ed., *Social Theories of Jacksonian Democracy* (New York: Bobbs-Merrill, 1954).

6. See Edmund Wilson, *The Shock of Recognition* (New York: Doubleday, 1943).

7. John Tomsich, *A Genteel Endeavor* (Stanford, Calif.: Stanford University Press, 1971).

8. Van Wyck Brooks, "The Literary Life," in Harold Stearns, ed., *Civilization in the United States* (1922; reprint, Westport, Conn.: Greenwood, 1971), p. 196.

9. For the letters tradition early in the century see Henry May, *The End of American Innocence* (New York: Knopf, 1959).

10. Brooks, "The Literary Life," pp. 190, 196.

11. Brooks, "The Literary Life," p. 191.

12. Lionel Trilling, Alfred Kazin, and Irving Howe all wrote essays about Wilson's influence and leadership.

13. Nathan Huggins, *Harlem Renaissance* (New York: Oxford University Press, 1971).

14. *NYT*, March 29, 1989, p. D25.

15. See the biographical sketches on Schumpeter and Simons in the *Dictionary of American Biography*, supplement 4. Schumpeter's influence is apparent on the work of Daniel Bell, and Frank Knight had an influence on Edward Shils at the University of Chicago. Edward Shils, *Center and Periphery: Essay in Macrosociology* (Chicago: University of Chicago Press, 1975), p. xxix.

16. The term *Trotskyist* has both a precise and an imprecise meaning, both of which are used by figures in this study. The term originally denoted a follower of the socialist principles advanced by Trotsky. But since Trotsky was Stalin's main adversary, Stalinists came to use *Trotskyist* as a derisive epithet for any socialist who did not follow Stalin. Just as the Stalinists disparaged most of their enemies on the left as Trotskyists, so the term often became a general label used by the left to refer to independent leftists.

17. For histories of the group in the pre-World War II period, see Alexander Bloom, *Prodigal Sons* (New York: Oxford University Press, 1986); Terry Cooney, *The Rise of the New York Intellectuals* (Madison: University of Wisconsin Press, 1986); Alan Wald, *The New York Intellectuals* (Chapel Hill: University of North Carolina Press, 1987); Stephen Longstaff, "The New York Intellectuals: A Study of Particularism and Universalism in American High Culture," Ph.D. dissertation, University of California, Berkeley, 1978; James Burkhart Gilbert, *Writers and Partisans* (New York: Wiley, 1968); Daniel Aaron, *Writers on the Left* (New York: Harcourt, Brace, World, 1961); John Patrick Diggins, *Up From Communism* (New York: Harper and Row, 1975); and the memoirs and autobiographies by members of the New York group, especially those by Podhoretz, Kazin, Howe, Barrett, Phillips, Bell, and Mary McCarthy.

18. Several authors have created "family trees" of the New York intellectuals; see Stephen Longstaff, "The New York Family," *Queen's Quarterly* 83(4):556–73, Winter 1976, p. 573. Also Daniel Bell, *The Winding Passage* (New York: Basic Books, 1980), pp. 127–29.

19. The following is a rough list of the New York intellectuals, arranged alphabetically. As there are legitimate disagreements over the membership of the New York group (some of those often included protest that no "group" even exists), this list is meant to be suggestive rather than exhaustive. Some of these figures are central to the group; others are more peripheral. An asterisk indicates a European intellectual who influenced the members' outlook, contributed to the group's publications, or took part in their organizations or conferences.

Daniel Aaron	David Bazelon
Lionel Abel	Daniel Bell
Hannah Arendt	Saul Bellow
*Raymond Aron	*Nicola Chiaromonte
William Barrett	Elliot Cohen

Lewis Coser
Midge Decter
Theodore Draper
F. W. Dupee
Jason Epstein
Joseph Epstein
Lewis Feuer
Leslie Fiedler
Emanuel Geltman
Nathan Glazer
Paul Goodman
Clement Greenberg
Elizabeth Hardwick
Michael Harrington
Murray Hausknecht
Robert Heilbroner
Gertrude Himmelfarb
Richard Hofstadter
Sidney Hook
Irving Howe
Alfred Kazin
*Arthur Koestler
Hilton Kramer
Irving Kristol
Melvin Lasky
Robert Lekachman
Seymour Martin Lipset
Mary McCarthy

Dwight Macdonald
Norman Mailer
C. Wright Mills
Reinhold Niebuhr
*George Orwell
Henry Pachter
William Phillips
Stanley Plastrik
Norman Podhoretz
Philip Rahv
David Riesman
Bernard Rosenberg
Harold Rosenberg
Isaac Rosenfeld
Meyer Schapiro
Arthur Schlesinger, Jr.
Delmore Schwartz
Philip Selznick
Edward Shils
*Ignazio Silone
Susan Sontag
*Stephen Spender
Diana Trilling
Lionel Trilling
Michael Walzer
Robert Warshow
Dennis Wrong

20. Talcott Parsons, "'The Intellectual': A Social Role Category," in Philip Rieff, ed., *On Intellectuals: Theoretical Studies/Case Studies* (New York: Doubleday, 1969), pp. 3–26; and Robert Brym, *Intellectuals and Politics* (London: Allen and Unwin, 1980), p. 12.

21. For this position see J. P. Nettl, "Ideas, Intellectuals, and Structures of Dissent," in Rieff, ed., *On Intellectuals*, pp. 57–134.

22. Edward Shils, *The Intellectuals and the Powers* (Chicago: University of Chicago Press, 1972), pp. 16–18; and Shils, *Center and Periphery: Essays in Macrosociology* (Chicago: University of Chicago Press, 1975), part two. Also see Daniel Bell, *The Cultural Contradictions of Capitalism* (New York: Basic Books, 1978), pp. 146–71; and Bell, *The Winding Passage*, pp. 324–54.

23. Quoted in Adam Gussow, "Bohemia Revisited: Malcolm Cowley, Jack Kerouac, and *On the Road*," *Georgia Review* 38(2):291–311, Summer 1984, p. 299. Also see Malcolm Cowley, *And I Worked at the Writer's Trade* (New York: Viking, 1978), pp. 201–3.

24. Lewis Coser, *Men of Ideas* (New York: Free Press, 1965), esp. pp. vii–xii; Harold Rosenberg, "The Intellectual and the Future," *Discovering the Present* (Chicago: University of Chicago Press, 1973), pp. 187, 190–95; Irving Howe, "A Mind's Turnings," *A World More Attractive* (New York: Horizon, 1963), pp. 283–87. Even some centrists in the group, such as Richard Hofstadter, thought of the intellectual as a questioner. See Richard Hofstadter, *Anti-Intellectualism in American Life* (New York: Knopf, 1963), pp. 25–33.

25. There are at least two ways to define the term *ideology*. As Raymond Williams has pointed out, the earlier meaning was used by Napoleon, in Williams's words, to signify "abstract, impractical or fanatical theory." This first meaning defined ideology as impractical, overheated, and false thinking. The later meaning was used by Marx to denote a false consciousness, an inverted view of reality, an illusion that a class harbors about itself and its goals. The New York intellectuals employed the first definition. They used *ideology* to mean an outlook that was utopian and abstract rather than practical, fanatically committed to an ideal rather than rationally analytical, an absolute vision that embodied total solutions rather than tentative hypotheses. Raymond Williams, *Keywords* (New York: Oxford, 1983), pp. 154–56.

26. Lionel Trilling, *The Liberal Imagination* (1950; reprint, New York: Harcourt, 1978), pp. 8–9.

27. Alfred Kazin, *Contemporaries* (Boston: Little, Brown, 1962), pp. 500–501.

28. *The New York Times* published a partial list of official sponsors of the Waldorf Conference, most of whom had merely given their names as an endorsement and had no active role in the conference. Some of the better-known names on the list include: Leonard Bernstein, Marlon Brando, Charlie Chaplin, Lee J. Cobb, Aaron Copland, W.E.B. DuBois, Albert Einstein, Howard Fast, Jose Ferrer, Will Geer, Jack Guilford, Dashiell Hammett, Lillian Hellman, Leo Huberman, Langston Hughes, Matthew Josephson, Albert E. Kahn, Garson Kanin, Corliss Lamont, Ring Lardner, Jr., Helen Lynd, Robert Lynd, Carey McWilliams, Norman Mailer, Thomas Mann, F. O. Matthiessen, Arthur Miller, Mitchell Miller, Kenneth Murdock, Clifford Odets, Eugene Ormandy, Dorothy Parker, Linus Pauling, Paul Robeson, Budd Schulberg, Artie Shaw, Paul Sweezy, Studs Terkel, Dalton Trumbo, Rexford Tugwell, Henry Wallace, Sam Wanamaker, and Frank Lloyd Wright. For the complete list see *NYT*, March 24, 1949, p. 4.

29. *NYT*, March 22, 1949, p. 1; March 24, 1949, pp. 1, 3. For other similar incidences see *NYT*, March 25, 1949, p. 19; March 26, 1949, pp. 1, 3.

30. *NYT*, March 30, 1949, p. 1.

31. Letter from Shapley to Hannah Dorner, February 11, 1949. Har-

242 / Notes to Pages 15–19

low Shapley Papers, Harvard University Archives, Cambridge, Mass., box 10b, HD file. Used by permission of the Harvard University Archives.

32. John P. Rossi, "Farewell to Fellow Traveling: The Waldorf Peace Conference of March 1949," *Continuity* 10:1–31, Spring 1985, pp. 6–7, 9.

33. *NYT*, March 16, 1949, p. 17; March 17, 1949, pp. 1, 4; March 21, 1949, p. 4.

34. *NYT*, March 22, 1949, p. 1; March 23, 1949, pp. 19, 1, 18. "Everybody Wars Over It," *Newsweek*, April 4, 1949, p. 19.

35. *NYT*, March 24, 1949, p. 2; March 23, 1949, p. 1.

36. Dwight Macdonald, "The Waldorf Conference," *Politics* 6(1):32A–32D, Winter 1949, p. 32D. Macdonald was referring to Frederick Schuman, professor of political science at Williams College and a participant in the conference.

37. Letter from Sidney Hook to Harlow Shapley, February 25, 1949. Shapley Papers, box 10c, "peace conference" file. There was considerably more maneuvering between Hook and the Program Committee than this summary suggests; see Neil Jumonville, "The Gray Dawn: The New York Intellectuals and the Function of Criticism," Ph.D. dissertation, Harvard University, 1986.

38. Howard Fast, "Cultural Forces Rally Against the Warmakers," *Political Affairs* 28:29–38, May 1949, p. 33.

39. Letter from Shapley to Emil Lengyel, March 12, 1949. Shapley Papers, box 10c, "peace conference" file. Also see *NYT*, March 20, 1949, p. 4. Irving Howe, "The Culture Conference," *Partisan Review* 16:505–11, May 1949, p. 510. Hook, "Peace Offensive," p. 693.

40. *NYT*, March 20, 1949, p. 4.

41. *Contemporary Authors*, vols. 9–12, first revision (Detroit: Gale Research, 1974), pp. 396–97. *Current Biography*, 1952 yearbook (New York: H. H. Wilson, 1952), pp. 269–70. Sidney Hook, *Political Power and Personal Freedom* (New York: Criterion, 1959), p. xv.

42. Milton R. Konvitz, "Sidney Hook: Philosopher of Freedom," in Paul Kurtz, ed., *Sidney Hook and the Contemporary World* (New York: John Day, 1968), pp. 18–19. Sidney Hook, "My Running Debate With Einstein," *Commentary*, 74:37–52, July 1982, p. 48.

43. *Current Biography*, pp. 269–70.

44. Irving Howe, *World of Our Fathers* (New York: Harcourt, 1976), pp. 283–85.

45. Sidney Hook, "The Philosophy of Morris R. Cohen," *The New Republic* 63:278–81, July 23, 1930, p. 278.

46. Hook, "Philosophy of Morris R. Cohen," p. 278. Konvitz, "Sidney Hook," pp. 18–19. See also the useful entry on Cohen in the *Encyclopedia of Philosophy*.

47. *Contemporary Authors*, p. 396. *Current Biography*, pp. 269–70. Konvitz, "Sidney Hook," p. 19.

48. Sidney Hook, "Breaking With the Communists—A Memoir," *Commentary* 77:47–53, February 1984.

49. John Dewey, *Democracy and Education* (New York: Macmillan, 1916). Lewis S. Feuer, "From Ideology to Philosophy: Sidney Hook's Writings on Marxism," in Kurtz, ed., *Sidney Hook and the Contemporary World*, pp. 38–44. Marx and Engels, *Basic Writings on Politics and Philosophy*, Lewis Feuer, ed. (New York: Doubleday, 1959), p. 245.

50. Richard Pells, *Radical Visions and American Dreams* (New York: Harper, 1973), pp. 149, 133–40.

51. John Dewey, *Characters and Events*, Joseph Ratner, ed. (New York: Holt, 1929), 1:74.

52. John Dewey, *Reconstruction in Philosophy* (1920; reprint, Boston: Beacon Press, 1957), chap. 8.

53. John Dewey, *Individualism Old and New* (New York: Minton, Balch, 1930), pp. 15–16, 32–36, 61, 72, and 115; Alfonso Damico, *Individuality and Community: The Social and Political Thought of John Dewey* (Gainesville: University Presses of Florida, 1978), p. 70.

54. John Dewey, *Democracy and Education* (1916; reprint, New York: Free Press, 1944), p. 99.

55. Dewey, *Characters and Events*, 2:849, 851.

56. Kurtz, editor's preface, *Sidney Hook and the Contemporary World*. Raziel Abelson, "Hook's Ethical Theory, Pure and Impure," in Kurtz, ed., *Sidney Hook and the Contemporary World*, pp. 203–4. Konvitz, "Sidney Hook," pp. 20, 22.

57. Dewey, *Characters and Events*, 2:731–32.

58. Dewey, *Reconstruction in Philosophy*, chap. 8.

59. Hook's article appeared in *The Social Frontier*, February 1938, and is quoted in Feuer, "From Ideology to Philosophy," p. 50.

60. For a discussion of philosophical absolutism and Hook's opposition to it, see Edward Purcell, Jr., *The Crisis of Democratic Theory* (Lexington: University Press of Kentucky, 1973), especially chaps. 1, 6, 8, 11, 13, and 14. Also see Morton White, *Social Thought in America: The Revolt Against Formalism*, rev. ed. (Boston: Beacon Press, 1957), especially chaps. 1, 2, 10, and the epilogue to the 1957 edition.

61. Sidney Hook, "The Integral Humanism of Jacques Maritain," *Partisan Review* 7(3):204–9, May–June 1940, p. 204; "The New Failure of Nerve," *Partisan Review* 10(1):2–23, January-February 1943.

62. Purcell, *The Crisis of Democratic Theory*, pp. 203, 218–19. Letter from Sidney Hook to the author, July 17, 1986.

63. Quoted in Konvitz, "Sidney Hook," p. 20.

64. Hook, "Breaking With the Communists," pp. 48–52.

65. William Phillips, *A Partisan View* (New York: Stein and Day, 1983), pp. 30, 45.

66. William Barrett, *The Truants* (Garden City, N.Y.: Doubleday, 1982), p. 84. Feuer, "From Ideology to Philosophy," p. 36.

67. Sidney Hook, "Ethereal Politics," *The Nation* 142:653–54, May 20, 1936.

68. Diggins, *Up From Communism*, pp. 169–70. Gilbert, *Writers and Partisans*, pp. 165, 202–3.

69. Sidney Hook, "The Future of Socialism," *Partisan Review* 14(1):23–36, January–February 1947, p. 24.

70. Sidney Hook, "Three Intellectual Troubadours," *The American Spectator* 18(1):18–22, January 1985, p. 21. Norman Podhoretz, *Breaking Ranks* (New York: Harper, 1979), p. 178. Philip Rahv, *Essays on Literature and Politics, 1932–1972*, Arabel Porter and Andrew Dvosin, eds. (Boston: Houghton Mifflin, 1978), p. 353.

71. Phillips, *Partisan View*, pp. 163–64.

72. Howe, *A Margin of Hope* (New York: Harcourt, 1982), p. 211.

73. Hook, *Political Power*, pp. 363–64.

74. Sidney Hook, "Living with Deep Truths in a Divided World," *Free Inquiry*, 3(1):30–31, Winter 1982–83, p. 31; Hook, *Political Power*, p. v.

75. Gunn, *Culture of Criticism*, p. 64.

76. Phillips, *Partisan View*, pp. 163–64.

77. Hook, "My Running Debate With Einstein," p. 48. *NYT*, March 20, 1949, p. 4.

78. Hook, "Peace Offensive," p. 694.

79. *NYT*, March 20, 1949, p. 4. Macdonald, "The Waldorf Conference," p. 32A.

80. Interview with Lewis Coser, Wellfleet, Mass., July 9, 1985. Interview with Sidney Hook, Wardsboro, Vt., July 15, 1985. Letter from Hook to the author, August 1, 1985.

81. Hook, "Peace Offensive," pp. 694–96. Macdonald, "The Waldorf Conference," p. 32A. "Summary of an Interview with Sidney Hook, 5 April 1972," in Job L. Dittberner, *The End of Ideology and American Social Thought, 1930–1960* (Ann Arbor, Mich.: UMI Research Press, 1979), p. 305.

82. *NYT*, March 25, 1949, p. 18. Macdonald, "The Waldorf Conference," p. 32A.

83. Fast, "Cultural Forces," pp. 32–33.

84. Joseph Lash, "Weekend at the Waldorf," *The New Republic* 120:10–14, April 18, 1949, p. 11. Hook, "Peace Offensive," p. 699.

85. *NYT*, March 21, 1949, p. 4. "The Shostakovich Gambit," *Newsweek* 33:22–23, March 28, 1949. "Everybody Wars Over It," p. 19. *NYT*, March 4, 1949, p. 2. Others who withdrew or were too "sick" to attend included Donovan McCune, professor of pediatrics at the College of Physicians and Surgeons at Columbia; Dr. Herbert Davis, president of Smith College; Marshall E. Dimock, professor of political science at Northwestern University; Dr. Lyle Borst, project leader at Brookhaven National Laboratory; Lisa Sergio, radio commentator; Canada Lee, a black actor;

and Franklin P. ("Information, Please") Adams, the radio personality who claimed he had been "a sucker."

86. *NYT,* March 25, 1949, pp. 1, 18. Fast, "Cultural Forces," p. 31.

87. Phillips, *Partisan View,* p. 149.

88. *NYT,* March 20, 1949, p. 4; March 22, 1949, p. 16.

89. *NYT,* March 23, 1949, p. 18.

90. *NYT,* March 27, 1949, pp. 1, 46; March 26, 1949, p. 3. Macdonald, "The Waldorf Conference," p. 32B. New York *Herald Tribune,* March 27, 1949, p. 1.

91. Anatole Shub, "Soviets Launch 'Peace' Drive in West, Concentrate on East," *The New Leader,* April 2, 1949, p. 3. *NYT,* March 27, 1949, pp. 1, 46. New York *Herald Tribune,* March 27, 1949, p. 42. UPI photos of Hook and Max Eastman speaking at the Freedom House conference are reproduced in Diggins, *Up From Communism,* following page 300.

92. Others who addressed the AIF conference were H. J. Muller, a Nobel Prize winner and professor of genetics at Indiana University; Max Eastman, who had already completed his journey from political left to right; Dr. Max Yergan, a founder and former chairman of the Council on African Affairs; and Morris L. Ernst, lawyer and a director of the ACLU. Completing the list were George Counts, professor at Teachers College and cochairman of the AIF; George Biddle, an artist; and Nicholas Nabokov, a music critic. *NYT,* March 27, 1949, pp. 1, 46; March 26, 1949, p. 3. New York *Herald Tribune,* March 27, 1949, p. 42. Macdonald, "The Waldorf Conference," p. 32B.

93. New York *Herald Tribune,* March 27, 1949, p. 42. Macdonald, "The Waldorf Conference," p. 32B. *NYT,* April 21, 1949, p. 6.

94. *NYT,* April 21, 1949, p. 6.

95. Dittberner, "Interview with Hook," pp. 306–7.

96. Diana Trilling, "An Interview With Dwight Macdonald," *Partisan Review* 51(1):799–819, anniversary issue, 1984–85, p. 801.

97. D. Trilling, "Interview with Macdonald," p. 799. Dwight Macdonald, *Memoirs of a Revolutionist* (New York: Farrar, Straus, 1957), pp. 6–7. *Current Biography,* 1969 yearbook (New York: H. H. Wilson, 1969), pp. 277–78.

98. D. Trilling, "Interview with Macdonald," pp. 800–801. Macdonald, *Memoirs,* pp. 8–9.

99. In the 1980s Cowley still felt that the animosity from the 1930s persisted. "I fought with the group(s) in 1938 and they never forgave me," he remembered. "For many years they have waged a vendetta against me and it continues in 1984; consult the summer and forthcoming fall numbers of the *Georgia Review*." Letter from Malcolm Cowley to the author, August 13, 1984. Cowley complained publicly that Kenneth Lynn and other neoconservative critics had accused him of an anti-American interpretation of the work of Ernest Hemingway in his introduction to

the Viking Portable Hemingway in 1949—an interpretation they said showed that Cowley took to literature in the postwar period his frustrations from an earlier unsuccessful totalitarian liberalism that opposed America and celebrated the Soviet Union. Malcolm Cowley, "Hemingway's Wound—And Its Consequences for American Literature," *Georgia Review* 38(2):223–39, Summer 1984.

100. Macdonald, *Memoirs*, pp. 6–7, 10. D. Trilling, "Interview with Macdonald," p. 803.

101. Macdonald, *Memoirs*, pp. 10–11. D. Trilling, "Interview with Macdonald," p. 803.

102. Macdonald, *Memoirs*, pp. 11–12. D. Trilling, "Interview with Macdonald," p. 800.

103. Macdonald, *Memoirs*, pp. 128, 147–48, 296, 307.

104. Macdonald, *Memoirs*, pp. 300, 298.

105. Macdonald, *Memoirs*, pp. 155, 158.

106. Letter from Cowley to the author, August 13, 1984.

107. D. Trilling, "Interview with Macdonald," p. 805.

108. Macdonald, "The Waldorf Conference," pp. 32A, 32B, 32C. Macdonald, "Misstatement and Bias?" (letter to the editor), *The Nation* 168:624–25, May 28, 1949.

109. Margaret Marshall, "Notes By the Way," *The Nation* 168:419–20, April 9, 1949.

110. Sidney Hook, "Waldorf Aftermath—Dr. Hook Protests" (letter to the editor), *The Nation* 168:511–13, April 30, 1949.

111. Fast, "Cultural Forces," p. 37. Letter from Albert E. Kahn to Harlow Shapley, March 1, 1949, in the Shapley Papers, box 10c, "peace conference" file. Used by permission of Mrs. Albert E. Kahn.

112. Kirchwey claimed that in addition to Cousins, editor of the *Saturday Review*, the conference had asked such noted anti-Communists as Bryn J. Hovde, president of the New School for Social Research; Trygve Lie, the secretary general of the United Nations; Isador Lubin, an economist who was a member of Roosevelt's brain trust; Gordon Clapp, chairman of the board of the Tennessee Valley Authority; Stacy May, associate professor of economics at Goucher College; Louis Wirth, professor of sociology at the University of Chicago; and Thomas Parran, former surgeon general of the United States, a founder of the World Health Organization, and dean of the Graduate School of Public Health at the University of Pittsburgh. Freda Kirchwey, "Waldorf Aftermath—Miss Kirchwey Replies," *The Nation* 168:511–13, April 30, 1949.

113. Freda Kirchwey, "Battle of the Waldorf," *The Nation* 168:377–78, April 2, 1949; and Kirchwey, "Waldorf Aftermath," p. 512.

114. Marshall, "Notes By the Way," pp. 419–20.

115. Hook, "Waldorf Aftermath," p. 511. Kirchwey, "Waldorf Aftermath," p. 512.

116. *NYT*, March 24, 1949, p. 2. Hook, "Peace Offensive," p. 706.

117. Theodore Brameld, "Conference Defended" (letter to the editor), *NYT*, April 3, 1949, section IV, p. 8.

118. Sidney Hook and George S. Counts, "Stand of the Liberals" (letter to the editor), *NYT*, April 3, 1949, p. 28.

119. Theodore Brameld, "Lessons of Cultural Meeting" (letter to the editor), *NYT*, April 19, 1949, p. 24.

120. Hook, "Waldorf Aftermath," p. 511.

121. Kirchwey, "Waldorf Aftermath," p. 512.

122. Marshall, "Notes By the Way," p. 419.

123. Barrett, "Culture Conference," p. 492. Macdonald, "The Waldorf Conference," p. 32D.

124. William Phillips, "The Politics of Desperation," *Partisan Review* 15(4):449–55, April 1948, p. 449.

CHAPTER 2

1. As early as 1949 Mary McCarthy, in her novella *The Oasis*, noted a split in the group—although she labeled it a division between realists and idealists (mostly in the realm of foreign policy, the war, and anti-Communism) rather than affirmers and dissenters. McCarthy portrayed "the realist party" led by Philip Rahv (instead of Hook), and the other circle as "the purist faction" led by Macdonald. See Mary McCarthy, *The Oasis* [1949] in *Cast a Cold Eye & The Oasis* (New York: New American Library, 1972), pp. 136–37.

2. Sidney Hook, "The Radical Comedians," *American Scholar* 54:45–61, Winter 1984–85, p. 46. James Gilbert, *Writers and Partisans* (New York: Wiley, 1968), p. 175.

3. Daniel Aaron later disagreed with Phillips and Rahv about why *Partisan Review* was suspended and then reborn. Phillips and Rahv portrayed themselves as tired of proletarian realism and committed to modernism in the mid-1930s, and disgusted at Communist party guidance of their literary magazine. Aaron, however, thought they were actually more sympathetic to proletarian realism than modernism in the early 1930s, and were only critical of the insufficiently good proletarianism in the Party magazines. According to Aaron, their switch to modernism and a revived *Partisan Review* contained an element of careerism: they felt it was time that they and their generation asserted themselves in a new way. Interviews with Daniel Aaron, Cambridge, Mass., June 16 and September 2, 1986.

4. Letter from Dwight Macdonald to Hook, December 6, 1938, DMP. Letter from Sidney Hook to the author, July 17, 1986. See also Gilbert, *Writers and Partisans*, pp. 201–3; and Macdonald, *Memoirs of a Revolutionist* (New York: Farrar, Straus, 1957), p. 13. The Dies committee in

the House of Representatives, chaired by Congressman Martin Dies, investigated leftist political connections in the late 1930s. It was the forerunner of the more famous House Un-American Activities Committee (HUAC), which was convened in 1947.

5. Letter from Sidney Hook to Richard Rovere, April 2, 1952, in the Norman Thomas Papers, Rare Books and Manuscripts Division, The New York Public Library, Astor, Lenox, and Tilden Foundations. Used by permission of the New York Public Library.

6. William Barrett, "The Truants: 'Partisan Review' in the 40's," *Commentary* 57:48–54, June 1974, p. 52.

7. Dwight Macdonald and Clement Greenberg, "Ten Propositions on the War," *Partisan Review*, July–August 1941, pp. 271–73. Philip Rahv, "Ten Propositions and Eight Errors," *Partisan Review*, November–December 1941, pp. 499–502.

8. Diana Trilling, "An Interview with Dwight Macdonald," *Partisan Review* 51(1):799–819, anniversary issue, 1984–85, p. 806. This intellectual struggle over the war is covered in much greater detail in Gilbert, *Writers and Partisans*, pp. 221–282. It is also apparent from Macdonald's correspondence with others, contained in the Macdonald Papers. See also Irving Howe, "The Dilemma of Partisan Review," *The New International*, 8(1):20–24, February 1942, pp. 21–22.

9. Interview with Sidney Hook, Wardsboro, Vt., July 15, 1985.

10. Letter from Philip Rahv to Dwight Macdonald, March 30, 1941, DMP.

11. Letter from Philip Rahv to Dwight Macdonald, November 11, 1941, DMP.

12. Quoted in Stephen Whitfield, *A Critical American: The Politics of Dwight Macdonald* (Hamden, Conn.: Archon Books, 1984), p. 51.

13. Sidney Hook, "The Failure of the Left," *Partisan Review*, 10(2):165–77, March-April 1943, pp. 168–71, 175.

14. Letter from Lewis Coser to Dwight Macdonald, April 20, 1942, DMP.

15. Howe, "The Dilemma of Partisan Review," p. 21.

16. Unprinted statement written by Macdonald, no date (probably in the spring or early summer of 1943), in DMP.

17. Letter from Philip Rahv to Dwight Macdonald, no date, DMP.

18. Letter from William Phillips to Dwight Macdonald, no date, DMP.

19. Comment from Gerald Sykes to Alfred Kazin, in Alfred Kazin's journal (hereafter referred to as AKJ), vol. 4, December 26, 1941. In the Henry W. and Albert A. Berg Collection, The New York Public Library, Astor, Lenox and Tilden Foundations. Used by permission of Alfred Kazin and The New York Public Library.

20. Letter from Philip Rahv to Dwight Macdonald, July 28, 1943, DMP.

21. Hook, "The Radical Comedians," pp. 45–46.

22. William Barrett, *The Truants* (Garden City, New York: Doubleday, 1982), pp. 83–85.

23. Richard Hofstadter, *Anti-Intellectualism in American Life* (New York: Knopf, 1963), p. 394.

24. On the masthead Macdonald printed *politics* in lowercase, but in his references to it within the magazine and his correspondence he capitalized the first letter: *Politics*. Conversation with Michael Wreszin, June 15, 1989.

25. According to Michael Wreszin, Nancy Macdonald was a powerful "catalyst" in Dwight's life, and without her he might have remained a Luce man and there might never have been a *Politics*. Letter from Michael Wreszin to the author, February 27, 1987.

26. Letter from Daniel Bell to the author, October 17, 1986.

27. Letter from Lewis Coser to Dwight Macdonald, August 20, 1943, DMP.

28. Walter W. Powell and Richard Robbins, "Lewis A. Coser: Intellectual and Political Commitments," in Powell and Robbins, eds., *Conflict and Consensus: A Festschrift in Honor of Lewis A. Coser* (New York: Free Press, 1984), pp. 6–7.

29. Bernard Rosenberg, "An Interview with Lewis Coser," in Powell and Robbins, eds., *Conflict and Consensus*, pp. 38–39, 50. Interview with Lewis Coser, Wellfleet, Mass., July 19, 1985. Letter from Coser to Macdonald, August 4, 1943, DMP. Letter from Lewis Coser to the author, October 1, 1986. The Shachtmanites were a subgroup of Trotskyists who followed Max Shachtman, an American Trotskyist leader. The Shachtmanites parted company with Trotsky's belief that societies were either capitalist or socialist, and concluded that there was a third possibility: bureaucratic collectivism. Trotsky, however, worried that such a proposal would undermine the Marxist revolutionary outlook. Perhaps it did. See Irving Howe, *A Margin of Hope* (New York: Harcourt, 1982), pp. 78–89.

30. Irving Howe, "Forming Dissent," in Powell and Robbins, eds., *Conflict and Consensus*, p. 61.

31. B. Rosenberg, "Interview with Coser," p. 40. Letter from Lewis Coser to Dwight Macdonald, July 22, 1948, DMP. Interview with David Riesman, Cambridge, Mass., November 23, 1984.

32. Interview with David Riesman, Cambridge, Mass., November 23, 1984. Letter from David Riesman to the author, July 27, 1986.

33. Interview with David Riesman, Cambridge, Mass., November 23, 1984.

34. Dwight Macdonald, *Discriminations* (New York: Grossman, 1974), p. 299. Letter from Dennis Wrong to the author, May 18, 1989.

35. Macdonald, *Discriminations*, p. 299. Bernard Rosenberg, "Interview with Coser," p. 49.

36. Daniel Bell's contribution to the Richard Hofstadter Project, pp.

32–33; from a transcript of a tape-recorded interview by William Keylor in April 1972 in New York. Columbia University Oral History Research Office, New York. Used by permission of Daniel Bell.

37. For a critical treatment of Schlesinger's political involvement, see Michael Wreszin, "Arthur Schlesinger, Jr., Scholar-Activist in Cold War America: 1946–1956," *Salmagundi* 63–64:255–85, Spring-Summer 1984.

38. AKJ, vol. 4, March 3, 1944; vol. 7, November 20, 1946, and February 1, 1948.

39. AKJ, vol. 7, May 17, 1948, and November 17, 1948.

40. Irving Howe, *Steady Work* (New York: Harcourt, 1966), p. 246. Howe, "Forming Dissent," p. 62.

41. Letter from Irving Howe to Dwight Macdonald, August 1, 1946; and letter from Irving Howe to Dwight Macdonald, August 12, 1946, DMP.

42. John Dewey, *Individualism Old and New* (New York: Minton, Balch, 1930), pp. 119–20.

43. John Dewey, *Characters and Events*, Joseph Ratner, ed. (New York: Holt, 1929), 2:757.

44. Dewey, *Individualism Old and New*, p. 118.

45. Hook remembered with amusement that Macdonald considered it a compliment if he was accused of being irresponsible; interview with Sidney Hook, Wardsboro, Vt., July 15, 1985. See Hook's sympathetic account of Macdonald in "The Radical Comedians." Hook claimed that he never took Macdonald seriously enough to regard him as a nemesis; letter from Sidney Hook to the author, July 17, 1986.

46. Interview with Irving Howe, New York, June 6, 1985. Hook maintained that *Partisan Review* had printed Howe's work only in order to get back at Hook. Rahv, Hook said, never liked Hook even when he agreed with him politically—partly because Hook tried to protect Phillips from Rahv. Letter from Sidney Hook to the author, July 17, 1986.

47. Lionel Trilling, "Young in the Thirties," *Commentary* 41(5):43–51, May 1966, pp. 45–47; and Trilling, "On the Death of a Friend," *Commentary* 29(2):93–94, February 1960.

48. Norman Podhoretz, *Making It* (New York: Random House, 1967), pp. 128–29.

49. L. Trilling, "On the Death of a Friend," p. 94.

50. Alexander Bloom, *Prodigal Sons: The New York Intellectuals and Their World* (New York: Oxford University Press, 1986), chapter 9. This is a good source for the background and history of *Commentary*.

51. Letter from Irving Howe to Dwight Macdonald, August 1, 1946; letter from Macdonald to Howe, August 13, 1946, DMP.

52. Midge Decter, in Bernard Rosenberg and Ernest Goldstein, eds., *Creators and Disturbers* (New York: Columbia University Press, 1982), pp. 356–57.

53. Letter from Hannah Arendt to Houghton Mifflin, December 24, 1946. A copy of this letter is in the Dwight Macdonald file, box 11, Hannah Arendt Papers, Manuscripts Division, Library of Congress, Washington, D.C.

54. AKJ, vol. 7, October 8, 1950.

55. See the intelligent essay on the Frankfurt School by David Held in Tom Bottomore et al., eds., *A Dictionary of Marxist Thought* (Cambridge, Mass.: Harvard University Press, 1983); and Martin Jay, *The Dialectical Imagination* (Boston: Little, Brown, 1973).

56. Letter from Michael Wreszin to the author, February 27, 1987.

57. Macdonald, *Memoirs*, pp. 191–92.

58. Macdonald, *Memoirs*, pp. 196–97.

59. Macdonald, *Memoirs*, pp. 311–13, 309–10.

60. Macdonald, *Memoirs*, pp. 27–28.

61. Macdonald, *Memoirs*, pp. 129–31.

62. Macdonald, *Memoirs*, pp. 5, 197, 201.

63. See Irving Howe, "The Human Factor," *The New Republic* 200(19):30–34, May 8, 1989.

64. Howe, *Margin of Hope*, pp. 1–7.

65. Howe, *Margin of Hope*, pp. 12–13, 22–23. For a good account of Alcove One, see Irving Kristol, "Memoirs of a Trotskyist," in *Reflections of a Neoconservative* (New York: Basic Books, 1983), pp. 3–13.

66. Robert Brym, *Intellectuals and Politics* (London: Allen and Unwin, 1980), pp. 14–18, 25, 67, 72–73.

67. Howe, *Margin of Hope*, p. 9.

68. Mary McCarthy began the autobiographical retrospective with *The Company She Keeps* (New York: Harcourt, 1942), a gossipy kiss-and-tell collection of stories about the crowd, a novelistic rather than analytical attempt to understand the group. She later published *Memories of a Catholic Girlhood* (New York: Harcourt, 1957). Alfred Kazin was the first to take an analytical approach to the group, with *Starting Out in the Thirties* (Boston: Little, Brown, 1962). Norman Podhoretz added his recollections in *Making It* (1967). Irving Howe offered his view in "A Memoir of the Thirties," in *Steady Work* (1966), and "The New York Intellectuals: A Chronicle and a Critique," in *Commentary* 46(4):29–51, October 1968. In the 1970s and 1980s there have been retrospective books and essays by Lionel Abel, William Barrett, Daniel Bell, Sidney Hook, Irving Howe, Alfred Kazin, Irving Kristol, Mary McCarthy, Norman Podhoretz, and William Phillips, among others.

69. Kazin, *Starting Out*, p. 4.

70. AKJ, vol. 4, September 17, 1941.

71. AKJ, vol. 4, March 30, 1942.

72. AKJ, vol. 4, February 28, 1942.

73. Irving Howe, *Celebrations and Attacks* (New York: Horizon, 1979), pp. 12–16, 18, 20.

74. AKJ, vol. 4, February 28, 1942.

75. Howe, *Steady Work*, pp. 358, 360.

76. Letter from Irving Howe to Dwight Macdonald, July 2, 1946, DMP. Howe, *Margin of Hope*, pp. 115–16.

77. Letter from Dwight Macdonald to Irving Howe, July 17, 1948; letter from Irving Howe to Dwight Macdonald, August 27, 1948, DMP.

78. Howe, *A Margin of Hope*, p. 59.

79. Howe denied that Hook ever influenced him or the group with his pragmatic orientation. I remain unconvinced. Howe and others in the group moved from ideological to pragmatic outlooks between the 1940s and the 1980s, a course that Hook took ten to fifteen years earlier. Interview with Irving Howe, New York, June 6, 1985.

80. Irving Howe, "The Rejection of Marxism," Alfred Kazin, "Some Answers," and Robert Gorham Davis, "Some Answers" (letters to the editor), *Commentary* 12:388–90, October 1951. Irving Howe, *A World More Attractive* (New York: Horizon, 1963), p. 265.

81. Howe, *World More Attractive*, pp. 252, 266–67, 278–79. Howe's article was the major criticism of what became known as the institutionalization of the intellectuals.

82. Howe, letter to the editor, *Partisan Review*, March–April 1954, p. 239.

83. David Riesman, "Our Country and Our Culture," *Partisan Review* 19:311–14, May–June 1952, p. 313. Interview with David Riesman, Cambridge, Mass., November 23, 1984.

84. Interview with Bernard Rosenberg, Wellfleet, Mass., July 25, 1985. Howe, *Margin of Hope*, pp. 211–18. B. Rosenberg, "Interview with Lewis Coser," p. 43.

85. Letter from Sidney Hook to Richard Rovere, April 2, 1952, Norman Thomas Papers. Used by permission of the Rare Books and Manuscripts Division, New York Public Library, Astor, Lenox and Tilden Foundations.

86. Interview with Lewis Coser, Wellfleet, Mass., July 9, 1985. Irving Howe, letter to the editor, *Commentary*, March–April 1954, p. 240. B. Rosenberg, "Interview with Lewis Coser," p. 42.

87. Letter from Irving Howe to Dwight Macdonald, May 8, 1949, DMP. See Irving Howe, "Magazine Chronicle," *Partisan Review* 16:416–27, April 1949. Jim Cork had written earlier for the magazine *Revolutionary Age*.

88. Letter from Irving Howe to Dwight Macdonald, May 8, 1949, DMP.

89. Letter from Dwight Macdonald to Irving Howe, May 21, 1949, DMP.

90. Letter from Dwight Macdonald to Alfred Kazin, November 26, 1960, DMP. Letter from Alfred Kazin to Dwight Macdonald, November 17, 1960, DMP.

91. Irving Howe, "The First 25 Years," *Dissent* 26:6, Winter 1979. Howe, *A Margin of Hope*, pp. 183–84. B. Rosenberg, "Interview with Lewis Coser," p. 41.

92. Lewis Coser, "The First 25 Years," *Dissent* 26:3–4, Winter 1979. Howe, "Forming Dissent," in Powell and Robbins, eds., *Conflict and Consensus*, p. 62. Letter from Irving Howe to Dwight Macdonald, March 1, 1953, DMP.

93. Howe, "Forming Dissent," p. 62. Coser, Howe, and Plastrik, in their contributions to "The First 25 Years," pp. 3–6. Interview with Lewis Coser, Wellfleet, Mass., July 9, 1985. Interview with Bernard Rosenberg, Wellfleet, Mass., July 25, 1985.

94. Interview with Lewis Coser, Wellfleet, Mass., July 9, 1985. B. Rosenberg, "Interview with Lewis Coser," p. 42. Coser, "The First 25 Years," pp. 3–4.

95. Howe, *Margin of Hope*, p. 235. Plastrik and Coser's contributions to "The First 25 Years," pp. 3–4. B. Rosenberg, "Interview with Lewis Coser," pp. 42–43. Interview with Lewis Coser, Wellfleet, Mass., July 9, 1985.

96. Letters from Irving Howe to Dwight Macdonald, March 1 and March 18, 1953, DMP.

97. Letter from Lewis Coser to Dwight Macdonald, November 16, 1953, DMP. For the circulation figure, see *Dissent*, Spring 1957, p. 98. Letter from Lewis Coser to Dwight Macdonald, December 4, 1955, DMP.

98. Two years later, in the Winter 1956 issue, the editorial board had added Emanuel Geltman and Bernard Rosenberg, and had dropped Harold Orlans. The most frequent contributors to *Dissent* between 1954 and 1960 (with the number of their contributions in parentheses) were Irving Howe (23), Lewis Coser (18), Bernard Rosenberg (10), Stanley Plastrik (10), Ben B. Seligman (8), Norman Mailer (7), H. Brand (7), William J. Newman (7), Michael Harrington (6), Harold Rosenberg (5), Henry Pachter (5), Michael Walzer (5), Helen Mears (5), Harvey Swados (5), C. Wright Mills (4), Paul Goodman (3), Travers Clement (3), and George Woodcock (2).

99. Howe, *Margin of Hope*, p. 237. Howe, "Forming Dissent," pp. 65–66.

100. Editors, "A Word to Our Readers," *Dissent* 1(1):3–4, Winter 1954.

101. Lewis Coser, "Young Man on the Make," *Dissent* 1(1):108, Winter 1954.

102. Irving Howe, "Does It Hurt When You Laugh?" *Dissent* 1(1):4–7, Winter 1954.

103. Glazer said that if he had not written this rejoinder, Elliot Cohen probably would have had someone else write it. In any case, according to Glazer, none of the other members of the *Commentary* staff would have

disagreed significantly with what he wrote. Letter from Nathan Glazer to the author, July 28, 1986. Howe, *Margin of Hope*, p. 236.

104. Nathan Glazer, "Philistine Leftism," *Commentary* 17(2):201–6, February 1954, pp. 201–2, 204.

105. Glazer, "Philistine Leftism," pp. 205, 202.

106. Interview with Nathan Glazer, Cambridge, Mass., May 21, 1985.

107. An example of the documentation of this change is Daniel Bell's *The End of Ideology* (1960; reprint, Cambridge, Mass.: Harvard University Press, 1988). That majority of the New York intellectuals who became neoconservatives continued this chronicling effort through the 1980s. For an example of the dissenters' reaction against the affirmers' documentation of a changing America, see Irving Howe, "America, the Country and the Myth," *Dissent* 2(3):241–44, Summer 1955.

108. *Contemporary Authors*, first revision, vols. 5–8 (Detroit: Gale Research, 1969), p. 443. Unless otherwise cited, the information in this biographical section is drawn from Glazer's unpublished autobiographical manuscript, "From Socialism to Sociology," which he generously provided me.

109. Letter from Nathan Glazer to the author, July 28, 1986.

110. Interview with David Riesman, Cambridge, Mass., November 23, 1984.

111. Interview with Nathan Glazer, Cambridge, Mass., May 21, 1985.

112. *Contemporary Authors*, vols. 5–8, p. 443.

113. Letter from Nathan Glazer to the author, July 28, 1986.

114. Nathan Glazer, "Negroes and Jews: The New Challenge to Pluralism," *Commentary* 38(6):29–34, December 1964; and Glazer, *Affirmative Discrimination: Ethnic Inequality and Public Policy* (New York: Basic Books, 1975).

115. This intellectual concern for pluralism and diversity has also been called "cosmopolitanism." See David Hollinger, "Ethnic Diversity, Cosmopolitanism, and the Emergence of the American Liberal Intelligentsia," *In the American Province* (Bloomington: Indiana University Press, 1985); and Terry Cooney, *The Rise of the New York Intellectuals* (Madison: University of Wisconsin Press, 1986).

116. Glazer, *Affirmative Discrimination*, pp. 4, 50–51, 75, 220.

117. AKJ, vol. 15, June 20, 1959.

118. Diana Trilling, "A Communist and His Ideals," *Partisan Review* 18:432–40, July–August 1951, pp. 434–35, 439–40.

119. Sidney Hook, "Our Country and Our Culture," pp. 569–70, 574.

120. Letter from Sidney Hook to Norman Thomas, June 24, 1954, Norman Thomas Papers.

121. Interview with Sidney Hook, Wardsboro, Vt., July 15, 1985.

122. Philip Rahv, "Our Country and Our Culture," pp. 304, 307–8.

123. Reinhold Niebuhr, "American Pride and Power," *American Scholar* 17:393–94, Autumn 1948. Reinhold Niebuhr, "The Sickness of American Culture," *The Nation* 166:267–70, March 6, 1948, p. 268.

124. Archibald MacLeish, "The Conquest of the United States," *A Continuing Journey* (Boston: Houghton Mifflin, 1967), p. 59. The reflex MacLeish described was later called a "purely reactive independence" by Jonathan Arac. "They live in history," he argued, "by their own repeated choice, as the 'anti-Stalinist' intellectuals, and this chosen negative independence continually acted to restrict their positive independence." Jonathan Arac, *Critical Genealogies* (New York: Columbia University Press, 1987), p. 309.

125. Howe, *World More Attractive*, p. 261.

126. Interview with Lewis Coser, Wellfleet, Mass., July 9, 1985. Interview with Irving Howe, New York, June 6, 1985.

127. Stanley Plastrik, "The Specter of Neutralism," *Dissent* 1(2):165–71, Spring 1954. Editorial statement, *Dissent*, Winter 1956, inside of front cover. Lewis Coser, "The New Turn in Russia," *Dissent* 3(2):124–28, Spring 1956, pp. 124–26. Irving Howe, "Notes on the Russian Turn," *Dissent* 3(3):309–13, Summer 1956, pp. 309–10.

128. Irving Howe, "Russia and the *Monthly Review*," *Dissent* 3(4):433–35, Fall 1956. See also Irving Howe, "The Choice of Comrades," *Dissent* 4(3):332–35, Summer 1957; and Lewis Coser, "Towards Dynamic Barbarism," *Dissent* 4(4):427–29, Fall 1957.

129. Howe, *Margin of Hope*, p. 205.

130. Harold Rosenberg, *Discovering the Present* (Chicago: University of Chicago Press, 1973), pp. 301–3. Letter from Sidney Hook to the author, July 22, 1985.

131. Irving Howe, "The Cold War and the West," *Partisan Review* 29:27–35, Winter 1962, pp. 28, 34–35.

132. H. Rosenberg, *Discovering the Present*, pp. 307–8.

133. Irving Howe, *Steady Work*, p. 247. For examples of the dissenters' criticism of Mills see Bernard Rosenberg, "Rebellious Orgmen & Tame Intellectuals," *Dissent* 5(2):119–24, Spring 1958; and Irving Howe, "C. Wright Mills' Program: Two Views," *Dissent* 6(2):191–96, Spring 1959, pp. 193–94.

134. C. Wright Mills, in Irving Howe and C. Wright Mills, "The Intellectuals and Russia," an exchange, *Dissent* 6(3):295–301, Summer 1959, pp. 295–97.

135. Howe, *World More Attractive*, pp. 263, 272. See editorial statement, inside of front cover, *Dissent*, Winter 1956. Howe, "Russia and the *Monthly Review*," pp. 434–35; "The Choice of Comrades," p. 335; and "A New Political Atmosphere in America?" *Dissent* 6(1):5–8, Winter 1959, p. 7.

136. Lewis Coser and Irving Howe, "Images of Socialism," *Dissent*

1(2):122–38, Spring 1954, pp. 130, 132–34. Lewis Coser, "What Shall We Do?" *Dissent* 3(2):156–65, Spring 1956, p. 164.

137. Ben B. Seligman, "The Economics of Joseph Schumpeter," *Dissent* 1(4):370–84, Autumn 1954, pp. 370–74; and Seligman, "Keynesian Economics—A Critique," *Dissent* 3(1):51–67, Winter 1956, pp. 62–67.

138. Ben B. Seligman, "Marxian Economics Revisited," *Dissent* 5(4):342–52, Autumn 1958.

139. Ben B. Seligman, "Socialism Without Marx," *Dissent* 6(3):258–74, Summer 1959, pp. 258–66. For a review and treatment of the theory of market socialism and its American reception, see Neil Jumonville, "Market Socialism: The Theory and Its Critics," unpublished bachelor's thesis, Reed College, 1977, in the Reed College library. John Kenneth Galbraith's *Affluent Society* was not radical enough for Seligman, although he thought it represented a useful radical liberalism; see Seligman, "Where Do We Go from Here?" *Dissent* 6(1):84–87, Winter 1959.

140. Seligman, "Socialism Without Marx," pp. 273–74.

141. The idea of market socialism originated in Austria in the 1890s with Friedrich von Wieser and his brother-in-law Eugen Bohm-Bawerk, and then was extended slightly by the Italian economists Vilfredo Pareto and Enrico Barone after 1908. But the first political economists to make it accessible in English were Mises, Hayek, and Schumpeter in the 1930s and 1940s. See Ludwig von Mises, *Socialism* (New Haven: Yale University Press, 1951); Friedrich Hayek, ed., *Collectivist Economic Planning* (London: Routledge, 1935); Hayek, *Individualism and Economic Order* (Chicago: University of Chicago Press, 1948); and Joseph Schumpeter, *Capitalism, Socialism and Democracy* (New York: Harper, 1942). On the Austrian school of economics and its tie to the Chicago school, see Lewis Coser, *Refugee Scholars in America* (New Haven: Yale University Press, 1984), pp. 139–42.

142. Frank Knight, *Freedom and Reform* (New York: Harper, 1947), pp. 134–39. See also Henry Simons, *Economic Policy for a Free Society* (Chicago: University of Chicago Press, 1948).

143. Henry Dickinson, *Economics of Socialism* (London: Oxford University Press, 1939); Oscar Lange, *On the Economic Theory of Socialism*, Benjamin Lippincott, ed. (Minneapolis: University of Minnesota Press, 1938).

144. Howe, *Margin of Hope*, pp. 238, 236.

145. Coser, "What Shall We Do?" pp. 156–63.

146. B. Rosenberg, "Rebellious Orgmen," p. 121.

147. Howe, "A New Political Atmosphere in America?" pp. 5–8.

148. Howe, *World More Attractive*, pp. 284–87.

149. Howe, *World More Attractive*, pp. 252–56, 258.

150. H. Rosenberg, *Discovering the Present*, pp. 168–69.

151. Granville Hicks, "Liberalism in the Fifties," *The American Scholar* 25(3):283–96, Summer 1956, p. 296.

152. Hook, "Our Country and Our Culture," pp. 573–74.

153. David Riesman, "Our Country and Our Culture," pp. 313–14.

CHAPTER 3

1. Sidney Hook, "Pragmatism and the Tragic Sense of Life" [1960], *Pragmatism and the Tragic Sense of Life* (New York: Basic Books, 1974), p. 16. Reinhold Niebuhr, *The Irony of American History* (New York: Scribner's, 1952), p. vii.

2. Granville Hicks, "Arthur Koestler and the Future of the Left," *Antioch Review* 5:212–23, Summer 1945, p. 214.

3. At a conference in 1987 several former New Left radicals from the 1960s publicly celebrated their conversion to conservatism. See Sidney Blumenthal, "Thunder on the New Right," *Washington Post*, October 19, 1987, pp. B1, B10. In 1989 Peter Collier and David Horowitz, former editors of the New Left *Ramparts*, published their remorseful jeremiad, *Destructive Generation: Second Thoughts About the Sixties* (New York: Summit, 1989). Horowitz appeared to be the most eager repenter of the New Left, with his "Nicaragua: A Speech to My Former Comrades on the Left," *Commentary* 81(6):27–31, June 1986; and "Still Taking the Fifth," *Commentary* 88(1):53–55, July 1989.

4. Joseph B. Matthews, *Odyssey of a Fellow Traveler* (New York: Mt. Vernon, 1938). Benjamin Gitlow, *I Confess* (New York: Dutton, 1940). Louis Budenz, *This Is My Story* (New York: McGraw-Hill, 1947). Elizabeth Bentley, *Out of Bondage* (New York: Devin-Adair, 1951).

5. Lionel Trilling, *The Middle of the Journey* (1947; reprint, New York: Harcourt, 1975), p. xxii.

6. Sidney Hook, "The Faiths of Whittaker Chambers," *New York Times Book Review*, May 25, 1952, p. 34. Irving Howe, *A World More Attractive* (New York: Horizon, 1963), p. 293.

7. Irving Howe, *Steady Work* (New York: Harcourt, 1966), p. 264. Philip Rahv, *Essays on Literature and Politics, 1932–1972*, Andrew Dvosin and Arabel Porter, eds. (Boston: Houghton Mifflin, 1978), pp. 317–19. Asked later whether his characterization of *Witness* as Dostoevskian had a respectful implication, Howe answered that *Witness* was a book written more by a Dostoevskian character than by a Dostoevskian writer—an important distinction, and hardly as complimentary. Interview with Irving Howe, New York City, June 6, 1985.

8. Rahv, *Essays*, p. 325. Richard Crossman, "The Hiss Case," *Political Quarterly* 24:396–403, October–December 1953, p. 403.

9. AKJ, vols. 5–6, September 13, 1952, and September 22, 1952. Members of the New York group who were religious, such as Kazin and Daniel Bell, felt that faith could coexist with rationality and liberal open debate.

10. *Reprint of Stenographic Transcript, Hearing Before Committee on*

Un-American Activities, House of Representatives, 83d Congress, first session, February 25–26, 1953 (Cambridge, Mass.: Harvard University Printing Office), p. 59.

11. Ignazio Silone, Arthur Koestler, and Louis Fischer, in *The God That Failed,* pp. 113, 74, 224. For a similar sentiment about Louis Budenz, see James T. Farrell, "Out of the Frying Pan," *The Nation* 164(1):368–70, March 29, 1947, p. 370.

12. Rahv, *Essays,* pp. 319–20. Howe, *Steady Work,* pp. 265–66. Sidney Hook, "Myths of Marx," *Saturday Review* 37:11–12, May 15, 1954, p. 12; "The Faiths of Whittaker Chambers," p. 35.

13. Howe, *Steady Work,* pp. 266–67; *World More Attractive,* p. 296. Chambers had portrayed Communism, with some justification, as introducing an order and plan to history, as making "careful measurements" about society. It dealt with action rather than utopian reflection, after all. Still, action, measurements, and plans do not preclude absolutism. See Goronwy Rees, "The Informer and the Communist," *The Spectator* 190:205–7, February 20, 1953, pp. 206–7.

14. Morton White, *Social Thought in America: The Revolt Against Formalism,* rev. ed. (Boston: Beacon, 1957); and Edward Purcell, Jr., *The Crisis of Democratic Theory* (Lexington: University of Kentucky Press, 1973).

15. John Dewey, *Reconstruction in Philosophy* (1920; reprint, Boston: Beacon, 1957), pp. 188–90, 192–93, 198; *Characters and Events,* Joseph Ratner, ed. (New York: Holt, 1929), 1:424.

16. Letter from Sidney Hook to the author, July 17, 1986.

17. Hook, "The Faiths of Whittaker Chambers," p. 34.

18. Sidney Hook, *Political Power and Personal Freedom* (New York: Criterion, 1959), p. 183.

19. Hook, *Political Power,* pp. 217, 222. In the 1980s Hook still felt that most people who gave up their Communist faith did not become reactionaries, but became social democrats like Silone or Koestler. Interview with Sidney Hook, Wardsboro, Vt., July 15, 1985.

20. I am using the term *anti-ideology* rather than *end-of-ideology,* because the latter refers to a perception that America was changing in the late 1940s and 1950s into a classless society in which ideology was no longer as necessary and ideological analyses or solutions were no longer very useful. Anti-ideology signifies an antagonism toward ideology as, in the New York group's view, a form of absolutist or a priori thinking. For the end-of-ideology debate, see Job Dittberner, *The End of Ideology and American Social Thought, 1930–1960* (Ann Arbor, Mich.: UMI Research Press, 1979); and Chaim Waxman, ed., *The End of Ideology Debate* (New York: Funk and Wagnalls, 1968).

21. Irving Kristol, *Two Cheers for Capitalism* (New York: Basic Books, 1978), chaps. 2, 12, 15, 18.

22. Trilling, *Middle of the Journey,* pp. x–xi, xxv.

23. Trilling, *Middle of the Journey*, p. 29.

24. Trilling, *Middle of the Journey*, pp. 93, 95.

25. Trilling, *Middle of the Journey*, pp. 115, 106, 117.

26. Trilling, *Middle of the Journey*, pp. 155–56.

27. Trilling, *Middle of the Journey*, pp. 173–74, 176.

28. Trilling, *Middle of the Journey*, pp. 333–34.

29. Trilling, *Middle of the Journey*, pp. 335, 337.

30. Diana Trilling, "Memorandum on the Hiss Case," *Partisan Review* 17:484–500, May–June 1950, p. 497.

31. Granville Hicks, "Liberals Who Haven't Learned," *Commentary* 11:319–29, April 1951, p. 329; "Mr. Hicks Replies" (letter to the editor), *Commentary* 12:87–88, July 1951; and *Where We Came Out* (New York: Viking, 1954), p. 178.

32. Hicks, "Liberals Who Haven't Learned," p. 329.

33. Hicks, "Mr. Hicks Replies," p. 88; *Where We Came Out*, p. 205.

34. Irving Howe, "America, the Country and the Myth," *Dissent* 2(3):241–44, Summer 1955, p. 241.

35. Crossman, "The Hiss Case," p. 403.

36. Lionel Trilling, *The Last Decade* (New York: Harcourt, 1979), p. 71.

37. Trilling, *The Last Decade*, pp. 83, 90–99.

38. Rahv, "Paleface and Redskin," in *Essays*, pp. 3–7.

39. *Contemporary Authors*, first revision, vols. 9–12 (Detroit: Gale, 1974), p. 904. Lionel Trilling, "From the Notebooks of Lionel Trilling," *Partisan Review* 51:496–515, Anniversary Issue, 1984–85, p. 496. Lionel Trilling, "Young in the Thirties," *Commentary* 41(5):43–51, May 1966, p. 46. James Burkhart Gilbert, *Writers and Partisans* (New York: Wiley, 1968), p. 166.

40. Lionel Trilling, "On the Death of a Friend," *Commentary* 29(2):93–94, February 1960. Norman Podhoretz, *Breaking Ranks* (New York: Harper, 1979), p. 174.

41. Irving Howe, *World of Our Fathers* (New York: Harcourt, 1976), p. 412. Diana Trilling, "Lionel Trilling: A Jew at Columbia," in Lionel Trilling, *Speaking of Literature and Society*, Diana Trilling, ed. (New York: Harcourt, 1980), p. 412.

42. *Contemporary Authors*, p. 904. D. Trilling, "Lionel Trilling," pp. 418–28.

43. Trilling, "Young in the Thirties," p. 47. William Barrett, *The Truants* (New York: Doubleday, 1982), p. 185.

44. D. Trilling, "Lionel Trilling," p. 413.

45. Barrett, *The Truants*, pp. 161–62.

46. Alfred Kazin, *New York Jew* (New York: Knopf, 1978), pp. 43, 47. Harold Rosenberg, *The Tradition of the New* (New York: Horizon, 1959), p. 242.

47. AKJ, vol. 23, October 20, 1968; vol. 8, November 1, 1951.

48. AKJ, vol. 23, October 20, 1968; vol. 15, April 26, 1959; vol. 8, August 18, 1955.

49. Letter from Sidney Hook to the author, July 17, 1986.

50. Trilling, "Notebooks," p. 503.

51. Barrett, *The Truants*, pp. 164–65. Irving Howe, *A Margin of Hope* (New York: Harcourt, 1982), pp. 231–32. Kazin, *New York Jew*, p. 192.

52. Trilling, *The Last Decade*, p. 239.

53. Barrett, *The Truants*, p. 168.

54. Podhoretz, *Breaking Ranks*, p. 283.

55. Norman Podhoretz, *Making It* (New York: Random House, 1967), p. 79. Rahv, *Essays*, p. 24.

56. Giles Gunn, *The Culture of Criticism and the Criticism of Culture* (New York: Oxford University Press, 1987), p. 27.

57. Lionel Trilling, *A Gathering of Fugitives* (1956; reprint, New York: Harcourt, 1978), pp. 108–9; *Beyond Culture* (1965; reprint, New York: Harcourt, 1978), pp. 131–32, 138–39, 146–47. For an especially good interpretation of Trilling's moral component to criticism, see Gunn, *Culture of Criticism*, pp. 23–24, 114–15.

58. Trilling, *Beyond Culture*, p. 147.

59. Trilling, *Gathering of Fugitives*, pp. 111–12; *Beyond Culture*, p. 129.

60. Lionel Trilling, *The Liberal Imagination* (1950; reprint, New York: Harcourt, 1978), pp. 3–4, 7–12.

61. Trilling, *Liberal Imagination*, pp. 25–27, 39–40. Gunn, *Criticism of Culture*, p. 27, argues that Trilling and Edmund Wilson were both "under the sway of Romantic challenges to eighteenth-century optimism," and "their view of human nature darkened under the influence of the modern Romantic legacy." To the contrary, Trilling was a central participant in the New York group's assault on romanticism and the constellation of values they associated with it.

62. Trilling, *Liberal Imagination*, pp. 172–86.

63. Trilling, *Liberal Imagination*, p. 194.

64. Trilling, *Liberal Imagination*, preface.

65. Interview with Daniel Bell, Cambridge, Mass., May 20, 1985.

66. Interview with Daniel Bell, Cambridge, Mass., May 20, 1985; and Bell, *The End of Ideology* (1960; reprint, Cambridge, Mass.: Harvard University Press, 1988), pp. 415, 441–42. See also Hook, "Pragmatism and the Tragic Sense of Life."

67. R. Alan Lawson, *The Failure of Independent Liberalism, 1930–1941* (New York: Putnam's Sons, 1971), pp. 105–6.

68. White, *Social Thought in America*, pp. 250, 252, 254–57, 263–64.

69. Trilling, *The Last Decade*, pp. 236–37.

70. For Trilling's use of Freud to get "beyond culture," see Gunn, *Culture of Criticism*, pp. 30, 34–35.

71. Lionel Trilling, "Seven Professors Look at the Jewish Student" (a symposium), *Commentary* 12:526–29, December 1951, p. 528.

72. Gunn, *Culture of Criticism*, p. 28.

73. Leslie Fiedler, *An End to Innocence* (Boston: Beacon, 1955), pp. 4, 8.

74. Hook, *Political Power*, p. 183; "The Faiths of Whittaker Chambers," p. 35.

75. AKJ, vols. 5–6, April 11, 1946.

76. Mary McCarthy, *On the Contrary* (New York: Farrar, Straus, 1961), pp. 75–76.

77. McCarthy, *On the Contrary*, pp. 76–77, 83.

78. McCarthy, *On the Contrary*, pp. 84, 99, 101, 103.

79. H. Rosenberg, *Tradition of the New*, pp. 221–22.

80. H. Rosenberg, *Tradition of the New*, pp. 222–25. For Rosenberg's other reflections on the ex-Communist confessors, see his "The Communist: His Mentality and His Morals," *Commentary* 8:1–9, July 1949, p. 1; and "The Case of the Baffled Radical" [1944], in *The Partisan Reader*, William Phillips and Philip Rahv, eds. (New York: Dial Press, 1946), p. 666.

81. Murray Hausknecht, "Confession and Return," *Antioch Review* 14:76–86, Spring 1954.

82. Hausknecht, "Confession and Return," pp. 76–77.

83. Hausknecht, "Confession and Return," pp. 79, 82–84, 86.

84. Letter from Everett Wilson to Hausknecht, November 24, 1953; letter from Paul Bixler to Hausknecht, November 25, 1953; letter from Paul Bixler to Hausknecht, February 24, 1954. I am grateful to Murray Hausknecht for making these and several unpublished papers available to me. Also interview with Murray Hausknecht, Long Island City, N.Y., June 24, 1985.

85. Louis Filler, "Confessions in a Democracy: Chambers and Budenz, for Example," unpublished paper, provided by Murray Hausknecht.

86. Murray Hausknecht, "Science and Intuition: A Rejoinder," unpublished paper, provided by Murray Hausknecht.

87. Interview with Murray Hausknecht, Long Island City, N.Y., June 24, 1985.

88. H. Rosenberg, "The Communist," pp. 3–4.

89. Hook, "Myths of Marx," p. 12.

90. NYT, July 13, 1978, p. D16.

91. NYT, July 13, 1978, p. D16. Letter from Harold Rosenberg to Dwight Macdonald, June 6, 1940, DMP.

92. NYT, July 13, 1978, p. D16. Seymour Krim, "Remembering Harold Rosenberg," *Commentary* 66:65–67, November 1978.

93. Mary McCarthy, *NYT*, May 6, 1979, section II, p. 12. *NYT*, July 13, 1978, p. D16. "Harold Rosenberg," *New Yorker* 54:80, July 24, 1978, p. 80. Krim, "Remembering Harold Rosenberg."

94. Saul Bellow, *Him With His Foot in His Mouth, and Other Stories* (New York: Simon and Schuster, 1984), pp. 82, 109, 121, 141, 112, 81, 113.

95. Bellow, *Foot in His Mouth*, pp. 113, 172.

96. Letter from Dwight Macdonald to Hannah Arendt, November 3 (no year), in the Dwight Macdonald file, Hannah Arendt Papers, Manuscripts Division, Library of Congress, Washington, D.C.

97. On Hulsenbeck's influence on Rosenberg, see James D. Herbert, "The Political Origins of Abstract-Expressionist Art Criticism: The Early Theoretical and Critical Writings of Clement Greenberg and Harold Rosenberg," *Stanford Honors Essay in Humanities*, vol. 28 (Stanford, Calif.: Stanford University Press, 1985), pp. 38–39.

98. H. Rosenberg, *Tradition of the New*, pp. 25–26; "Preface to the Second Edition," *Tradition of the New*, p. 5.

99. Herbert, "Political Origins of Abstract-Expressionist Art Criticism," pp. 25–29.

100. H. Rosenberg, *Tradition of the New*, pp. 81, 83.

101. Harold Rosenberg, *The De-Definition of Art* (New York: Horizon, 1972). See also Lionel Trilling, *The Last Decade*, pp. 134–35.

102. H. Rosenberg, *Tradition of the New*, pp. 11–12.

103. H. Rosenberg, *Tradition of the New*, pp. 28–29, 7, 11, 76.

104. H. Rosenberg, *Tradition of the New*, p. 6.

105. Jerome Klinkowitz, *Rosenberg, Barthes, Hassan: The Postmodern Habit of Thought* (Athens: University of Georgia Press, 1988), pp. 3–4, 6, 9.

106. Letter from Dwight Macdonald to Harold Rosenberg, June 7, 1938, DMP.

107. Krim, "Remembering Harold Rosenberg," p. 66. According to Nancy Macdonald, Dwight's first wife, the tension between Rosenberg and her husband was not usually that bad. Letter from Michael Wreszin to the author, February 27, 1987.

108. Rosenberg would not have expected different treatment from Bell or Hook. He had long been a thorn in the side of the affirmers, satirizing and criticizing them, and he had written caustically of Bell's *The End of Ideology* (see Rosenberg, *Tradition of the New*, pp. 254–55, 258). But Bell did not single out Rosenberg for criticism; Bell thought that Rosenberg, Macdonald, Hausknecht, and Shils were all overrated later as important influences within the group.

109. Interview with Daniel Bell, Cambridge, Mass., May 20, 1985.

110. Interview with Sidney Hook, Wardsboro, Vt., July 15, 1985. Letter from Sidney Hook to the author, July 22, 1985.

contemporary popular culture, and therefore the British cultural studies movement refused "either to isolate the pre-industrial and pre-literate folk or to make categorical distinctions between different phases of internal and autonomous, sometimes communal, cultural production." Williams, *Keywords*, p. 137.

15. Shils, "Daydreams and Nightmares," pp. 590, 593, 606.

16. Kazin, AKJ, vol. 15, May 29, 1958. Also interview with Alfred Kazin, New York, June 6, 1985.

17. Macdonald, letter to the editor, *Sewanee Review*, pp. 354–55. See also Macdonald in *Mass Culture*, p. 69.

18. Lewis Coser, "Nightmares, Daydreams, and Prof. Shils," *Dissent* 5:268–73, Summer 1958, p. 271.

19. Coser, "Nightmares," pp. 271–72.

20. Interview with Bernard Rosenberg, Wellfleet, Mass., July 25, 1985; with Lewis Coser, Wellfleet, Mass., July 9, 1985; and with Nathan Glazer, Cambridge, Mass., May 21, 1985.

21. Herbert Gans, *Popular Culture and High Culture* (New York: Basic Books, 1974), p. 45.

22. John O'Brian, Introduction to *Clement Greenberg, The Collected Essays and Criticism*, John O'Brian, ed. (Chicago: University of Chicago Press, 1986), 1:xix, 253.

23. *Contemporary Authors*, vols. 1–4, first revision (Detroit: Gale Research, 1967), p. 393. O'Brian in *Clement Greenberg*, 1:xix–xx, 253–54.

24. O'Brian in *Clement Greenberg*, 1:xx. Greenberg, *Art and Culture*, p. 230.

25. O'Brian in *Clement Greenberg*, 1:xx–xxi. Greenberg, *Art and Culture*, pp. 232, 231. Letter from Clement Greenberg to Erle Loran, February 1, 1944, Erle Loran Papers, Archives of American Art—Smithsonian Institution. Letter from Clement Greenberg to the author, September 21, 1986.

26. Letter from Clement Greenberg to Erle Loran, February 1, 1944. Later Greenberg could not recall which article he referred to in his letter to Loran. Letter from Clement Greenberg to the author, September 21, 1986.

27. William Phillips, *A Partisan View* (New York: Stein and Day, 1983), pp. 65–66. William Barrett, *The Truants* (New York: Doubleday, 1982), p. 138.

28. Letters from Clement Greenberg to the author, November 8, 1986, and September 21, 1986.

29. Letter from Greenberg to Erle Loran, February 1, 1944.

30. O'Brian in *Clement Greenberg*, 1:xxi.

31. O'Brian in *Clement Greenberg*, 1:xviii–xix.

32. Quoted in James D. Herbert, "The Political Origins of Abstract-

Expressionist Art Criticism: The Early Theoretical and Critical Writings of Clement Greenberg and Harold Rosenberg," *Stanford Honors Essay in Humanities*, vol. 28 (Stanford, Calif.: Stanford University Press, 1985), pp. 4–5. Herbert makes a strong argument that Greenberg was influenced by Trotsky's artistic individualism.

33. Herbert, "Political Origins of Abstract-Expressionist Art Criticism," pp. 2–3, 6, 8.

34. Casey Blake, "Aesthetic Engineering," *Democracy* 1(4):37–50, October 1981, pp. 46, 41.

35. Letter from Daniel Bell to the author, April 24, 1987.

36. O'Brian in *Clement Greenberg*, 1:xxiii.

37. Barrett, *The Truants*, pp. 136, 143, 150. O'Brian in *Clement Greenberg*, 1:xxiv.

38. O'Brian in *Clement Greenberg*, 1:xxii.

39. Letter from Clement Greenberg to James Laughlin, December 9, 1954, in the Clement Greenberg Papers, on loan to the Archives of American Art—Smithsonian Institution. Used by permission of the Archives of American Art—Smithsonian Institution. See also H. Rosenberg, *Tradition of the New*, pp. 23–39. Greenberg confirmed that it was this essay of Rosenberg's at issue; letter from Clement Greenberg to the author, September 21, 1986.

40. Letter from Clement Greenberg to the author, November 8, 1986.

41. Greenberg said the de Kooning scuffle was at Dillon's rather than at the Cedar Tavern, where Abel placed it. Greenberg also said the incident was not as Abel related it—although he declined to give the circumstances. He reported that de Kooning was known as a prevaricator. Letter from Clement Greenberg to the author, September 21, 1986. Lionel Abel, *The Intellectual Follies* (New York: Norton, 1984), p. 212.

42. Barrett, *The Truants*, pp. 58, 41–42. Greenberg denied the Rosenberg story; letter from Clement Greenberg to the author, September 21, 1986.

43. O'Brian in *Clement Greenberg*, 1:xx. Herbert, "Political Origins of Abstract-Expressionist Art Criticism," p. 29. Letter from Irving Howe to Dwight Macdonald, August 1, 1946, DMP.

44. Norman Podhoretz, *Making It* (New York: Random House, 1967), p. 101. Letter from Clement Greenberg to the author, November 8, 1986.

45. Podhoretz, *Making It*, pp. 129–30.

46. Greenberg, *Art and Culture*, p. 15.

47. Editors, "Our Country and Our Culture," *Partisan Review* 19(3):282–326, May–June 1952, p. 285.

48. Bernard Rosenberg in *Culture for the Millions?* Norman Jacobs, ed. (Princeton, N.J.: Van Nostrand, 1961), p. 163; and "A Symposium on TV," *Dissent* 7:297–98, Summer 1960.

49. Edward Shils, "What Is a Liberal, Who Is a Conservative?" *Commentary* 62:95–97, September 1976, p. 96.

50. Daniel Bell said Shils was "influential" to the group from "a distance," but "close enough at times" to be considered a "cousin." But he also cautioned that Shils's importance to the group should not be overrated. According to Bell, few of the New York intellectuals knew him. Shils did play a role in the Congress for Cultural Freedom, but he either ignored or was antagonistic toward most members of the New York group other than Irving Kristol. His real influence, Bell reported, was as an advisor to foundations and individuals—yet most people were afraid of Shils's sharp tongue and kept away from him. Daniel Bell, *The Winding Passage* (New York: Basic Books, 1980), p. 129; and letter from Daniel Bell to the author, October 9, 1986.

51. Steven Lukes, a sociologist at Oxford, describes Shils as "Parsons's collaborator and a structural functionalist to the bone." Steven Lukes, "The Theoretical Polemics of Anti-Ideology," *American Journal of Sociology* 84(1):186–90, July 1978, p. 186.

52. James D. Stolzman, "Edward Shils on Consensus: An Appreciation and Critique," *British Journal of Sociology* 25(1):3–14, March 1974, pp. 3–5.

53. Edward Shils, *Center and Periphery: Essays in Macrosociology* (Chicago: University of Chicago Press, 1975). Also see Stolzman, "Edward Shils," pp. 5–8.

54. Lukes, "Theoretical Polemics," pp. 186–87.

55. Edward Shils, *The Constitution of Society* (Chicago: University of Chicago Press, 1982), pp. xxx, xxii.

56. Shils, "What Is a Liberal," pp. 95–96; *Constitution of Society*, pp. x, xx.

57. Abel, *Intellectual Follies*, p. 69. Bell, *Winding Passage*, p. 231.

58. Shils, *Constitution of Society*, pp. xxiii, xii, xiv, xxiv–xxv.

59. Phillips, *A Partisan View*, pp. 254–55.

60. Shils, "What Is a Liberal," p. 96. Bell, *Winding Passage*, p. xx.

61. Shils, *Constitution of Society*, p. xxix.

62. Macdonald, *Against the American Grain*, p. 34. In 1985 members of the New York group disagreed about whether their mass-culture criticism had been elitist or not. Nathan Glazer, Sidney Hook, and Alfred Kazin thought it had been elitist; Murray Hausknecht, Irving Howe, and Bernard Rosenberg thought it had not. Author's interviews with Nathan Glazer, Cambridge, Mass., May 21, 1985; Murray Hausknecht, New York, June 24, 1985; Sidney Hook, Wardsboro, Vt., July 15, 1985; Irving Howe, New York, June 6, 1985; Alfred Kazin, New York, June 6, 1985; and Bernard Rosenberg, Wellfleet, Mass., July 25, 1985.

63. Williams, *Keywords*, pp. 112, 114–15.

64. Interview with Sidney Hook, July 15, 1985.

65. By *cultural pluralism* I am not referring to ethnic pluralism and diversity, which the New York group always supported strongly, but rather aesthetic pluralism and diversity. Herbert Gans calls this a prolif-

eration of "taste cultures" in his *Popular Culture and High Culture*. Kenneth Roberts terms this arrangement "taste publics" in his "Culture, Leisure, Society—The Pluralist Scenario," in Tony Bennett et al., eds., *Culture, Ideology and Social Process* (London: Batsford, 1981), p. 272. Raymond Williams, in *Keywords*, p. 89, traces the concept of a plurality of "cultures" within a national culture to the work of Johann Herder in the late eighteenth century.

66. William Phillips in *Culture for the Millions?* pp. 192–93.

67. Ernest van den Haag and Sidney Hook in *Culture for the Millions?* pp. 160–61, 165.

68. David Riesman in "Our Country and Our Culture," pp. 311–14. Herbert Gans was later influenced by Riesman, with whom he studied.

69. Hook in *Culture for the Millions?* p. 160.

70. Williams, *Keywords*, p. 96.

71. On the academic character of the younger intellectuals see Russell Jacoby, *The Last Intellectuals* (New York: Basic Books, 1987).

72. Williams, *Keywords*, p. 90; *Marxism and Literature* (New York: Oxford University Press, 1977), p. 13.

73. Raymond Williams, *Television: Technology and Cultural Form* (New York: Schocken, 1975), p. 121; *Problems in Materialism and Culture* (London: NLB, 1980), p. 48; *Marxism and Literature*, pp. 136–38.

74. On Williams's contributions to the outlook of the young, see Michael Denning, "'The Special American Conditions': Marxism and American Studies," *American Quarterly* 38(3):356–80, bibliography issue 1986, p. 372; Richard A. Peterson, "Revitalizing the Culture Concept," *Annual Review of Sociology* 5:137–66, 1979, p. 137; Sherry B. Ortner, "Theory in Anthropology Since the Sixties," *Comparative Studies in Society and History* 26(1):126–66, January 1984, p. 149; and Stuart Hall, "Cultural Studies and the Centre: Some Problematics and Problems," in Stuart Hall et al., *Culture, Media, Language* (London: Hutchinson, 1980), p. 19.

75. E. P. Thompson, *The Making of the English Working Class* (1963; reprint, New York: Vintage, 1966). See also Herbert Gutman, *Work, Culture, and Society in Industrializing America* (New York: Vintage, 1977), and the interview with Herbert Gutman in Harry Abelove et al., *Visions of History* (New York: Pantheon, 1983), pp. 187–216.

76. Hall, "Cultural Studies," pp. 21, 40; on the relation between cultural studies and the New Left, see pp. 17, 25. For Hall's definition of culture, see Bennett et al., *Culture, Ideology and Social Process*, pp. 53–54.

77. See Giles Gunn, *The Culture of Criticism and the Criticism of Culture* (New York: Oxford University Press, 1987), chap. 3; Jonathan Arac, *Critical Genealogies* (New York: Columbia University Press, 1989);

Terry Eagleton, *Literary Theory: An Introduction* (Minneapolis: University of Minnesota Press, 1983); and Stuart Hall, "Cultural Studies: Two Paradigms," in Bennett et al., *Culture, Ideology and Social Process*, pp. 19–37. On Geertz, see Gunn, chap. 5.

78. John Patrick Diggins, "Dusting Off the Old Values," *New York Times Book Review*, March 15, 1987, p. 11; Gunn, *Culture of Criticism*, p. 194. For an example of the movement of this postmodernist outlook into the discipline of history, see Hayden White, *Tropics of Discourse* (Baltimore: Johns Hopkins University Press, 1978).

79. Susan Sontag, *A Susan Sontag Reader* (New York: Vintage, 1983), pp. 102–103, 98–99.

80. Sontag, *Sontag Reader*, p. 108.

81. In *The Agony of the American Left* (New York: Knopf, 1969), Lasch was critical of both the Old Left (chaps. 2 and 3) and the New Left (chap. 5).

82. Studies of the therapeutic culture include Philip Rieff, *The Triumph of the Therapeutic* (New York: Harper, 1966); Tom Wolfe, "The Me Decade and the Third Great Awakening" [1976], *The Purple Decades* (New York: Farrar Straus, 1982), pp. 265–93; Warren Susman, "Personality and the Making of Twentieth-Century Culture" [1979], *Culture as History* (New York: Pantheon, 1984), pp. 271–85; Christopher Lasch, *The Culture of Narcissism* (New York: Norton, 1979), pp. 27–70; and Richard Fox and T. J. Jackson Lears, eds., *The Culture of Consumption* (New York: Pantheon, 1983).

83. For the antimodernist outlook see T. J. Jackson Lears, *No Place of Grace: Antimodernism and the Transformation of American Culture, 1880–1920* (New York: Pantheon, 1981); and Robert Brym, *Intellectuals and Politics* (London: Allen and Unwin, 1980), p. 19.

84. Lasch's antimodernist complaint against the New York group was seconded by his student Casey Blake, who criticized Clement Greenberg for moving from radicalism to modernism and for trying "to reconcile art with industrial society." Blake's criticism of Greenberg reveals a connection between hostility to the industrial modernization and organization of society, on one hand, and hostility to artistic modernism as an expression of that industrial rationalization, on the other. Casey Blake, "Aesthetic Engineering," pp. 46, 41.

85. Christopher Lasch, "Mass Culture Reconsidered," *Democracy* 1(4):7–22, October 1981, pp. 10, 12–13.

86. Lasch, "Mass Culture Reconsidered," pp. 11, 7.

87. Lasch, "Mass Culture Reconsidered," p. 11.

88. Henry Steele Commager, "On the Way to 1984," *Saturday Review*, April 15, 1967, p. 82.

89. Gans, *Popular Culture and High Culture*, pp. 7, 55–56. Whether people are ascending or descending in status, as Richard Hofstadter

pointed out, individuals or groups can become anxious about their relation to the rest of the community.

90. Quoted by Dwight Macdonald in *Mass Culture*, p. 61. Quotes in the next paragraph are from p. 64.

91. John Clarke, Stuart Hall, Tony Jefferson, and Brian Roberts, "Sub Cultures, Cultures and Class," in Bennett et al., *Culture, Ideology and Social Process*, pp. 76, 78.

92. For this argument, see Neil Jumonville, "In Their Own Hand," *Boston Review* 9(5):22–24, October 1984.

CHAPTER 5

1. James McKenzie, "An Interview with Gary Snyder," in *The Unspeakable Visions of the Individual*, vol. 5, Arthur Knight and Kit Knight, eds. (California, Pa., 1977), p. 141.

2. McKenzie, "Interview with Snyder," p. 141.

3. Ellen Frankfort, *The Voice* (New York: Morrow, 1976), pp. 214–18.

4. Norman Mailer, "The White Negro: Superficial Reflections on the Hipster," *Dissent* 4(3):276–93, Summer 1957, pp. 285–86.

5. Norman Podhoretz, "The Know-Nothing Bohemians," *Partisan Review* 25:305–11, Spring 1958, pp. 307–8, 313–15.

6. Norman Podhoretz, "The Beat Generation" (response to a letter to the editor), *Partisan Review* 25:476–79, Summer 1958, p. 476. Paul Goodman, *Growing Up Absurd* (New York: Random House, 1960), pp. 64, 175.

7. Mailer, "The White Negro," pp. 280, 284.

8. AKJ, vol. 15, August 31, 1957. Also see the reaction to Mailer's essay in Richard Hofstadter, *Anti-Intellectualism in American Life* (New York: Knopf, 1963), pp. 422–23.

9. Podhoretz, "Know-Nothing Bohemians," pp. 316–18.

10. James McKenzie, "Interview with Allen Ginsberg," *The Unspeakable Visions of the Individual*, vol. 8, Arthur Knight and Kit Knight, eds. (California, Pa., 1978), p. 10.

11. Mailer, "The White Negro," pp. 278–80; Mailer in Norman Mailer, Jean Malaquais, and Ned Polsky, "Reflections on Hipsterism," *Dissent* 5(1):73–81, Winter 1958, p. 76.

12. Ned Polsky in "Reflections on Hipsterism," p. 78. Paul Goodman, *Drawing the Line* (New York: Free Life, 1977), p. 140; *Growing Up Absurd*, pp. 112, 175.

13. AKJ, vol. 15, August 31, 1957.

14. Irving Howe, *A World More Attractive* (New York: Horizon, 1963), pp. 95–96.

15. Delmore Schwartz, "Present State," *Selected Essays of Delmore Schwartz* (Chicago: University of Chicago Press, 1970).

16. McKenzie, "Interview with Snyder," p. 141.

17. Podhoretz, "The Beat Generation," p. 477; "Know-Nothing Bohemians," pp. 307–8. McKenzie, "Interview with Ginsberg," p. 10.

18. As Paul Goodman pointed out, the Beats had a similar problem in their attempt to form a bond with the poor. The bohemians came from middle-class backgrounds but rejected those values and morals. The poor, on the contrary, had no patience with the Beats' sexual and racial nonconformity and aspired to middle-class respectability. Goodman, *Growing Up Absurd*, pp. 64–65.

19. Norman Podhoretz, *Doings and Undoings* (New York: Farrar, Straus, 1964), pp. 108–11; *Breaking Ranks* (New York: Harper, 1979), p. 28.

20. *Contemporary Authors*, vols. 9–12, first revision (Detroit: Gale, 1974), p. 720.

21. Norman Podhoretz, *Making It* (New York: Random House, 1967), pp. 7–9, 18, 28.

22. Norman Podhoretz, "Why 'The God That Failed' Failed . . . ," *Encounter* 60:28–34, January 1983, p. 28.

23. Podhoretz, *Making It*, pp. 41–42.

24. Podhoretz, *Making It*, p. 3.

25. Podhoretz, *Doings and Undoings*, p. 259.

26. Robert Brustein, "Who's Killing the Novel?" *The New Republic* 153(17):22–24, October 23, 1965, pp. 22–23.

27. Podhoretz, *Doings and Undoings*, pp. 13–18. Alfred Kazin, *On Native Grounds* (New York: Reynal and Hitchcock, 1942), pp. 457–65.

28. Podhoretz, *Breaking Ranks*, pp. 188–89.

29. Norman Podhoretz, "My Negro Problem—and Ours" [1963], in Podhoretz, ed., *The Commentary Reader* (New York: Atheneum, 1967), pp. 376–87. Nat Hentoff, "Cool, Like Blocked," *The Nation* 198(13):298–300, March 23, 1964, pp. 299–300.

30. Podhoretz, "My Negro Problem," pp. 376–87.

31. Norman Podhoretz, "A Note on Vietnamization," *Commentary* 51(5):6–9, May 1971.

32. Norman Podhoretz, "The New Hypocrisies," *Commentary* 50(6):5–6, December 1970, p. 6; "A Minor Cultural Event," *Commentary* 53(4):7–10, April 1972, p. 7.

33. William Phillips, *A Partisan View* (New York: Stein and Day, 1983) pp. 244–45.

34. Brustein, "Who's Killing the Novel?"

35. Norman Podhoretz, "Reflections on Earth Day," *Commentary* 49(6):26–28, June 1970; "The New Hypocrisies," *Commentary* 50(6):5–6, December 1970; "Adversaries or Critics?" *Commentary* 51(3):6–7, March 1971; "A Certain Anxiety," *Commentary* 52(2):4–10, August 1971; "Liberty and the Liberals," *Commentary* 52(6):4–6, December 1971; "A Minor Cultural Event," *Commentary* 53(4):7–10, April 1972; "Between Nixon and the New Politics," *Commentary* 54(3):4–8, September 1972.

36. Norman Podhoretz, "Laws, Kings, and Cures," *Commentary* 50(4):30–31, October 1970.

37. Norman Podhoretz, "The Present Danger," *Commentary* 69(3):27–40, March 1980, p. 27. See also Norman Podhoretz, "Making the World Safe for Communism," *Commentary* 61(4):31–41, April 1976.

38. Podhoretz, "Why 'The God That Failed' Failed," p. 34.

39. Norman Podhoretz, "If Orwell Were Alive Today," *Harper's* 266:30–37, January 1983, pp. 30, 35, 37. See also Norman Podhoretz and Christopher Hitchens, "An Exchange on Orwell," *Harper's* 266:56–58, February 1983.

40. Podhoretz, "A Certain Anxiety," p. 10.

41. Podhoretz, "Between Nixon and the New Politics," p. 8.

42. Christopher Hitchens in Podhoretz and Hitchens, "An Exchange on Orwell," p. 58.

43. Conor Cruise O'Brien, "Trop de Zèle," *New York Review of Books* 33(15):11–14, October 9, 1986, pp. 12–14.

44. The sociologist Robert Brym has suggested that when students are not well integrated into national political parties they are more likely to become radical. Further, where repression is only moderately high or inconsistently applied, radicalism reaches a peak. It might be argued that the students in the early 1960s had already become disenchanted with established politics—by their contact with the civil rights movement, the Cold War, and the beginnings of the Vietnam War—and consequently had no desire to be integrated into the political parties. It also seems likely that the students did feel moderate and inconsistent repression against their political agendas at Berkeley and Columbia. Robert Brym, *Intellectuals and Politics* (London: Allen and Unwin, 1980), p. 17.

45. Tom Hayden et al., "The Port Huron Statement" [1962], in *The American Left: Radical Political Thought in the Twentieth Century*, Loren Baritz, ed. (New York: Basic Books, 1971), pp. 393–94.

46. Podhoretz, *Breaking Ranks*, p. 197. Nathan Glazer, "On Being Deradicalized," *Commentary* 50(4):74–80, p. 75.

47. "The Young Radicals: A Symposium," *Dissent* 9(2):129–63, Spring 1962, pp. 129–30, 132, 136, 141–42.

48. Lewis Coser in "The Young Radicals," pp. 159–62.

49. Irving Howe, *A Margin of Hope* (New York: Harcourt, 1982), pp. 291–93. Interview with Murray Hausknecht, Long Island City, N.Y., June 24, 1985.

50. Interview with Murray Hausknecht, Long Island City, N.Y., June 24, 1985.

51. For the New York group's involvement in the Berkeley protests, see Neil Jumonville, "The Gray Dawn: The New York Intellectuals and the Function of Criticism," Ph.D. dissertation, Harvard University, 1986, pp. 341–45.

52. Nathan Glazer, "What Happened at Berkeley," *Commentary* 39(2):39–47, February 1965, p. 47.

53. Daniel Bell, in Daniel Bell and Irving Kristol, eds., *Confrontation: The Student Rebellion and the Universities* (New York: Basic Books, 1969), pp. 72–74.

54. From Richard Hofstadter's contribution to the "Columbia Crisis 1968" project, in the Columbia University Oral History Research Office, New York, pp. 1–2. This is a transcript of a tape-recorded interview of Hofstadter on May 15, 1968. Used by permission of the Trustees of Columbia University in the City of New York.

55. Diana Trilling, *We Must March My Darlings* (New York: Harcourt, 1977), p. 87.

56. Bell, *Confrontation*, p. 83. Hofstadter, "Columbia Crisis 1968," p. 7.

57. Hofstadter, "Columbia Crisis 1968," pp. 6, 4–5.

58. Bell, *Confrontation*, p. 83.

59. Hofstadter, "Columbia Crisis 1968," pp. 4–5.

60. Hofstadter, "Columbia Crisis 1968," p. 10. D. Trilling, *We Must March*, p. 123.

61. Sidney Hook, "Three Intellectual Troubadours," *The American Spectator* 18(1):18–22, January 1985, p. 22.

62. Sidney Hook, *Academic Freedom and Academic Anarchy* (New York: Cowles, 1970) p. 91.

63. Bell, *Confrontation*, pp. 101–2.

64. Dwight Macdonald, *Discriminations* (New York: Grossman, 1974), pp. 456–57.

65. D. Trilling, *We Must March*, p. 90. Bell, *Confrontation*, p. 98.

66. Howe, *Margin of Hope*, pp. 314–15.

67. Interview with David Riesman, Cambridge, Mass., November 23, 1984.

68. Howe, *Margin of Hope*, p. 306.

69. Irving Howe, *Steady Work* (New York: Harcourt, 1966), pp. 39–40.

70. Hook, *Academic Freedom*, pp. 66–67, 121, 126.

71. Bell, *Confrontation*, pp. 80, 101, 107.

72. Glazer, "What Happened at Berkeley," p. 47.

73. Howe, *Steady Work*, p. 112.

74. Seymour Martin Lipset and Gerald Schaflander, *Passion and Politics* (Boston: Little, Brown, 1971), pp. 203–4.

75. *Contemporary Authors*, vols. 1–4, first revision (Detroit: Gale, 1967), p. 65. Job L. Dittberner, "Interview with Daniel Bell, May 1972," in *The End of Ideology and American Social Thought: 1930–1960* (Ann Arbor, Mich.: UMI Research Press, 1979), p. 309.

76. Daniel Bell, *The End of Ideology* (1960; reprint, Cambridge,

Mass.: Harvard University Press, 1988), p. 299; "First Love and Early Sorrows," *Partisan Review* 48(4):532–51, p. 534. Dittberner, "Interview with Bell," pp. 309–10.

77. Dittberner, "Interview with Bell," pp. 310–11. Interview with Nathan Glazer, Cambridge, Mass., May 21, 1985. Letter from Daniel Bell to the author, July 22, 1987.

78. Howard Brick discusses Bell's leftist economic and political journalism in *Daniel Bell and the Decline of Intellectual Radicalism* (Madison: University of Wisconsin Press, 1986). Letter from Bell to the author, July 22, 1987.

79. Daniel Bell's contribution to the "Richard Hofstadter Project," in the Columbia University Oral History Research Office, New York, pp. 1–2. This is a transcript of a tape-recorded interview of Bell in April 1972. Used by permission of Daniel Bell and the Columbia University Oral History Research Office. See also Dittberner, "Interview with Bell," p. 314.

80. Dittberner, "Interview with Bell," pp. 320, 318. Letter from Bell to the author, July 22, 1987.

81. Letter from Dwight Macdonald to Daniel Bell, November 26, 1946, DMP. The year of the letter is uncertain.

82. Bell, *End of Ideology*, p. 305.

83. Letter from Daniel Bell to the author, October 17, 1986.

84. Letter from Bell to the author, July 22, 1987; letter from Dwight Macdonald to Daniel Bell, April 8, 1947, DMP. The year of this last letter is uncertain.

85. Bell, "Richard Hofstadter Project," pp. 1–3; *The Winding Passage* (New York: Basic Books, 1980), p. xi; *The Radical Right* (New York: Doubleday, 1963), p. xi. Letter from Bell to the author, July 22, 1987.

86. Bell, "Richard Hofstadter Project," p. 4. Dittberner, "Interview with Bell," pp. 324–25. *Contemporary Authors*, vols. 1–4, first revision (Detroit: Gale, 1967), p. 65. Bell, *Winding Passage*, pp. xi–xii. The *Commentary* job had first been offered to Kristol, who turned it down; then it was offered to Bell, and then to Podhoretz. Bell suggests that Mills opposed his being hired at Columbia for personal reasons resulting from an "ugly episode" that Bell and Hofstadter witnessed when Mills left his wife in 1945. Letter from Bell to the author, July 22, 1987.

87. Bell, *Winding Passage*, pp. xii–xiii. Bell's interests evolved over the decades and he left some of his early socialist enthusiasm behind, yet he always carried with him the romance of those earlier political battles. This is apparent in his "First Love and Early Sorrows," a 1981 essay whose title refers not to a former amour but rather the creation of his political outlook. A continuing enthusiasm for the earlier polemics is also apparent in his afterword to the 1988 reprint of *The End of Ideology*.

88. Hook, "Three Intellectual Troubadours." Interview with Daniel Bell, Cambridge, Mass., May 20, 1985.

89. Interview with Daniel Bell, Cambridge, Mass., May 20, 1985. Interview with Sidney Hook, Wardsboro, Vt., July 15, 1985.

90. Hook, "Three Intellectual Troubadours." Bell, *End of Ideology*, p. 449; the original edition of the book does not carry this statement.

91. Letter from Bell to the author, July 22, 1987. See also Bell, *End of Ideology*, pp. 415, 441.

92. Bell, "Richard Hofstadter Project," p. 11. Letters from Daniel Bell to the author, October 17, 1986, and July 22, 1987.

93. Bell has said that "given my orientation and interests, I never accepted the Parsonian system, though I fully appreciated the scope of his theoretical efforts. . . . I have always argued that sociology cannot be fully formalized, for to do so would be to detach it from history and institutions—in the way that neo-classical Walrasian economics tries to do (and which was Parsons' model)." Letter from Bell to the author, July 22, 1987. See also *End of Ideology*, pp. 413–14.

94. Stuart Hall, one of the leaders of the cultural studies movement at the University of Birmingham in Britain, has argued that when American sociologists such as Bell gave up on the concepts of "totality" and ideology in culture, the new approaches by the New Left in anthropology, literary theory, and social history filled that gap—and that culture studies, sympathetic to the popular culture that the New York group rejected, bound the new approaches together. "One way of thinking of Cultural Studies," Hall proposed, "is as the intellectual space where the convergences between these displaced traditions occurred." Stuart Hall, "Cultural Studies and the Centre: Some Problematics and Problems," in Stuart Hall et al., eds., *Culture, Media, Language* (London: Hutchison, 1984), pp. 20–21.

95. Richard Hofstadter, *The Progressive Historians* (New York: Knopf, 1968), pp. 444n., 450–52. The consensus school was closely allied to the "myth-symbol school" of American studies in that the latter searched for common themes in the American "mind," an approach that its critics have argued stressed the unity and consensus in the American identity. The myth-symbol writers also had much in common with the New York intellectuals since both groups challenged the formalist preoccupations of the New Critics and the academy. As Giles Gunn has pointed out, the myth-symbol approach opposed "the tendency of so much critical study during the 1940s and 1950s to restrict the whole meaning of verbal texts to an analysis of their specific metaphorical or linguistic properties," and fought "the temptation to define ideas in isolation from the actual circumstances to which they are a response." Giles Gunn, *The Culture of Criticism and the Criticism of Culture* (New York: Oxford University Press, 1987), p. 158.

96. Hofstadter, *Progressive Historians*, pp. 451–52.

97. Brick, *Daniel Bell*, pp. 19, 107. Nathan Liebowitz, *Daniel Bell and the Agony of Modern Liberalism* (Westport, Conn.: Greenwood, 1985),

p. 4. Of course, much of the intellectual community (particularly the New York group) faced the same hard "contradictory" choices as Bell, which makes it harder to appeal to contradiction as an explanation of what is unique about his thought. Further, contradiction is central to the thought of most intellectuals—though not usually to the same degree as found in Bell.

98. Bell, "First Love and Early Sorrows," pp. 536–38.

99. Bell, "First Love and Early Sorrows," pp. 550–51.

100. Bell, *Winding Passage*, p. xiv. See also Daniel Bell, *The Coming of Post-Industrial Society* (New York: Basic Books, 1973), pp. 10–13; and *The Cultural Contradictions of Capitalism* (New York: Basic Books, 1978), pp. xvi–xviii.

101. Bell, *Cultural Contradictions*, pp. xxx–xxxi, xvi–xviii.

102. Bell, *Cultural Contradictions*, pp. xi–xv. Much of the rest of *Cultural Contradictions* is Bell's restatement of Joseph Schumpeter's point that, in Schumpeter's words, "capitalism creates a critical frame of mind which, after having destroyed the moral authority of so many other institutions, in the end turns against its own; the bourgeois finds to his amazement that the rationalist attitude does not stop at the credentials of kings and popes but goes on to attack private property and the whole scheme of bourgeois values." Schumpeter similarly claimed that "unlike any other type of society, capitalism inevitably and by virtue of the very logic of its civilization creates, educates and subsidizes a vested interest in social unrest." Joseph Schumpeter, *Capitalism, Socialism and Democracy* (1942; reprint, New York: Harper, 1975), pp. 143, 146.

103. Daniel Bell, "Our Country—1984," *Partisan Review* 51(1):620–37, Anniversary Issue, 1984–85, pp. 630–37. Also letter from Daniel Bell to the author, May 27, 1987.

104. Bell thought much of their difference was in temperament—not so much the content of the views as the way they were held. "Norman," Bell believed, "has always had an argumentative, even 'Bolshevik' temperament; and a coarse streak to boot." Letter from Bell to the author, July 22, 1987.

105. Bell and Kristol, *Confrontation*, pp. x, 106–7.

106. James F. Petras and Michael Shute, "Berkeley '65," *Partisan Review* 32(2):314–23, Spring 1965, pp. 316, 315. For an example of a scholarly criticism of the group's fear of democratic masses, see Michael Paul Rogin, *The Intellectuals and McCarthy* (Cambridge, Mass.: MIT Press, 1967).

107. Interview with Daniel Bell, Cambridge, Mass., May 20, 1985.

108. David Riesman has provided an interesting insight into the factors underlying his own fear of the masses. In addition to national and international events and leaders—such as the Nazi uprising in Germany, and Huey Long, Father Coughlin, and Senator Joseph McCarthy at

home—part of the fear stemmed from the social and intellectual tension within American culture. "I early became aware of resentment of the expert in such things as anti-fluoridation fights," he remembered, "and now the animal rights groups. People who say: get those university people. One thing that's been both puzzling and dismaying to me in both the counterculture and the New Left is how many professors who would be vulnerable have led the charge." A final reason was personal. "I had that strong feeling, I think, because I could never fight in school, and didn't have the physical endurance. When I was a teen I was the poorest ballplayer. When I spent a year of grad school in Tucson I was the poorest rider. So I was afraid of the other boys, physically. They would torment me. I was always unsuccessful. But also I had a fear of the mob." Interview with David Riesman, Cambridge, Mass., November 23, 1984.

109. The quotes here and in the following two paragraphs are from Daniel Bell, "Richard Hofstadter Project," pp. 25–29.

110. On Coughlin's anti-Semitism see Richard Hofstadter, *The Paranoid Style in American Politics* (New York: Knopf, 1965), pp. 68–69; and Alan Brinkley, *Voices of Protest* (New York: Knopf, 1982), pp. 269–73.

111. Lionel Trilling, *Beyond Culture* (1965; reprint, New York: Harcourt, 1978), pp. 3–4, 16, 23–24.

112. Lionel Trilling, *Beyond Culture*, preface.

113. Bell, *Cultural Contradictions*, p. 143.

114. Bell, "Richard Hofstadter Project," pp. 27–28.

115. Paul Goodman, in Irving Howe, ed., *Beyond the New Left* (New York: McCall, 1970), pp. 86–89, 95.

116. Hook, *Academic Freedom and Academic Anarchy*, pp. 25–26.

117. For good examples of this outlook see Bell, *Confrontation*, pp. 94–95, and Nathan Glazer, "On Being Deradicalized," *Commentary* 50(4):74–80, October 1970, p. 75.

118. Nathan Glazer, "The New Left and Its Limits," *Commentary* 46(1):31–39, July 1968, pp. 32–33, 35, 39.

119. Howe, *Steady Work*, pp. 68–69.

120. Howe, *Beyond the New Left*, pp. 46, 50.

121. Dennis Wrong, response to letters to the editor, *Commentary* 51(3):22–30, March 1971, pp. 26, 24.

122. Irving Kristol, *Reflections of a Neoconservative* (New York: Basic Books, 1983), pp. 27–28.

123. Bell and Kristol, *Confrontation*, p. xii.

124. Hook, *Academic Freedom*, p. xvii.

CHAPTER 6

1. Alfred Kazin, "Saving My Soul at the Plaza," *New York Review of Books* 30(5):38–42, March 31, 1983, p. 38.

2. Kazin, "Saving My Soul," p. 38.

3. Kazin, "Saving My Soul," p. 41; Kazin's ellipses.

4. Kazin, "Saving My Soul," p. 41.

5. Irving Kristol, *Reflections of a Neoconservative* (New York: Basic Books, 1983), pp. x–xii. For another mention of ideology and the French Revolution, see Daniel Bell, *The End of Ideology* (1960; reprint, Cambridge, Mass.: Harvard University Press, 1988), p. 419.

6. Fundraising circular from the Committee for the Free World, over the signature of Midge Decter, April 1987.

7. Soon after Hook's death, the breakdown of Communism in Eastern Europe began. Much of Hook's opposition to totalitarianism had been predicated on its irreversible nature; it would forever preclude the existence of a system of choices, he believed, and choice is essential to a pragmatist. What might Hook have said in the face of the democratization in Eastern Europe? Moreover, will future generations judge that the dissolution of Communism was due partly to the battle for intellectual freedom that Hook and the New York group had waged against it? Or was the system destined to fall anyway? Finally, at the beginning of the 1990s, with Communism no longer the palpable threat it once was, is the New York group's antiabsolutism outdated and ready to be retired? Or is antiabsolutism a perennial need in the defense of freedom—now to be mustered, in the name of liberal tolerance and tentative truths, in the fight against the fanaticism of nationalistic, ethnic, and religious zealots? Perhaps it is fitting that Hook departed at such a watershed moment, leaving another generation to wage the conflicts of the new era.

8. James Atlas, "The Changing World of New York Intellectuals," *New York Times Magazine*, August 25, 1985. For the argument that follows, see also Neil Jumonville, "Laments for the Last Intellectual," *Boston Review* 13(6):11–14, December 1988.

9. Russell Jacoby, *The Last Intellectuals* (New York: Basic Books, 1987).

10. Harold Rosenberg, *Discovering the Present* (Chicago: University of Chicago Press, 1973), p. 190.

Index

About the Author

Neil Jumonville was born in 1952 and raised in Portland, Oregon, where he received his bachelor's degree from Reed College in 1977. He earned a master's degree at Columbia University in 1979 and then worked as an editorial intern at *The Nation* magazine. In 1987 he received his Ph.D. in the History of American Civilization from Harvard University. His essays and reviews have appeared in the *New York Times, Die Zeit, The New Leader,* the *Journal of American Culture, Boston Review,* and *Queen's Quarterly.* He has taught American intellectual history in the History and Literature program at Harvard. Currently he and his wife, Lynn, live in Tallahassee, Florida, where he is a member of the history department at Florida State University.

Compositor: Graphic Composition, Inc.
Text: 10/13 Aldus
Display: Aldus
Printer: Maple-Vail Book Mfg. Group
Binder: Maple-Vail Book Mfg. Group